HOBBES
A BIOGRAPHY

Thomas Hobbes (1588–1679) is now recognized as one of the fathers of modern philosophy and political theory. In his own time he was as famous for his work in physics, geometry, and religion. He associated with some of the greatest writers, scientists, and politicians of his age: Ben Jonson, Galileo, and Charles II. The list of his enemies is no less impressive: Robert Boyle, René Descartes, and Edward Hyde, the earl of Clarendon.

His life was a long, rich, and intensely controversial one. On the eve of the English Civil War he fled the king's enemies and settled in France, where he wrote his masterpiece, *Leviathan*. Ten years later, fearing the French Catholic clergy, he returned to England, only to have Anglican bishops try to have him burned at the stake as an atheist fifteen years thereafter. The controversy surrounding his life never abated: the Catholic Church placed his books on the Index, and Oxford University dismissed faculty for being Hobbists.

A. P. Martinich has written the completest and most accessible biography of Hobbes available. The book takes full account of the historical and cultural context in which Hobbes lived, drawing on both published and unpublished sources. It will be a great resource for philosophers, political theorists, and historians of ideas. The clear, crisp prose style will also ensure that the book appeals to general readers with an interest in the history of philosophy, the rise of modern science, and the English Civil War.

A. P. Martinich is Professor of Philosophy at the University of Texas at Austin. He is the author or editor of nine books, including *The Two Gods of Leviathan: Thomas Hobbes on Religion and Politics* (Cambridge University Press, 1992).

Hobbes

A Biography

A. P. Martinich

PUBLISHED BY THE PRESS SYNDICATE OF THE UNIVERSITY OF CAMBRIDGE
The Pitt Building, Trumpington Street, Cambridge, United Kingdom

CAMBRIDGE UNIVERSITY PRESS
The Edinburgh Building, Cambridge CB2 2RU, UK http://www.cup.cam.ac.uk
40 West 20th Street, New York, NY 10011-4211, USA http://www.cup.org
10 Stamford Road, Oakleigh, Melbourne 3166, Australia

First published 1999

Printed in the United States of America

Typeface Ehrhardt 10.5/13 pt   *System* MagnaType™ [AG]

*A catalog record for this book is available from
the British LIbrary.*

Library of Congress Cataloging-in-Publication Data
Martinich, Aloysius.
Hobbes : a biography / A.P. Martinich.
p.   cm.
Includes bibliographical references and index.
ISBN 0-521-49583-0 (hc.)
1. Hobbes, Thomas, 1588–1679. 2. Philosophers – England –
Biography. I. Title.
B1246.M38   1999
192 – dc21
[B]   98-36567
CIP
ISBN 0-521-49583-0 hardback

To Carol, John, and Mary, again

Contents

Preface

Self-interest originally moved me to study Thomas Hobbes in a serious way. Shortly after I finished my doctoral dissertation, Isabel Hungerland, who was a member of my committee, asked whether I was willing to translate the first part of Hobbes's *De Corpore*. Someone else was originally scheduled to do it as a companion to her commentary on Hobbes's theory of meaning and signification. When that did not work out, Isabel turned to me because of my knowledge of Latin and work in the philosophy of language. As wide as my knowledge of the history of philosophy was, I knew very little about Hobbes. But she had a publisher lined up for the translation and I already anticipated the pressure on assistant professors to publish, so I accepted the offer. Eventually, my translation and a commentary on it was published (in 1981), with a long introduction by Hungerland and George Vick.

Because I considered Hobbes's work on logic and the philosophy of language to be dull and not especially original or cogent, I thought that I had ended my involvement with him. Several years later, I was gently coerced into giving a graduate seminar on Hobbes because I was "supposed to be an expert on Hobbes since you published a book on him." I was not thrilled by the prospect, but I knew that *Leviathan* was thought to be a great work and I had never read much of it. To my surprise, I enjoyed the book and the seminar went well. So I decided to incorporate Hobbes into my introduction to the philosophy of religion and to teach additional seminars on him. My reading of the standard secondary works on Hobbes's philosophy bothered me. They did not seem to adequately fit the text or the historical context. The more I read the more excited I became about Hobbes's thought and the more convinced I was that my interpretation of Hobbes was better than the standard ones. Eventually, this research resulted in the publication of *The Two Gods of Leviathan:*

Thomas Hobbes on Religion and Politics (1992). In addition to his theoretical aims in political philosophy, Hobbes, as I saw him, wanted to reconcile orthodox Christian doctrine with modern science, and to show that authentic Christianity was not politically destabilizing. His project was, as I think it was bound to be, a failure, but I believe that he never realized that. Nothing in the way he lived his life suggests anything other than that he was a devoted member of the Church of England.

Narrow self-interest has long since ceased to be my motive for studying Hobbes. It is now almost pure intellectual delight. The more I studied his philosophy, life, and his historical context, the more fascinated I became.

I am gratified that Hobbes is no longer the object of interest primarily for philosophers. Much of the best recent work on Hobbes has been done by historians of politics and science and political scientists. They have taught me a lot.

I want to thank Terence Moore, who invited me to take on this project in 1994. Dr. Andrew Thrush, an editor for the History of Parliament Project, allowed me to read drafts of the biographies of the first and second earls of Devonshire. Kay Walters, assistant librarian at the Athenaeum Club, London, allowed me to read Charles Blount's copybook. Some or all of my manuscript was read by the following people at various stages of completion: Jo Ann Carson, Gregory Dickenson, Margaret Duerkson, Matthew Evans, Loyd Gattis III, Kinch Hoekstra, David Johnston, Cory Juhl, Fred Kronz, Brian Levack, Leslie Martinich, Max Rosenkrantz, and George Wright.

Introduction

The organization of every intellectual biography is a compromise between chronological and topical order. I have chosen to have a chronological organization dominate the topical. Consequently, the same general topic is sometimes treated in more than one place, for example, Hobbes's political philosophy and scientific views. My goal is to give the reader a sense of time; philosophers, and even historians, often tend to ignore it. I am interested in conveying when and where Hobbes first came up with certain ideas and how they relate to his other ideas. So I give *The Elements of Law, Natural and Politic* and his commentary on Thomas White's *De Mundo* much more prominence than other writers do. My purpose also explains why his dispute with John Bramhall over the issue of free will is discussed in the chapter on the 1640s even though it did not begin to be published until the 1650s. I have also given more space than I otherwise would have to materials and topics that have recently come to light, are currently being hotly discussed, or are less well known even to those with some knowledge of Hobbes's life and works. These include certain essays probably written by him in the late 1610s, his trip through the Peak District in 1626, his first major psychological and political treatise, *The Elements of Law*, and the translations he did of the *Iliad* and the *Odyssey* late in his life. Since information about Hobbes's life before the age of forty is scarce, the first two chapters concentrate on the milieu within which he lived.

Although scholars now generally recognize that Hobbes's own life was highly social and "commodious," as he would say, most people still think that it was solitary, poor, nasty, and brutish, if not short. One goal of my book is to correct that misimpression. Although I disagree with much of what Hobbes taught, the man and his thought remain exceptionally fascinating. I hope my readers will come to share my fascination.

This book is the result of scholarship, but it is not a work of scholarship, because it lacks the full apparatus and requisite jousting with opponents. I have provided fairly complete notes to Hobbes's works and have acknowledged my secondary sources when this is appropriate or essential. I have not given page references to quotations taken from Hobbes's autobiographies, "Vita Carmina Expressa" (written about 1672, when he was eighty-four) and "Prose Life" (dictated about 1676), nor to John Aubrey's biography. With a couple of exceptions, I have not given references to unpublished sources, such as letters and manuscripts in archives. When it was convenient, references to closely occurring quotations have been gathered into one note. I have recorded my debts to various scholars in the *Two Gods of Leviathan, A Hobbes Dictionary* (Oxford, 1995), and *Thomas Hobbes* (London, 1997). In addition to my previous work in libraries, I have done additional research for this book in the Bodleian Library, the British Library, the Athenaeum (London), and the Humanities Research Center, University of Texas at Austin.

Spelling and punctuation in quotations have usually been modernized, but not Americanized. The few exceptions occur where the sense or flavor of the text demands the original. Book titles are almost always unchanged.

Double quotation marks are used when someone's speech is being quoted; single quotation marks are used when words, phrases, or sentences are being mentioned and also as so-called scare-quotes.

I have occasionally supplied my own translation for some of the Latin texts, even when I refer the reader to a published translation.

A Note on Dates

In the seventeenth century, England followed the Julian calendar rather than the more accurate Gregorian calendar because it did not want to calculate time according to the Roman Catholics. The Julian calendar was ten days behind the Gregorian calendar, which was already in use in most countries on the Continent. Thus, December 10 in England would be December 20 in France. A date according to the Julian calendar is also known as Old Style in contrast with one of the Gregorian calendar, which is New Style. It is conventional to retain the Old Style dates for events that occurred in the British Isles. Dates for events that involve the Continent in a significant way will be given in the form: December 10/20.

There is one further complication. In England, the new year was taken to begin on March 25. The choice of this date is connected with the vernal equinox and also the fact that it was the mythic date of the Annunciation, that is, the day on which the Virgin Mary became pregnant with Jesus. (Christmas Day comes exactly nine months later.) It is the convention among historians to give the year in which an event occurred as if the year began, as it does now, on January 1. Here are two examples where being clear about what system of dating is involved will avoid confusion. Some books report that Hobbes graduated from Magdalen Hall in February 1607. By our convention, the correct date is February 1608. Also, Charles I was beheaded on January 30, 1648, according to seventeenth-century sources. But according to our convention, it occurred on January 30, 1649.

Chronology

Malmesbury and Magdalen Hall, 1588–1608

Our Saviour, the Man-God, was born fifteen hundred and eighty eight years ago. The renowned enemy fleet was standing in Spanish ports, soon to perish in our waters. It was early spring. The fifth day of April was beginning. It was then I was born, a little worm, in Malmesbury. I received baptism from my father, a minister, and he gave me his name. ("Vita Carmine Expressa")

Mother

Fear invaded England months before the Spanish Armada set sail. Rumors that the Armada was on its way were circulating as early as December 1587. As spring approached, Hobbes's pregnant mother became more anxious. Many thought that the Spanish were the Antichrist or his agent. And everyone knew that the end times would be filled with wars and rumors of war.

For more than a century learned men had been predicting that 1588 would be "climacteric." Philip Melanchthon, Martin Luther's theologian, had made 1518 the start of the final age, which would end after seventy years, supposedly the same number of years as the Babylonian Captivity. The calculations marking 1588 as a terrible year in world history were based on numbers supplied by the apocalyptic books of Revelation and Daniel, and confirmed by a passage in Isaiah. Some of the prophecies would be recorded by Francis Bacon in his essay "Of Prophesies." What if 1588 was to be the beginning of the end of the world? The Book of Revelation had said that women with child would suffer especially horribly. Hobbes's mother could not have known that the Armada would not leave Spain until May, that a wind would blow it off course, that another attempt would be needed, that the Armada would not reach England until July and would be resoundingly defeated by both the weather and the English navy.[1] Given the information available to her and the possibly catastrophic consequences of an invasion, she would have been perfectly justified in being afraid. In any case, Hobbes reported that it was this fear that prematurely induced his mother's labor and caused him to be born between four and six in the morning on Good Friday, April 5, 1588, in the village of Westport, just outside of Malmesbury, Wiltshire.

His traumatic birth affected Hobbes for the rest of his life. He thought that the circumstances of his birth explained "my hatred of the enemies of my country." In his verse autobiography, written eighty-four years later, he wrote: "For the rumor went everywhere through our towns that the last day for the nation was coming by fleet. And at that point my mother was filled with such fear that she bore twins, me and together with me fear."

Hobbes was the second child of his mother. John Aubrey, Hobbes's earliest biographer, says that she came from a yeoman's family, named Middleton, from the village of Brokenborough, Wiltshire; but no records of such a family exist. Virtually nothing more is known about her, but there are some speculations. Arnold Rogow mentions that a Thomas Hobbes married an Alice Courtnell on May 3, 1578, in the parish of St. Martin, Salisbury, not far from Malmesbury and speculates that this couple may be Hobbes's parents. If 'Alice' was not the name of Hobbes's mother, then 'Anne' may have been since that was the name of Hobbes's sister. The mother's principal duty, aside from the care of the children, was the maintenance of the family house, a stone-and-tile structure that included a buttery and two rooms on a second floor. Aubrey described it as "the farthest house on the left hand as you go to Tedbury leaving the church on your right." The house stayed in the family at least for two more generations. It no longer stands.

Father

Hobbes was named after and baptized by his father. Thomas Hobbes senior was a semiliterate clergyman. He could read the Bible and the Sunday sermons and not much more. Aubrey calls him one of the ignorant "Sir Johns" of the Elizabethan church. Late in life Hobbes contrasted the seditious clerics who preached their own sermons with the law-abiding ones who read the prescribed sermons. When he mentions that the latter were called "dumb dogs," one gets the impression that he is thinking of his own father and thought that they were mocked unfairly.

Hobbes senior matriculated at Brasenose College, Oxford, in April 1587, supposedly at the relatively superannuated age of forty. (There is some uncertainty as to the accuracy of this date since there is also a document that lists his age as thirty-two in 1589.) It may be dubious that a grown man with a family would be starting university, but there are two likely explanations. One is that his bishop might have sent him there as part of the Elizabethan effort to upgrade the clergy. Another is that he may not have been a student at all but a so-called privileged person, someone employed by the college. Even janitors fell into the category of privileged persons. The city of Oxford did not like the category because all privileged persons were outside the jurisdiction of the city and could get away with shenanigans that citizens could not. The colleges had only an indirect interest in disciplining bad behavior in the city.

Thomas senior already had a son and so was presumably married. It is an open question whether his wife was with him in Oxford or still in the area around Malmesbury. Since she probably became pregnant in August 1587, Thomas senior's stay at Brasenose would not have been very long. He never got a degree and almost surely would have been back home for his son's birth the next spring.

According to Aubrey, one of the father's positions was that of vicar of Westport, where he was paid sixty to eighty pounds per year. Current historians dispute this. The father is described in the Wiltshire Record Office as the curate of the nearby village of Brokenborough. And Rogow, who argues that Thomas senior was a member of the lesser clergy, estimates his annual pay as closer to ten pounds. By comparison, Hobbes's future salary as an employee of the noble Cavendish family would be eighty pounds annually in addition to other income such as gifts from his master and royalties from his books.

All of the surviving stories about Hobbes's father indicate that he was an irresponsible and unpleasant fellow. Aubrey calls him "choleric" (bad tempered). On two occasions his parishioners at the village of Brokenborough complained that he did not give the required number of sermons. Part of the problem was the father's residence at Westport. The bridge between Westport and Brokenborough was often flooded by the Avon, so the father could not get to the church. His parishioners wanted him to reside in their town, as previous curates had, and he refused.

According to another story, the father fell asleep during a worship service and was heard to mutter, "Clubs are trump."

Then there are the stories that reflect badly on the father. A clergyman of Westport angered the father at the church door, "so Hobbes struck him and was forced to fly for it and . . . in obscurity beyond London, died there." There is more to the story. It began in October 1603, when the father was the defendant in a libel suit brought by another clergyman. The claim was that he had called Richard Jeane "a knave and an arrand knave and a drunken knave and one that would have killed his brother minister Mr. Andrewes." The court found for Jeane, and Thomas senior was ordered to do public penance. He did not present himself on the designated day but reportedly "carried himself contumaciously."[2] Back in court, Jeane had Thomas senior declared "contumacious and . . . excommunicate accordingly." Thomas senior would not let bad enough alone. In February 1604, he confronted Jeane in a churchyard and accused him of instigating the excommunication. Jeane denied it and walked away. Thomas senior followed and swore at Jeane before punching him "with his fist under the ear or about the head and stroak off his hat and made him let fall his cloak from his back all which the said Mr. Jeane suffered until the said Hobbes hanged about him and would not desist from striking the said Mr. Jeane and then he [Jeane] in his own defense stroke the said Thomas Hobbes and shaking him off from him threw him to the ground."[3] Soon after this, the father left the area for the environs of London, as mentioned above. Because Oxford, where Hobbes had already started his university studies, would not have been far out of Thomas senior's way as he traveled from Malmesbury to London, he could have visited his son. But whether he made the effort, we will never know. The father simply disappeared from history.

Since this unfortunate incident occurred after Hobbes had left home, he may have escaped the worst embarrassment caused by his father's behavior. But as a young teenager in 1603, he still probably would have been mortified. Although there is no excuse for the behavior of Thomas senior, it was not unusual for the times. The church canons for 1604 forbade clergymen to frequent taverns and alehouses and insisted that they not "give themselves to . . . drinking or riot, spending their time idly by day or by night, playing at dice, cards or tables, or any other unlawful game." Clearly, there was a genuine problem with clerical behavior. The puritan "Survey of the Ministry" for Essex in 1586 found that out of 335 clerics, 173 were "ignorant and unpreaching ministers" and a dozen of "scandalous life." One or more of the offenders was "a gamester, alehouse haunter, drunkard, very ridiculous preacher, dicer, carder, a pot companion, [and] incontinent." One minister "had a child by his maid and is vehemently suspected to have lived incontinently with others."[4]

Brother and Sister

Hobbes had an older brother, Edmund, and a younger sister, Anne. Edmund, named for an uncle who died when Hobbes was eighteen years old, grew up to be a glover, like his other uncle, Francis. Edmund presumably did not leave the area around Malmesbury. He was not particularly well educated, yet he understood some Greek even into old age. He was not quite as tall as Hobbes, who was almost six feet. Since Edmund died at about the age of eighty, Thomas senior reportedly at the age of eighty-three, and Hobbes himself at ninety-one, they must have come from sturdy stock, even though Hobbes himself was sickly as a child.

Edmund had three children. One was a male, Francis, apparently named after his uncle. He was left a total of about eighty pounds a year income by the combined generosity of his father and Hobbes; he was an alcoholic who abused his wife.

About Hobbes's sister, Anne, as about their mother, little is known. She married Thomas Lawrence, had seven children, and inherited her father's house. Two of Anne's children, Mary (Tirell) and Eleanor (Harding), were given bequests from Hobbes's will. Although women play a minor role in what we know of Hobbes's life, they are a significant part of his will. In addition to his two nieces, he left two hundred pounds to an orphaned girl, entrusted to his care, and ten pounds to one Mary Dell.

Uncle Francis

After Thomas senior abandoned the family, Hobbes was supported by his uncle Francis, who served in Malmesbury as burgess and as alderman (the chief magistrate of the town). In addition to supporting Hobbes at Magdalen Hall, Uncle Francis left Hobbes a pasture, Gaston ground, which earned sixteen pounds a year. Uncle Francis was a successful glover. Leather goods were one of the specialties of the area. Stratford is not far from Malmesbury, and William Shakespeare was the son of a glover as well.

Malmesbury and Westport

The place that Hobbes considered his hometown, Malmesbury, is in southwestern England, in the Cotswolds. In the seventeenth century, it was an average-size town of about one thousand residents. Two tributaries of the River Avon almost completely encircle Malmesbury. One, now known as Ingleburn, approaches from the north; the other, known as the River Avon, approaches from the south. They join just east of town. Hobbes lived outside the town in the village of Westport, so named because it began at the western gate of Malmesbury. One road from Malmesbury went through Westport to Gloucester; another went to Bristol. Brokenborough, where Hobbes's father was a curate, was a little over a mile to the west; Charlton, where, according to Aubrey, the father held another clerical position, was slightly over a mile to the northeast.[5] The church of Westport, dedicated to Saint Mary, was impressive, given the size of the village; its steeple may have stood taller than the one in Malmesbury. The church was destroyed by the parliamentary army during the Civil War in order to prevent it from being used as a fortress by the royalists. The church that eventually replaced it was described as being "like a stable," but Hobbes never saw it, because his last trip to his hometown was in 1634.

In his verse autobiography, Hobbes expressed quite a bit of pride in Malmesbury. Standing on a steep hill, it was an ancient town, whose origins date back to the mid-seventh century, when an abbey was founded there. By the ninth century, it was a local trading center. It had a charter as a borough that sent two representatives to the House of Commons. The bones of King Aethelstan (tenth century) are buried there. Hobbes also mentions a monk of Malmesbury Abbey, Saint Aldheim (late seventh, early eighth century), who founded the first Latin school. Unfortunately, Hobbes does not mention the medieval historian William of Malmesbury, to whom we owe the story that the philosopher John Scotus Erigena, a resident of the abbey, was stabbed to death by his students with their pens. Malmesbury had been an important wool producer until the middle of the sixteenth century. Its economic condition declined with the woolen industry. In 1663, Hobbes tried to get the king to endow a free school at Malmesbury, and he had Aubrey look for a suitable location on at least one of his many visits to Wiltshire. In the end, the prospective school could not get funded, and so the idea died.

As a boy, Hobbes was playful enough but sometimes melancholy. When he smiled, his eyes became little more than slits in his face; when he became angry, they opened as wide as "chestnuts." His black hair earned him the nickname "Crow." In later life, Hobbes had male pattern baldness and the remaining hair, left to grow to collar length, turned white.

Robert Latimer

Hobbes went to school in Westport at the age of four and stayed until the age of eight. Having learned to read and do elementary arithmetic, he went to school in Malmesbury with "Mr. Evans, the minister of the town." But the great educational influence on Hobbes's life was Robert Latimer, described as a "good Grecian," who had a school in Westport.[6] Latimer graduated in 1591 with a B.A. from Magdalen Hall, which would be Hobbes's own undergraduate school about a decade later, and received his M.A. in July 1595 from Magdalen College. Hobbes began taking classes with Latimer about 1596. According to Aubrey, Latimer was nineteen or twenty at the time. But, since he received his B.A. in 1591, it is more plausible that he was about twenty-four.

Later Latimer became a minister of Malmesbury and then rector at Leigh-de-la-mere (Leigh Delamere). He had taken a liking to Hobbes, and the feeling must have been mutual since decades later Hobbes went out of his way to find his old teacher in a village some distance away. The instruction that Hobbes received from Latimer went on until about nine o'clock at night. Shortly before going off to Oxford, Hobbes presented to Latimer a translation he had done of Euripedes' *Medea* into Latin iamb. The play seems to have deeply affected Hobbes. Later in life, he regretted not having kept a copy of these adolescent efforts. He refers to *Medea* four times in his writings, more than to any other non-Homeric literary work. Once is in *Leviathan*, when he warns against unrealistic expectations of creating a better government by altering the existing one: "those that go about by disobedience, to do no more than reform the commonwealth, shall find they do thereby destroy it; like the foolish daughters of Pelias, in the fable; which desiring to renew the youth of their decrepit father, did by the counsel of Medea, cut him in pieces, and boil him, together with strange herbs, but made not of him a new man."[7]

Scholars owe quite a bit to Latimer, because it was through him that Aubrey met Hobbes. Aubrey became an important antiquarian who wrote

biographies of many of the greatest Stuarts and a history of the city of
Oxford. It is easy enough to excuse the occasional factual errors he makes
because of the richness of his anecdotes and physical descriptions. He
wrote the first and, without doubt, the liveliest biography of Hobbes. If it
had not been for Aubrey, Hobbes would have a somewhat ghostly or at
best skeletal appearance in history. Aubrey reminisced about the July or
August of 1634, when he was eight years old:

> Hobbes came into his native country to visit his friends, and amongst others he
> came to see his old Schoolmaster, Mr. Latimer at Leigh Delamere, when I was
> then a little youth at school in the church. . . . Here was the first place and time I
> ever had the honor to see this worthy man, who was then pleased to take notice of
> me, and the next day came and visited my relations. He was a proper man, brisk,
> and in very good equipage; his hair was then quite black. He stayed at Malmes-
> bury and in the neighborhood a week or better.

He seems to have been quite full of himself and dropped the name of Ben
Jonson, poet and raconteur. It is possible that Hobbes saw himself in the
eight-year-old Aubrey. It is also fortunate that Hobbes came that summer
to see Latimer, because the teacher died later that year.

Oxford

Hobbes chose to continue his education at Magdalen Hall, Oxford. He
went there probably in 1602 but possibly in 1603. There would be no
question at all if the record of his matriculation had survived, but because
it does not, we must speculate. The evidence for the exact year is contradictory. The argument for 1603 is this: It is a hard fact that he was
graduated in February 1608. In his prose autobiography, he says that he
remained at Oxford for five years. Five from 1608 is 1603. This is the year
that Aubrey gives, and it is likely that he arrived at his date just as we now
have, by subtraction. We know that Aubrey did not have firsthand information of the year, because a marginal notation in his manuscript reminds
him to ask Anthony Wood for the year. But there is reason to doubt that
1603 was the year Hobbes matriculated, because he would have been
fifteen years old at the time and this does not square with what he himself
says in both of his autobiographies: that he went to university at the age of
fourteen. (Some translations of his autobiographies translate a tricky
passage as saying that he matriculated in his "fourteenth year," that is, at
the age of thirteen; but I think fourteen is the correct understanding of

the Latin.) Fourteen is also more plausible on other grounds. The average entering age for students at Magdalen Hall was over sixteen. Only three students whose admission is recorded between 1601 and 1603 were as young as fourteen years of age. Most were sixteen to eighteen, with one as old as twenty-one.

Although younger than most of his classmates, Hobbes was adequately prepared. His education had begun at the age of four and had included six years of Latin and Greek before going to Oxford. And he was precocious.

On the assumption that he went to Oxford in 1602, stayed for five years, and graduated in 1608, there is a missing year to account for. A plausible explanation involves the interaction between the plague and graduation requirements. A student did not actually complete the requirements for the bachelor of arts degree until he went through a series of public and ritualistic academic exercises. The most important of these was the "determination," a formal disputation pitting the candidate against two bachelors of arts. (The range of topics was broad, as we shall see.) Determinations were held only during Lent. Often when an epidemic raged, the university would cancel the public academic exercises, without automatically suspending the requirements to perform them. Obviously, these cancellations caused a backlog of students to be "determined" the next year. Some students might be excused from them altogether through a successful petition, and some might receive permission to perform them in private. But exceptions were usually given to clergymen and to the sons of gentlemen. Hobbes was neither. For the most part, students simply had to wait until the next year to complete their requirements, and this could well have happened to Hobbes. If so, then he would have completed his course work in 1607, missed the opportunity to determine that year because of the epidemic, and then determined the next. There were, in fact, epidemics in both 1606 and 1607. Epidemics occurred relatively frequently in Oxford. Hygiene was poor; dunghills littered the streets; the food was sometimes spoiled; and the water was polluted. Rather than risk death, the timid and sickly Hobbes might well have chosen to return to Westport at the first hint that the plague might interfere with the university exercises. Admittedly, this is speculative, but it seems neatly to explain how Hobbes might have arrived at Oxford at the age of fourteen, stayed five years, as he says he did, and graduated in February 1608.

Granted that we know little about when Hobbes went to Oxford, it is

plausible that he arrived in early April. There were four terms: Mich-
aelmas, which usually began in October; Hilary, which began in January;
Easter, which began just after Easter; and Trinity, which began in May or
June. The starting times would vary from year to year, depending on
epidemics and the date of Easter. August, September, and the beginning of
October were vacation time. Students matriculated anytime from October
through July, although most arrived at the beginning of a term. Aubrey
says that Hobbes matriculated near the beginning of the year. Because in
England the year was taken to begin on March 25, this would mean late
March or early April, probably at the start of the Easter term. April 5,
1602, would have been when Hobbes turned fourteen. If Hobbes's first
year at Magdalen Hall began in April and ended in late July, it would have
eased the stress of entering university at a relatively young age.

When Hobbes first arrived at Magdalen Hall, the first thing that would
have been done was to enter his name in the buttery-book although he
was probably not aware that this was being done. The buttery-book was a
ledger in which were entered a student's expenses. Students sixteen years
of age and older were required to sign a pledge affirming that they
subscribed to the Thirty-nine Articles, the Book of Common Prayer, and
the Royal Supremacy.[8] Subscription to the Thirty-nine Articles was also
one of the many terminal requirements for the B.A. In addition, Hobbes
would have been assigned to a tutor who was responsible for his overall
education. But some tutors were irresponsible or incompetent, and he
never mentions his tutor's name.

A student was not only expected but required to attend lectures according to the statutes. The practice may have been more lax, and by
Hobbes's own account he did not attend regularly. In the first year,
grammar was taught on Tuesday and Friday at 8:00 A.M., rhetoric and
logic on Monday and Thursday at the same time; metaphysics was introduced in the second year. The lectures were supposed to prepare the
student for a series of logical disputations, in which he initially would
have to defend some thesis against the objections of two more advanced
students and then progress to being one of the objectors. A variation of
these exercises is depicted on the lowest panel on the title page of *Leviathan*. Hobbes reports with some sense of reverse pride that when he
arrived at Oxford he was placed in the most elementary ("the lowest")
class of logic. He mocks the young instructor, too young to grow a beard,
who lectures him in a very solemn voice. What the instructor is gravely

pronouncing are the mnemonic names of the figures of the syllogism, which are nonsense when strung together: *Barbara celarent darii, ferio barlypton, Caesare camestres festino baroco darapti.* Hobbes may have thought about how such Latin words were extensions of the scholastic hocus-pocus that he often railed against in his later years.

Hobbes learned his logic slowly and preferred to prove things in his own way. This trait of intellectual independence would remain with him his whole life, sometimes to his glory, as when he applied himself to political philosophy, and sometimes to his detriment, as when he tried to square the circle and double the cube. In addition to logic, Hobbes learned about Aristotelian physics. Everything in the world was explained in terms of matter and form. 'Species', that is, appearances of things, flew through the air. When they land in the eyes, you see, and when they land in the ears, you hear. Many effects were caused by Sympathy or Antipathy. Other explanations were given that were beyond Hobbes's comprehension and belief, as he wrote in his autobiographical poem.

Recently, Quentin Skinner has detailed the rhetorical works that students were supposed to read and master as undergraduates in late Tudor and early Stuart England and has concluded that Hobbes was both very well informed and deeply influenced by this work.[9] I am slightly dubious. Hobbes possibly read most of what was required, but whether it had an effect on him at that time or whether it came to have an effect on him later in life is less certain. He bragged that he spent much of his time in other pursuits, such as catching jackdaws. His interest in being away from the classroom and study is also indicated by the "great delight" he took in going to bookshops to gape at maps of the heavens and the earth. He enjoyed marking the course that the sun took across the sky from the spring to the winter. And he traced the paths that Sir Francis Drake and Thomas Cavendish took in their travels around the globe. He was fascinated with the areas marked "terra incognita" and fantasized about the people and the monsters that lived in those regions. He wanted to know about these unknown lands.

When a student had completed his twelve terms of lectures and preliminary disputations, there remained a complex set of rituals that he had to go through before he received his B.A. Oddly, even after that degree was granted, one further requirement had to be satisfied: to give a "determination," as was mentioned earlier. In a determination, the candidate was required to defend a certain proposition. Two senior members of the college would propose objections to the proposition. The candidate had to respond to these objections and defend whatever additional propositions he committed himself to in his responses. At the end of the session, the moderator "determined" the question by giving the correct answer and commenting on the course that the debate had taken. Three questions about Aristotle's philosophy were asked, and the candidate had to answer all of them. In 1608, the following two sets of questions were used in the Faculty of Arts:

1. Whether it would be better if there were one language throughout the world than the various languages of the diverse nations.
2. Whether a new inundation of water [over the whole earth] would be a greater catastrophe than all of it freezing.
3. Whether anyone thinks that he is stupid.

1. Whether ignorance is the mother of arrogance.
2. Whether the earth is a magnet by nature.
3. Whether it is appropriate for a woman to listen to moral philosophy.[10]

As far as the questions asked, Hobbes could have done worse. Questions from other years included the following: whether the sea was salt, whether women were happier than men, whether gold could be made from baser metals, whether impudence was more tolerable than shyness, and a man's rights in the taming of a shrew.[11] Many of the questions are intriguing even today, such as, whether the death of the mind is worse than the death of the body.

Most of a student's life was spent outside of the lecture hall. It was customary for a fellow of a college to sleep with about five students in a large room. The students would sleep on trundle beds beneath and around the master's bed. Smaller rooms were used for study. The wake-up bell was rung at 5:00 A.M. during the summer and 6:00 A.M. during the winter. A light meal was provided for breakfast. Beer was the drink that was served. Lunch was at 11:00 A.M. and supper at 5:00 P.M. The early morning routine probably did not bother Hobbes. He used to enjoy waking early to catch jackdaws, as mentioned earlier. He would tie lead weights with thick twine, smeared with birdlime and baited with bits of cheese. When the jackdaws took the bait, Hobbes yanked the twine. The sticky weights would attach to the bird, preventing it from flying away. Nothing is said about what Hobbes then did with the birds. The image of his hunting stayed with him. In *Leviathan*, he would compare a person who confuses his definitions with "a bird in lime-twigs, [which] the more he struggles, the more belimed."[12]

Sixty years later, in *Behemoth*, Hobbes said that students were "debauched to drunkennesss, wantonness, gaming, and other vices."[13] Given that Hobbes had not been to Oxford for at least decades, the evidence for his remark is usually taken to be a very old memory of how things had been when he was at Magdalen Hall. Hobbes certainly intends the remark to be a stinging criticism of the universities, and most scholars agree that Oxford must have been a very decadent place. I am more sanguine about the condition of the universities. Drunkenness, wantonness, gaming, and other vices were part of my undergraduate experience and those of my friends at various universities, and nothing has changed over the past forty years, judging from the experiences of my students and my children. Of course there are degrees of drunkenness and wantonness, but without better evidence, I am reluctant to judge that Oxford in 1605 was worse than Oxford (or the University of Texas) in 1998.

Since Hobbes was fourteen when he went to Magdalen Hall, his report about the debauchery of Oxford might have been more a reflection of how he first experienced the behavior of his older fellow students than how things really were. There is an enormous difference between the interests and sensibilities of a fourteen-year-old and a sixteen-year-old.

We do not know which students Hobbes associated with at Magdalen Hall. With five students sleeping to a room, it is plausible that a student would either bond with the others and form a close relationship, or withdraw into himself in order to preserve his privacy. There is no evidence that Hobbes kept up with any of his Oxford schoolmates. He started out two to three years younger than most of his classmates. As a fourteen-year-old among students who were between sixteen and twenty, he may have found the experience traumatic. He was also sickly and that could have made him an easy target for jokes or physical abuse. These considerations may partially explain his solitary activities of catching birds and looking at maps; and the maps, he says, inspired flights of fantasy, which further insulate a person from others.

Perhaps he sought out the few other students who were about the same age as he. After a couple of years, he might have come upon Roger Manwaring, from All Souls College, who was two years younger than he. Manwaring would later get in trouble with Parliament for his extreme royalist views. He would preach that Charles I was an absolute sovereign. Since there were only about 2,500 students at Oxford at the beginning of the seventeenth century, it is plausible that Hobbes would have known some students outside of his own hall.

One of the highlights of Hobbes's stay at Oxford must have been the visit of James I in late August 1605. All of Hobbes's references to that king in his writings are favorable, and he suggests that the English Civil War might never have happened if James's desire to unite England and Scotland into "Great Britain" had been satisfied. Much of Hobbes's mature political writings sound like a philosophical version of what James said of himself throughout his reign. James's book, *Basilikon Doron*, written for his son Prince Henry, was reprinted in England soon after the death of Elizabeth. The sonnet that summarizes the book says:

> God gives not Kings the style of Gods in vain,
> For on his Throne his Scepter do they sway:
> And as their subjects ought them to obey,
> So Kings should fear and serve their God again;
> If then ye would enjoy a happy reign,
> Observe the Statutes of your heavenly King,
> And from his Law, make all your Laws to spring:
> Since his Lieutenant here ye should remain,
> Reward the just, be steadfast, true, and plain,
> Repress the proud, maintaining aye the right,
> Walk always so, as ever in his sight,
> Who guards the godly, plaguing the profane:
> And so ye shall in Princely virtues shine,
> Resembling right your mighty King Divine.

Several of the themes of this poem were emphasized by Hobbes later. The sovereign is accountable only to God, not to his subjects. A king should make his laws compatible with the laws of nature, which are the same as the laws of God. The subjects of a king all suffer from the sin of pride, because all human beings, as the descendants of Adam and Eve, are "the sons of pride." In his greatest work, Hobbes says that he calls the sovereign 'Leviathan', because that monster in the Book of Job is said to be the "king of the sons of pride." Hobbes also says that Leviathan or the sovereign is "a mortal God, to whom we owe, under the immortal God, our peace and defense." The idea that kings are gods is very strong in James's "Speech to the Lords and Commons of the Parliament at Whitehall": "Kings are justly called gods for that they exercise a manner or resemblance of divine power upon earth. For if you will consider the attributes of God, you shall see how they agree in the person of a king." We cannot simply extrapolate backward and say with certainty that Hobbes's attitude about James in the 1640s and 1650s was the same as his attitude in the early 1600s. But there is no evidence that Hobbes was ever a political rebel, even as an adolescent, so he may have always been an admirer of James. In any case, even if he did not have a special affection for James in 1605, the inherent interest and spectacle of a relatively new monarch, visiting a student's university, were great.

The preparations for James's visit were elaborate. The Oxford officials were especially eager to impress James both because he had become king of England only two years earlier and because he preferred Cambridge to Oxford. The king was attended by his queen, Anne of Denmark, and Prince Henry. (The prince stayed in Magdalen College, which was next to Magdalen Hall.) The preparations were elaborate. All the windows, casements, pumps, and gates to the city were newly painted; the streets were swept and repaved. A decree was issued requiring all members of the university to wear gowns, hoods, and caps, as appropriate to their status. They were also admonished "diligently" to attend the ordinary lectures as long as the king was in residence. Students who made "any outcries or indecent noise about the hall, stairs, or within the quadrangle of Christ Church" if they could not get into the plays put on for the king would be imprisoned and otherwise punished.

The king's arrival was the occasion for several examples of the absurd rivalry between town and gown and between Oxford and Cambridge. The king was supposed to be greeted outside the city walls, first by representatives from the university, and then by those from the city. The university officials stopped at "Aristotle's well," but were then asked by the lord chamberlain to move farther ahead because too much dust was blowing around the area. They rode up to a meadow and dismounted in order to wait for the king. Then they saw representatives from the city ride past them. The university officials complained to the chancellor; the chancellor complained to the lord chamberlain; the lord chamberlain consulted with the mayor; the mayor sent two aldermen to explain to the chancellor that they had not seen the university officials in the meadow and that no offense was intended. The incredulous chancellor said that the city officials should not have gone ahead. He thought, probably rightly, that the city officials intended to upstage the university men by greeting the king first. But when their plan was discovered, they retreated to their appropriate place in the rear. The king's arrival proceeded with great pomp and no acrimony. Inside the university grounds, the students and teachers stood on one side of the street; other people stood on the opposite side. An oration was made in Greek. Queen Anne, something of a social bumbler, said she enjoyed the speech because she had never heard Greek before.

A monarch's presence at a university was unusual enough to draw scholars even from Cambridge. But it was jealousy, not collegiality, that brought them there. The perceptions of the Cambridge men about what went on were jaundiced, as evidenced by the verse description one of them wrote about the king's procession into Oxford:

> To Oxenford the King is gone,
> With all his mighty Peers
> That hath in grace maintained us
> These four or five long years.
> Such a King he hath been
> As the like was never seen;
> Knights did ride by his side,
> Evermore to be his guide;
> A thousand Knights, and forty thousand Knights,
> Knights of forty pound a year.

The king's retinue was large, but not that large. In the last two lines, the author was referring to James's enforcement of an ancient law that Englishmen who owned land worth at least forty pounds a year in income were required to become knights. Knighthood required a payment to the king. Because of inflation, forty pounds was a relatively insignificant amount of money; so many people of quite modest means had thrust upon them the dubious honor of being a knight. James's motives were purely pecuniary. He wanted the money to supplement the inadequate funds he received from Parliament.

Once he was settled in, a large part of the king's visit was taken up by lectures and disputations. James was an intellectual and liked these academic debates. He often interjected his own opinion and gave his own "determination" of the issue. At other times, he simply muttered, "Tush, tush, away, away," to indicate his disagreement or boredom.[14] Among the topics debated during James's visit were whether saints and angels know the secret thoughts of people, whether infants suck in the habits of their wet nurses along with the milk, whether a minister of the church is required to fulfill his normal duties during a plague, and whether the imagination can cause real effects. James was an ardent opponent of smoking, and another question of debate was whether smoking was healthy for people. (Pity the scholar who affirmed it, except that it was the king's own physician, Sir William Paddy, who was probably a ringer.) In moral philosophy, two questions were debated. The first was whether it is better to protect one's borders or to enlarge them. The other would become an important part of Hobbes's most intellectually important years: whether justice and injustice exist only in the law or in nature also.

James Hussey, who may have been the principal of Magdalen Hall at the time, was one of six teachers to argue the negative side of the question whether a judge must follow the ordinary legal procedures that would lead to the conviction of a person that the judge privately knows is innocent. Eventually, the king decided the issue for himself:

Any judgment that violates the judge's integrity and unviolate purity of his conscience in performing his duty as a judge or what God requires of him is a false judgment. On the other hand, he is required by his sovereign always to follow proper procedure in his official capacity and to execute his duty in obedience and fidelity to the laws and statutes of the king. Now since he often encounters difficulty in the process of rendering his judgment, difficulties arising from opposing accounts of the truth, and from the fact that the evidence presented may conflict with the judge's own personal thoughts, these are the things that can be done in this situation.

In order that the judge may know in what manner he may conduct himself in rendering judgment I therefore resolve thus: it is chiefly the judge's work (responsibility) to bring the truth to light for his sovereign or his king by means of his own personal deliberations and thus make his decisions on the basis of his own truth. But if in exerting himself greatly, he effects or accomplishes too little, let him exercise his capacity of judge to summon witnesses in private and thus in whatever manner preserve his conscience pure in advancing the truth in order to check [hold off] the longer the loss of conscience and truth in his role of judge.

James left Oxford at the end of August. Little more than two months later, the Gunpowder Plot was discovered. A group of Roman Catholics had conspired to blow up the king, queen, Prince Henry, and both houses of Parliament all at once. They had dug a tunnel from the cellar of the house next door to the Parliament building. Under the building, Guy Fawkes had planted twenty barrels of gunpowder, covered with iron bars to maximize the effect of the explosion. Crowning the entire works were a large number of faggots or bundles of sticks. The plot was discovered because one of the conspirators sent a letter to his relative warning him not to go to Parliament. The relative turned over the letter to the earl of Salisbury, who launched an investigation. When the investigators went down to the cellar, there was Guy Fawkes standing guard over the faggots. Yet it was not until a more thorough search was conducted the night before Parliament was to assemble that the explosives were uncovered. The Gunpowder Plot immediately became infamous throughout England. The students at Oxford must have felt a special closeness to the incident since James had been with them so recently. Sixty years later, when Hobbes wrote his history of the English Civil War, he cited the Gunpowder Plot, "the most horrid act that ever had been heard of before," as a cause of the war even though he did not think that war was inevitable until many decades later. His reasoning was convoluted: The Roman Catholics were a cause of the war because it was thought that they would be happy if the pope's authority were reestablished in England, to the detriment of the king.

Shakespeare's *Hamlet* was performed in Oxford in 1607, but we do not know whether Hobbes attended. He never mentions Shakespeare and says very little about theater even though Ben Jonson became a good friend of his.

The Principals of Magdalen Hall

It is not clear who was the principal of Magdalen Hall when Hobbes arrived there. It was probably James Hussey, as mentioned earlier. But there is some evidence that he did not become principal until sometime after 1605. In any case, he was made chancellor of the bishopric of Sarum and knighted by James in 1619. He died of the plague on July 11, 1619, the day after he returned to Oxford. Blame for starting an epidemic in Oxford at that point was pinned on him. We are more certain about who was principal when Hobbes graduated. It was John Wilkinson, a staunch Calvinist.

Hobbes graduated with a bachelor of arts degree on February 5, 1608.[15] He "determined" during the Lenten term of that year. While Oxford had opened up a new, larger world to the poor, provincial Cotswold boy, an even larger and more exciting world was about to be opened up to him.

2

Tutor and Companion, 1608–1620

At that time he [William Cavendish] was subject to the authority of his father. I served him diligently for twenty years; he was not only a master, but a friend as well. This was by far the most agreeable period of my life, and now I often have pleasant dreams of it. ("Vita Carmine Expressa")

Bess of Hardwick

Hobbes must have been a good and respectable student, because the principal of Magdalen Hall recommended him to the rich and influential Cavendish family of Hardwick Hall, probably in early 1608. This was about the same time that the true founder of that great family, the redoubtable Elizabeth Hardwick (aka Bess of Hardwick and Bess the Builder), died in her ninth decade of life. Even if Hobbes never met her, he may have seen her body since she was lying in state for three months. Her ghost at least continued to watch over her Derbyshire and Nottinghamshire estates for decades after that. Hobbes eulogized her in the late 1620s in his poem *De Mirabilibus Pecci*. He attributes her great wealth to "her candor," which he thinks explains why she had so many powerful friends. In fact, she had powerful friends because she was powerful.

Hobbes does not even mention her Cavendish husband. There were three others besides. Through these four judicious marriages and some aggressive litigation, Bess acquired prodigious wealth and became one of the richest people in England. Her first husband, a cousin of hers, died not long after the wedding. His death benefited her financially. Her second husband was a William Cavendish, with whom she had eight children, six of whom survived birth. Buying and selling lands wisely, Beth consolidated her property in the Midlands. One of the acquisitions was Chatsworth, the future seat of the earls of Devonshire, Hobbes's patrons.

Cavendish, who would jump at anything he considered an opportunity, did not oppose his wife's wise land strategy. He had made a fortune from the dissolution of the monasteries through the good graces of Thomas Cromwell. After the fall of Cromwell, Cavendish switched political allegiances and made another fortune in Ireland. Under Henry VIII, he eventually rose to be treasurer of the royal chamber. While Bess was firmly committed to the country life, Cavendish's business and personal preference was for London. When Mary I succeeded Edward VI in 1553, Cavendish not surprisingly converted to Roman Catholicism and retained his post as treasurer. It was not that Cavendish was unprincipled; rather, his principle was opportunism. But because all good things must come to an end, a suspicious deficit in the royal accounts a few years later led to his downfall. He died in October 1557, just before Mary could punish him. This was fortunate in that it gave Bess some time to maneuver out of the lawsuits that were pending against her recently deceased husband.

And death was not finished smiling on Bess. Queen Mary died the next year and was succeeded by Bess's friend Elizabeth I. This gave her even more time and a better chance at resolving legal problems her late husband had left her. Her substantial lands were jeopardized by the penalty that had been levied against his estate as punishment for his official misconduct. Her way out of this problem and to greater riches was again to be a happy combination of marriage and death. Her third marriage was to the wealthy Sir William St. Loe, who became Chief Butler of England. He settled Bess's debt to the crown for a small fraction of the amount owed. She also persuaded him to will all of his property to her and her children even though he had children from a previous marriage. Then he died.

Ah, death, where is thy victory? Bess had not lost a husband, she had gained more land. It was also an opportunity for another marriage. Her fourth marriage was the coup de grâce. George Talbot, the sixth earl of Shrewsbury, was a recent widower and a rich neighbor: a perfect mate. When they married in 1557, Bess, still bewitching at forty, became countess of Shrewsbury. Now she had both wealth and social standing. But not even money and a title were enough for Bess. She convinced Shrewsbury to marry his eldest son to one of her daughters and one of his daughters to one of her sons. She thus became mother-in-law to two of her stepchildren. This was an ingenious way to keep her property all in the family. The marriage of her daughter to Shrewsbury's eldest son was especially fortunate, because her silent business partner, Death, carried off that husband. Eventually, Shrewsbury's younger son and Bess's daughter became Lord and Lady Shrewsbury.

Bess also succeeded in marrying her daughter Elizabeth to Charles Stuart (earl of Lennox), a descendant of Henry VII and thus a genuine, if remote, heir to the throne of England. Thus Bess was a potential "queen mother-in-law." Queen Elizabeth was furious that a royal marriage had been concocted without her approval and put Bess into the Tower of London for three months. But at the end of that time, Bess was free, and her daughter was still married to a Stuart. The daughter of that marriage was Arabella Stuart, who had an exciting but sad life. She became a virtual prisoner of Bess, was part of a plot to set herself on the throne, was imprisoned by James I, and went insane before dying at age forty in 1615.

Although the marriage between Bess and Shrewsbury began happily, two years later it was put under a strain. Mary, Queen of Scots, and the queen's rival for the throne, had been put under house arrest in the custody of Shrewsbury. Eventually, this would stretch out to more than fifteen years and become an emotional and financial burden for Shrewsbury. Mary was a politically dangerous friend, and, despite her precarious state, she wanted to be treated like a queen. Her entourage consisted of forty or more people. It was necessary for political and health reasons to shuttle her back and forth between several of Shrewsbury's residences, including Chatsworth.

After a time, rumors were spread that Shrewsbury and Mary were having an affair. Bess knew that the rumors were false and complained to Queen Elizabeth about being a wronged woman, but only when it served her purposes. The marriage of Bess and Shrewsbury had been deteriorating for some time. The emotional death blow to the marriage was precipitated by a dispute over – what else? – land. Shrewsbury had given his stepsons William and Charles a good bit of land. When he discovered that they, with Bess's connivance, had used the lands solely for their own benefit, that is, not sharing any of the proceeds with him, he sued to have the gift revoked. Bess and sons countersued. The sides in the incestuous suit were complicated by the fact that Bess's oldest son, Henry, sided with Shrewsbury and Shrewsbury's eldest son, Gilbert, sided with Bess. The dispute was protracted and vicious. Shrewsbury once complained that she had called him "knave, fool, and beast to his face, and mocked and mowed at him."[1] Once when Shrewsbury tried to enter Chatsworth, his stepson

William Cavendish (the future first earl of Devonshire), holding a halberd and packing a pistol in his belt, stopped him at the door. Shrewsbury retaliated by vandalizing the grounds. He broke windows, trampled the gardens, and befouled the fish ponds.

Bess needed the queen's sympathy in order to bolster her legal case. Her chance came when the queen asked how Mary, Queen of Scots, was doing. Bess replied, "Madam, she cannot do ill while she is with my husband, and I begin to grow jealous, they are so great together."[2] The ruse worked. After protracted legal wrangling, the queen decided the issue herself largely to the advantage of Bess. Injury had been added to insult. Having been humiliated and bested by his wife, Shrewsbury felt he could no longer live under the same roof with her. He referred to her as his "very wicked and malicious wife" and cursed his wedding day. Speaking to Queen Elizabeth later, he thanked her for delivering him of two devils, his wife and Mary, Queen of Scots. He died in 1590, but Bess continued to exact her revenge by living well.

One of the sources of tension between Shrewsbury and Bess had been her ambitious construction projects. She was refurbishing and enlarging Chatsworth (a predecessor to the stupendous structure now there). She also built the magnificent houses of Oldcotes and Worksop in Nottinghamshire. But her greatest architectural achievement, and something of an Elizabethan marvel, is Hardwick Hall,. The west face of the building is mostly glass. It has fifty windows, each of which contains between six and sixteen leaded glass panes. Many of these windows, however, are blocked by fireplaces inside the house. It is three stories high and has sixty rooms. Hobbes probably occupied a room on the second floor next to the rooms of his tutee.

Hobbes had a particular affection for architecture during the 1610s and 1620s, or at least gives that impression. The simplest explanation for that affection was the importance it had to his employers and his exposure to their estates. In the essay "A Discourse of Rome," probably written by Hobbes around 1615, the author praises architecture as one of the most pleasing of human works. In addition to satisfying "our own present invention," buildings provide posterity with "perpetual remembrances, and memorials of their progenitors, adding present content to ourselves, perpetuating reputation in the world, remaining as living monuments of our magnificence, and beneficent expressions of our greatness."[3] A finer tribute to Bess could not have been written.

Answering the charge that great buildings are "superfluous," Hobbes says, "First this Art of Architecture is honorable in all men's esteem, and profitable to ourselves. Next, it keeps us busied in thought and action and so diverts us from delights more dangerous. Then upon occasion it enables us in the use of fortification. Fourthly, it gives a kind of extraordinary delight to ourselves, when we see those things which before we had but formed in conceit made visible."

Bess's houses also had exquisite gardens, and in one of his rare rhapsodic moments Hobbes writes:

[T]he delicacy of Gardens be of inestimable consideration, where a man's mind may receive such content, and his eye such diversity of objects, as in nothing more. If a place of delight and pleasure content our minds, it may be here satisfied with the beauty of walks, sweetness and diversity of flowers, melody of birds, and the like. . . . If one would contemplate the wonders of nature, here he may find all things necessary and pleasurable, healthful or hurtful for man. If we be inclined to any serious study or meditation here is the place where our thoughts cannot be perturbed nor diverted nor our senses unsharpened, because they continually meet with such variation.[4]

Aubrey said that Hobbes belonged to the melancholy type of person, and alluding specifically to that type, Hobbes writes that "the privacy and solitude of this place [a garden], the murmuring of the waters, fills us with a strange kind of satisfaction."

It may be appropriate to leave Bess of Hardwick with a poem written to her by Sir Horace Walpole:

> Four times the nuptial bed she warmed,
> And every time so well performed,
> That when death spoiled each Husband's billing,
> He left the Widow every shilling.
> Sad was the dame, but not dejected;
> Five stately Mansions she erected
> With more than Royal pomp, to vary
> The prison of her Captive Mary.
> When Hardwick's tow'rs shall bow their head,
> Nor Mass be more in Worksop said;
> When Bolsover's fair fame shall tend,
> Like Oldcotes, to its mould'ring end;
> When Chatsworth tastes no Candish bounties,
> Let fame forget this costly Countess.

The Cavendishes

Two great lines of Cavendishes would descend from Bess. The one at Chatsworth through Hobbes's first employer, her son William (1552–1626), would become the earls and dukes of Devonshire. The one at Welbeck in Nottinghamshire through her son Charles (1552–1617) would become the earls and dukes of Newcastle.

There were Cavendishes galore in Hobbes's life, especially William Cavendishes. It is worth setting them all down in order to forestall confusion. Bess's second husband, William, has already been mentioned. Her son William (hereafter 'Cavendish'), also already introduced, would become a baron in 1605 and first earl of Devonshire in 1618. He was the one who in 1608 had hired Hobbes to tutor his son, still another William. This William (hereafter 'William'), who was only two years younger than Hobbes, became the second earl of Devonshire in 1626, when his father died. The second earl in turn had a son William (hereafter 'Devonshire'), who would become the third earl of Devonshire and whom Hobbes would also tutor.

This is not the end of the Cavendishes who mattered to Hobbes. In some ways, more important than his employers at Chatsworth were their relatives at Welbeck. Only two need to be mentioned now. The first is, as one might have guessed, another William Cavendish, the marquis and later duke of Newcastle (hereafter 'Newcastle'). He is historically the most significant of the Cavendishes. He was at one point governor to the Prince of Wales, the future Charles II, and commanded Charles I's troops in the north during the Civil War, but left England in disgrace after the defeat at Marston Moor. Newcastle was interested in the new science. He associated with Marin Mersenne and his circle in France and had his own small group of amateur scientists in his chaplain Robert Payne, Payne's friend Walter Warner, and Newcastle's brother Charles, not to mention Hobbes himself.

When Hobbes first went to Hardwick Hall as an employee of Cavendish, Chatsworth was owned by Cavendish's older brother Henry. By that time Henry was alienated from his mother because he had supported his stepfather Shrewsbury against Bess and her other sons. Because he died without any legitimate children – he provided for his illegitimate children generously – Chatsworth passed over to Cavendish in 1616. This branch of the family then alternated living at Chatsworth and Hardwick, about fifteen miles apart, when they were not living in London or touring. Chatsworth, which is situated on higher ground, was favored during the summer, Hardwick Hall during the winter.

Hobbes's duties with the Cavendishes of Chatsworth and Hardwick during the first two decades of employment were not onerous. Although he technically began as William's tutor, he was more of a companion. In 1608, Hobbes was twenty and William eighteen. Sometime later, Hobbes evolved into William's secretary. According to Aubrey, it was William himself who requested a tutor about the same age as he. The reasoning was that William would "profit more in his learning if he had a scholar of his own age to wait on him than if he had the information of a grave doctor." William's reasoning was self-serving: He wanted a friend and companion more than a tutor.

Although it is not completely certain, it is plausible that William was the "William Cavendish" at St. John's College, Cambridge, who received an M.A. from that institution in July 1608. (The other possibility is that this William Cavendish is Newcastle.)[5] One reason for thinking that this William Cavendish is not our William is that ours was already married, and students were not permitted to be married. However, there are rules, and then there are the things that are done. Cambridge would have been very happy to have the son of the earl of Devonshire and not to discover what was then strictly a paper marriage. His bride was only twelve years old and not ready to cohabit with him. One reason for thinking that our William was at Cambridge is that Hobbes himself incorporated at Cambridge in 1608. (Incorporation was a courtesy extended to graduates of other universities that gave a person certain privileges in the adopted university.) Rather than holding that Hobbes incorporated at Cambridge and then got the position with the Cavendishes, I think it is simpler to maintain that he incorporated at Cambridge in order to be with William.

Hobbes may well have been at Cambridge six months or more and would have met various Cambridge men. One of them was very probably Robert Mason, who was at St. John's College in 1608 and who later corresponded with Hobbes. Hobbes accompanied William from Cambridge to Hardwick Hall in November 1608, and there is no hard evidence that Hobbes ever revisited that university.[6]

Christian Cavendish (née Bruce)

William's child bride, whom he married before receiving his M.A. from Cambridge, was Christian, the daughter of Edward, Lord Bruce of Kinloss, Scotland. Lord Bruce was one of the few Scotsmen to serve James at the highest level of government. James was good to Bruce, because Bruce had been good to him. The Scotsman had been one of the most effective negotiators in behalf of James's claim to the throne of England.

It was not William's idea to marry Christian. He himself was in love with an older woman, Margaret Chatterton, who had been one of the ladies attending Bess of Hardwick. There is no love like one's first love. But Cavendish had no intention of letting a little thing like love interfere with a marriage that would end up being financially beneficial to him. After all, he was the progeny of "marrying Bess." James I had probably proposed the marriage as a way of rewarding Bruce. The terms were worked out by the fathers, but Cavendish, being a bit tight with his money, had to be prodded by the king into giving the couple a more generous wedding gift. This is one version of the wedding story. There is another version, according to which it was the scheme of Arabella Stuart; and it was accomplished very quickly, according to the earl and countess of Arundel.

The ritual bedding of the bride and groom was traumatic, not only because William loved someone else, but also because of Christian's young age. William's uncle Henry, writing to his brother-in-law, the earl of Shrewsbury, said that "Wylkyn" (William's nickname) and Christian were "bedded together to his great punishment some two hours." Afterward, William led the life of a bachelor for years to come. Christian bided her time and would eventually show herself to be more responsible, more resourceful, and more competent than he. After his death, she would pull the family together, rescue it from financial ruin, and rebuild its greatness.

The emotional problems aside, William and Christian started off their marriage securely. At the prompting of James I, Cavendish reportedly gave the couple £7,000; James himself may have thrown in another £3,000. James would continue to be a benefactor to young William. He knighted him, though probably for a price, at Whitehall the next year.

Hobbes and William Together

Hobbes and William do not seem to have made much use of the well-stocked library at Hardwick Hall, notwithstanding Hobbes's praise for the learning of his employer. As a tutor, he should have been teaching William the classical languages. Although he gives the impression in his verse autobiography that he continued his humanistic studies when he took his position with the Cavendishes, we also know that he discovered a few years later that he was losing his ability to read Greek and Latin.

Most of William's time was devoted to the leisurely pursuits of a young aristocrat of the age, both in the country and in town. And Hobbes had no choice but to suffer the same delights. In an essay, "Of a Country Life," published in a book that will be discussed in Chapter 3, William, possibly with Hobbes's assistance, wrote, "All field delights, as hunting, riding and hawking, commendable, if used with moderation, are properly belonging only to this [i.e., a country] life."[7] These activities strengthen one's body and prepare one for war. Fine sentiments, but both William and Hobbes seemed to hawk and hunt immoderately, and neither was a soldier.

Its title notwithstanding, William's essay on country life also celebrates life in the city, "where generally the most refined and judicious men be likeliest to be found." The city gives people knowledge of their own times and access to "the great men and guiders of the state."[8] William, and so Hobbes, had many opportunities to mingle with the great men of England. William almost certainly would have taken Hobbes with him to Whitehall for his knighting. Hobbes had several other opportunities to see or be in the presence of the king. James I was at Derby and at Nottingham in August 1609. William participated in the games conducted during the installation of Charles as Prince of Wales in 1616. The next year the king was at Worksop and Pomfret, estates owned by the Talbot line of Bess's descendants, and it would have been unneighborly not to include the other side of the family. Both Cavendish and William were official mourners at the funeral of Queen Anne, on May 13, 1619, at Westminster Abbey. James I was at Welbeck, the principal home of William's cousin Newcastle, on August 10, 1619, and would be there again in August 1624. One special reason for thinking that William, and hence Hobbes, was at Welbeck in 1619 was that the king on that occasion knighted Sir Sutton Coney, who was William's half brother-in-law. In August 1619, the Prince of Wales (the future Charles I) visited Hardwick

Hall. Hobbes probably would have been present, though inconspicuous, at the dinners in the prince's honor.

In addition to expanding one's cultural and political horizons, a city gives people access to many avenues for squandering money. And William walked down most of them. Hobbes's job was to borrow the money that paid for the strolls. Aubrey described the situation: "His [Hobbes's] lord, who was a waster, sent him up and down to borrow money and to get gentlemen to be bound for him [William], being ashamed to speak for himself. He [Hobbes] took colds, being wet in the feet. . . . Notwithstanding he was well-beloved; they loved his company for his pleasant facetiousness and good nature." William was as much the friend of Hobbes as he was his master. Emotional bonding of this sort often occurs when young men are involved in hunting, drinking, and wenching, much more than in studying or conducting business. If Hobbes had been only a tutor to William, then he certainly would have been let go by the Cavendish family after several years. As a tutor, he was not an essential employee. As a boon companion, he was.

The Addled Parliament, 1614

Like almost every Stuart Parliament of the seventeenth century, the king's intentions in calling Parliament in 1614 were frustrated. The Addled Parliament, so called because it did not pass one substantive act, was dissolved after only eight weeks in existence. It ended somewhat acrimoniously, with the House of Commons declaring that until "it shall please God to ease us of these Impositions [taxes], whereby the whole kingdom doth groan, we cannot, without wrong to our country, give your Majesty that relief which we desire."[9]

The Parliament was not a great success for William either, who was one of the two members representing the county of Derbyshire. His only speech in the Commons was one that he read from a prepared text in support of the naturalization of two Scotsmen. It was the performance of an amateur. Sir John Savile shamed him when he asked that Cavendish be instructed that it was inappropriate to read a speech.

But at least William would not have been lonely in Parliament. His father sat in the House of Lords; his cousin Newcastle represented East Retford; and Gervase Clifton, a neighbor and friend of Newcastle, was a representative for Nottinghamshire. William, and so possibly Hobbes, may also have become acquainted at this time with Francis Bacon, who was an important agent for the king in Parliament. Bacon would become an important figure in William's correspondence soon after.

The First Tour of the Continent

It was customary for rich young English gentlemen to take a grand tour of the Continent, and for most it would be the only time that they set foot in Europe, especially if they did not go off to one of the wars. Hobbes, as a tutor, would eventually go to the Continent on three of these tours. The first trip was with William. The second would be with the son of Gervase Clifton; the third, with William's son, the future third earl of Devonshire.

Until recently, it was generally thought that the first of these tours began in 1610. William had received official permission to leave England that year. Also, Hobbes says in his autobiography that he went to the Continent the year after he began working for the Cavendishes, and people tend to remember such things, even when they are very old. Finally, William had a motive to go that year since his cousin Newcastle was in Italy. All of this notwithstanding, there is now strong evidence that Hobbes and William did not go to the Continent before 1614. In October of 1610, Henry Howard, the earl of Northhampton, recommended to the bailiffs and burgesses of Bishop's Castle that they select William to represent them in Parliament, in order to fill the vacancy caused by a death. It is scarcely credible that Northhampton would have nominated someone who was out of the country to serve in a parliament that had begun in 1604 and was now in its last stages. Also, William collected his allowance in London several times between 1611 and 1613. Further, William and Hobbes were mourners at the funeral of William's father-in-law in the Rolls Chapel, London, in February 1611. (In addition to its evidential value as to the whereabouts of Hobbes and William, it is significant that Hobbes was included as a named mourner, albeit one of the least prominent ones, after only three years of employment.)[10] As a final bit of evidence, William was a member of the Addled Parliament of 1614.

Of course, this evidence is not conclusive. It is possible to construct all sorts of hypothetical journeys to get William and Hobbes out of and back into England in order to attend parliaments and funerals. But since there is no evidence of these sojourns, such hypotheses are unwarranted. The most sensible view is that William and Hobbes did not leave England until 1614, just after the dissolution of the Addled Parliament.

Although the year of their departure may be doubted, their presence in Venice in September 1614 is certain. William went with Henry Parvis (or Purvis), a merchant, to Rome and then to Naples in October and later stayed with Parvis in Venice until the end of April 1615. William and Hobbes were probably in Rome during October and November 1614. This first tour seems to have been largely an Italian journey although we know that they returned by way of Paris in the summer of 1615.

Concerning their time in Rome, the best evidence about it comes from the essay "A Discourse of Rome" (hereafter "Of Rome"), possibly written by Hobbes and published in 1620 in the same volume as William's essay, "Of a Country Life." My guess is that Hobbes wrote it soon after his return to England as a way of showing William's father that his money had not been completely wasted in sending the two young men to the Continent.

The writing is perfunctory, and the essay has all the enthusiasm, insight, and emotion of an adolescent's first writing assignment of the fall semester, "What I Did during Summer Vacation." Here are some representative samples:

The River Tiber runs through the town, and within this compass are those seven Hills so famously known, all of one side the River, upon which old Rome was built. And still there be some Palaces on them; but the City, as it is now, is more built in those spaces, as Campus Martius, etc. which before were left vacant. . . . There is also the Statue of Marcus Aurelius in brass, and upon horseback, not anciently here, but removed hither from a more obscure place, by Paul III, Pontifex Maximus. . . . Here is also the great Amphitheater, but now extremely ruinate, where the most public shows and sports were usually shown.[11]

Cavendish was fortunate that Hobbes could not take photographic slides to be shown in the living room.

Hobbes dutifully reports some of the great art that he saw, but he is disturbingly unaffected by it. Here is his complete description of Michelangelo's *Pietà*: "On the left hand in a Chapel where the Canons sing their Office is the Statue of Our Lady, and Christ in her arms, cut in Marble by the most famous Painter Statuist in the World, Michelangelo." That is it. Not one word about its aesthetic merits or his own emotional response to it. His description of the Sistine Chapel is similarly desiccated: "There is also a private Chapel of the Popes where the high Altar is set out by Michelangelo's curious [i.e., detailed] description of the day of Judgment."[12] Unfortunately, Hobbes's disappointing performance cannot be excused as adolescent indifference. He was in his late twenties, not his teens.

As part of his travelogue, Hobbes describes the seven major churches of Rome. What is odd about the description is that, in spite of Hobbes's avowed appreciation for great edifices, there is little to nothing about their architecture. His focus is on their alleged relics. Without a hint of sarcasm, he reports the following:

This Church [Santa Maria Maggiore] is famous for these relics. The bodies of Saint Matthew, and Saint Jerome, which lied here buried, . . . And the picture of our Lady drawn, as they say, by Saint Luke. . . . Amongst other relics [in Santa Croce], there is a part of the Cross, from whence it took the name, and one of the thorns of that crown, which was in derision set upon our Savior's head. . . . The heads of Saint Peter and Saint Paul be here [in St. John Lateran] retained for relics. . . . [In the Sanctum Sanctorum] is also conserved the Ark of the Old Testament, Aaron's Rod, The Sudatorium, which is a napkin, with which in the way to the cross Christ wiping his face, there remained in it his picture; the table upon which Christ celebrated his last supper, and one little glass of his blood.[13]

Is Hobbes so naive as to accept all of these claims as true? No, not completely: "I must profess for myself that I am not so credulous as to tie my belief to these miraculous reports; nay, I am so far from it that I esteem *most* [my emphasis] of them rather feigned than true." Most? That implies that some of the alleged miracles are genuine. This same implication is present in what he says shortly after: "Some have such stony hearts and leaden heads that they cannot conceive (beyond themselves and nature, as they term it) any supernatural, or powerful government in their life and actions, nor any heaven besides their sensuality."[14]

The alleged miracles that he considers most dubious are the quotidian ones: "For example, if a man going down a pair of stairs, by chance his foot should slip, he would presently make a miracle of it and say, that in that instant he called upon Saint Francis, or San Carlo, or some other Saint, by whose prayers he was relieved, that otherwise he had maimed himself, or lost his life." Hobbes thinks that to attribute miracles to saints diminishes "the power and glory of God."[15] Thirty years later, he would maintain the same position in *Leviathan*. Rather than miracles, Hobbes preferred to found his religious faith on the Bible. He was a true Protestant.

When Hobbes tries to be profound, he often sounds sophomoric. Near the beginning of "Of Rome," he wonders how a great city could have been founded where the soil is as poor as it is. His speculation is that its poorness in fact was beneficial: "ease and delicacy of life is the bane of noble actions, and wise counsels." People who live in a beautiful area have no motivation to change their condition. No one in such a situation is impelled to "advance his own honor or the good of his country." He continues:

[A] life of pleasure does so besot and benumb the senses, and so far effeminate the spirits of men, that though they be naturally prone to an active life, yet custom has brought them to such a habit, that they apprehend not any thing farther than the compass of their own affections; [they] think nothing beyond their own enjoyments.

Consequently, Hobbes believes that "a place of hardness and a life exercised in actions of valor and not idleness" are necessary to produce the "bravest men" and "greatest fortune." (This is a somewhat odd sentiment for the tutor of a spendthrift to express.) Hobbes asks rhetorically, "Cannot virtue and poverty be together? Cannot an unfruitful Country yield men full of worthiness, and Valour?"[16]

Hobbes may have been responding to part of the beginning of Machiavelli's *Discourses on the First Ten Books of Titus Livy*. Machiavelli wrote:

[T]he question arises whether it would not be better to choose a barren place in which to build cities so that men would have to be industrious and less given to idleness, and so would be more united because, owing to the poor situation, there would be less occasion for discord. . . . Since, however, security for man is impossible unless it be conjoined with power, it is necessary to avoid sterile places and for cities to be put in very fertile places, where, when expansion has taken place owing to the fruitfulness of the land, it may be possible for them both to defend themselves against attack and to overcome any who stand in the way of the city's greatness. . . . I maintain, then, that it is more prudent to place a city in a fertile situation, provided its fertility is kept in due bounds by laws.[17]

If Hobbes is taking on Machiavelli, then he has lost the contest, because his own position is implausible and doesn't refute Machiavelli's arguments.

Hobbes visited the Capitoline hill, where "almost nothing remains but the memory." He catalogs several of the famous statues that he saw, like that of Marcus Aurelius on horseback, the she-wolf suckling Romulus and Remus, and the boy taking a thorn out of his foot, "looking so earnestly and pitifully that a man would think he had some sense of pain." Later he mentions the statues of Laocoön and some by Phydias and Praxiteles. Other sites are mentioned such as the Pantheon, about which Hobbes dryly comments that it once was "dedicated to all the Gods, and now converted to the honor of all the Saints." There is no sense of condemnation here. But the memory must have stayed with him and became mixed with disgust in *Leviathan.* Roman Catholics reinterpreted works of art representing pagan deities as representations of Christian figures. Their practice was "to make that an image of the Virgin Mary, and of her son our Savior, which before perhaps was called the image of Venus and Cupid; and so of a Jupiter to make a Barnabas, and of Mercury a Paul, and the like."[18]

Although he was impressed by the greatness of Rome and its artifacts, Hobbes saw it as suffused with paganism. The mistake made by superstitious religion, that is, "Religion exercised in false worship," is that it tries to represent the "incorruptible God into the likeness of a corruptible man." The attempt is against "Reason and Religion." Hobbes would get into trouble later for seeming to define superstition differently in *Leviathan:* "fear of powers invisible, . . . not allowed."[19] But in "Of Rome," there is nothing objectionable in his definition and his very Protestant abhorrence for superstition.

The pope at this time was Paul V. Of him, Hobbes writes:

[H]e is descended of no great family [the Borgheses of Siena], an Italian born, and exercised the former part of his life, before his Papacy, in the office of a Judge. He was made Cardinal by Clement the eighth, and Pope by the difference of the two great factions in that conclave of Montalto and Aldobrandino, both striving to make one of their own creatures, yet finding the other opposition too strong, were in the end forced to make a neutral.[20]

Although living a retiring life, the pope uses more pomp on public occasions and requires more obeisance than the proudest prince. With journalistic objectivity, Hobbes reports that the purpose of such displays is "to stir up reverence in the beholders, and devotion in their hearts, and that as all outward respects be used to honor the Princes of the world, so there ought to be much more to the Pope, being head of the Church." One can imagine that if Hobbes had seen the pope in 1650 or even 1640, he would not have objected to his behavior since by then he would have maintained that the pope is a genuine secular and spiritual sovereign, with all of the rights and prerogatives of any other sovereign. His principal complaint would be with the pope's pretension to being the spiritual sovereign of all Christians. In 1614, however, Hobbes was a more conventional Protestant, intent on criticizing the pope as any kind of religious leader. He thinks that "the sumptuousness of the Pope, and the pride of his government, is one token of the falsity of their [Roman Catholic] doctrine."[21]

The same objection applies to bishops and cardinals, often referred to as 'princes of the Church':

When they [bishops and cardinals] profess sanctity and strictness of life; who will believe him, when, after he has gotten to be a Bishop or Cardinal, he is found to be as proud, seditious and covetous as the rest? . . . When the Pope, to show his humility upon the Maundy Thursday, washes the feet of the poor, and in the meantime is attended with Cardinals and Ambassadors, some giving him water, some the towel, others holding his train, himself carried into, and out of the room, as if he were too good to tread on the earth, what man can be so stupid that discerns not his pride? Thus you may see what contrariety there is betwixt their profession and practice. . . . [I]t is strange to see their pride, every one esteeming himself of equal rank with any prince, and are served with a kind of extraordinary pomp, using their rooms of audience, clothes of estate, as princes do, and when they go to Consistory, you shall have one of them attended by their friends and followers with 20 or 30 coaches, and at least 200 or 300 *Staffieri* or footmen.[22]

The only cardinal exempted from Hobbes's criticism is Robert Bellarmine, described as "a little lean old man," who lives "more retired."[23] Hobbes's apparent respect is curious. Bellarmine was one of the pope's chief propagandists against James I, one of the prosecutors against Galileo, and one of the chief apologists for papal supremacy. Hobbes must have been quite affected by Bellarmine, since in addition to being one of the few people mentioned by name in "Of Rome," Hobbes would pay him the honor of refuting his views about the Roman Catholic Church thirty-five years later in *Leviathan*. Indeed, the attention that Bellarmine gets in that book is practically incomparable. Bellarmine is one of only two cardinals that Hobbes took special note of at an evening service on November 1 (All Saints' Day), 1614. He might have seemed especially noteworthy to Hobbes because he had recently criticized James I for taking repressive measures against Roman Catholics in retaliation for the Gunpowder Plot.

The other cardinal mentioned as being at the All Saints' Day service was Domenico Tosco, who had almost been elected pope before Paul V emerged as the compromise candidate. As Hobbes tells the story, Tosco actually had forty-five of the sixty votes cast and was sitting in the chair of Peter, when Cardinal Baronius, a man of integrity, intervened: "Will you choose him [Tosco] head of the Church that cannot speak a sentence without that scurrilous byword of the Lombards (*Cazzo* [a slang word for penis])? What a shame will this be in our election?"[24] Tosco's defenders said that he merely spoke like a Lombard, but Baronius's objection was sustained.

Concerning that thorn in the side of Protestants, papal indulgences, Hobbes writes, "When . . . we pay for them, what man can think the Pope has so much interest in God, as to make him pardon us, for his profit?" In *Leviathan,* Hobbes would return to the theme that sin is not a commodity. Attacking the "satisfaction theory" of redemption, according to which a debt incurred for sinning has to be paid off, Hobbes said, "sin cannot be taken away by recompense; for that were to make the liberty to sin a thing vendible,"[25] that is, something that can be bought and sold. An astute theological point.

In the last part of "Of Rome," Hobbes gives advice to his countrymen. He recommends that people who have written against Roman Catholicism should not go to Rome at all. Hobbes's other recommendations are similarly sensible: Do not argue about religion; especially do not defend the Church of England; do not give scandal in their churches; know a language other than English so that one can hide the fact that one is English; do not pretend to be a Roman Catholic unless absolutely necessary; do not go during Holy Week, because each resident must prove that he has "confessed, communicated and the like" according to the Roman rite. Finally, if a person becomes sick, the physician has to swear within three days that the patient has "confessed and communicated."[26] If the patient does not, then he and his party are turned over to the Inquisition. Perhaps the point of this information is this: While in Rome, don't get sick.

Ten Essays of William

Shortly after returning to England in 1615, William presented his father with a manuscript containing ten essays in the style of Francis Bacon. This is not surprising. After completing a tour of the Continent, it would make sense for William to show his appreciation to Cavendish by providing him with some sort of evidence that he had matured intellectually. The choice of topics may have been dictated partially by the success of Bacon's *Essays,* published in a second edition just a few years before (1611) and the possible personal acquaintanceship that William may have had with Bacon during the Addled Parliament. The *Essays* have the following titles:

1. Of Arrogance
2. Of Ambition
3. Of Affectation
4. Of Detraction
5. Of Self-Will
6. Of Masters and Servants
7. Of Expenses
8. Of Visitations
9. Of Death
10. Of Reading Histories

Some scholars have claimed that notwithstanding William's representation of them as his own and his dedication of them to his father, they were in fact written by his tutor, Hobbes. This seems to me to be wishful thinking. Bacon's and Cavendish's essays belong to the same genre but are not in the same class. There is no reason to think that William was incapable of achieving the modest heights of thought and shallow depths of sentiment expressed in the essays. Also, William had already published a long essay, "Against Flatterie," in 1611, and had dedicated it to his father-in-law. Of course, one could maintain that Hobbes himself is the author of that essay, too. (But what an irony if William had his employee write against flattery.) Even if the manuscript is in Hobbes's handwriting, as Leo Strauss maintains, that would show only that Hobbes transcribed them, an entirely appropriate job for a secretary.

In one way it would be wonderful to have Hobbes's thoughts recorded when he was in his late twenties. But there is no good reason to think that these ten essays are his. Some of what resemble sentiments and opinions in *Leviathan* were sentiments and opinions that other people would have espoused. In another way, it is fortunate that these essays do not seem to be by him, for it would be hard to explain how the author of the banalities of the essays could have developed into the author of *De Cive*, *Leviathan*, and *De Corpore*. None of this is meant to imply that Hobbes had no hand in the essays. Since he was both a secretary and friend to William, Hobbes may well have made suggestions about them. He could have polished some of the prose, inserted some phrases that sound especially like him, and provided some inspiration for the thought.

These ten essays, written for the private enjoyment of Cavendish, would take on a public life five years later when they would be included in an anonymous collection called *Horae Subsecivae*, which will be discussed in Chapter 3.

Very little detail is known about Hobbes's activities between the latter part of 1615 and the end of 1620. He seems to have been bothered by his realization that his facility in Greek and Latin had seriously deteriorated since leaving Oxford. He resolved to resurrect them by reading dramatists, poets, and historians. He also tried his hand at Latin composition. His goal was to develop a style "not flowery" but "perspicuous and easy to understand." He wanted his words to "be congruent with" the ideas he wanted to express. This stylistic ideal fit well with his later scientific aspiration.

International Affairs: The Correspondence with Micanzio

While they were in Venice, William and Hobbes had met Fulgentio Micanzio, the secretary to Paolo Sarpi, Venice's state theologian and chief theorist in its battle with Rome over religious independence. England favored Venice because it was opposing the leader of the international Roman Catholic conspiracy. Venice favored England because Spain, the fist of the papacy and an immediate threat to Venice, was traditionally England's enemy. "The enemy of my enemy is my friend," according to the muddled political maxim.

Soon after William was back in England, he and Micanzio struck up a correspondence that went on for years. My guess is that Micanzio's interest in William was largely based on the interests of Venice. Micanzio was forty-five years old when the correspondence began, whereas William was only twenty-five. Micanzio was probably acting to some extent on behalf of his mentor, Sarpi. The distinguished historian William Bouwsma thinks that Sarpi "probably had a hand" in writing the letters and was "almost certainly privy" to their contents.[27] Also, Micanzio had other English correspondents, most notably, the one-time ambassador to Venice, Sir Dudley Carleton. The style and content of the letters also suggest that Micanzio was trying to get William to influence James I to change English foreign policy, either directly or indirectly. In his first letter, Micanzio says that he expects William to receive it when William is "back in court."

Micanzio may have had a dual strategy. He probably hoped that William could influence James directly, but if William could not do it, then Bacon could. In his third letter Micanzio thanks William for "relating to Sr. Francis Bacon how much I esteem his judgment and learning." Micanzio has learned so much from Bacon's *Essays* that, as he says, "I find myself very much carried away to love and honour him."[28] As extravagant as his praise is of the essays and the *Advancement of Learning*, Micanzio rarely says anything substantive about them. He was probably being diplomatic. What he wanted was to be in Bacon's good graces in order to motivate him to influence the king to send assistance to Venice. That's how diplomacy sometimes works. Criticism would hurt those chances, and even reporting what he liked about the essays ran the risk of showing that he had misunderstood them. None of this is to imply that Micanzio did not genuinely admire Bacon. Both were antischolastic, and the quality of Bacon's thought is unmistakable. The point is that people can have many motives for praising someone, and when the object of praise is in a position to advance one's own interests, it is plausible that one motive is to effect just that.

Seventy-five letters from Micanzio to William between 1615 and 1628 survive in translation. Micanzio says that he is writing in Italian because his Latin is poor. He may well have been speaking ironically. It is hard to believe that an educated Italian cleric of the time would not have been competent in Latin. His allegedly poor Latin may have been a way of snubbing his nose at the papacy. Micanzio was more of an Italian, a Venetian Italian, of course, than a Roman Catholic. The letters were translated by Hobbes. The substance of most of them concerns the military campaigns of the Thiry Years War as they affected Venice and the political intrigues connected to the war. Carl von Clausewitz's remark that war is an extension of politics by other means could have been inspired by the history of Italy during this period. William's own letters no longer exist, and with rare exception it is difficult or impossible to figure out what he was saying from the content of Micanzio's.

Hobbes's rejection of scholasticism may have been reinforced by hearing Paolo Sarpi attack it. Sarpi was a nominalist and probably a materialist. Like Hobbes, he rails against abstract talk in philosophy. Sarpi's ecclesiological views were also very close to those that Hobbes would argue for in *Leviathan*. He believed in state churches and did not believe that there was any Catholic Church, apart from the cluster of national Catholic churches.

From 1616 until 1622, Micanzio used a carrot-and-stick approach when talking about James I. He combined praise for the king's great attributes with criticism of him for not sending troops to relieve the Venetian forces at war with Ferdinand. When the Thirty Years War broke out in 1618, Micanzio's criticisms became even harsher. After James I gave his son-in-law Frederick reason to think that his bid to become king of the Holy Roman Empire would be supported by England, in fact little more than moral support was forthcoming. When they were in their most extreme need, James even prevented his daughter and son-in-law from taking refuge in England. (More will be said about Frederick's troubles in the next chapter.)

Micanzio was especially upset because Ferdinand had been harassing Venice. He feared that Spain would conquer all of Italy. He was disappointed in James on almost every front. In May 1617, James had gone to Scotland to promote the Scottish episcopate, as well as to impose the liturgy of the Church of England on the Scots. Micanzio was disturbed. Bishops were just like the pope as far as he was concerned. In 1620, Micanzio would report rumors that "England will be converted to Roman Catholicism and that the Prince of Wales has already converted." Sounding like he is whistling in the dark, Micanzio says that he does not believe it.

When Micanzio was trying to influence Bacon, it was all carrot. After receiving a copy of Bacon's *De Sapientia Veterum*, Micanzio writes, "I find that Gentleman is so full of knowledge and learning Politique, – moral and divine that the abundance of his breast is communicated to whatsoever he reads." The praise is fulsome and vacuous. Micanzio never says what precisely impresses him about Bacon. Micanzio worked hard to have

Bacon's essays published in an Italian translation. He says that their imminent publication in 1618 was squelched by a "Friar" who objected to something in Bacon's essay "Of Religion." Publication eventually occurred the next year. Bacon appreciated Micanzio's praise and efforts on his behalf and began his own correspondence with him. Micanzio's interest in and admiration for Bacon was unaffected by Bacon's dismissal as lord chancellor and conviction for corruption and official misconduct.

For a long time, James had aspirations of becoming the head of a reunited international Christian community. As part of that grand illusion, Marc D'Antonio, De Dominis, the archbishop of Spalato (Split, Dalmatia) defected from the Roman Catholic Church and went to England to seek his fortune in the Church of England. Dalmatia at that time was a satellite of Venice, and Micanzio was quick to praise De Dominis ("a man of great integrity") to William. When his investment for advancement in the Church of England underperformed, he returned to the fold of the Roman Catholic Church. By 1622, De Dominis's reputation was quite bad, and Micanzio criticized the "besotted" rogue for "his ambition and avarice." De Dominis was a "mountebank," someone who traveled from place to place trying to promote himself through devious means.

The First Earl of Devonshire

Before his fall from English grace, De Dominis had some kind of connection with William. But the nature and closeness of it is not clear. Something that De Dominis reported to Micanzio led the latter to think that William had "advance[d] to a higher degree of honor." He may well have been confusing William with his father Cavendish, who had been created first earl of Devonshire in early August 1618. He was one of a number of peers created in Salisbury, during one of the king's progresses. Since Salisbury is in Wiltshire, Hobbes's home county, it is likely that Hobbes was present. The earldom cost Cavendish £10,000. It was not his first purchase of a peerage. In 1605, he had paid Arabella Stuart £2,000 to have her nominate him to become a baron. Although it was rare for anyone other than the king (or Buckingham during James's reign) to nominate, the sale of titles of honor during the reign of James was not. Peerages were for sale. Although there were fewer than 60 peers when Elizabeth I died in 1603, there were more than 80 by 1615 and more than

120 by 1628.[29] The number of earls, of which Cavendish was one, more than doubled. James was selling nobility in order to supplement the money he got from Parliament. Because it was not practically possible to create new peers indefinitely, James created a new rank, baronet, higher than a knight and lower than a baron. (The rank was Bacon's brainchild.) In order to maintain its value, like a commemorative plate from the Franklin Mint, baronets were made in a limited edition of two hundred. There might have been a saying, 'If you're so rich, why aren't you a peer?' Anyway, Cavendish could easily afford the payment for an earldom.

Sir Walter Raleigh, a sick and broken man, was also at Salisbury when Cavendish was elevated. Even though his time was almost up, the explorer, adventurer, and anti-Spaniard must have been a fascinating and revered figure for Hobbes, who had marveled at the exploits of such adventurers in his youth. Raleigh had recently returned from his failed raid on the Spanish colony at Guiana. He was questioned by the chancellor and other commissioners about the matter. His behavior had jeopardized the possibility of a marriage between Spanish and English royalty. Spain wanted such a marriage in order to move England away from an alliance with the Netherlands. The Spanish ambassador, who had protested the expedition before it had begun, insisted that Raleigh be executed. Raleigh had spent all of his goodwill and had no reasonable defense for his actions. He was beheaded in October.

A Comet, 1618

An isolated incident will bring this chapter and phase of Hobbes's life to a close. Although he would not become seriously interested in science until the 1630s, Hobbes was fascinated by a comet that appeared in mid-December of 1618. Writing decades later, he recounted that he saw it when its tail seemed to be at its greatest length:

I thought that its head was burning, for it seemed as though the illumination of the night air was projected from that fire. I pondered the fact that neither the comet itself nor its mane could at that time have fallen within the shadow of the earth unless the comet was indeed near to the earth (because the sun was about 20 [degrees] in Sagittarius but the comet was more to the north than Arcturus was.) I did not know what to make of this, nor, when I had read other authors, did I subsequently find anything but grounds for doubt. Let me openly profess my ignorance of the formation and nature of comets – not only do I know nothing for sure, but also I do not put forward any conjecture worthy of consideration.[30]

Hobbes must have been moved to research the phenomenon of comets because he then recounts the observations and theories of many astronomers, Peter Apian, Cornelius Gemma, Tycho Brahe, and Rothomann. There is a sense of relief in his report that none of them has a good explanation of comets either. Ignorance too loves, company.

3

Secretary and Humanist, 1621–1629

Now for his [Thucydides'] writings, two things are to be considered in them: truth and elocution. For in truth consists the soul, and in elocution the body of history. The latter without the former is but a picture of history; and the former without the later unapt to instruct. Let us see how our author has acquitted himself in both. ("Of the Life and History of Thucydides")

During the 1620s, a large part of Hobbes's life was occupied with serving as William's secretary, improving his own literary skills, and deepening his knowledge of history. As secretary, Hobbes helped William with his work as lord-lieutenant of Derbyshire, as a member for the Parliaments of 1621 and 1624, and as a stockholder in the Virginia Company. At the same time, Hobbes was improving his Latin and Greek, most notably, translating Thucydides' *History of the Peloponnesian War*, writing at least one long poem and possibly some essays, and sometimes working as a secretary to Francis Bacon. These activities are the subject of this chapter.

Horae Subsecivae

In 1620, an anonymous collection of essays was published, *Horae Subsecivae* (*Leisure Time*). It is divided into two parts. The first part contains twelve short essays, called "Observations." Ten of these are almost identical to the ten essays that William presented to his father in 1615. The other two, "Of a Country Life" and "Of Religion," are new to the book. The authorship of all of these essays has been attributed to various people: William himself, Grey Brydges (Lord Chandos), William's older brother Gilbert, Francis Bacon, and Hobbes. As explained in the preceding chapter, William is the most likely author. The second part of the book contains four longer essays, called "Discourses." One of these is a variant of the "Discourse of Flatterie" that William had dedicated to his father-in-law, Lord Bruce, in 1611. The other three are "Of Rome," which also was discussed in the preceding chapter, "A Discourse upon the Beginning of Tacitus," and "Of Laws." The same problem of authorship concerns these essays. The standard scholarly view now is that Hobbes is their author. The evidence is that the three essays are stylistically similar to each other and to some of Hobbes's other writings; they are compatible with Hobbes's experience and interests; they are published with essays by William; and there is no better candidate for authorship. Also, if William and Hobbes are severally the authors of the essays, then there is a simple explanation for the anonymity of the collection. Friend or not, it would have been unprecedented for a nobleman to share authorship with his employee. This notwithstanding, it is somewhat odd that when he came to reminisce wistfully in his verse autobiography about his years with William and where he was bold enough to call himself William's friend, Hobbes did not mention that they had contributed essays to the same book, even if he would not have dared to claim coauthorship. (Perhaps Hobbes was embarrassed by their quality.) A related oddity involves William's correspondence with Micanzio. Why would William, who knew of Micanzio's great love of Bacon's essays, fail to mention or to offer his own to him?

Since "Of Rome" was already discussed in Chapter 2, only the remaining essays, both of which deal with politics broadly construed, will be discussed here. My guess is that the latter two essays were written after "Of Rome," because he would be more likely to write about his trip soon after its completion than later, and because the themes of the latter two essays are closer to those that occupied Hobbes in the 1620s. However, since "Upon the Beginning of Tacitus," preceded "Of Rome," it may be the earlier piece.

Scholars have very different opinions about the intellectual merit of the essay on Tacitus and on laws. On one end of the spectrum are people who consider both small gems; at the other end of the spectrum, where I stand, are those who think they are shocking disappointments. As I indicated in Chapter 2, it is hard to understand how the author of pieces as pedestrian as these could ever have come to write masterpieces like *De Cive* and *Leviathan*. The fact that Hobbes produced "Of Tacitus" in his early thirties and *De Cive* in his early fifties is one of the strongest arguments I can think of for adult education.

In downplaying the quality of the essays on Tacitus and on laws, I am not suggesting that they should be ignored. The essays merit our attention partly because Hobbes's judgment of the Roman historian might be compared with his judgment of Thucydides, who he thought was the greatest historian of all time, and partly because we can get some sense for where Hobbes was intellectually between 1616 and 1620.

"Of Tacitus"

Let us begin our look at the two essays with "A Discourse Upon the Beginning of Tacitus" (hereafter "Of Tacitus"). The essay in fact has the character of a school exercise. My guess is that it is part of Hobbes's attempt to improve his facility in Latin, combined with a growing interest in contemporary politics that was nurtured by the study of ancient history. Some years later, Hobbes would translate Thucydides' *History of the Peloponnesian War*. Compared to his mature love of Thucydides, his interest in Tacitus must be considered an early infatuation.

Tacitus was very popular in the sixteenth and seventeenth centuries. His cynicism, realism, and skepticism were appealing to people who saw the old world crumbling and were not clear about what would replace it. He was influential in late Tudor and early Stuart England. Elizabeth I read his works, and James I alluded to him in the 1603 edition of his *Precepts on the Art of Governing*. Both Prince Henry and Prince Charles read Tacitus as well. Francis Bacon had a high regard for Tacitus, as both a historian and a stylist. He refers to his "pointed, concise style," which was also referred to as "plain style." (It is possible that Hobbes aspired to a style "not flowery" but "perspicuous and easy to understand" through the influence of Tacitus directly or possibly through Bacon.) Hobbes's friend Ben Jonson used Tacitean language in his play *Sejanus* (1603). Even William Laud, the archbishop of Canterbury, quoted Tacitus just before his execution.[1] Given the cultural milieu and Hobbes's respect for James, Bacon, and Jonson, it is not surprising that Hobbes read and wrote something about Tacitus. Yet, this fact does not entail that Tacitus had a great effect on him though a few of Tacitus's sentiments were carried over into *Leviathan*. The evidence suggests just the opposite. The commentary on Tacitus is one of Hobbes's earliest intellectual efforts; he abandons the commentary after writing on less than 1 percent of it, in contrast to his translation of Thucydides' entire *History of the Peloponnesian War,* more than 200,000 words long, and Hobbes never again refers to Tacitus except for one mention near the end of his life. One reason that Hobbes may have left him behind in his later life is that Tacitus's sympathies were with the republicans.

"Of Tacitus" begins with the first line of the *Annals:* "Urbem Romam a principio Reges habuere." Hobbes appropriately translates it as, "The City of Rome was at the first governed by kings." This is better than the more literal translation, "Kings governed the city Rome from the beginning," because by making "Urbem Romam" the opening words, the historian indicates that the focus of his story is Rome itself, not the kings. One disappointment of Hobbes's commentary is that he does not say anything about the rhetorical elements of Tacitus's prose. Why would he not, if rhetoric had a strong attraction for him at this time?

Hobbes purports to cover six topics in "Of Tacitus": (1) an enumeration of the different forms of Roman government; (2) the personality appropriate to a historian; (3) the way Augustus acquired supreme power; (4) the advantages of naming one's successor; (5) how Livia, Augustus's wife, plotted to promote her children; and (6) what happened after Augustus died. However promising these topics may seem to be, the execution of them is by and large unsuccessful because the actual structure of the essay is determined mostly by the individual sentences and phrases of the opening paragraphs of Tactitus's text. Hobbes quotes a sentence or clause and then comments on it. This strategy is characteristic of an inexperienced author or one who has not mastered the material. The opening ten sections are devoted to commenting on the following passages:

> The city of Rome was at first governed by Kings.
> Liberty and the Consulship Lucius Brutus [were] brought in.
> Dictators were chosen but upon occasion.
> The *Decemviri* passed not two years.
> Neither did the Consulary authority in Tribunes of the Soldiers remain long in force.
> The domination of Cinna and Sulla did not long endure.
> The power of Pompey and Crassus soon passed into Caesar.
> The forces of Lepidus and Antonius came into the hands of Augustus.

Who, when the whole State was wearied with civil discords, received it under his government with the Title of Prince.

But of the ancient people of Rome, both the prosperous, and adverse estate has been recorded by renowned Writers.

With topics like these, is it any wonder that the commentary does not sparkle? What these sentences invite and what Hobbes in large part provides is a fleshing out of these historical bones.

My remarks about Hobbes's modest intellectual achievement in these essays are not meant to imply that the essays do not have their moments. Some of the epigrammatic passages are quite successful:

[I]t is contrary to the dignity of a Prince to take notice of that fault which he is not able to amend.

Augustus had hitherto dealt with the State, as one that tames wild horses; first, he did beat and weary them; next, took care not to frighten them with shadows; then showed them hope of ease, and made provision of corn for them; and now he begins gently to back [mount] the State.

That purse that was heaviest, that bribe that was greatest, carried the cause. Justice was not seen, but felt; a good bribe was their best advocate.

[H]ope is the whetstone of man's desires.[2]

Several of these epigrams are paraphrases of Tacitus's own words or at least echo his sentiments. A few of these sentiments also got carried over into *Leviathan* as when Hobbes wrote:

To have received from one to whom we think ourselves equal greater benefit than there is hope to requite disposes to counterfeit love, but really secret hatred and puts a man into the estate of a desperate debtor . . . For benefits oblige, and obligation is thraldom, and unrequitable obligation perpetual thraldom, which is to one's equal hateful.

That opinion always struck me as odd until I read Hobbes's translation of Tacitus:

When once they [benefits] exceed that [being requitable] they are an intolerable burden, and men seldom are willing to acknowledge them; for who but a man of desperate estate will set his hand to such an obligation as he knows he never can discharge. . . . So that great services procure many times rather the hatred than the love of him they are done unto.[3]

Here is another example. In *Leviathan*, Hobbes says, "To have done more hurt to a man than he can or is willing to expiate inclines the doer to hate the sufferer. For he must expect revenge or forgiveness, both which are hateful." In "Of Tacitus," he says, it is "the property of human nature to hate those they have wronged; so also is it on the contrary to love those to whom they have been beneficial." Tacitus is translated as saying: "For benefits increase the love of the bestower more than of him that receives them: for as it is . . . the property of human nature, to hate those they have wronged; so also is it on the contrary, to love those to whom they have been beneficial."[4]

Viewed from the perspective of his later political thought, many of Hobbes's views in "Of Tacitus" are surprising. He says that "the first form of government in any state is accidental."[5] This contrasts with the view he would express in the *Elements of Law, Natural and Politic* (1640), where he would maintain that democracy is the earliest and least stable form of commonwealth. Also, in all of his political works, he maintained that monarchy is the best form. Even though Hobbes knew that governments were not necessarily monarchical, it is hard to believe that he would ever say in his later political writings that monarchy is an accident. On the contrary, most governments are monarchies, Hobbes would say, because they are the most stable ones. Other royalist theorists, such as Robert Filmer, would use the pervasiveness of monarchy in the most ancient times to argue that monarchy is the original and ultimately only justifiable form of government. Even John Locke, for whom monarchy was only one form of government among others, thought that it was natural for it to be the earliest. Later in "Of Tacitus," Hobbes again demeans monarchs when he says that their historians have to lie about the monarch's bad actions in order to avoid being censored.

But Hobbes is not antiroyalist in this essay. After acknowledging Romulus as the founding king of Rome and dutifully enumerating the succeeding kings, he explains that the rule of consuls arose from the assassination of Tarquinus Superbus due to a private dispute. And the Romans were no more satisfied with the successive governments than they had been with their kings. The rule of kings is not worse than other forms. People are difficult to rule and rarely satisfied. Hobbes implies that the supposed democratic governments of the Romans were de facto oligarchies, just as he would in *Leviathan*.

One of the strikingly un-Hobbesian elements of this early essay is his sympathetic treatment of liberty. In the essay, he says that the Romans lost their "liberty" when Augustus took over, and he often implies that this loss was disastrous. Hobbes repeats the fable of the horse that, in order to escape a deer, became a slave to a man who put a bridle on him. The horse "could never after recover his former liberty." The mistake that the Romans made, according to Hobbes, was to allow a man to control the entire military might of the nation under the pretext of defending the citizens when he in fact intended to promote himself by turning the soldiers "to our [!] destruction." But if there is one thing that is clear about his later political view it is that having a monopoly on military might is part of the essence of sovereignty. In *Behemoth*, written during the Restoration, he would partially explain the English Civil War as the result of the division of the army between Parliament and Charles. In *Leviathan*, liberty clearly takes a diminished role. He says explicitly that the citizens of no state are freer than those of any other: "There is written on the turrets of the city of Lucca in great characters at this day, the word *Libertas;* yet no man can thence infer that a particular man has more liberty or immunity from the service of the commonwealth there than in Constantinople. Whether a Commonwealth be monarchical, or popular, the freedom is still the same."[6]

Sometimes "Of Tacitus" intermixes un-Hobbesian and traditional Hobbesian themes, as when he praises liberty and denounces civil war in the same sentence. He freely talks about tyranny in the essay because he thinks that some states are freer than others. In contrast, the mature Hobbes would come to disapprove of this use of the word 'tyranny'. For him, monarchy is the best form of government. 'Tyranny' and 'monarchy' denote the same thing; the difference between the words is merely one of usage, not signification. 'Tyranny' connotes the speaker's negative opinion of monarchy.

Tyranny is disliked because a person and not the laws rule. The young Hobbes had this sentiment himself. He lamented the condition in which "great men grow once too mighty for the laws." He thought that men with authority should have coercive power only for the purpose of enforcing the laws, and the latter seem to have an independent existence. Hobbes sarcastically quotes the proverb "Laws are like Spiders' webs, only to hold the smaller Flies."[7] In contrast, the mature Hobbes of

Leviathan pooh-poohed the idea that there was any sense to being ruled by laws and not men. He said that only the sovereign makes the laws, so whatever the sovereign says is law.

Just as strong as his condemnation of loss of liberty is his condemnation of civil war; it is the worst thing that can happen to a state. The only ones who benefit from civil war are "desperate unthrifts that they may cut their creditors' throats without fear of the gallows, men against whom the law and the sword of justice makes a fearful war in time of peace."[8] What this sentiment lacks in comparison with his later political theory is a theoretical underpinning. Although the young Hobbes condemns civil war, the condemnation does not yet fit into any large-scale view of the world, which view would not develop until the early 1640s.

It is not surprising that in *Leviathan* a mature Hobbes would maintain that to ensure stability obedience is the primary virtue of any subject. After all, according to the Judeo-Christian tradition, the essence of sin is disobedience. When Adam and Eve ate the forbidden fruit, the ruin that they brought upon themselves and their descendants happened because they disobeyed God. In contrast, a younger and more recalcitrant Hobbes makes much less of that virtue in "Of Tacitus." There he somewhat derisively maintains that obedience is "the greatest virtue" only for subjects of a monarch. It has that primacy under monarchy because the subjects have lost their liberty. Thus, the function of subjects under such a rule is to "apply themselves wholly to the arts of service, whereof obsequiousness is the chief."[9]

In *Leviathan,* Hobbes would often argue against the idea that a person could serve two masters. He was most concerned about the presbyterian policy of separating religious from secular authority. The problem of serving two masters is present in an unfocused way in "Of Tacitus." Hobbes says that Rome faced a crisis of government when Livia and her two sons shared power: "For it is a hard matter to serve and please well one Master: but to please two or more, when there is, or may be, betwixt them competition or jealousy (leaving out that one of them is a woman) is altogether impossible."[10]

Hobbes has been categorized as a Machiavellian because of his commentary on Tacitus and aspects of the discourse in "Of Rome." Certainly some of the sentiments in the essay can be described as Machiavellian, such as his remark that "it is not wisdom for one that is to convert a free State into a Monarchy, to take away all the show of their liberty at one blow, and on a sudden make them feel servitude, without first introducing into their minds some *previae dispositiones,* or preparatives, whereby they may the better endure it." But, beyond sharing the realism of Machiavelli, I do not see any special resemblance.

"Of Laws"

The remaining essay from *Horae Subsecivae* that might have been authored by Hobbes is "Of Laws." Its purpose is to discuss the nature and basic types of law. Hobbes says that law is "the straight and perfect rule by application whereunto, right and wrong are discerned and distinguished one from another." When sketching his history and development of law among the Romans, Hobbes makes clear that he thinks law does not have to be a command. The common law has the status of law in virtue of its necessity, of which a sign is the fact that it is "grounded upon ancient customs."[11] This contrasts with his definition of law in *Leviathan:* Law is command. The laws of nature can be considered genuine laws in that they are the commands of God; and civil laws are the commands of the sovereign.

It is not clear what Hobbes meant by "straight and perfect rule" in the essay, although it may suggest that these rules have some objective character, independent of the will of human beings. This suggestion is reinforced by the clause, "whereunto right and wrong are discerned." Similarly, when Hobbes says in the essay that the equal administration of justice is "the true knot that binds us to unity and peace amongst our selves and disperses all such violence and unlawful courses as otherwise liberty would insinuate,"[12] he gives the impression that justice is logically prior to government. This early doctrine is quite different from that of *Leviathan,* in which justice is usually viewed as something artificial, a construct of political society. According to Hobbes, good and evil in civil society are defined by laws, and they are the result of the sovereign's choice. Justice and injustice are the keeping and breaking of covenants, respectively. Sometimes he says that there is no such thing as justice in the state of nature, even when there are covenants.

In "Of Laws," Hobbes takes a strong stand against injustice. When someone breaks the law, "there is no other satisfaction left to the world or the party offended than the punishment of the offender." Punishment is necessary because just as "it encourages men in their just and lawful actions, so it abates the insolency of others who be only bridled with the fear of punishment." Without punishment, "the worst men by wickedest courses were most likely to make great fortunes, and to carry the greatest sway, which would so discourage men honestly disposed that they would neither have will nor power nor confidence to labor for the public."[13] This part of the essay could have been preached before the king by one of his chaplains.

One of the most important aspects of the essay "Of Laws," as regards Hobbes's intellectual development, is the fact that the laws are put ahead of sovereigns. Laws, he says, are "so great and absolute that men otherwise could not be distinguished from unreasonable creatures." Laws are, in effect,

the princes we ought to serve, the captains we are to follow, the very rules by which all the actions of our life be squared and disposed. They are the bulwarks and defenses to keep them in safety and peace that no unjust thing be done against them, that by the laws men may be made good and happy, and that the punishment of offenders should appear to proceed from a necessity forced rather than a will voluntary.[14]

In *Leviathan*, the priority of princes and laws would be reversed. Since laws are the commands of princes [sovereigns], they do not exist without a prince whether it be a divine prince [God] or a human one. And any law that a prince makes can be nullified by him.

One of the key ideas in Hobbes's later political philosophy, that of the laws of nature, is hardly mentioned in "Of Laws." Instead he refers to "fundamental laws, upon which the fabric of a commonwealth and people be grounded and built, . . . [and which] in no case will admit innovation." But he thinks that most laws change over time, because time "is the greatest innovator."[15] In fact, to preserve the old laws when new conditions obtain, he sagely observes, is to introduce a change, because the old laws only made sense in regulating the old conditions. The law originated in ancient Rome as the will and command of princes; later it evolved into a codified set of rules to which most nations give at least some authority. England's own civil law, in contrast with the common law, was based on Roman law.

International Affairs, 1620–28

Much of William's political involvement during the 1620s and thus much of Hobbes's interest is reflected in the correspondence between William and Micanzio that continued until 1628. Micanzio's letters of 1620 are primarily concerned with two matters. One is the reception of Sarpi's book *The History of the Council of Trent*, which showed up the duplicity and fallibility of the Roman Catholic Church. Predictably, it was condemned at Rome. The other, which requires some explanation, is the fate of Frederick, the elector of the Palatinate, who was the son-in-law of James I. Frederick accepted the invitation of some Protestant rebels to become emperor of the Holy Roman Empire. (The strongest claimant was the Spanish-backed Roman Catholic Ferdinand II.) Frederick's own claim was as weak as his army. His delusion of emperorship was complemented by his delusion that his father-in-law could be trusted to support him militarily. Almost all that James sent were promises. Frederick's grand design on the Holy Roman Empire was smashed by his defeat at White Mountain (1620).

Micanzio's two items – Sarpi's book and Frederick's misadventures – were related. Sarpi's book was a successful intellectual attack on the Catholicism of Rome, but the attack of Frederick was an unsuccessful military attack against that same Catholicism. In effect, Micanzio was reporting that while Venice was doing its job, England was not. James had implied that he would send an army to support Frederick's claim to the throne, but then reneged. James was a lover, not a fighter.

Micanzio wanted to know what James was now going to do to help Frederick. He was unable to comprehend James's inaction. As Frederick's situation continued to deteriorate, Micanzio reported rumors that England would be converted to Roman Catholicism and that the Prince of Wales had already converted. When Micanzio says that he does not believe it, one has the sense that he means, "Please tell me it isn't so."

In January 1621, James opened a new Parliament. Buckingham and the Spanish faction opposed it, but James saw it as a necessity for financial reasons. Micanzio was dubious about its prospects, but William was optimistic and remained so long after an ordinary person would have seen that no good was going to come of it. In May, William informed Micanzio that Bacon had been removed as chancellor. William was still optimistic about Parliament and Micanzio still pessimistic. Although Bacon would never again have political power, Micanzio never lost interest in or respect for him. Many of his letters end with a request for William to give his regards to Bacon.

When Frederick's fortunes further deteriorated, James called the prorogued Parliament back into session in November 1621. But instead of staying in London, he went to Newmarket to play. James presumptuously expected Commons to vote him money to support Frederick. Commons did not trust James and was not about to give him any money. Its members rightly saw that James could not both fight Spain for the Palatinate and have it as a friend; he could not both tolerate Roman Catholicism in England and try to stamp it out on the Continent. And how could he think of marrying his son to the Spanish infanta?

In December, the House of Commons presented James with a document that specified its reservations about his policies. James was furious. He decided to dissolve Parliament. In his council chamber, he announced his decision and called for the journal book of the Commons. He ripped out the page that contained the "Protestation" and soon dissolved Parliament. When Micanzio learned of the dissolution, he said that he had never had any hope for it, and he attributed a large part of the failure to James's desire for a Spanish match between Charles and the infanta.

James's slide into disrepute had been long coming, and it is hard to explain William's optimism of the year before, unless he was merely putting on a happy face for the unhappy Venetian. Not long after the end of Parliament, William returned to his estates in Derbyshire and caused a gap in correspondence. Micanzio was disturbed by the silence. When the correspondence resumed, he made a point of complimenting William on his supposedly astute analysis of English affairs. But he still thinks that William is too optimistic. He is convinced that Spain has the upper hand and that the situation of Venice and England will deteriorate. It is clear that Micanzio is worried about England being at peace when the rest of Europe is at war, because he says just the opposite and then adds that he hopes that England's peace does not cause greater troubles.

Occasionally, there was some opportunity for wry humor. The pope that succeeded Paul V was a Jesuit and wanted to honor his order by canonizing some of its heroes, such as Ignatius Loyola, Philip Neri, and Francis Xavier. The Jesuits were hoping for a miracle to confirm their divine calling, when much to their chagrin some scaffolding fell down, killing one and injuring eight. At first, all of the casualties were believed to be Jesuits, and there was no pious explanation for the incident. Their morale soared later when it was supposedly discovered that the dead man had been a Protestant.

In addition to his work as the translator of Micanzio's letters, Hobbes's involvement in William's political activities is confirmed by a letter that survives from Robert Mason of St. John's College, Cambridge, who later became secretary to the duke of Buckingham. Written in a familiar, chatty style, its contents concern some of the same international affairs that Micanzio reported on. Mason expresses his sympathy for Sir Horace Vere, the leader of a failed expedition of English volunteers who had gone to help Frederick. There is some indication that Hobbes is more discreet about peddling tales than Mason. That is what I infer from Mason's request that Hobbes "be as free with me as you see that I am with you" and his willingness to have rumors reported to him that may originate "at sixth, seventh or fiftieth hand."[16]

Like many politically interested young men, Mason and presumably Hobbes were interested in the diplomatic intrigues even more than the fighting. The Roman Catholic Spaniards wanted to arrange a marriage between Charles, the Prince of Wales, and the infanta, in order to diminish the likelihood of James sending aid to his Protestant son-in-law. In time, there would be a personally and diplomatically silly courtship between the prince and the infanta. In early 1623, Charles and Buckingham had initiated the reckless plan of traveling incognito through France to Spain in order to negotiate the marriage agreement that had been dragging on for many years. What they did not seem to appreciate was that once in Spain, they were de facto hostages, not to mention the inherent dangers of traveling in foreign countries. Predictably, after months of posturing by Charles, he insincerely agreed to the Spanish terms for a marriage, left Spain with the promise to marry the infanta by proxy, and arrived back in London in October. The English were overjoyed by his return because Charles was not married to a Catholic. Enjoying their new popularity with the people, Charles and Buckingham urged James to call a new Parliament in order to get the money needed to start a war against Spain. James was unenthusiastic, but he was a sick and broken man. Parliament eventually opened in February 1624.

Mason, like Micanzio, was also interested in the prodigal De Dominis (the former archbishop of Spalato) and mentions his recent departure for Rome. He doubted the sincerity of De Dominis's return to the bosom of the Roman Catholic Church: "he has long since dyed himself in such a color of Reformation as all the holy water in Rome cannot wash out of him." Micanzio of course had more at stake than Mason in the actions of De Dominis. De Dominis's double-crossing decision to abandon the Church of England and to return to Rome was a long, sharp thorn in Micanzio's side because it undermined the chances of uniting England with antipapal Catholics in Italy. Micanzio said that De Dominis "is already canonized in all the world for one of the most wicked men that ever lived" and is "resolute to do all the evil he can." When he heard that De Dominis had told the pope that he had never really abandoned Roman Catholicism and had only criticized Rome to ingratiate himself with the English so that he could spy on them, Micanzio was beside himself with rage. He railed that De Dominis "confounds himself every day more [than before] . . . in fictions, lies, and infamy." When the Prince of Wales had gone to Spain, the Spanish thought that his intention must have been to convert to Roman Catholicism. When the news reached Italy, it was embellished with the rumor that all of England would be converted to Roman Catholicism. Micanzio reported that De Dominis crowed that his "predictions are come to pass," and he "magnifies his own merits and says he spoke truth when he said he had reduced [won over] the king [James I] and the principal of the Court to his religion."

Unable to criticize the prince directly, Micanzio does so implicitly: "For the reverence due to so great princes require that we should suppose all to be wisely done which they do and that it should be done with wisdom and advice; at least they should be allowed thus much, that it should be held for done for some ends." With sarcasm oozing from his words, he specifically excludes the possibility that Charles is motivated by "his pleasures and dissoluteness." The "end of so deep a knowledge" as the prince possesses must be "some great purpose not seen by others."

Close to despair because Frederick has been defeated and because of rumors that James intends to extend toleration to Roman Catholics, Micanzio ended one letter: "God guides us through ways known to himself." The expressions of resignation to God become more frequent in 1623: "God's judgments are both just and secret. . . . God do his will and encline us to the obedience thereof. . . . But I confess that God has made his judgment to man impenetrable." There are few things more effective in bringing people to God than despair.

Things went from bad to worse for Micanzio in the succeeding months. He reported that "the pope is so impotent of brain that the cardinal nephew is absolutely pope" and the nephew is pursuing his own policy, not that of the pope. Then his mentor Sarpi died. Rome was certain that James I would convert to Catholicism. Micanzio had no alternative but to "find out this riddle" by waiting until "the event" played itself out. In a letter of June 1623, William reassured Micanzio that there was nothing to fear from Charles's trip to Spain. Unfortunately, we do not know exactly what William said because we have only Micanzio's expression of relief.

I have my doubts that William was anywhere near as forthcoming as Micanzio was. For example, William did not report the arrival of the Prince of Wales in London to Micanzio. Also, although Parliament opened in mid-February, Micanzio did not know about it even in late March. When he did learn of it, he perfunctorily expressed his happiness that it had opened, but was pessimistic about what it might achieve. Again, Micanzio's instincts are right. James's infirmity was evident. Charles and Buckingham were in effect exercising the monarchical power. Parliament was asserting its voice. James was disgusted by all of it. He fulminated against what he perceived as Parliament's insolence in petitioning him to break his treaties with Spain. But in the end, Charles and Buckingham and Parliament got what they wanted: a war with Spain and an alliance with France.

Charles's First Parliament, 1625

William does not seem to have been a very good correspondent during the early part of this year. Shortly before James's death in March 1625, Micanzio complained that he had not heard from him for a long time, even though William was apparently in London. Funeral preparations for the king were elaborate, and burial was delayed until May. William's father was listed as one of the fourteen "assistants to the chief mourner," the chief mourner being King Charles himself. Since sons of earls were also included in the funeral, it is a safe assumption that William was there and hence that Hobbes was in the area also.

By English law, the monarch never died. When one human being who had the office of king died, the successor immediately became king, even though the coronation ceremony, and even the known identity of that person, might be delayed months or even years. So Charles, the surviving son of James, became king on March 27, 1625.

One of the first bits of business of a new king was to call Parliament. Normally, Parliament would give the monarch the right to collect "tonnage and poundage," that is, an excise tax on wine and grain, for life. From the very beginning, many things would not be normal during Charles's reign. The circumstances surrounding the opening of Charles's first Parliament were inauspicious. England was at war with Spain, an army sent to help Frederick met with disaster, and Parliamentarians were becoming even more dissatisfied with Buckingham. It was not a good time to ask Parliament for relatively large amounts of money to meet his commitments, but Charles had no choice.

William and Hobbes were probably in London at least by April 1625, since that was when Parliament had been scheduled to begin. But it was prorogued until June. William represented Derbyshire while his father sat in the House of Lords. Like the Parliament of 1621, the one of 1625 was very concerned about religion in England. It wanted the recusancy laws against Roman Catholics enforced. Charles was in a bind. If he persecuted the Roman Catholics, then he would break the terms of his wedding contract with France. If he did not persecute them, he would not get his money. He acted in his near-term interests and promised to punish the Catholics. But for his efforts, Charles did not get the usual lifetime grant of money from tonnage and poundage, an excise tax on imported wine and grain. Instead, Parliament voted tonnage and poundage for only one year.

In early July, most members of Parliament left London because the plague was raging. Parliament was formally prorogued on July 11. Given his disposition, Hobbes would have left town with the others if he had any choice in the matter. Parliament reassembled at Oxford in August. Buckingham came under fierce attack, and Charles dissolved his first Parliament, coming away with insufficient money and lingering ill will from the Parliamentarians.

Not being able to think of a better remedy for his financial problems, Charles called a second Parliament for early 1626. When that one failed, he was forced to become more imaginative. He continued to collect tonnage and poundage as if he had a right to do so. He thought that if the money would not come to him, then he would go to the money. He also resorted to forced loans.

Forced loans had been used by previous monarchs, notably Elizabeth, but they were never popular; and Charles, being less lovable than the Virgin Queen, encountered more opposition. Even William, who was lord-lieutenant of Derbyshire and thus responsible for collecting the forced loan, initially refused to pay it. He was the first to sign a reply of July 18, 1626, of the Derbyshire justices, refusing to give Charles I the "free gift" that he asked for. In doing so, William was acting in the tradition of his paternal grandfather (one of Bess's husbands), who had refused to accede to a forced loan instigated by Elizabeth. William eventually went along with the program, however. As his secretary, Hobbes helped to collect the loans.

Absolute Sovereignty

In addition to the inherent dislike of taxes, an important part of the revenue controversy concerned an ingrained belief of most wealthy Englishmen, namely, that property rights were part of the common law and did not depend upon the monarch. At the behest of the king, who was looking for support for his policy wherever he could, two clerics, Roger Manwaring and Robert Sibthorpe preached an absolutist doctrine of sovereignty, contrary to the belief in inviolable property rights. According to them, the king derived his right to govern directly from God, and so, as Manwaring said, "nothing can be denied" to kings even if what is commanded is harsh or unfair. Parliament punished Manwaring for his loyalty to the king and to the doctrine of absolute sovereignty, but the king rewarded him soon enough after that.

Hobbes came to virtually the same conclusion as Manwaring but from different premises. It is not clear when he first had these thoughts. They were written down in *The Elements of Law, Natural and Politic* (1640), but he may have had them much earlier. Hobbes told Aubrey that Manwaring "preached his [Hobbes's] doctrine." The context suggests that Hobbes meant that Manwaring was influenced by Hobbes. Since Manwaring made a stir in the mid-1620s, Hobbes may have been referring to his own views at that very time. Although there is no direct evidence for their association, it is plausible that they would have conversed. The two men overlapped as students at Oxford and were almost the same age. Manwaring was a chaplain to the king, and Hobbes was sometimes at court with William. Although Hobbes was not a divine right theorist, he sometimes used that kind of language for rhetorical purposes (even in the last years of his life), and one can imagine him using it with Manwaring.

Hobbes's real theoretical position, which he first made clear in 1640, was that private property does not exist in the state of nature because everyone has a right to everything. The ideas of "mine and thine" (*meum et teum*) make sense only under the rule of a sovereign. John Selden, who befriended Hobbes in 1652, did not accept this view. Selden said that if Sibthorpe were right, then "there is no *Meum* or *Teum;* no man in England has any thing of his own."[17] Hobbes thought that that was ultimately the truth. He would come to be strongly criticized by many people, including loyal royalists, for holding the Manwaring-Sibthorpe view. It is one of Lord Clarendon's main criticisms of him.

In addition to his work as lord-lieutenant, William also served in the Parliaments of 1621 and 1624. Since his father was a member of the House of Lords, it was not hard for William to be elected to the House of Commons. 'Selection' may be a better word than 'election' because the person chosen to represent a county or borough was usually negotiated among the richest and most influential men of the area. Given the overwhelming wealth of the Cavendish family in Derbyshire, it was easy for William to be selected. He served as a member until he ascended to the House of Lords upon the death of his father in 1626.

William was a better courtier than politician. He participated in the functions of court, including the installation of Charles as the Prince of Wales and the marriage of Charles and Henrietta Maria. When Charles was crowned king in 1625, William's eldest son, the future third earl of Devonshire, was made a Knight of the Bath. Part of William's success at court is attributable to his absurdly lavish expenses. His house in London, which sat on the present site of Devonshire Square in Bishopsgate, was described as looking more like a prince's court than a subject's.

The Virginia Company Meetings, 1622–24

In 1615, Cavendish had become one of the grantees of the Bermudas or Somer Islands and an original member of the "Company of the City of London for the Plantation of the Somers Islands," an offshoot of the Virginia Company.[18] One of the eight 'tribes' of the Virginia Company was called the Devonshire Tribe. Cavendish's son William would later become a governor of the Bermudas Company. On June 19, 1622, Hobbes became directly involved with the company when William gave him one share in it. Since each shareholder received one vote no matter how many shares he held, it seems plain that Cavendish's motive was to enhance his own influence over the company. It is revealing that Hobbes atttended only those meetings at which William was also present, except for the period between July 1623 and February 1624, when William was in hiding for reasons that will be explained below. Hobbes's toadyish participation is confirmed by the accusation of Sir Nathaniel Rich that some shareholders were packing votes with "a number of friends, allies and confidants ready to assist with their votes." By the time Hobbes joined the company, it had been in dire financial straits for some time and was divided into two factions. William was aligned with the one led by Edwin Sandys, who had taken over as treasurer in 1619, while Rich was aligned with the one led by Sir Thomas Smith (Smythe), who had lost control of the company to Sandys and his party.

As part of a supposed reform measure in late 1622, Sandys and some of his allies were to be given exorbitant salaries in order to get the company, ironically, on sound financial footing. The Smith coalition was furious. Commenting on the fulminations of one of these, William declared that his opponent had spoken, not "out of present passion and heat, but upon premeditate intention to raise a Combustion."[19] By 1623, the tide had turned again. The Sandys faction was in the minority, and the end of the company was inevitable. As the company was being dismantled, Sandys's faction lashed out at the opposition. In May 1623, William presented a report in which he calumnied Robert Rich, earl of Warwick, for his activities in the company. Warwick counterattacked and had William, Sandys, and two others put under house arrest for violating the privy council's order to avoid inflammatory statements. At a July meeting, Warwick accused William of lying. The pride of an aristocrat demanded that William challenge Warwick. Since dueling had been outlawed in England, the two decided to hold the event in the Netherlands on August 1. The plot was thick. Both William and Warwick were well known in England, and the duel was caused by the infamous Virginia Company business. The duel even became known to Micanzio through one of his sources. He wrote to William: "I have heard of a certain quarrel your Lordship has with a great person by which I have been ever troubled expecting the event. And praying earnestly unto God that the end thereof may be such as may be fully to your reputation and without any hurt in any of the goods which either nature, fortune or god has granted to you. Amen." Fortunately, no one got hurt. The privy council intervened and ordered the arrest of both parties. While Warwick managed to get to Ghent in modern-day Belgium, William, moving at a snail's pace, was apprehended in Shoreham, Sussex.

One reason that the duel never came off was that William's wife, Christian, and the countess of Warwick were friends, and they "joined hands in a plea to the government to prevent the duel."[20] Personal relations in Stuart England were every bit as complicated and crazy as they are today. Warwick's son later married William's daughter Anne. And still later, but mercifully after her death, Anne's only son married Oliver Cromwell's youngest daughter.

Dueling occupied an ambiguous position in early Stuart England. Its public character conflicted with its private status. James I had outlawed it, yet sometimes it remained the only way that a gentleman could preserve his honor. Hobbes commented in *Leviathan:* "And at this day in this part of the world private duels are and always will be honorable, though unlawful, till such time as there shall be honor ordained for them that refuse and ignominy for them that make the challenge. For duels also are many times effects of courage; and the ground of courage is always strength or skill, which are power." But duelers are in a double bind: "For example, the law condemns duels; the punishment is made capital. On the contrary part, he that refuses a duel is subject to contempt and scorn without remedy, and sometimes by the sovereign himself thought unworthy to have any charge or preferment in war." Because of this bind, Hobbes concluded that duelers "ought not in reason to be rigorously punished, since part of the fault may be discharged on the punisher."[21] To my knowledge, this is Hobbes's only criticism of James I, and it is mild enough.

Sandys and his allies, which included William and Hobbes, were the party out of favor with James I. Hobbes probably hated being in this position. The Spanish ambassador to James's Court, Count Gondomar, painted the members of the Virginia Company as potential rebels. He told the king: "That though they might have a fair pretense for their meetings, yet he would find in the end that court would prove a seminary for a seditious Parliament." We saw in Chapter 1 that Hobbes indicated that he always hated the Spanish, largely for ruining the occasion of his birth; and Gondomar's behavior, which he probably knew about, would have intensified his hatred. Nonetheless, he agreed with the substance of Gondomar's remark. In *Behemoth,* he would write that merchants are "the first encouragers of rebellion." Since their only interest is "to grow excessively rich by the wisdom of buying and selling,"[22] they consider any taxation to be a political grievance. The principal reason for the existence of the Virginia Company was money or "private gain," as Hobbes called it. The behavior of the principals among both factions was motivated by greed, and that generated a broad range of duplicitous and self-serving behavior. The combination of the venality of the proceedings in the Company and its problems with James I may explain why Hobbes never refers to his participation in it in any of his published works. There is only one perfunctory allusion to the Virginia Colony and Somer Islands in "Of Laws" and one in *Leviathan.* In the latter work, he cites the Company in arguing for the superiority of monarchical governments:

[W]hen there were colonies sent from England to plant Virginia and Somer Islands, though the government of them here were committed to assemblies in London, yet did those assemblies never commit the government under them to any assembly there; but did to each plantation send one governor. For though every man, where he can be present by nature, desires to participate of government; yet where they cannot be present, they are by nature also inclined to commit the government of their common interest rather to a monarchical then a popular form of government.[23]

Hobbes's association with Sandys was only practical. In theoretical matters, they were at opposite ends of the spectrum. Sandys believed that natural reason was superior even to the sovereign and that private property was a natural right. He was also an ally of the great common-law lawyer Edward Coke, whose theory Hobbes believed was inherently seditious. Hobbes eventually wrote *A Dialogue between a Philosopher and a Student of the Common Laws of England* in order to refute Coke.

One of the happy side effects of Hobbes's participation in the meetings of the Virginia Company was the opportunity it gave him to associate with some of the most powerful and interesting men of his time, although, given his social standing, he would not have been hobnobbing with them. And his membership gave him a convenient introduction to several members of the Great Tew circle in the 1630s. At least two members of the board, Sir Dudley Digges and John Selden, would become prominent members of the circle. Other important members had close relations on the board. George Sandys was the brother of Edwin Sandys; and two of Edward Hyde's relatives had been members of the board. Given their opportunities for meeting both at board meetings and at Great Tew, it is plausible that Aubrey is mistaken when he says that Hobbes did not meet Selden until after *Leviathan* was published. Instead, that is when a close friendship may have begun. We at least know that Hobbes was already enthusiastic about Selden's published work by 1636 when he wrote to Newcastle: "All I study is a [*sic*] nights, and that for a little while is the reading of certain new books, especially Mr. Selden's *Mare Clausum*."[24]

In light of Hobbes's early interest in exploration and his membership in the Virginia Company, it is somewhat surprising that his information about North America is so limited and his beliefs so distorted. In *Leviathan*, he would write that the condition of the American Indians is one example of the state of nature. (The other two are cases of civil war and wars between nations.) Believing that the Indians were in the state of nature could have supplied Hobbes with one justification of the institution of the colony: There is no mine or thine in the state of nature. A person has a right to whatever he can keep. He might have held this doctrine in an inchoate form in the 1620s. Self-serving justifications are credible ones. There were other justifications available. In his sermon to the Virginia Company, which Hobbes probably attended, John Donne says that land that is not filled by inhabitants is free to anyone who is able to "possess it."

James I seems to have justified colonization by the right of conquest. In 1621, he gave a speech in Parliament in which he said that "conquests are ordered by the will of the conqueror," and thus Virginia is not part of the crown of "England." It is his personal belonging and not subject to the laws of Parliament. Hobbes himself would have had no problem with the justification if he held in the 1620s the same view that he would express in his political works. About colonies, he would say that they could be established by inhabiting an unoccupied area or a land "made void . . . by war."[25] War is justified to establish a colony because people not under the same sovereign are in the state of nature with respect to each other, and in that condition everyone is an enemy to everyone else. Of course the purpose of colonization is to increase one's wealth in order to better ensure one's survival.

Sir Francis Bacon

Aubrey reports that Hobbes served as a secretary to Francis Bacon for some time. The standard view has been that this was during the early to mid-1620s, after Bacon was dismissed as chancellor for taking bribes and before the publication of the third edition of his *Essays* in 1625. But events that have already been mentioned make an earlier date also possible. Hobbes could already have encountered Bacon in 1614, when both Bacon and William served in Parliament. From Micanzio's letters to William, we know that William at least, and hence probably Hobbes, had dealings with Bacon by late 1615. Finally, the account books at Chatsworth show that Hobbes was with Bacon by May 1620.

To some extent, the legal problems that led to Bacon's disgrace and fall from power were due to the personal animosity of Buckingham and Edward Coke. In 1597, Bacon had lost out to Coke in a contest for the hand in marriage of Lady Hatton. She refused Bacon's proposal before accepting one by Coke. Two decades later, Bacon had tried to interfere in the marriage of Coke's daughter to Buckingham's younger brother. In addition to these personal conflicts, Bacon also had intellectual reasons to dislike Coke, the great defender of the thesis that the common law was superior to everything, even the king. Hobbes shared this dislike for Coke's view, as mentioned earlier. Hobbes may also have had a dislike for Buckingham, whose policies were often opposed by William. Also, Buckingham interfered with Newcastle's attempt to marry Coke's daughter. She married Buckingham's brother.

Some modern commentators excuse Bacon's corrupt behavior as lord chancellor by appealing to the principle that "everyone did it," *it* being the taking of bribes. The defense is weak. Bacon's judges knew what the normal level of corruption was, and so they came to the right decision in convicting Bacon of in effect sinking below that level. He was fined £40,000 and prohibited from ever sitting in Parliament again. Bacon's own defense of himself is no better. He claimed that his decisions were not influenced by the money he accepted from the interested parties. At its best, this defense admits to malfeasance. Bacon does not even meet the liberal criterion of an honest politician in Prohibition-era Chicago, that is, one who "when he's bought, he stays bought."

Bacon was arrogant and often self-serving. Not even his friends liked him. When he eventually died, his wife did not need more than three weeks to grieve since she married his butler at the end of that period.

Hobbes's duties to Bacon included taking dictation and also helping with the translation of some of the essays into Latin for the international market. Aubrey says that Bacon enjoyed having Hobbes around him: "His lordship would often say that he better liked Mr. Hobbes's taking his thoughts, than any of the other, because he understood what he wrote, which the others, not understanding, my Lord would many times have a hard task to make sense of what they writ." Understood them he may have, but Bacon's radical empiricism in science is at the opposite pole from Hobbes's rationalism. For Hobbes, although scientific terms should denote material objects, scientific propositions are not empirical, but universal and necessarily true.

It would be a mistake to infer from Hobbes's service to Bacon that he liked him. Many people do good work for bosses they do not like. Hobbes would not have had much, if any, say in the decision to work for Bacon. Bacon never mentioned Hobbes, and Hobbes mentioned Bacon only once, in *Decameron Physiologicum*, a book published the year before he died.[26] William Harvey and Hobbes liked each other, and Harvey did not like Bacon. He said that Bacon wrote philosophy like "a Lord Chancellor." Hobbes, who is the source for the story about the circumstances of Bacon's death, may have intended it as something of a sly attack on Bacon's scientific method. Riding in a coach in March 1626, the empiricist decided to test the hypothesis that cold would delay decomposition. He stopped his coach in order to buy a chicken from a woman who then killed it for him. Bacon himself presumably stuffed the chicken with snow but almost immediately developed bronchitis; he died shortly after. There is no report about how long the chicken was preserved. Hobbes's moral may be that not only are experiments often useless, they can be dangerous.

It has recently been suggested on the basis of supposed stylistic similarities that Hobbes wrote some of Bacon's essays, just as Bacon was supposed to have written Shakespeare's plays. I am dubious. I do not think that there was substantial influence of thinking between Hobbes and Bacon. Each had enough ideas of his own that neither needed to pilfer from the other. But there may have been some borrowing of ideas and phrases. In particular, Hobbes may have gotten from Bacon the idea, expressed in *De Corpore*, that scientific knowledge has power as its goal ("Scientia propter potentiam").[27]

They also had similar views about definitions. In *The Advancement of Learning* (1605) Bacon had written:

[C]ertain it is that words, as a Tartar's bow, do shoot back upon the understanding of the wisest, and mightily entangle and pervert the judgment. So as it is almost necessary, in all controversy and disputations, to imitate the wisdom of the mathematicians, in setting down in the very beginning the definition of our words and terms, that others may know how we accept and understand them, and whether they concur with us or no. For it comes to pass, for want of this, that we are sure to end there where we ought to have begun, which is, in questions and differences about words.[28]

In *Leviathan* Hobbes wrote:

By this it appears how necessary it is for any man that aspires to true knowledge, to examine the definitions of former authors; and either to correct them, where they are negligently set down, or to make them himself. For the errors of definitions multiply themselves according as the reckoning proceeds, and lead men into absurdities, which at last they see, but cannot avoid, without reckoning anew from the beginning, in which lies the foundation of their errors. From whence it happens, that they which trust to books do as they that cast up many little sums into a greater, without considering whether those little sums were rightly cast up or not; and at last finding the error visible, and not mistrusting their first grounds, know not which way to clear themselves, but spend time in fluttering over their books; as birds that entering by the chimney, and finding themselves enclosed in a chamber, flutter at the false light of a glass window, for want of wit to consider which way they came in. So that in the right definition of names lies the first use of speech; which is the acquisition of science: and in wrong, or no definitions, lies the first abuse; from which proceed all false and senseless tenets; which make those men that take their instruction from the authority of books, and not from their own meditation, to be as much below the condition of ignorant men, as men endued with true science are above it. . . . Nature itself cannot err; and as men abound in copiousness of language, so they become more wise, or more mad than ordinary. . . . For words are wise men's counters, they do but reckon by them; but they are the money of fools, that value them by the authority of an Aristotle, a Cicero, or a Thomas, or any other doctor whatsoever, if but a man.[29]

But whether this similarity is coincidence or influence is hard to say. Bacon's essay "Of Cunning" begins:

And certainly there is a great difference between a cunning man and a wise man, not only in point of honesty, but in point of ability. There be [some] that can pack the cards, and yet cannot play well; so there are some that are good in canvasses [intrigues] and factions, that are otherwise weak men.[30]

Hobbes may have tried to improve on the passage in *Behemoth*, when he wrote:

If craft be wisdom, they were wise enough. But wise, as I define it, is he that knows how to bring his business to pass, without the assistance of knavery and ignoble shifts, by the sole strength of his good contrivance. A fool may win from a better gamester by the advantage of false dice, and packing of cards.[31]

A more interesting case of possible influence concerns psychological analyses of myths. In *De Sapientia Veterum* (*On the Wisdom of the Ancients*), Bacon gives fascinating interpretations of the meanings of thirty-one myths. For example, after rehearsing the myth of Prometheus, Bacon writes in part:

Prometheus clearly and expressly signifies Providence: and the one thing singled out by the ancients as the special and peculiar work of Providence was the creation and constitution of Man. . . . The chief aim of the parable appears to be that Man, if we look to final causes, may be regarded as the center of the world; insomuch that if man were taken away from the world, the rest would seem to be all astray, without aim or purpose to be like a besom [a kind of broom] without a binding, as the saying is, and to be leading to nothing. For the whole world works together in the service of man, and there is nothing from which he does not derive use and fruit. . . . Nevertheless we see that man in the first stage of his existence is a naked and defenseless thing, slow to help himself, and full of wants. Therefore, Prometheus applied himself with all haste to the invention of fire, which in all human necessities and business is the great minister of relief and help; insomuch that if the soul be the form of forms and the hand the instrument of instruments, fire may rightly be called the help of helps and the means of means. For through it most operations are effected, through it the arts mechanical and the sciences themselves are furthered in an infinite variety of ways.[32]

I think that Hobbes may have imitated Bacon's type of analysis in the preface to *De Cive*. There, he summarized the myth of Ixion, who tried to seduce Juno at a feast. Ixion had been invited by Juno's husband, Jupiter, the king of the gods. Trying to grasp her, Ixion clutched a cloud and gave birth to the centaurs, half horse and half human, "a fierce, a fighting, and unquiet generation." Hobbes analyzed the myth in this way. Justice, like Juno, is "the sister and wife of the supreme." Allowing a subject into the councils of state is like making justice a prostitute for them. Embracing their own "false and empty" opinions of justice, private men have "begotten those hermaphrodite opinions of moral philosophers, partly right and comely, partly brutal and wild, the causes of all contentions and bloodsheds."[33]

De Mirabilibus Pecci

William became the second earl of Devonshire when his father died in February 1626. In August of that year, William, Hobbes, and several other men made an excursion through the Peak District (the English Alps) northwest and west of Chatsworth. Hobbes wrote a Latin poem, *De Mirabilibus Pecci*, commemorating the event. It was eventually published in 1636 and much later translated and published anonymously as "The Wonders of the Peak" (1678). The English subtitle, "Commonly Called the Devil's Arse of Peak," is sensationalistic and unjustified. There is no such Latin subtitle, and the exploration of the Devil's Arse is a minor part of the poem.

Its literary merits are not great, and much of the content is conventional. Hobbes records all of the standard myths and stories about the Peak. (The interested reader should compare Hobbes's poem with Michael Drayton's 1622 edition of *Poly-Olbion*.) Even Hobbes, at least in his later years, considered his poem to be something of an embarrassment. When his nemesis John Wallis mocked him in the 1660s for having written it, Hobbes did what he virtually never did to his critics: he conceded the point. Nonetheless, because of his reputation as a philosopher, it continued to be read into the eighteenth century. Its value for us is that it is one of the very few documents from the 1620s that speaks firsthand about his life.

The poem begins with a celebration of Chatsworth, situated on the Derwent River, near the Peak. (The current Chatsworth replaced the house that Hobbes is describing at the beginning of the eighteenth century.) There is a hill behind the house that protects it from the eastern wind but also blocks out the morning sun. At the foot of the hill is an artificial lake that captured the water that runs down from the mountains. Both in front of and behind the house are gardens, which Hobbes describes in loving detail. Two fish-filled ponds built parallel to each other catch the rays of the sun. From the ponds the land slopes upward to the main entrance of the house.

This was the work of a woman, Elizabeth of Shrewsbury, who built "many, great palaces," he says. But her greatest building was the many great descendants that she produced. One of these was Hobbes's master, William. Although he was a spendthrift, it was Hobbes's duty as his personal poet laureate to misrepresent this fact. Hobbes says that the earl spent money on his friends freely, but not extravagantly.

William's wife, Christian, knew otherwise. She is briefly praised as springing from a race of kings, the Bruces of Scotland. Of their three children, Hobbes calls the two boys "angelic." But before them, he mentioned their daughter, Anne, who was "cherished by the gods." A special affection seems to have existed between her and Hobbes. When Hobbes left the service of the Cavendishes after the death of William, one of Hobbes's correspondents noted that Anne "does most very kindly commend herself to you and wishes you a safe and speedy return."[34] She married Robert Rich and died in 1638 at the age of twenty-six. Both Sidney Godolphin and Edmund Waller eulogized her in poems, as did John Gauden, the future ghost author of *Eikon Basilike*. In "Upon the Death of my Lady Rich," Waller lamented,

> That Death should license have to rage among
> The fair, the wise, the virtuous, the young,
>
> . . . .
>
> A skillful eye at once might read the race
> Of Caledonian monarchs in her face,
> And she had sweet humility; her look and mind
> At once were lofty, and at once were kind.
> There dwelt the scorn of vice, and pity too,
> For those that did what she disdained to do;
> So gentle and severe, that what was bad,
> At once her hatred and her pardon had.
> Gracious to all; but where her love was due,
> So fast, so faithful, loyal, and so true.

To return to *De Mirabilibus Pecci*, Hobbes's declaration that Chatsworth is the first and greatest of the wonders does not square with certain other lists. For example, Drayton in *Poly-Olbion* included Peak Forest, not Chatsworth, as one of the wonders. Hobbes's motives of naming Chatsworth are obvious. However, Chatsworth, rather than Peak Forest, is on later lists. Either Drayton is wrong or Hobbes's poem established Chatsworth as a wonder.

The celebration of the Cavendish land and family obscures the fact that the poem had begun in medias res. The Peak contains seven wonders. Chatsworth is only one of these (the palace). The rest of the poem describes the other six. Since many other geologic and man-made sites are described, some of which appear to be no less wondrous than the official wonders, it would be impossible to know precisely which were the official seven wonders if Hobbes did not flag them in footnotes:

one palace: (1) Chatsworth
one mount: (2) Mam Tor
one pit: (3) Elden Hole
two fonts: (4) St. Anne's (5) *Fons aestuans* (Weeden Well)
two caves: (6) The Devil's Arse (7) Pool's Hole

Jonathan Swift, in *A Tour through the Whole of England* (1724–26), was completely unimpressed with these so-called wonders: "I cannot but, after wondering at their making wonders of them, desire you, my friend, to travel with me through this howling wilderness in your imagination, and you shall soon find all that is wonderful about it." Hobbes can be forgiven for his enthusiastic description of the seven wonders, if forgiveness is needed. He was celebrating his employer's area; it had been his adopted home for more than a decade, and he was nowhere near as well traveled in England as Swift was. Finally, I think the wonders are quite nice.

Hobbes was unfortunately vague about who precisely went on the excursion. While the occasion for it was to satisfy the curiosity of "certain people eager (*promptis*) to learn the causes of things," Hobbes does not say who these people were or whether they went on the excursion. When he says "we" left the house, the only ones explicitly mentioned are a guide and a servant. Only later in the poem is there hard evidence that William himself was in the party. From another source, I infer that Newcastle and probably three others were in the party.

The hills and rockiness of the area made the Peak remote even for the Cavendishes. Most of the local residents never ventured more than a few miles from their village. Setting off on a morning in August 1627, during the harvest time, the travelers rode northwest, first to Pilsley and then to Hassop. The steep ride up the Peak begins at this point. The horses are exhausted by the time they reach the top. Although they were less than 1,500 feet above sea level, as they were during the entire trip, the climb was arduous because the hills in that area are steep and rocky. Positioned above the clouds, they still have a diminishing, geometrical view of their starting place. The Derwent looks like a crooked line, and Chatsworth is a point.

A little farther on, they came upon lead mines that deeply cut into the ground like wounds. Lead mining was quite active in this area during the seventeenth century, and William had a financial interest in some of the mines. Hobbes alludes to the practice of piling up wood against a hill and burning it until the rock fractured from the intense heat. The practice eventually had to be restricted because the smoke polluted the air. Mining was difficult and dangerous, and it made a poor living for the people. A century later, Swift reported finding a family that lived in a cave. The husband was a miner who earned five pence on a good day. Here he describes one who had just climbed out of one of the mines: "For his person, he was lean as a skeleton, pale as a dead corpse, his hair and beard a deep black, his flesh lank, and, as we thought, something of the color of the lead itself, and being very tall and very lean he looked, or we saw him ascend *ab inferis*, fancied he looked like an inhabitant of the dark regions below, and who was just ascended into the world of light." The man's dialect was unintelligible to Swift, and he needed an interpreter to translate what the man said. The conditions were probably about the same in Hobbes's time. The villages in the areas were also often hit by epidemics that so depopulated the area that the owners had a difficult time getting enough people to work the mines.

Hobbes is repelled by the tangle of sordidness: the poverty of the people, the destruction of the land, and the economic motivation. "Poverty has damned" the people to work the mines. When Hobbes and his party come upon the area, two men had just been crushed in a mine collapse: "they had dug their own Sepulcher." One has already been excavated: "Look, a corpse dug up from the earth lays at our feet." The sight of the man reminds Hobbes of his own mortality ("nostique monet meminisse"). The other miner, still interred, will have to wait for the resurrection at the end of the world before he is released from the rocks. Village gawkers look at the corpse and watch the digging. Two women are sobbing. Widows. One an old wife, the other a bride. Hobbes has no words to express his grief: "Let them mourn. We resume our trip." The terse words convey ineffable sorrow.

They now travel in a more northerly direction, passing many small villages. Only Hope is mentioned. Hobbes indicates that they arrive in the early afternoon. Although they are only ten miles from Chatworth as the crow flies, they have probably gone about twenty-five miles over rugged ground. My guess is that Hobbes has compressed time and that this is their second day on the road. I doubt that they could have watched the recovery of the bodies and gotten to Hope in half a day.

They then begin another tiring climb up a mountain. After reaching the top, Hobbes offers some comic relief when he says that it would then be easy to get to the village beneath them by falling off the cliff, but they prefer to take the well-worn path. The village of Castleton commands a view of the valley below. The ruins of a Norman castle, Peveril, is nearby. From there they proceed to the second wonder of the Peak, the Devil's Arse, partially so-called because the rocks supposedly look like the buttocks of a person bending over. The rocks are enormous and between them is a very deep cavern, in which the sun never shines. They are awed by how the rocks can support such a height without columns, and they praise "the eternal geometer." The party enters the cave on horseback and sees other horses inside, tall hay stacks and tiny streams. They hire a local girl to guide them. Hobbes, who was in his early thirties at the time, comments that she was "pretty enough, and very much a girl." They explore as much as they can before being stopped by a river that wells up from the ground.

After leaving the Devil's Arse, they go to the third wonder, Mam Tor (also known as Shivering Hill and Sandy Hill). It rises precipitously to a height of 200 feet (about 1,700 feet above sea level). The hill is made of sandstone with shale layers interlaced. When the hill becomes saturated with water and whipped by the wind during the summer or when the ice in it thaws in the spring, parts of it on the side facing Castleton fall off and cause rock slides, which form hillocks at the foot of the tor. Mam Tor "gives birth to" other tors. This explains the origin of its name. 'Mam' means mother. Punning on 'Mam', Hobbes suggests that 'Maimed Tor' would be a more appropriate name. He reports the popular belief that Mam Tor does not diminish its mass even though it has been shedding its sides. This is supposedly part of his search for the causes of the seven wonders. He expresses some skepticism about this ("mirabile dictu, / Constaret si certa fides") and offers his own explanation. The pile of sand, formed from the falling debris from the mountain, shows that the process will continue until Mam Tor is completely leveled.

They next cross Peak Forest, which has been deforested. Peak Forest was well known for its large population of deer. It was a cliché to say that the deer would trample dogs and men when they were frightened. Hobbes observes that the deer are imprisoned by the rock works, which exposes them to the harsh winds in the winter and the scorching sun in the summer. Hobbes laments the destruction that humans sometimes wreak on the earth.

The destination of the party is now the fourth wonder, Eldon (Elden) Hole, which is about two miles from Buxton. How can its shape be described? Hobbes's Muse whispers it in his ear. While the poem itself says only that its shape is obscene, a discreet footnote says that it has the same shape as a woman's genitals ("foveae os, forma cunnoedes"). I will not speculate on where the bachelor Hobbes received his information about the shape of a woman's privy parts. Less anatomically, Eldon Hole may be described as a gash in a gently sloping plain. In Hobbes's day, the gash would have been about ninety feet in length and half that in breadth. Two or three feet into it, there were craggy rocks and the hole narrowed to only a few feet in length and width. (Eldon Hole is now a bit longer and wider. Modern explorations have discovered that it is 245 feet deep.) Its sides are very sheer. The hole was reputed to be bottomless. Hobbes again reports that he does not accept the local, mythic explanation. He and his companions approach the steep edge carefully and look down into the hole nervously. They throw stones into it and wait a long time for the sound of them hitting. At first they think they have hit its bottom, but then realize that they have been deceived. Even rolling a large boulder into the hole fails to make its way to the bottom. It seems to reach all the way down to hell ("ad inferos"), Hobbes seems to conclude. Since Hobbes stated in *Leviathan* that he thought that hell was on earth, his stated conclusion may not be entirely figurative.

Hobbes tells a long story about how Lord Dudley came to this cave and wanted to know how deep it was. He had a peasant climb into the hole with a rope one hundred yards long, tied around his waist. The peasant carried a basket of stones; his mission was to drop a stone and listen for the sound it made when it hit bottom in order to calculate its depth. When the peasant was lifted up, he was out of his mind. Whether it was from fear or the twisting of the rope or images of hell, or some imp of hell, Hobbes cannot say. What he knows is that the man raved and convulsed for eight days before he died.

The fifth wonder is unnamed by Hobbes and described only as a fountain with two mouths. Others refer to it as "a flowing and ebbing well," Tideswell or Weeden Well. The marvel of it is that the water periodically gushes out of the mouths with great force (although only the larger one is worth looking at, according to Hobbes) and then recedes. Hobbes speculates on the cause of this phenomenon. It is not due to the moon or to the same cause as the tides. (Hobbes did not know that the moon causes tides.) He thinks that the swiftly moving subterranean water enters a narrow channel. The air on the other side prevents the water from coming in immediately; but when a large amount of water has backed up, it surges through the narrow channel like soldiers streaming through narrow gates. Once the surplus water has gushed out of the fountain, the water level goes down and the process begins again. During droughts, there is hardly enough water for the process to occur at all. (Although he was singularly unimpressed with the well, Swift repeated Hobbes's explanation of the phenomenon.) Since it is quickly getting dark, the travelers hurry on.

The sixth wonder is the mineral baths or the fountain of St. Anne at Buxton. Shrewsbury occasionally took Mary, the exiled Queen of Scots, to these baths for medicinal purposes. They are a mixture of hot and cold springs, with an average temperature of eighty-one degrees Fahrenheit. Probably alluding to the gospel story of the cured lepers, who did not return to thank Jesus, Hobbes refers to the ungrateful people who, having been cured by the miraculous waters, walk away thoughtlessly. Among the marvelous powers of the baths is that previously barren women, unaccompanied by their spouses, can become pregnant in them. Hobbes does not think about other possible explanations for how this could happen.

He explains with great delight how enjoyable it was for the exhausted travelers to soak in the waters. Having been dried in towels, they eat a sumptuous meal of soup, lamb, a young chicken, and buttered peas. They drink ale because no wine is available. They sleep and then soak in the waters again before going the short distance – just a quarter of a mile – to the last wonder, Pool's Hole (now Pool's Cavern), "another of the wonderless wonders of the Peak," according to Swift, who I think is quite unfair.

It is named for a thief who used to lure unsuspecting travelers to his lair, where he would rob and murder them. Hobbes and his party hire another guide to take them through the cave.

The entrance is very small and can be entered only by getting down on hands and knees. They scuttle like crabs to get through the narrow opening. But once inside, they find themselves in a large cavern. The cave continuously drips water that forms stalagmites and stalactites. One that looks like a slab of bacon is commented on by numerous visitors. Even more impressive than the rock formations is the eerie glow caused by the candlelight reflecting off the ceiling and walls. A late-seventeenth-century tourist, Celia Fiennes, describes it as "glistering like diamonds or stars." Swift's description, written a few decades later, is even better, but oddly dismissive: "the light of the candles reflected by the globular drops of water, dazzle upon your eyes from every corner; like as the drops of dew in a sunny-bright morning reflect the rising light to the eye, and are as ten thousand rainbows in miniature." Swift is not impressed for the odd reason that the same effect would not be achieved if the cave were seen in daylight and if the walls were not covered with slime. That is like not being impressed with rainbows because they would not occur without light being refracted through raindrops.

From Pool's Hole, Hobbes and his party return to Buxton to eat and then make their way back to Chatsworth via the villages of Sheldon, Ashford, and Shelmarton.

The poem is aesthetically unsatisfactory for several reasons. First, Hobbes and his companions rarely appear in it. Second, Hobbes gives virtually no indication of how the travelers reacted to their experiences. Third, although the purpose of the excursion was allegedly scientific, not much is made of that in the poem. Fourth, Hobbes gives very little sense of time. It is not clear how many days they were on the road. Hobbes mentions only one night. The most precise time cited is the nine hours that they slept during (what I take to be) their second day on the road. It is likely that it took at least three days and two nights. This estimate is based on both actual distances and Hobbes's description of the "paces" that they traveled, where conventionally one thousand paces equals a mile. Finally, the transitions from one incident to the next are slight or non-existent. Nonetheless, the poem has its charms, and I hope to have conveyed some of them.

The Death of William

Only about a year after the Peak excursion, William, the second earl of Devonshire and Hobbes's friend for twenty years, died on June 20, 1628, at the age of thirty-eight, in Devonshire House, London. One person listed the cause of death as too much good living. Hobbes would memorialize his former master in his own autobiographical poem by alluding to the general resurrection: "believe me, [he is] destined to return on the last day." The spendthrift William left his estate in a precarious state. Just ten days before he died, a bill allowing him to sell part of his estates to pay off some debts passed the House of Commons. Hobbes remained in the Cavendish household through the summer. William left a widow, three children, and a very large debt. It would take Christian several years to get his estate into a healthy financial condition.

Thucydides' *History of the Peloponnesian War*

Sometime during the 1620s, Hobbes translated Thucydides' *History of the Peloponnesian War*. It was published in 1629 but registered with the Company of Stationers of London on March 18, 1628, three months before William died. Not even death was strong enough to prevent Hobbes from dedicating the work to his beloved William, "now in heaven." It is not known when he had begun it or how long it took. In his preface, Hobbes says that he had laid it aside for a long time after it was finished. This could have been two or three years. The process of translation itself could have taken a year or two. These assumptions would suggest that Hobbes started the translation soon after Charles's troubles with Parliament began. He probably considered the work a political act. Even if he had started the work as early as 1620 with no special purpose, he could have come to see his translation as a political act when circumstances would tend to give it that character.

As an employee of the Cavendishes, Hobbes had few options for political activity, translation being one of them because it had the advantage of having deniability built into it. If a reader liked Thucydides' words, Hobbes could take a certain credit for them. If a reader did not like them, Hobbes could disavow them as being only the author's.

What Hobbes liked most about Thucydides was his supposed preference for monarchy and disdain for democracy. During the rule of Pericles, Athens was in fact a monarchy, although technically it was a democracy. The great danger of democracy is the abuse of rhetoric by demagogues. Hobbes has Thucydides say:

The received value of names imposed for signification was changed into arbitrary [ones]. For inconsiderate boldness was counted true-hearted manliness; provident deliberation, a handsome fear; modesty, the cloak of cowardice; to be wise in every thing, to be lazy in every thing. A furious suddenness was reputed a point of valor . . . He that did insidiate [plot], if it took, was a wise man; but he that could smell out a trap laid, a more dangerous man than he. But he that had been so provident as not to need to do the one or the other, was said to be a dissolver of society. In brief, he that could outstrip another in the doing of an evil act, or that could persuade another thereto that never meant it, was commended.[35]

Thucydides is exploiting a deep point about language, one that was familiar to ancient rhetoricians. A current way of explaining the phenomenon is this: There is a difference between the meaning of a word and the criterion that people employ to apply the word; and this has consequences for how a word is used. The phrase 'true hearted manliness' never meant inconsiderate boldness, even though that was the criterion that was used to apply the phrase to someone. Hobbes wanted his readers to apply the lessons of Thucydides' history to their own time. The rhetoric of the king's enemies was threatening the stability of the nation.

Hobbes took the conventional view that "the principal and proper work of history" is "to instruct and enable men, by the knowledge of actions past, to bear themselves prudently in the present and providently towards the future."[36] And no one wrote history better than Thucydides. One of his virtues was that he did not preach any morals in his own voice; instead, he let the narrative itself illustrate the moral that the reader could then draw for himself: "the narration itself does secretly instruct the reader."[37] Another is that his narrative is so perspicuous that, as Plutarch says, he "makes his auditor a spectator." He puts the reader "in the assemblies of the people and in the senate, at their debating; in the streets, at their seditions, and in the field, at their battles."[38] This sentiment is similar to the one expressed in the essay "Of Reading History" (1620), probably by William, but possibly influenced by Hobbes: "This kind of history therefore which I hold most necessary and profitable may be written . . . by joining together both times, persons, places, counsels, and events. And this is that History that adds (if it be read with attention and understanding) so much strength to a man's knowledge and judgment."[39]

In sum, good history requires two things: truth and elocution. Truth is the soul of history; without it a history is merely the image of reality. Hobbes says little more about truth than that the historian needs to be objective and to have access to information about his subject. He is more concerned about elocution. Elocution is the body of history, and without it history will not instruct.

Hobbes divides elocution into two parts: "disposition" and (literary) style. By disposition, he means the method or way in which the history is presented. Thucydides has an introduction ("exordium") that gives the prewar history of Greece and then the initial causes of the war. The rest of the history is structured by treating individual years as units and dividing each year into a summer and winter. Within this general framework of annual and semiannual segments, Thucydides has a substructure. (1) Each significant campaign is introduced with a statement of the "grounds and motives" for the action. (2) Then follows a narrative of the action. (3) Finally, he gives his "judgment." Almost forty years later Hobbes would in effect adopt the same substructure for the whole of *Behemoth*, his history of the English Civil War. What makes Thucydides' prose great history, according to Hobbes, is his ability to wrap (1) and (3) into the narrative itself. Unlike moralizing historians, Thucydides does not digress to make his points. In this dimension, Hobbes's *Behemoth* is a failure. Only Hobbes's stock characters A and B speak; A is knowledgeable and, one might say, pedantic; B is inexperienced and docile. It is completely lacking in drama.

Concerning style, Hobbes quotes Cicero's praise for Thucydides' writing before rendering his own judgment that it excels in "pithiness and strength." Although Dionysius of Halicarnassus praised Thucydides' style in general, he prefers that of Herodotus and has specific criticisms of Thucydides. Hobbes thinks the criticisms are unfair. He points out that whereas Herodotus chose a subject he could not have had good information about, Thucydides wrote about what he lived through. The events Herodotus wrote about were fables that "delight more the ear . . . than satisfy the mind with truth." The events that Thucydides relates are not pretty, but they are true: "[And] men profit more by looking on adverse events than on prosperity: therefore by how much men's miseries do better instruct than their good success, by so much was Thucydides more happy in taking his argument than Herodotus wise in choosing his."[40] Hobbes is especially irritated that Dionysius criticizes Thucydides for not showing partiality for his own countrymen, the Athenians, and for not beginning and ending the history with noble or happy events. Hobbes says, "There was never written so much absurdity in so few lines."[41] Thucydides did exactly what he should have done, namely, to explain the causes of the war and to report the course that it took.

Dionysius also criticizes Thucydides for making years his historical units since it sometimes requires breaking off the story of some siege to pick up events elsewhere. In other words, Dionysius thinks that history should be treated more thematically than chronologically. Each individual campaign or siege should have formed a unit. Hobbes rejects this position. He says that if Thucydides had written according to Dionysius's principles, then "he had sewed together many little histories and left the Peloponnesian war, which he took for his subject, in a manner unwritten; for neither any part nor the whole could justly have carried such a title."[42]

In a section titled "Of the Life and History of Thucydides," Hobbes raises the question of whether Anaxagoras and Thucydides were atheists. He thinks that they were not and explains the popular belief that they were by the fact that their opinions were "of a strain above the apprehension of the vulgar." Thucydides was smart enough to see that the heathen religion "was vain and superstitious" and that was "enough to make him an atheist in the opinion of the people." In effect, most ancient Greeks took to be an atheist anyone who "thought not as they did of their ridiculous religion." Thucydides took the middle course, being "on the one side not superstitious, on the other side not an atheist."[43]

Hobbes would later apply this same point to two words that were often misused in his own time: 'atheist' and 'heretic'. The former means a person who does not believe in God; the latter means a person who believes a false doctrine with respect to a religious denomination. But a favored criterion for being an atheist in the early modern period was a person who taught a doctrine that the speaker believed led to atheism. And a favored criterion for being a heretic was a person who believed something different from what the speaker believed. Hobbes in effect would make this point in *A Dialogue of the Common Law*, written about 1668, when he wrote that heresy is "a singularity of doctrine or opinion contrary to the doctrine of another man or men."[44] He knew well enough that that was not the meaning but the way the word was used. The proper criterion for the use of 'atheist' would occupy Hobbes decades later when he debated Bishop John Bramhall.

If we accept that Hobbes was sensitive to the pernicious confusion that resulted from employing an inappropriate criterion for a word, then what he would say about superstition in *Leviathan* makes sense. Superstition, he wrote, is fear (of invisible powers) that is not allowed (by people or the government). There are all sorts of obvious objections to raise against this if it is taken to be a definition, and it did not take long for Hobbes's critics to put them into print. But if what he says is intended as a sardonic remark about the inappropriate criterion that people use for applying the word, then it is sensible and clever.

Hobbes thought of his translation as a work of scholarship. He brags in the preface that Thucydides' history had never before been translated from Greek into English and that he had used the critical edition of Aemilius Porta. Two poets, the renowned Ben Jonson and the Scottish émigré Robert Ayton, had commented on and praised his translation before its publication. Hobbes himself drew the map of Greece that accompanied the text, no doubt a way of satisfying his long fascination with remote places. The translation was something of a swan song to the humanistic phase of his life (1602–29), although he did not know it at the time. William's death forced Hobbes to make changes in his life. He moved out of the world of Chatsworth/Hardwick for a time and into the pioneering world of the new science.

4

Early Scientific Studies and Religious Views, 1629–1640

And the physical universe seemed to me the only true thing in the entire cosmos, although falsified in many ways. ("Vita Carmina Expressa")

Taking Leave of the Cavendishes

Hobbes was in sound financial shape when William died. He would not have had to work again if he had not wanted to. But his home was with the Cavendishes, and no doubt he would have preferred to stay with them in some capacity. There are several versions and conjectures about why Hobbes left their employment. According to one, there was no work to do since William's children were still too young to need a tutor. The new earl of Devonshire (hereafter 'Devonshire') was only ten years old. It would make sense then for Christian to let Hobbes go as part of her comprehensive plan to get the estate's finances back in order. There is only one problem with this otherwise plausible account: Christian seems to have hired George Aglionby (Eglionby) to instruct her children about the same time that Hobbes left. Aglionby, who was also connected to the Newcastle Cavendishes, eventually became a member of the Great Tew circle, a correspondent of Hobbes, and a successful churchman.

There are other problems with the 'no-work-for-Hobbes' explanation. Hobbes says that he was "too much disregarded."[1] That remark suggests, not that he was not needed, but that he was no longer wanted. As soon as William died, Hobbes became nothing more than a secretary to a dead man; his status plunged and his ego would have been bruised. Of course, the widow's estates were extensive, her financial problems prodigious, and if she had trusted Hobbes's character and competence, she would have wanted to keep him for his expertise. The fact that she did not leads me to conjecture that she may have laid some blame on him for letting William jeopardize the family fortune and no doubt for having participated in some of the excesses of her spendthrift husband. The mere sight of him could have raised in her unpleasant memories or worse. Perhaps he was not fired but quit when he saw himself frozen out. There is no way to be certain.

In any case, Hobbes had no problem getting a position with Sir Gervase Clifton. Newcastle, who was a friend and neighbor of Clifton, may have helped Hobbes get the job. At least a large part of the Cavendish household seems to have felt genuine regret at Hobbes's departure. Through a letter written by Aglionby to Hobbes more than a year after his departure from the Chatsworth Cavendishes, William's daughter, Anne, wishes him "a safe and speedy return." She was about eighteen at the time. Aglionby says she "is (you know) fair & ripe, and tis pity she is so long a forbidden fruit." She died too young, in 1638.

Aglionby himself and three other members of the Cavendish household, Mr. Ramsden, Mr. Robert Gale (chaplain to Christian Cavendish), and Mrs. Stradling, also express their love or affection for Hobbes. In his letters to Clifton, Hobbes always asks that his regards be sent to various people in Derbyshire or Nottingham. So Hobbes's personal friendships survived whatever trouble he may initially have had with Christian following the death of William.

The Second Tour of the Continent

Hobbes's new employer, Sir Gervase Clifton, was one of the wealthiest and hence most influential landowners in Nottinghamshire. He was a member of the House of Commons in all the Parliaments between 1614 and 1626, as well as the Long Parliament. He was a royalist and voted against the bill of attainder presented against Strafford. During the Civil War, he served the king at Newark and Oxford. He hired Hobbes to accompany his son, also named 'Gervase', on his Grand Tour. They were accompanied by three servants and Walter Waring, a neighbor's son. It was fortunate that Gervase had someone about his own age along. Hobbes could no longer act as a companion as he had on his first trip a decade earlier. He was now foremost a tutor. On his first tour of the Continent, he had been in his early twenties in the company of someone roughly his own age. On this second tour, he was in his early forties, a person of some experience both as a traveler and secretary. Young Gervase was about seventeen.

Hobbes, who should also have been acting as a chaperone, did not keep the feral Gervase on a short leash. Gervase was a ne'er-do-well who would eventually be disinherited by his father. When his mother was dying in 1639, his father lamented that young Gervase was already coveting the inheritance that her death would bring. Clifton reported that as soon as he turned his back, Gervase made "a prey of all my convertible goods within doors and without." Later that year, he was arrested for "many robberies."[2] If Hobbes himself had been a young adult, he might have found Gervase's shenanigans amusing; but as a mature man, he did not. The fact that Hobbes was first awakened to modern scientific thinking on this trip also suggests that he let Gervase go his way in order to give himself time to go on his own.[3]

A surviving letter from Hobbes to Clifton traces part of their itinerary. From Paris, they went to Lyons and then Geneva, where they arrived in April 1630. Their goal of getting to Italy, the standard destination of Grand Tours, was frustrated by the fighting of the war of the Mantuan succession, one of the many subwars constituting the Thirty Years War. When two Englishmen invited them to go together to Italy, Hobbes declined because he was afraid that they might catch the plague. Hobbes's cautious nature served him well. Instead, they moved on to Orleans.

The Discovery of Geometry, 1630

It was probably in Geneva that Hobbes had his geometrical epiphany. As Aubrey records it:

Hobbes was in a gentleman's house in which a copy of Euclid's *Elements* lay open on a desk. When he read proposition 47, he said, "By G——, this is impossible". So he read the demonstration of it, which referred him back to such a proposition; which proposition he read. *Et sic deinceps*, that at last he was demonstratively convinced of that truth. This made him in love with geometry.

Some scholars doubt the truth of this story. They think that Hobbes must have studied Euclid at Oxford, and it is too neat that the book should just happen to have been opened to proposition 47, that is, the Pythagorean theorem. Hobbes probably did have some prior interest in and knowledge of geometry. We have already seen that in *De Mirabilibus Pecci* he compared Chatsworth to a point, and the Derwent to a line; and he referred to God as the eternal geometer. But I also accept Aubrey's story. First, there is a difference between learning something and being struck by its power and importance. I learned symbolic logic as an undergraduate but only appreciated it as a graduate student. Second, if a gentleman has an edition of Euclid displayed, it is probably a fine edition. It will be open not at random but to some significant page; and there is no better-known geometric theorem than Pythagoras's. Rare editions of Bibles are often open to the Twenty-third Psalm ("The Lord is my Shepherd; I shall not want") for the same reason. It is much catchier than, say, 1 Chronicles 2:10–12: "And Ram begat Amminadab, and Amminadab begat Nahshon, prince of the people of Judah. And Nahshon begat Salma, and Salma begat Boaz. And Boaz begat Obed, and Obed begat Jesse," and so on.

The importance of geometry on Hobbes's philosophy can hardly be exaggerated, although there are scholars who grossly underestimate it. According to Hobbes, natural science should take the form of geometrical demonstrations. Axioms in the form of definitions, according to Hobbes, should be laid down and then necessary inferences drawn from them. Science would consequently be certain, a priori, and necessary.

Since these definitions are stipulated, they have to be true. They are *analytic,* in the argot of later philosophy. As we saw earlier, Bacon also had emphasized the importance of definitions for science. Perhaps now Hobbes did not merely acknowledge that importance with his lips but experienced it when he read those connected proofs. What came to impress Hobbes was not so much the axioms, theorems, and proofs of geometry itself, but the method of connecting one thing with another on a foundation that could not be doubted. It was the method, not the substance, of geometry that staggered him.

This was the initial revelation of the power of a geometrical method. His complete understanding and theory of definition, however, would not mature for several more decades. Its explicit and large-scale treatment would appear in *De Corpore* (1655).

Hobbes's intention was to stay in Geneva until September 1630, partially because it was away from the fighting of the Thirty Years War. He wanted to go to Italy for the winter but thought that the war would make that impossible.

Politics in England

Letters from England kept Hobbes informed about the latest political wrangling. People were upset about the way Charles had handled the Petition of Right, a list of grievances drawn up by Parliament about such matters as arbitrary imprisonment, taxation without parliamentary consent, and the forced billeting of soldiers. After stubbornly resisting it, he claimed that it was nothing but a restatement of some traditional liberties of Englishmen and consistent with his sovereignty. Also, he dissolved Parliament in 1629, and no other Parliament would meet until 1640. This is the period that has been called alternatively 'the Personal Rule' and 'the Eleven Years Tyranny' of Charles I, depending on one's politics. Charles's position on absolute sovereignty was so extreme for the late 1620s that sometimes it was hard to tell sincere defenses of it from satire. A tract written by Sir Robert Dudley in 1614 in support of James I's claims to absolute sovereignty was circulated again in 1629. When Thomas Wentworth, the future earl of Strafford, saw a copy, he mistook it for a caricature of his own position and ordered the arrest of those responsible for spreading it around. In fact, five people were arrested and prosecuted in Star Chamber.

The Return to the Cavendish Family

During Hobbes's absence from the Derbyshire Cavendishes, Christian must have come to think better of Hobbes. She rehired him shortly after he returned from the Continent in the autumn, and he was back at Hardwick at the beginning of November 1630. Clifton had recommended him, and the two men corresponded for years to come. Hobbes was able to resume employment with the Cavendish family for two basic reasons. One was that Devonshire was now old enough to benefit from Hobbes's tutoring. For seven years Hobbes taught him Latin, rhetoric, logic, astronomy, and geometry. The other and more important reason was that Christian's financial wizardry had substantially improved the family's situation. Her skill was as impressive as that of Bess of Hardwick, her grandmother-in-law. She won all thirty of the lawsuits that she had initiated in her plan to repair the damage that her husband had done to his land holdings. Her success led the king to quip, "Madam, you have all my judges at your disposal."[4] Still, it took more than a decade to solve all of the problems.

Although Christian had rescued the family fortune, technically her son Devonshire owned the larger part of the fortune.[5] The legal issues were complicated, and mother was set against son. During the late 1630s, both relied on Hobbes for advice, but Christian did not realize this. She was furious when she found out that Hobbes had been advising Devonshire without her knowledge or permission. She felt that he had favored Devonshire over her. As his employer and the mother of her son, she believed that Hobbes's uncompromising loyalty should have been to her.

Hobbes had been put into a virtually impossible situation. He had to steer a course between the Scylla of Devonshire and the Charybdis of Christian. In a document titled "A Narrative of Proceedings both Public and Private concerning the Inheritance of the Right Hon. William, earl of Devonshire, from the time of the decease of his Grandfather to this Present," Hobbes vindicated his behavior. He explained that Devonshire had come to him for advice about what to do about his fears that his mother had used his estate for her own profit in the course of paying off William's debts. The fear was caused by Christian's request in 1638 that Devonshire sign a statement that released her of all responsibility in her dealings for him during his minority. Devonshire wanted to have an audit done in order to substantiate his fears and also threatened to leave home. Hobbes, according to the document, agreed not to tell Christian about Devonshire's plans in exchange for Devonshire's promise not to leave home or to do anything "but what should become a good and dutiful son." He also persuaded Devonshire to sign the statement that Christian had prepared. Hobbes also gave his opinion that certain properties, owned by Devonshire but controlled by Christian, most significantly, the Devonshire house in London, should not be used to help pay off William's debts. This opinion was directly against Christian's interests.

In order to forestall the accusation that he had profited from the advice he had given Devonshire, Hobbes added this testimony to his document:

The said Thomas Hobbes hath counseled him [Devonshire] and does still counsel him to continue so, and not to commence any suit against her. And for this information the said Thomas Hobbes neither has received nor demanded, nor expects any reward but only the testimony of having performed the part of a faithful tutor, and to be justified against aspersions to the contrary.

Christian continued to have suspicions, but eventually she was reconciled to Hobbes.[6]

Hobbes's interest in the politics of the day continued. In late 1632, the king issued a proclamation commanding all nonresidents of London not having compelling business there to leave the city for their own homes. Charles was concerned about the possibility of riots. Englishmen were unhappy with the king's policies.

In late spring, 1633, Charles headed north to be crowned king of Scotland. He stopped at Welbeck Abbey to be feted by Newcastle. Ben Jonson was hired to write "The King's Entertainment at Welbeck," and the total cost to Newcastle for the king's visit was the prodigious amount of almost £2,000. While it is difficult to make a fair conversion from seventeenth-century values to our own, I think $1,500,000 is a reasonable estimate. If this seems excessive one should remember that Charles's entourage was enormous. Five physicians and surgeons, including William Harvey, accompanied him. So numerous was the party that the earl of Arundel took care of some of the overflow at Worksop Manor. A central part of Jonson's entertainment was a dialogue between two characters, Accidence (a schoolteacher in the area) and Fitz-Ale, "Herald of Darbie, Light and Lanthorne of both Counties [Derbyshire and Nottinghamshire]." There was no office of county herald, but Hobbes certainly qualified as a distinguished member of both counties since he had served William, had published his translation of Thucydides a few years before, and was an important member of Newcastle's circle. It is possible that Hobbes played Fitz-Ale because the parts were performed by gentlemen of the county and Fitz-Ale carries a report of "Wonders of the Peake." Hobbes's poem *De Mirabilibus* would have been known to a large part of the audience. Finally, Accidence recites a poem about Fitz-Ale, which begins,

> Saint Anne of Buxton's boiling well,
> Or Elden, bottomless, like hell:
> Pool's hole, or Satan's sumptuous arse,
> (Surreverence) with the Mine-men's farce.

These are four of the seven wonders of the Peak about which Hobbes wrote. Whether Hobbes acted in Jonson's entertainment or not, he very probably was present, and he would soon have to endure more elaborate courtly productions.

In January 1634, Hobbes was in London in the company of the Devonshire Cavendishes: Devonshire himself, Christian, her daughter, Anne (now Lady Rich), Anne's husband (Robert Rich, eldest son of the earl of Warwick), and Christian's brother (Lord Elgin), among others. They were in large part occupied with courtly things, sometimes participating in masques. Hobbes expresses some boredom or disgust for the frivolity of the court. Devonshire participated in Thomas Carew and Inigo Jones's famous masque *Coelum Britannicum,* which the master of entertainment, Henry Herbert, described as "the noblest masque of my time to this day, the best poetry, best scenes, and the best habits [costumes]."[7] Between November 1633 and February 18, 1634, seventeen theatrical productions were produced. Shakespeare's works were something of a favorite. Four of his plays, *Richard III, The Taming of the Shrew, Cymbeline,* and *The Winter's Tale,* were presented. But Hobbes never mentioned Shakespeare in any of his works.

In March, plans were being made for Devonshire, who was now seventeen, to leave England for a tour of the Continent. Whether they would leave in a few weeks or spend the summer in Oxford and leave England in the fall was undecided. Hobbes was afraid that Oxford would be suffering a plague during the summer as it often did. He must have had chilling memories of it from his student years. In the end, they may well have gone to Oxford, because in July or August, Hobbes visited his hometown, which was much closer to Oxford than to London or Hardwick.

As far as we know this was the last visit Hobbes ever made to Malmesbury, but it was a fateful one. Hobbes's old teacher Robert Latimer had moved on to a position at Leigh-de-la-mere, where he had become the teacher of John Aubrey. Only eight years old at the time of the meeting, the young Aubrey may well have reminded Hobbes of himself at that age, being taught by the very same teacher. That is the likely explanation for why Hobbes, who was forty-six years old, took a liking to Aubrey. The bachelor Hobbes, who visited Aubrey's relatives, may have had avuncular feelings for him.

The Third Tour of the Continent, 1634–36

Beginning in the fall of 1634, Hobbes accompanied Devonshire for two years on his Grand Tour of France and Italy. This was Hobbes's third visit and by far the most important one of these intellectually, because it put him into the company of some of the leading scientists of the time. By his own account in the "Prose Life," his interest in science began with puzzles about the mechanics of sensation:

[A]t a meeting of learned men, when mention was made of the cause of sensation, somebody asked "What is sense?" and he did not hear any reply; he wondered how it could come about that people who, on account of their alleged wisdom so scornfully despised other men, should yet have no knowledge of the nature of their own senses. From that time on he thought frequently about the cause of sensation; and by good fortune it occurred to him that if all physical things and their parts were at rest together, or were always moved in a similar motion, the distinctions between all things would be removed, and so, consequently, would all sensation. So that therefore *the cause of all things was to be sought in the differences between their motions.*[8]

He was now deeply interested in scientific issues, and he definitely held that all that exists, including all human cognitive processes and actions, was nothing but motion. He was particularly interested in optics and hence in telescopes. This at least partially explains his meeting with Galileo during this trip. More important, he met Marin Mersenne, who promoted the interaction of some of the best intellectuals of the seventeenth century, including René Descartes and Pierre Gassendi.

Hobbes also had religio-political interests in the 1630s that would intensify as the decades rolled on. In France, he was reading John Selden's *Mare Clausum,* which maintained that the North Atlantic belonged to England, in opposition to the Dutch view that the seas were open to all that sailed them. Selden's title is a false echo of Hugo Grotius's *Mare Liberum,* which had defended the Dutch position. Another book read about the same time, probably Peter Heylyn's *The History of the Sabbath* (1636), argued that the commandment to keep holy the Lord's day was not part of the eternal law and could be altered by human beings. Hobbes worried that once ordinary people found out that one of the ten commandments was not a divine command they would think that the other nine also were not. Later, he would worry about public debate about predestination. It might lead people to think that they could lead any kind of life they liked because their salvation did not depend on good works. That, he thought, would be disastrous for society.

Hobbes and Devonshire were in Paris from October 1634 until August 1635. From there they moved south, going to Lyons, Venice, Rome, and Florence. They were in Rome on December 16, 1635, and probably stayed there through March 1636. They were in Florence in 1636, in

Paris on June 1, and back in England in October. (Hobbes's claim in his verse autobiography that he returned in 1637 is incorrect.)

Hobbes probably met Galileo in Florence in the spring of 1636. Galileo was technically under house arrest for publishing *Dialogue concerning the Two Chief World Systems* (1634). In fact, he lived a comfortable life in the houses of various friends. Hobbes was already interested in telescopes and other scientific issues. His attitude was firmly practical. Walter Warner, an associate of Newcastle and also interested in telescopes, had a theory about an "infinite" magnifying glass. Hobbes was not impressed. He doubted that such a glass could be constructed, and if it could not be constructed, the theory had no value: "if it cannot be practiced, 'tis worth nothing."[9] Twenty years later, he would criticize the mathematical discoveries of Ludovicus van Cullen and Willebrordus Snellius about pi, because they were of no practical benefit.[10] It is possible that this attitude was instrumental in causing his disastrous attempts at squaring the circle. Hobbes actually succeeded in devising a method for constructing a square that approached the area of a circle. But the area was never exactly the same. Perhaps deep down, Hobbes did not care about the minute discrepancy.

Hobbes's speculations about the physical universe took wing during this visit to Europe. As indicated earlier, it was at this time that he finally decided that the only things that exist are bodies and that human sentient experience, that is, the qualitative or phenomenal feel of life, is simply the complex motions of tiny bodies inside the human organism. Sensations are no different in kind from mirror images. As he said in his verse autobiography, "Fancies are the offspring of our brain; they are not outside us, and there is nothing within us except motion."[11] In *De Corpore* (1655), Hobbes would write: "Sense, therefore, in the sentient can be nothing else but motion in some of the internal parts of the sentient, and the parts so moved are parts of the organs of sense."[12] In his verse autobiography, he claims that he took no notes during this period because his teacher, namely, nature herself, "was always at my side." In saying this, he may have been trying to shore up his claim that he had thought of the same ideas as Descartes, but earlier, even though he had not made any record of his discoveries. Hobbes's defense has one sad drawback. What counts as significant in the history of science or philosophy is not simply who thinks of something first but who first makes his discoveries known publicly and has an impact on his profession.

Hobbes met Mersenne after returning to Paris from Italy. Mersenne was impressed with Hobbes's ideas and met with him on a daily basis. Mersenne also introduced Hobbes to other intellectuals, such as Gassendi, and Kenelm Digby, if Hobbes had not made Digby's acquaintance earlier. As Hobbes says in his verse autobiography, "From that time on, I too was counted among the philosophers."

Some of Hobbes's speculations during this third trip now strike us as ludicrous, but one at least is worth mentioning in order to get a sense for how difficult theorizing is at the beginning of a science. Hobbes considers the question of why it is that a man remembers less about his own face, which he often sees in a mirror, than about the face of a friend whom he has not seen for a long time. The question had been posed by his correspondent. Instead of questioning the truth of this putative fact, Hobbes conjectures that remembering something is a function of both how often and how long a person sees it. Each person sees his own face often but not for very long in comparison with that of a friend, whom one may see infrequently but for a long time. The impression made by two hours of uninterrupted perception of something is stronger than the impression made by two hours of intermittent perception of the same object. Pleased with the ingenuity of this answer, Hobbes invites his correspondent to ask another question: "Therefore, if this resolution of your first Question seem probable, you may propound another, wherein I will endeavor to satisfy you, as also in anything of any other Nature you shall command me, to my utmost power, taking it for an honor to be esteemed by you."[13]

The Return to England, 1636

Hobbes was back in England with Devonshire in October 1636. He initially stayed at Christian's house at Byfleet (Byflete), Surrey. His tutoring of Devonshire was over. He was nearing fifty years of age and could have gotten by without any remunerative employment. But he felt some commitment to help Christian and Devonshire if they needed him, and they wanted him to stay on as a "domestic." His own desire was to devote as much time as he could to his scientific studies. Residing at Welbeck with Newcastle seemed at this point to be the best way of doing that, and Newcastle was eager to have him. He was confident enough of his standing with Newcastle to ask whether he might continue his work at Welbeck: "and therefore I mean, if your Lord forbid me not, to come thither as soon as I can and stay as long as I can without inconvenience to your Lord."[14] Hobbes's departure from Byfleet was delayed, apparently by an epidemic. Hobbes said that, before setting out, he wanted to wait until the epidemic passed, which he estimated would be about a month. It was not his own health that he was concerned about, the altruistic Hobbes wrote, but that of Newcastle's family. Hobbes would be staying in "common inns," and there was no telling what diseases one might pick up in them.

A good indicator of Hobbes's standing with Newcastle is the familiarity of his prose style in writing to him. Nursing a cold at Christmas, 1636, Hobbes explains the dilemma of being in a house filled with people: "I have a cold that make me keep my chamber and a chamber (in this throng of Company that stay Christmas here) that makes me keep my cold."[15] The "throng" that Hobbes is referring to was Christian, her mother, brother and sister-in-law, Devonshire, Devonshire's brother (Charles), Devonshire's sister (Anne), and Anne's husband, Lord Rich.

Digby and the Devils of Loudun

Hobbes was probably still at Byfleet when he received a letter in January 1637 from Kenelm Digby, who was in Paris. In addition to reporting troop movements in the area between various forces of the Thirty Years War, he included a copy of a letter about his observations of the notorious "Devils of Loudun" (the subject of Ken Russell's 1971 film *The Devils*). In 1632, a group of Ursuline nuns at Loudun in France claimed to have become possessed through the machinations of a local priest. The priest was duly burned at the stake two years later, but the possessions did not end, probably because it was good for tourism. Weekly exorcisms attracted visitors from a long distance. The writhing nuns were still active in 1637.

Digby had visited them with Walter Montague, the younger son of the earl of Manchester, who had been so moved by an earlier experience of the bedeviled nuns that he had converted to Roman Catholicism. The nuns acted as respectfully as the devils would allow. They obeyed all the requests that Digby made of them in his investigation, except those that he gave mentally; they could not read his mind. He was ambivalent about the truth of the alleged possession. At one point, he concluded that the weight of evidence favored possession. The strongest evidence for the genuineness of the satanic possession in his view was the fact that it was implausible for so many people, otherwise known to be honest and sensible, to "keep up such an unflagging conspiracy so cleverly and so unanimously, in order to sustain for so many years a fraud which brings them no advantage and which requires them to endure so much labor and discomfort every day." He thinks that such behavior is "more than human patience and determination could sustain."[16] Digby underestimated the nuns. But he also recognized that people are inclined to believe a supernatural explanation for bizarre behavior, especially when they were able to witness it. It is this consideration that leads him to suspend his judgment about the matter, even though he witnessed the prioress's miraculous writing. When she would say a holy name, the letters of the name would be spelled out in red spots on her hand.

Perhaps Digby should not have been so skeptical. In August of that year, he fell from a horse and broke his arm. A friend had written to him at just about the time of his fall with a premonition of "some such misadventure" and had sent him her scarf as an aid. The letter and scarf arrived six days after the fall. Digby asks Hobbes what he thinks of such a case of human "foreknowledge or present knowledge at a distance."[17] Digby offers two hypotheses. One is that the soul, being a spirit, has all knowledge within it, and occasionally mistily perceives the future. The other is that the soul may be able to deduce a particular future fact about an object that one has earlier perceived. Unfortunately, no correspondence from Hobbes survived in which he might have given his opinion either about the devils or foreknowledge. As a determinist, Hobbes would have some theoretical sympathy with deducing later events from earlier ones. What he would not have had sympathy with is the idea that such a deduction could be made from an isolated object or that the soul contained the kind of scholastic "species" that Digby believed in.

Charles Cavendish, Brother of Devonshire

Devonshire's younger brother, Charles, who had a lot of his father, William, in him, deserves an extended aside. He was as wild as he was adventurous. He was getting into trouble in Paris during his Grand Tour, and Hobbes, probably at the request of Christian, played Dutch uncle in a letter to him in August 1638. He urged Charles at some length not to get himself into a duel. Sounding like Polonius, Hobbes admonished him thusly:

[A]void all offensive speech, not only open reviling but also that satirical way of nipping that some [people] use. The effect of it is the cooling of the affection of your servants & the provoking of the hatred of your equals. . . . [A noble person should aim to] encourage inferiors, to be cheerful with one's equals & superiors, to pardon the follies of them one converses withall, & to help men of [sic] that are fallen into the danger of being laughed at.[18]

He tells Charles that he should not take offense at the insults of anyone who does not have a substantial reputation. It is important to be insulted only by the right sort of person.

Hobbes also admonishes Charles not to make fun of people. Anyone, Hobbes said, can make jokes at the expense of another person; it does not show any intelligence. It does not make sense "to lose a friend though the meanest in the world for the applause of a jest." Hobbes had a grim view of humor. He thought that when people "mock and laugh" at "other men's infirmities"[19] they are in fact in love with themselves. In *The Elements of Law, Natural and Politic* he would explain this:

Men laugh often (especially such as are greedy of applause from every thing they do well) at their own actions performed never so little beyond their own expectation; as also at their own jests: and in this case it is manifest that the passion of laughter proceeds from a sudden conception of some ability in himself that laughs. Also men laugh at the infirmities of others, by comparison of which their own abilities are set off and illustrated. Also men laugh at jests the wit whereof always consists in the elegant discovering and conveying to our minds some absurdity or another. And in this case also the passion of laughter proceeds from the sudden imagination of our own odds and eminence, for what is else the recommending ourselves to our own good opinion by comparison with another man's infirmities or absurdity? For when a jest is broken upon ourselves, or friends of whose dishonor we participate, we never laugh thereat. I may therefore conclude that the passion of laughter is nothing else but a sudden glory arising from sudden conception of some eminency in ourself, by comparison with the infirmities of others or with our own formerly.[20]

Worse, since they are judging themselves to be superior, they are putting themselves in the same class as these unfortunate people:

Whereas to fall in love with one's self upon the sight of other men's infirmities, as they do that mock and laugh at them, is the property of one that stands in competition with such a ridiculous man for honor. They are much deceived that think mocking [is] wit.[21]

Hobbes's admonition here may not be clear. It depends on a philosophical point: Two objects can be ranked or compared only if they belong to the same category; that is why it is wrong to compare apples with oranges. So, to be superior to a laughable person, according to Hobbes, puts one in the same category as the laughable person; and that is nothing to be proud of. In short, it is beneath a gentleman to laugh at another person.

Joking is usually thought of as a social activity. People are more inclined to laugh when they are in a group, more inclined to laugh with their friends than strangers, and inclined to bond emotionally with those with whom they laugh. But for Hobbes, joking is an expression of the natural unsociableness of human beings. In *De Cive,* he would say that when people get together "for pleasure and recreation of mind, every man is wont to please himself most with those things which stir up laughter, whence he may, according to the nature of that which is ridiculous, by comparison of another man's defects and infirmities, pass the more current in his own opinion." He then continues: "it is manifest they are not so much delighted with the society, as their own vain glory. But for the most part, in these kinds of meetings we wound the absent; their whole life, sayings, actions are examined, judged, condemned. . . . And these are indeed the true delights of society."[22] Quentin Skinner has shown very strong similarities between Hobbes's views about humor and those in Aristotle, Cicero, and Quintilian. Hobbes's views were probably inspired or at least influenced by Aristotle and Cicero and could also have been influenced by numerous Renaissance thinkers who adopted the ancient views.[23]

Hobbes's last admonition to Charles Cavendish, namely, to "profess no love to any woman which you hope not to marry or otherwise to enjoy,"[24] seems strange. What kind of behavior is Hobbes warning Charles to avoid? Perhaps Hobbes is reacting to the Cavalier ethos of professing love indiscriminately, even when no follow-up action is intended. Hobbes expresses his confidence that Charles will take his advice to heart. In fact, there is no evidence that Charles dueled or womanized after receiving Hobbes's letter.

But repressing the urges Hobbes warned against may have aroused other desires in Charles. He eluded his tutor and went off to fight with the French army when it was in Luxembourg. Later, he traveled alone in the East, through Constantinople, Alexandria, and Cairo, before coming home via Malta and Spain. After a short time in England, he left to fight for the prince of Orange. When the English Civil War broke out, he immediately joined the king's army. Fighting with reckless abandon and great distinction, he was killed at Gainsborough in 1643. Knocked from his horse, he was either shot or stabbed as he lay on the ground. According to one account, he "died magnanimously, refusing quarter, and throwing the blood that ran from his wounds in their [Cromwell's soldiers'] faces that shed it."[25] He was twenty-three.

A Briefe of the Art of Rhetoric

For most of his life, Hobbes was either antagonistic to or ambivalent about rhetoric. He received some training in rhetoric at Magdalen Hall, although he does not mention it in his autobiographies. After his scientific phase began in the 1630s, he was openly antagonistic. Rhetoric aimed at persuasion by any means; science aimed at the truth. Science did not need eloquence because it consisted of indubitable premises and validly drawn inferences. Rationality ought to be sufficient to move people to think and act in the right ways. The increased opposition to the king's policies in the 1630s and 1640s stiffened Hobbes's opposition to rhetoric. He thought that demagogues used rhetoric to inflame the passions of the people against law and order. Rhetoric was the instrument of rebels.

But the rebels won. So, after the Civil War, Hobbes came to accept that although rhetoric could easily be abused, it was necessary for any writer who hoped to convince people and to move them to act in the right way. Rhetorical devices, such as metaphor, still come in for criticism in *Leviathan*, but Hobbes suffuses that book with rhetorical elements, much to the pleasure of generations of readers.

Although Hobbes was not happy with the standard use of rhetoric, his duties as a tutor to Devonshire obligated him to teach it. His pedagogy was laudable. He summarized Aristotle's *Rhetoric* in a Latin translation and then dictated it to Devonshire as an exercise in Latin comprehension. Thus the unpleasant but necessary task of teaching rhetoric could be combined with the useful instruction of Latin. Devonshire's exercise book, the cover of which contains many scribblings of his own name and that of his tutor, still exists among Hobbes's papers at Chatsworth. Perhaps Hobbes thought that his labors with Aristotle's rhetoric could spare other people the potentially corrupting activity of reading that book. This is not to say that Hobbes thought poorly of Aristotle's book. On the contrary, Aubrey reports Hobbes saying that while "Aristotle was the worst teacher that ever was, . . . his *Rhetoric* and *Discourse of Animals* was rare." In any case, Hobbes anonymously published a translation of his Latin summary under the title *A Briefe of the Art of Rhetoric* in 1637. It was a cheap edition in a small format, published by Andrew Crooke, whose firm would later become Hobbes's official publisher in England. The book was reprinted three times in the seventeenth century. In the edition of 1651, it was printed with several other rhetorical works. One of these, "The Art of Rhetorick Plainly Set Forth," mistakenly came to be attributed to Hobbes and is included in Molesworth's edition of Hobbes's works.

Leo Strauss thought that Hobbes's work on Aristotle's rhetoric was crucial to his intellectual development.[26] There is no doubt that Hobbes carried over many of the psychological concepts in Aristotle to his own writings. For example, in *A Briefe of the Art of Rhetoric,* Hobbes defines envy as "grief for the prosperity of such as ourselves, arising not from any hurt that we, but from the good that they receive";[27] and in *The Elements of Law,* he says that envy is "grief arising from seeing one's self exceeded or excelled by his concurrent, together with . . . pleasure conceived in imagination of some ill-fortune that may befall him."[28] Examples could be multiplied. I think, however, that these borrowings are not deep. Hobbes's philosophy would not be substantially different if Aristotle had not been the source of these analyses. For example, Aristotle, in Hobbes's summary version, says that what "is lasting (is a greater good) than that which is not lasting."[29] In *De Homine,* Hobbes said that if goods and evils are compared, then what lasts a long time is better other things being equal."[30] The thoughts are the same, but Hobbes did not need Aristotle to have them. Aristotle's alleged influence would be impressive if he had said that short-term goods are better than long-term ones and Hobbes had followed him in holding that opinion. The publication of *A Briefe of the Art of Rhetoric* was a way of saying good-bye to humanistic studies. He was already deeply involved in scientific investigations with Newcastle and his circle.

The Newcastle Circle

The primary interest of the Welbeck circle was optics. Hobbes's first unequivocal statement of his view that light is nothing but the motion of bodies and that perceptions of light and color are "nothing but the effects of that motion in the brain" occurs in a letter to Newcastle of October 1636.[31] The principal members of the Welbeck group of scientists were Newcastle's brother Charles (b. 1591), Robert Payne (1596–1649), Walter Warner (c. 1558–c. 1643), and Hobbes, not to mention Newcastle himself.

Charles Cavendish was intelligent, short, amiable, and physically deformed; his spine seems to have been bent. Clarendon wrote: "In this unhandsome or homely habitation [Charles's body], there was a mind and a soul lodged that was very lovely and beautiful; cultivated and polished by all the knowledge and wisdom that arts and science could supply it with."[32] Knighted in 1619, Charles was elected to Parliament three times. He was a good mathematician and corresponded with many important scientists, such as Descartes, William Oughtred, and John Pell.[33] Charles was a good friend to Hobbes and Hobbes to him. I do not think that Hobbes had the same affection for Warner.

Warner, who had been friendly with Sir Walter Raleigh and had some connection with Richard Hakluyt during the 1580s, later became financially secure through a pension given to him by the earl of Northumberland. In the late 1620s and 1630s, he was working on problems involving refraction and the construction of telescopes. Hobbes's criticism of Warner's work on telescopes has already been mentioned. Something more should be added to it. About Warner's theoretical solutions to practical problems, Hobbes says sarcastically that it would be easy to solve the problem of how high to make a bridge long enough to traverse the ocean. Simply make the height of the arch be equal to the breadth of the ocean. But since no one could build a bridge that big, the solution is pointless. Hobbes wrote that when Warner shows how a telescope can be made that can burn an object a mile away, the result is pointless because it would have to be "bigger than any constructible magnifying glass."[34] Hobbes's opinion that too much was being granted to Warner may have had some effect because the next year Payne wrote to Warner that "the theorems you take for principles, undemonstrated, require demonstration."[35]

That there was something personal in Hobbes's criticism of Warner is confirmed by an incident of 1636. When Hobbes was staying at Byfleet in December 1636, he excused his failure to visit Warner, who was living eight miles away, sometimes because the frost and sometimes because the floods "made the ways impassible for any but very rank riders, of which I was never any."[36] Perhaps. But I think that affection would have improved either the roads or Hobbes's horsemanship. Also, when Hobbes was feuding with Seth Ward during the mid-1650s, Ward twice claimed that Hobbes had pilfered some of his ideas from Warner. The fact that Warner had only an underground reputation and the fact that Ward repeats the charge of plagiarism suggest that the latter knew that he could get Hobbes's goat by promoting Warner's ability. In *Six Lessons to the Professors of the Mathematicks*, Hobbes responds to the charge of plagiarizing Warner's work at some length. He ends by writing:

In all my conversation with him [Warner], I never heard him speak of anything he had written or was writing *De penicillo optico*. And it was from me that he first heard it mentioned that light and color were but fancy. Which he embraced presently as a truth, and told me it would remove a rub he was then come to in the discovery of the place of the image.[37]

Although Hobbes once said that Warner was as "able" as anyone in optics, he criticized him in another letter for calling his results "demonstrations" when they were no more than conjectures. Also, Hobbes thought that Warner would not be able to give a good account of the passions and faculties of the soul. He thought his own prospects for success were much better and said so.

What accounts for Hobbes's reservations about Warner? Jealousy or fear of competition may have had something to do with it, just as it did in his relations with Descartes. Also, it would later become public knowledge that Warner sometimes took credit for Harvey's discovery of the circulation of the blood. Even if Harvey may have gotten a hint of the idea from Warner, the details of Harvey's views cannot be found in Warner's work, and so Harvey rightly deserved the credit for the discovery. Not only would Hobbes be suspicious of someone who took credit for someone else's discovery, but Harvey was his friend.

Warner's opinion of Hobbes seems to have been better than Hobbes's opinion of him. Writing to Payne, Warner said:

I pray you by any means send it to Mr. Hobbes, together with my hearty love and service, or whatsoever else you shall receive from me that may be thought worth the communicating, if it please you to impart it to him, you shall do me a pleasure. For I have found him free with me, and I will not be reserved with him; if it please God I may live to see him again.[38]

In contrast with his feelings for Warner, Hobbes liked Payne greatly. In a letter to Newcastle of August 1635, Hobbes said that his love for Newcastle was "of the same nature"[39] as it was for Payne. Since Hobbes is complimenting a peer, his affection for Payne must have been known to be great. Hobbes not only liked Payne, he esteemed his abilities. He told Charles Cavendish that Payne's prospects for making a magnifying glass were better than Warner's. Other scientists also valued Payne. He is often mentioned in the correspondence of some of the greatest names of Stuart England as a talented scholar. Payne met George Morley, one of the future stalwarts of Great Tew, at Oxford in 1618. He was hired by Newcastle in 1630. Although officially a chaplain, in fact he served as Newcastle's secretary. A letter survives from Ben Jonson, who praises Payne's help in putting on an entertainment for the king. During the interregnum, Payne corresponded with his good friend Gilbert Sheldon, the future archbishop of Canterbury. Payne told Sheldon that the Anglican clerics in Charles II's court had made a big mistake in alienating Hobbes and that Sheldon would not have acted in the same way. Unfortunately, very little more is known about Payne's life because his sister burned his papers shortly after his death.

An anonymous manuscript from the Newcastle circle, "A Short Tract on First Principles," is sometimes attributed to Payne. The work consists of about twenty printed pages divided into three sections. Each section begins with "Principles" and is followed by "Conclusions" drawn from them. Some of the principles from the first section are these:

1. That whereunto nothing is added and from which nothing is taken remains in the same state it was.
2. That which is no way touched by another has nothing added to nor taken from it.
3. Agent is that which has power to move.
4. Patient is that which has power to be moved.
11. An agent produces nothing in the patience but motion or some inherent form.

From these principles, the author infers the following conclusions:

5. That which now rests cannot be moved unless it be touched by some Agent.
7. Every agent working produces motion in the patient.

10. Nothing can move itself.

12. Every effect produced has had a sufficient cause (else it had not been produced) and every sufficient cause . . . is a necessary cause.

In the second section, he adds only one principle: "Every agent that works on a distant patient touches it either by the medium or by somewhat issuing from itself, which thing so issuing let be called 'species'." The third section introduces the idea of "animal spirits," which are defined as the "instruments of sense and motion." And phantasms are "the similitude of image of some external object, appearing to us after the external object is removed from the sensorium."[40]

But another candidate for the authorship of this work is Hobbes. He would talk about animal spirits in one of his early commentaries on the work of Descartes and continued to use the term in his scientific works. That, of course, is far from decisive. Several other scientists talked about "animal spirits." One of these was Warner, and he has been suggested as the tract's author. I am confident that this suggestion is incorrect. Both the content and literary style of the document point away from Warner. The preeminent expert on Warner's thought, Jan Prins, thinks that Hobbes wrote it before he ever met Warner.[41]

Richard Tuck thinks that "The Short Tract" may be by Payne but cannot be by Hobbes because it contains too much Aristotelianism. In fact, it does not contain a great deal of Peripatetic thought; what it does contain is easily accounted for by the fact that if it is by Hobbes, it is one of his earliest scientific works, possibly the earliest, and as such, it naturally would contain some Aristotelian elements. Even thinkers who aspire to complete originality cannot escape their early training, at least not immediately. So even if Hobbes was trying to blaze a new conceptual trail, it is likely that he would be cutting it with some of the same tools he had been given as a youth. Also, he was not strongly anti-Aristotelian in his written work until the early 1650s. Whether "The Short Tract" is by Hobbes or Payne, it nonetheless gives a good idea of the kind of thinking characteristic of the Newcastle circle.

The Great Tew Circle, 1634–40

From about 1634 until the beginning of the Short Parliament, a group of young men used to meet to discuss a variety of intellectual subjects.[42] They are known as the Great Tew circle because they met at the Oxfordshire estate of Great Tew, owned by the de facto leader of the group, Lucius Cary, Viscount Falkland. The house, about twelve miles from Oxford, was accessible to a large number of university scholars. It also had an excellent library, which itself attracted many people. Clarendon described Great Tew as "a college situated in a purer air" and "a university bound in a lesser volume." Thomas Triplet in an introduction to Falkland's *Discourse of Infallibility* wrote: "Great Tew [was] so valued a mansion to us: for as when we went from Oxford thither, we found ourselves never out of the University."[43] Some who initially came to study may have been drawn into the sparkling conversation, which in turn enticed other people to come. Hobbes's longtime acquaintance and eventual critic Clarendon wrote that the conversation was "enlivened and refreshed with all the facetiousness of wit and good-humour, and pleasantness of discourse, which made the gravity of the argument itself (whatever it was) very delectable." For example, in the course of a serious theological discussion George Morley, later bishop of Winchester, was asked what Arminians held. He answered: "All the best bishoprics and deaneries in England." Others echoed that sentiment, including Hobbes, who may have heard Morley say it. In his debate over free will, Hobbes quipped that his opponent, John Bramhall, later bishop of Armagh, became an Arminian because it was "the readiest way to ecclesiastical promotion."[44] (Roughly, an Arminian was a follower of the Protestant Dutch theologian Arminius, who maintained that human beings have free will.)

Some of the leading members of the Great Tew circle, according to Aubrey, were William Chillingworth, John Earles, George Aglionby, Charles Gataker, Sir Henry Rainesford, Sir Francis Wenman, George Sandys, Ben Jonson, and Edmund Waller. From other sources we know that Edward Hyde, Gilbert Sheldon, George Morley, and Henry Hammond were also members. Sidney Godolphin, Abraham Cowley, and Sir John Suckling visited from time to time as well. The Roman Catholics Kenelm Digby and Wat Montagu may have been there too. Almost all of these people were directly or indirectly acquainted with Hobbes, who most likely visited Great Tew at least occasionally.

Hobbes's introduction to some of the central members came through his involvement in the Virginia Company. Sandys, Dudley Digges, Rainesford, and Selden were connected with the Virginia Company. A Sir Walter Raleigh, not *the* Sir Walter Raleigh, another member of the Great Tew, was the son of a Virginia Company adventurer, and a "Carew

Rawleigh" was at a meeting that Hobbes attended. His introduction to others could have come initially through his association with Newcastle, who, for example, was the patron of Ben Jonson and a friend of Waller. Clarendon, in his scathing critique of *Leviathan*, said that Hobbes was one of his oldest "friends." It would be hard to guess how the friendship might have begun if not at Great Tew.

Hobbes could not have been present at the creation of the circle because he was on the Continent from late 1634 until late 1636. I have already suggested that he was probably at least an occasional visitor. Whether Hobbes qualifies as a member of the circle or not depends on the standard that is used. Since there were no dues or membership cards, there is no definite criterion to be applied. Given his interests, ability, personal associations, and possible access to Great Tew, it is plausible to count him as a member of the outer circle.

Religion at Great Tew

The favorite topic of conversation at Great Tew was religion. Several members had converted back and forth between the Church of England and Roman Catholicism. Falkland himself was alienated from his mother because she had converted to Roman Catholicism and did not intend to rest until she converted her entire household. (She succeeded with all of her children except for Falkland, who took refuge at Great Tew.) William Chillingworth wrote his famous *Religion of Protestants* (1638) there. Anthony Wood reported that Hobbes said that Chillingworth was like "a lusty fighting fellow that did drive his enemies before him, but would often give his own party smart back blows."[45] Hobbes meant it as a compliment since he too thought that while the Church of England was far superior to Roman Catholicism, on the religious right, and Presbyterianism, on the religious left, there were problems with it that needed to be corrected. For Chillingworth, the Bible alone was authoritative on religious issues. And what the Bible was silent about, reason could decide. His view was intended to be a modest reconciliation of the claims of faith and reason in the face of doctrinal multiplicity. This godson of Archbishop William Laud was sometimes accused of heresy by partisans of one sect or another. He died a captive of the parliamentary army, and at his funeral, his puritan adversary Francis Cheynell interrupted the ceremony by throwing a copy of *The Religion of Protestants* into the grave containing the corpse: "Get thee gone then thou cursed book, which has seduced so many precious souls . . . get thee gone into the place of rottenness, that thou mayest rot with thy author, and see corruption. So much for the burial of his errors."[46] In fact, *The Religion of Protestants* later came to be embraced by many officials of the Church of England, and its title was appropriated by the great church historian Patrick Collinson for his best-known book. Today's heresy is tomorrow's orthodoxy.

The central members of Great Tew were reformers in politics and religion. Hobbes was a reformer too, but his reforms usually went in a different direction. They preferred a liberalized theology, often Arminian, to Hobbes's brand of Calvinism, although some of them, such as Morley, were Calvinists. And they preferred a limited monarchy, not the absolute sovereignty championed by Hobbes. Falkland, like Hyde, was a major opponent of the king at the start of the Long Parliament; but both eventually sided with the king, and Falkland died fighting for the king.

Hobbes might well have thought that one of Falkland's supposedly royalist actions was one of the most disastrous to the king. In 1642, Parliament presented Charles with the Nineteen Propositions, which expressed their dissatisfaction with his policies. Seeing his power slipping away, Charles for the first time abandoned his pretension to being an absolute monarch. He allowed Falkland to write the response to the Nineteen Propositions in his name. In that "Reply," Falkland wrote that the English monarch was a limited one:

In this kingdom the laws are jointly made by a king, by a house of peers, and by a House of Commons chosen by the people, all having free votes and particular privileges. . . . And this kind of regulated monarchy . . . may not make use of his high and perpetual power to the hurt of those whose good he has it. . . . the House of Commons . . . is solely entrusted with the first propositions concerning the levy of money . . . and the impeaching of those who for their own ends . . . have violated the law. . . . And the Lords, being trusted with a judiciary power, are an excellent screen and bank between the prince and people, to assist each against any encroachment of the other, and by just judgments to preserve that law which ought to be the rule of every one of the three.[47]

In *Leviathan*, Hobbes would come to write that one of the worst mistakes a sovereign can make is not to claim all the rights that he needs to govern; and these prominently include the exclusive right to tax and to judge. The king had made exactly that mistake in his Reply. His opponents saw the

Reply as a sign of weakness, not goodwill. Hobbes never explicitly criticized the Reply to the Nineteen Propositions. Perhaps he knew that Falkland was its author and did not want to tarnish the reputation of a person whom he admired.

Chillingworth's presence at Great Tew must have been particularly offensive to Falkland's Roman Catholic mother. After Chillingworth had briefly converted to Catholicism, she had taken him into her London house as an ally. Her relish for having the godson of Archbishop Laud in her home soured when she discovered him one night undermining the Catholic faith of one of her daughters. He was expelled from the house and ended up at Great Tew, where he became one of the most powerful apologists for the Church of England.

The standard charge against the theology of the Great Tew circle was that it was "Socinian." The term was applied promiscuously; or, to use the terminology of the preceding chapter, the criterion applied for its use often did not well serve its cognitive meaning. The cognitive meaning of 'Socinian' is a follower of Faustus Socinus, a theologian who denied the doctrine of the Trinity. But the term was often applied to any opponent who purported to use reason in matters of religion. So it was mostly a term of abuse. Because of their rationalism in theology, the members of Great Tew met the criterion of their enemies, even though the narrower cognitive content of the word does not describe them. Also, even though Chillingworth professed to follow reason, he, like Hobbes, also affirmed that there may be truths above reason.

Hobbes agreed and went even further in defending the compatibility of faith and reason. In *Leviathan*, he would write: "For though there be many things in God's Word above Reason, that is to say, which cannot by natural reason be either demonstrated or confuted, yet there is nothing contrary to it." When it looks as if there is a conflict, "the fault is either in our unskillful interpretation or erroneous ratiocination."[48] But Hobbes's broad Socinianism was married to an even more dominant fideism. All that human reason can prove about God is that he exists. Virtually everything that people correctly believe about God had to come from divine revelation and is not even literally true, although Hobbes sometimes suggests that it is literally true that God is infinite and omnipotent. At any rate, Hobbes thinks that human talk about God should not aspire to be descriptively true. Theology is not and cannot be a science because the powers of human reason are too meager. The goal of human talk about

God ought to be to honor him; so what we say about him should be determined by what counts as praise.

Hobbes's fideism is part of a respectable aspect of Reformation Protestantism. Martin Luther in the *Babylonian Captivity of the Church* had urged Christians not to "dabble too much in philosophy" and to make "reason captive to the obedience" of Christ's words even when we cannot understand them. Chillingworth gave the appearance of endorsing Luther's admonition: "restore Christians to their just and full liberty of captivating their understanding to Scripture only."[49] But he did not mean by this what Luther did. He wanted tolerance for theological discussions. In *Leviathan,* Hobbes echoed Luther's and Chillingworth's language but again meant something different: "But by the captivity of our Understanding is not meant a Submission of the Intellectual faculty to the Opinion of any other man, but of the Will to Obedience, where obedience is due."[50] He favored dictated doctrine. Although it is possible that Hobbes came to favor a somewhat tolerant attitude toward religious diversity after the Restoration – after all Charles himself had tolerationist leanings – he was not a proponent of it in *Leviathan.*

Hobbes wanted to insulate almost all religious language from conflict with reason. In contrast, Falkland was one of the most radical of the broad Socinians. He professed to follow reason wherever it leads: "I profess myself not only to be an anti-Trinitarian but a Turk [Muslim] whensoever more reason appears to me for that than for the contrary." He was comfortable with this claim because he in fact did not find any logical problem with the Trinity. Clarendon endorsed Falkland's view of the strength and helpfulness of reason in religious matters. In a book that was predominantly a reply to Hugh Cressy, a former member of Great Tew who had gone over to the enemy Roman Catholic Church, Clarendon in effect attacked Hobbes at one point. He maintained that even when some religious doctrine is out of the reach of reason, for example, when it is "thought to be true, when it is not, and [thought] that some things are above reason which are not, reason shall contribute more to that obedience that is requisite than any stupid resignation to . . . authority." Eventually, Chillingworth's view became respectable. In 1662, Bishop John Gauden, who was the ghostwriter of Charles I's posthumous bestseller *Eikon Basilike,* wrote: "Nothing is by Scripture imposed upon us to be believed which is flatly contradictory to right reason and the suffrage of all our senses."[51]

The Socinianism of Great Tew was in the spirit of Erasmus, Richard Hooker, and Hugo Grotius.[52] Erasmus was the paradigm of the slightly skeptical, largely irenic Christian intellectual, admired by the central figures at Great Tew. Hooker was admired by Chillingworth, Clarendon, Hales, Cressy, and Earle. In the sixteenth century, he tried to give a foundation for the Church of England grounded on what was still then the best available theory, Aristotelianism. In the seventeenth century, Hobbes tried to do the same thing grounded upon what was becoming in his own day the best available theory, the modern science of Galileo and his friend William Harvey. Concerning Grotius, Richard Tuck has recently shown the extent to which Hobbes's political philosophy should be seen as continuing a tradition that begins with that Dutchman. Grotius was read extensively at Great Tew, so Hobbes would have been exposed to his views there (as well as elsewhere), like it or not.[53] (Hobbes never mentions Grotius, and I speculate that it was because Hobbes wanted to look as original as possible, and because he took a dim view of Grotius's Arminianism.)

Skepticism in Religion

One of the characteristics typically ascribed to the Great Tew circle is skepticism. The term is appropriate, but their skepticism was not Cartesian, philosophical, or methodological. It was based not on abstract possibilities of error but on the historical fact that limited or conflicting evidence, combined with human fallibility, often made truth elusive. I think the term 'empirical' or 'historical' skepticism is apt here. After the religious hegemony enjoyed by Roman Catholicism in Europe had been broken, the issue of orthodoxy became vexing. The question What is the truth that Christianity teaches? devolved into the question What is the criterion for recognizing the truth that Christianity teaches? The first answer to the latter question was that the Bible is the criterion. But this answer has all sorts of problems that were soon noticed: Which texts actually make up the Bible? Whose interpretation of the Bible is correct, given that the meaning of the texts is not obvious? In other words, what criterion of interpretation should be applied when using the Bible as the criterion of truth?

One strategy was to study the tradition of Christian teaching. The working criterion for truth would in effect become this: Any doctrine that was universally and always taught must be true. Unfortunately, historical research on the church fathers, some of it conducted by members of the Tew circle, uncovered that virtually no doctrine satisfied the criterion. Chillingworth wrote: "some Fathers against others, the same Fathers against themselves, a consent of Fathers of one age against the consent of Fathers of another age."[54] One of the advantages of the Church of England, according to many of those at Great Tew, was that it was not burdened by the theology of a Thomas, a Luther, or a Calvin. It was a kinder, gentler church. So one solution to the skeptical problem was to avoid altogether the kind of doctrinal pronouncements that kept theologians at war with each other.

From these general worries about doctrine, two issues can be distinguished. One is the essence of Christianity. Given that the church fathers disagree about most issues, does any doctrine satisfy the criterion of universal adherence? The other concerns how nonessential doctrinal disputes will be settled. Given that people with a cultural and national tradition will inevitably want a doctrine richer than that provided by the essence of a religion, how will religious disputes be settled? I think that we can reconstruct something very close to the answers that Hobbes gave to these issues within the context of the Tew circle. Hobbes's participation in the discussions there would have occurred between 1637 and 1639 and members of the circle were preoccupied with national affairs from early 1640 onward. So it is plausible that what Hobbes wrote about the essence of Christianity and the proper method of resolving disputes in *The Elements of Law*, completed not later than April 1640, expresses his reflections on what he had heard at Great Tew.

Concerning the first issue, Hobbes asserted that the essence of Christianity is the proposition that Jesus is the Christ. The formulas 'Jesus is the Messiah', 'Jesus is the Son of God', 'Jesus is the only begotten son of God', 'Jesus is the Holy One of God, the forgiver of sins, and is risen from the dead', and other familiar professions of Christianity are explications of the one, simple truth of Christianity. Hobbes would repeat this view in *Leviathan* and in some of his later polemical treatises.

Hobbes's judgment about what counts as the essence of Christianity is a doctrine that all the church fathers would agree to. But Hobbes does not justify that proposition by means of a historical study. Like an unreconstructed Protestant, he derives it from the Bible itself. Chillingworth had written: "by the 'religion of Protestants', I do not understand the doctrine of Luther, of Calvin, of Melancthon; nor the confession of Augusta, or Geneva, nor the Cathechism of Heidelberg, nor the Articles of the Church of England. The Bible, I say, the Bible only, is the religion of Protestants!"[55] Hobbes's biblical exegesis is elaborate. For our purposes, it is enough to mention just two of his main texts: "But these things are written, that ye might believe, that Jesus is the Christ, the Son of God, and that believing, ye might have life through his name" (John 20:31); and "Jesus . . . said unto them, 'This is the work of God, that ye believe in him, whom he hath sent'" (John 6:28–29). Hobbes's view, controversial in his own day, was picked up in the late seventeenth century by John Locke and the Latitudinarians, and many contemporary theologians concur with his exegesis.

Although Hobbes grounds his views about the essence of Christianity in the Bible, he does not think that an exclusive reliance on the Bible will avoid religious controversies among Christians. Chillingworth wanted civil toleration for a wide variety of interpretations of the Bible. Hobbes disagreed. A person does not really "submit himself to Holy Scripture that does not submit himself to some[one] or other for the interpretation thereof; or why should there be any church government at all instituted, if the Scripture itself could do the office of a judge in controversies of faith?"[56] The Bible, as we said, is not self-interpreting.

Some churchmen objected that Hobbes had watered down Christianity. In effect he had two replies. One is that Jesus himself had said that his "yoke is easy" (Matthew 11:30). Either Jesus spoke falsely, or the essence of his doctrine is simple. The essentials have to be learnable in the time it takes to die from crucifixion, since the Good Thief won a heavenly award in just that span of time. Hobbes rightly thinks that it is absurd to maintain that a person would have to have the recondite and technical theological knowledge that some theologians claim is required: "Beware lest there be any man that spoil you through philosophy and vain deceits, through the traditions of men, according to the rudiments of the world" (Colossians 2:8). Indeed, what many theologians consider necessary truths about religion seem to be unintelligible.

Hobbes's second reply is that most of what his opponents want to count as necessary to Christianity, namely, the propositions of the early Christian creeds, are in fact acknowledged by him as being entailed by the fundamental proposition that Jesus is the Christ and hence are also essential. In *The Elements of Law*, Hobbes maintains that the fundamental proposition entails that Jesus is God, the only begotten son of God, sent by God, forgiver of sins and redeemer of the world. In later works, Hobbes would make even stronger claims about what was entailed by the fundamental proposition. It was all the articles of the early Christian creeds, including those about the Trinity. Presumably, these propositions do not need to be believed explicitly. My guess is that Hobbes was trying not to sit on the theological fence but to be on both sides at the same time. On the one hand, he wanted to make what is essential to Christianity simple enough for anyone to be able to believe it and also to forestall disagreement among sects over the essentials. On the other hand, he wanted to accommodate the elaborate and traditional doctrine of Christianity that the Church of England had acknowledged in accepting the ancient Christian creeds and in formulating the Thirty-nine Articles. Hobbes's mind has the religious suppleness of any good child of Anglicanism. He professes both that salvation comes by faith alone and the importance of good works. Good works, however, have to be understood as "endeavors" or the "will" to do the right thing. The supposed genius of the Church of England is the accommodating strategy of *sic et non*, 'yes and no', 'both . . . and . . . ' rather than 'this and not that'. The project, it seems to me, was laudable, but not persuasive either to his contemporaries or ours.

This brings us to the second issue, namely, how doctrinal disputes about nonessential matters could be settled. Hobbes knew that human beings could not be content with the essence of Christianity. Human curiosity about the origins of things and their fear of their future determines that they must fill in at least some of the surrounding conceptual territory. That explains the existence of "sects, Papists, Lutherans, Calvinists, Arminians, &c," in the seventeenth century just as it did the existence of "Paulists, Apollonians, and Cephasians," in Paul's Corinth.[57] And the modern sects as much as the Pauline sects were a source of dissension. The doctrines and practices that distinguish one sect from another are all "superstruction," in contrast with the fundamental points of faith "necessary to salvation."[58] The inevitable disputes that would arise in the formation and evolution of a religion could not be simply ignored or tolerated, contrary to what other members of the Great Tew circle thought. Some mechanism was needed to resolve them. The Roman Catholic Church had a wonderful device for Christians living in the papal states, the doctrine of papal infallibility. But this device would not work in England or France or Germany, or anywhere else for that matter, because the pope, according to Hobbes, had no authority over Englishmen, Frenchmen, or Germans. What Hobbes supported in England was the complementary doctrine of monarchical infallibility.

Chillingworth's earlier conversion to Roman Catholicism had been inspired by this reasoning: Since (1) there must be an infallible guide for Christians and since (2) there was no guide other than the Roman Catholic Church, the Roman Catholic Church must be infallible. He soon came to believe that the first premise (1) was false. He thought that there was no infallibility for humans; moral certainty was the most that could be attained through the use of reason. Hobbes thought the fault in the argument lay in the second premise (2). In fact, each Christian nation has an infallible guide, namely, its sovereign. According to the terms of the covenant by which a sovereign is established, the subject transfers to the sovereign the right to make decisions about everything that pertains to self-preservation, and that includes religious behavior. Since the sovereign, by hypothesis, is a Christian, he professes and commands the fundamental point of faith necessary for salvation. So no subject need fear for his eternal salvation by obeying the sovereign. Whatever else the sovereign commands as regards religion is mere superstructure and cannot threaten the subject's future existence. And the subject owes it to the sovereign to obey whatever religious commands he issues that do not threaten his life: "So that faith and justice do both concur thereto."[59]

Hobbes's theological solution to the problem of the criterion had two great advantages over most of its English rivals. First, it had the political consequence of fitting the English constitution. Second, it had the philosophical consequence of solving the empirical or historical skepticism. Since that kind of skepticism was genuine and justified, it could have no epistemological solution. (This skepticism should thus be contrasted with typically philosophical skepticism, such as Cartesian doubt, which is not genuine and thus looks for an epistemological solution when in fact none is possible.)

Hobbes's solution was juridical. An authority was needed to stipulate what would count as true Christian doctrine; and the sovereign is that authority. The pronouncements that settle religious controversy have two components: one is the propositional content that expresses the doctrine itself; the other is the 'force' with which that content is expressed. These two components are distinguishable in a sentence like 'I declare (or define) that Jesus Christ is God'. The phrase, 'I declare (or define)' expresses the force of the utterance; it shows that the whole utterance makes it the case that the content of the declaration is true in virtue of being appropriately uttered by a person in authority. The clause, 'Jesus Christ is God' expresses the content. The whole sentence operates in the religious sphere just as 'I declare that the Olympic Games are open' and 'I find the defendant guilty' operate in the athletic and judicial spheres, respectively. (Declaratives are true in virtue of the institutional facts they create, not natural ones.)

Opponents of this kind of solution think that it smacks of artificiality and conventionalism. Although these objections were not explicitly raised against Hobbes's doctrine, what he could have replied is fairly clear: What is artificial is typically good; what is natural is typically bad. The civil government, hierarchy, and property rights are artificial and good. The state of nature, equality, and absence of property are natural and bad. The laws of nature are good, but largely because they direct people to construct an artificial state and instruct them about how to behave in one. Concerning conventionalism, Hobbes would maintain that the human condition does not allow for anything more than that. People who wrap themselves in the flag of right reason really mean that their own reasoning ought to prevail. Hobbes does not deny that there is a fact of the matter concerning many or all of the issues that divide people. His point is that people have no alternative but to defer to the decision of the authority that they choose to maintain peace, because it is impossible to get widespread agreement about what the truth is by having each person use his own natural reason. There is no good alternative to conventionalism. For Hobbes, the power of reason is relatively modest in matters of religion: "A man therefore ought not to examine by reason any point, or draw any consequence out of Scripture by reason, concerning the nature of God Almighty, of which reason is not capable. And therefore St. Paul, Rom. 12:3, gives a good rule, 'That no man presume to understand above that which is meet to understand.'"

Freedom of Conscience

Recently, some scholars have maintained that Hobbes had some enthusiasm for freedom of conscience. Taken in an artificially narrow sense, they are right. Conscience, being "a man's settled judgment and opinion,"[60] according to Hobbes, is free in that nothing can prevent a person from believing what he does. But this is not the usual sense of freedom of conscience. First, since people are not free to believe what they do believe – their beliefs are forced on them by their experience – it is odd to say that beliefs are free. Second, the justification of freedom of conscience usually is premised on the belief that conscience is a kind of knowledge or at least sacrosanct. Hobbes disagrees on both points. People who appeal to the judgments of their consciences think that "they know the truth of what they say,"[61] when in fact it is merely their opinion. Third, freedom of conscience usually entails the moral right to act according to one's beliefs. But Hobbes has no sympathy for this latter view. In *The Elements of Law* he lists this doctrine as one of six causes of rebellion. He seems to think that advocacy of freedom of conscience is a ploy to get the unsuspecting on a slippery slope:

> But the truth is apparent, by continual experience, that men seek not only liberty of conscience, but of their actions; nor that only, but a farther liberty of persuading others to their opinions; nor that only, for every man desires that the sovereign authority should admit no other opinions to be maintained but such as he himself holds."[62]

Even as early as *The Elements of Law* Hobbes noted that "no human law is intended to oblige the conscience of a man," unless, that is, the person wants to act on his conscience. People do not have the right to move their "tongue or other part of the body"[63] in any way that violates a law. He also advocated "rooting out" the opinion that a person should not act against his "private conscience."[64] Subjects owe their sovereign obedience, and this obligation is not mitigated by the claims of conscience.

The religiously based defenses of freedom of conscience seemed particularly wrongheaded to Hobbes. He had the Bible on his side. He quoted numerous passages to this effect: "Submit yourselves unto all manner of ordinance of man, for the Lord's sake, whether it be unto the king, as unto the superior, or unto governors, as unto them that are sent by him for the punishment of evildoers" (1 Peter 2:13–14). Hobbes compares subjects to servants and children in order to go on to quote Paul: "Children, obey your parents in all things; servants, be obedient to your masters according to the flesh in all things" (Colossians 3:20–22). These injunctions are categorical: Obedience is required in all things. For Hobbes a Christian cannot experience any conflict in a Christian commonwealth. Religious and secular authority are united. The sovereign is the head of the Church of England. This is not to say that there are no limits on the authority of the sovereign. Christians are "forbidden to obey" any command that entails the "denial of that faith which is necessary to our salvation."[65] He maintained the same position in *Leviathan*.

In *The Elements of Law*, Hobbes says that among Christians, there is disagreement about what ecclesiastical organization Jesus wanted people to follow and what the foundation for religious authority is. He describes the live options: "the question is, whether he [Jesus Christ] speak unto us by the pope or by convocation of bishops and ministers or by them that have the sovereign power in every commonwealth."[66] In other words, the options are between Roman Catholicism, *iure divino* episcopalianism, *iure divino* presbyterianism, or Erastianism, that is, the doctrine that the ministers of the church derive their authority from the civil sovereign. Hobbes defended Erastianism, as did the judicious Richard Hooker, who had pointed out that every English subject was a member of the Church of England and that only members of the Church of England were English subjects. From this Hooker inferred that the English sovereign was the head of the English Church. Although the argument is fallacious, it was persuasive.

Hobbes's reasoning leads to the same conclusion but along different paths. First, he draws a lesson from the Bible. Secular and religious sovereignty for the Jews were united in Moses. His rule was challenged twice. Once Aaron and Miriam claimed sole religious authority in virtue of being priests, and once a group of rebellious Jews, who claimed that the people had an independent authority, claimed authority over Moses. On both occasions, people in effect claimed that their "private consciences" had the ultimate authority in religious matters. Since God sided with Moses in both cases and punished his challengers, Hobbes concludes that secular and religious authority are united in the sovereign. Second, Jesus, who was the king of the Jews and of heaven, united secular and religious authority in himself as well. The decision to choose twelve apostles was motivated by the number of the tribes of Israel, united under Moses. In later years, Hobbes would retract the claim that Jesus had been or was now the king of anyone. Rather, he would come to hold that Jesus will be king when he returns to earth. This latter doctrine makes the kingship of Jesus eschatological and also politically irrelevant in the following sense. If Jesus is not now a king, then his kingship does not ground the authority of the sovereign (although sovereignty may still be dependent on God in some other way).

It is clear that the authority of the high priest resided in Moses, because he appointed Aaron to that post: "Moses . . . was to Aaron a God, and Aaron to him a mouth."[67] As Aaron was only the mouth of Moses, he was subordinate to him. Jesus did not even appoint a high priest; he himself was both high priest and king. Given that he was the "sacrifice" of human salvation, how could there be anyone, other than himself, worthy to make the offering? Hobbes then asserts that Jesus has "annexed the priesthood to those whom he had appointed to govern in the church."[68] After the Ascension, "the hierarchy of the church" consisted of apostles and two ranks of elders. After the death of the apostles, the name of the higher elders was changed to 'bishop' and that of the lower elders to 'priest': "And thus the government of bishops has a divine pattern in the twelve rulers [of the tribes] and seventy elders of Israel, in the twelve apostles and seventy disciples of our Savior."[69]

To this point, Hobbes's doctrine is very conservative, and his readers may have expected his specification of whom he thought Jesus had "appointed to govern in the church" would be similarly conservative. They were in for a surprise. The mission of the apostles and their successors was "to preach unto them that Jesus was the Christ, to explicate the same in all points that concern the kingdom of heaven, . . . but by no means to compel any man to be subject to them."[70] In terms that he would come to use in *Leviathan*, they had the right of counsel, not of command. The laws of the kingdom of heaven apply only to conscience. Because religious ministers of various ranks, from bishop to priest, have only the job of counseling and teaching people, they do not have coercive authority. The only sanction that Christian ministers can impose on wayward members is excommunication, and that involves nothing more than advice to avoid their company. In particular, "our Savior gave no authority to his apostles [or their successors] to be judges over them."[71] It follows that "in no case can the sovereign power of a commonwealth be subject to any authority ecclesiastical."[72] Hobbes represents his position not as a defense of sovereign power over religion but as a necessity for a decent human life: "If . . . kings should command one thing upon pain of death, and priests another upon pain of damnation, it would be impossible that peace and religion should stand together."[73]

To say that the sovereign is the only person with the authority to settle religious disputes with pronouncements is not to say that he does not need or ought not to depend on experts in religion to counsel him about the content that he ought to declare. In *De Cive*, Hobbes took the middle-of-the-road view that, whereas only the monarch had the authority to make the pronouncement, the content of pronouncement should be determined by the theological authorities. Many in the hierarchy of the Church of England liked *De Cive* because it included a place for them within a powerful theoretical structure.

In *Leviathan*, Hobbes's view changed dramatically. Having been abused by some of the clerics closest to Charles II in the exiled court after 1649 and with the episcopal Church of England brain-dead – both the archbishoprics of Canterbury and York were vacant – Hobbes came to think that the sovereign did not need to follow the judgments of the religious experts, although he could if he wanted to. I do not want to say that Hobbes's ill treatment by the clerics or the vegetative condition of the Church of England caused Hobbes to change his mind – to do so could be an instance of the fallacy of *post hoc, ergo propter hoc;* but many have interpreted Hobbes's change of mind in exactly that way.

Chillingworth's and Great Tew's opposition to elaborate doctrinal orthodoxy did not entail that Christianity had no doctrine at all. Chillingworth distinguished between what was revealed because it was necessary for salvation and what was necessary because it was revealed. The former category contained those doctrines that everyone needed to understand and could understand. Hobbes was the first to adopt the formula 'Jesus is the Christ' as that kernel of Christian truth. The establishment theologians of the Restoration church condemned Hobbes for watering down doctrine. Yet, decades later, Locke and the Latitudinarians adopted Hobbes's formula, without attribution. Clarendon, writing in the early 1670s, criticized clerics who confusedly thought many inessential points of religion were actually essential. For Clarendon, the essential point about religion in relation to the Civil War was political. His only objection to the chapter of *Leviathan* in which Hobbes denied that there was any genuine distinction between spiritual and temporal realms was that it was too short. Hyde liked Hobbes's observation that the distinction was intended to make men "see double." What B. H. G. Wormald says of Clarendon might just as well be said of Hobbes: "[He believed that] Religion of State was law and politics. . . . As a subdivision of the temporal, the ecclesiastical realm rightly belonged to the prince. When outside the prince's control and in the hands of the clergy, it was equally political, but wrongful."[74]

Although Hobbes did not toe what might be considered the party line of Great Tew, intellectually he was at home there. The members of Great Tew, like Hobbes, were intelligent, learned, and witty. They were as open-minded as could be expected given their historical situation, or, if not open-minded, at least open to debating their views. If anything made Hobbes out of place at Great Tew, it was his age. Almost all of the associates were at least a decade younger than Hobbes. In 1637, most were in their late twenties or early thirties while Hobbes was nearing fifty.

The Plan of *Elementa Philosophiae*

Although Hobbes would not publish any part of it until 1642, he devised the plan of his *Elementa Philosophiae* (*Elements of Philosophy*) in the late 1630s. The work was supposed to be a comprehensive treatment of reality that would reduce everything to one of three kinds of things: body, man, and citizen. So, *Elementa Philosophiae* was to be a trilogy: one section devoted to physics, one section to human nature, and one section to political philosophy. It would take until 1658 before all three sections were published. The word 'section' is chosen advisedly, because it is Hobbes's word for the three books, and Richard Tuck has shown that Hobbes's use of that word is an important clue for figuring out when Hobbes developed his physics.[75] The first book of *Elementa Philosophiae* to be published was the envisioned third section, *De Cive* (1642). Because of its popularity, a second, expanded edition was published in 1647. The second book to appear, more than a decade later in 1655, was the logically first section, *De Corpore*. The third book to appear was the logically second section, *De Homine*, in 1658.

All three parts were originally written and published in Latin. *De Cive* and *De Corpore* were also published in translation during Hobbes's life-time. However, there is some mystery surrounding the translations, and some of their titles are confusing. *De Cive* was published in translation in 1650 as *Philosophical Rudiments concerning Government and Society*, al-though it too is usually referred to as *De Cive*. Scholars disagree about whether Hobbes did the translating. The majority view today is that he did not, and I concur. Concerning *De Corpore*, a translation of it appeared a year after the Latin version. Scholars again disagree about whether

Hobbes translated it. My inclination is to think that he translated part, but not all of it. Concerning *De Homine*, it has not yet been translated as a whole although a translation of a significant portion of it was published in 1972. It is worth summarizing the information:

ELEMENTA PHILOSOPHIAE (*Elements of Philosophy*)

1. *De Corpore* (1655; published in translation in 1656)
2. *De Homine* (1658; not translated until 1972, and then only in part)
3. *De Cive* (1642, revised and expanded edition 1647; published in translation in 1650 as *Philosophical Rudiments concerning Government and Society*)

If the genealogy of Hobbes's trilogy is not complicated enough, there is more. In the late spring of 1640, before any of these works appeared, Hobbes circulated *The Elements of Law, Natural and Politic* in manuscript. In 1650–51, it was published in two parts with the titles, *Humane Nature* and *De Corpore Politico*. The similarity of these names to that of sections of *Elementa Philosophiae* can make one's head swim. In fact, the titles of these two books of 1650–51 were chosen by the publishers to lead the buyer to think that he was getting sections of *Elementa Philosophiae*. And, as a matter of fact, their content is very similar to that of the corresponding sections of the proposed trilogy.

Diaspora

The Great Tew circle as an intellectual center was destroyed by the English Civil War. Virtually all the members were loyal to the king when they were forced to choose a fighting side. Falkland and Godolphin died in battle, Chillingworth in prison, and Aglionby during a plague. Waller escaped to the Continent after his plot to seize London for the king failed. Clarendon, Morley, and others eventually went into exile and continued to associate even after the Restoration. But the circle had been broken.

Newcastle, who had been appointed governor to Prince Charles in 1638, was dismissed from that position in 1641, when he became a political liability to the king. (He participated in a plot to free Strafford from the Tower of London.) While he commanded the royalist forces in the north during the first part of the Civil War, he fled to the Continent after the defeat at Marston Moor. He saw Hobbes in Paris in 1645, for the first time in five years.

The war scattered other friends of Hobbes. Devonshire himself was not a fighter. After he was impeached along with eight other peers for supporting the king, he fled to the Continent not long after the fighting broke out. His brother, Charles, who had already proved himself to be a brave or reckless soldier, stayed and fought. He died at the battle of Gainsborough in 1643. Christian was devastated. She urged her sole surviving child, Devonshire, to return to England, compromise ('compound') with the parliamentary government, and save as much of their wealth as possible. The strategy worked. After returning to England, he spent most of his time during the remainder of the Civil War at Latimers, Buckinghamshire. Hobbes kept in contact. In September 1646, he was helping Devonshire find a tutor for his six-year-old son, William, the eventual fourth earl and first duke of Devonshire. At the request of Samuel Sorbière, Hobbes was willing to recommend M. du Prat. During the period of the Commonwealth, Devonshire moved from Latimers to Hardwick. (The earl returned to Chatsworth at the Restoration.)

Devonshire and his mother, Christian, saw the captured king as he was being moved from one place to another by the New Model Army. He spent one night in their house. Christian did what she could to promote the king's cause. She corresponded in cipher with the duke of Hamilton and others on the king's behalf. She moved to London in 1650 and participated in efforts to get the king restored. Charles II was grateful and occasionally dined with her in the 1660s. For some reason, the king was not so well disposed toward Devonshire, who was not welcome at court during the Restoration; so he rarely visited London. This caused a bitterness in his son William. Eventually, that son supported the exclusion of the duke of York from the succession, and as a reward for his support of William of Orange, he became the first duke of Devonshire.

5

The Elements of Law, Natural and Politic, 1640

It was now A.D. 1640, when an amazing plague swept through our land, as a result of which countless of our learned men later perished. Whoever was infested by this plague thought that he alone had discovered divine and human right. ("Vita Carmine Expressa")

The Short Parliament

Charles I's invasion of Scotland in 1639 in order to enforce the use of the Prayer Book had been a fiasco. He could not keep an adequate army together. One of his problems was the perennial Stuart one of insufficient money. Charles sensibly believed that only Parliament could provide him with the money he needed to raise an army and unsensibly believed that it might. In preparation for calling the first parliament to be held for more than a decade, he met with various people who he thought would support him. Devonshire may have been one of them. In January 1640, Devonshire, accompanied by his gentleman, met with the king.[1] It is plausible that Hobbes was the gentleman. There is no record of the topic of discussion, but it very likely would have included politics, possibly even a prospective role for Hobbes, for not long after that meeting, Devonshire put Hobbes forward as a candidate for the House of Commons. Given Devonshire's wealth and stature, his nomination would have great weight. But not great enough. The burgesses (the electors) would not accept him: "Derbymen are resolved to give no way to the election of Mr. Hobs."[2] Hobbes must have been fairly controversial, but there is no surviving evidence to explain why. Losing an election was an embarrassment, and, given Hobbes's high opinion of himself, he no doubt felt slighted. He never became so practically engaged in politics again. His career as a political theorist committed to the cause of the king was just about to begin, however.

The Short Parliament opened in April. The king wanted money to renew his war against Scotland, but a majority of members wanted to handle first things first, and what was first in their minds were their grievances about ship money, forced loans, coat and conduct money, and so on, the very things they had complained about more than a decade earlier. Neither side would compromise, and the king dissolved Parliament. Both sides were more bitter and frustrated than before. To Parliament, the king was untrustworthy; to the king, Parliament was insubordinate.

The date of the dedication of Hobbes's *The Elements of Law, Natural and Politic* is May 9, 1640, four days after the close of Parliament. Decades later he would remember *The Elements* as causing a stir among Parliamentarians. He cited their irritation with him as one of the chief reasons why he left England shortly after the opening of the Long Parliament later the same year. Given the brief time between the end of the Short Parliament and the dating of *The Elements,* some scholars wonder how Hobbes's work could have affected Parliamentarians. Actually the gap poses no problem. Some early and possibly incomplete versions may have been circulating in April and the first days of May. The British Library and Chatsworth have several copies of *The Elements* in more and less complete versions. Also, although the Tudor and early Stuart parliaments are aptly described as events rather than institutions, many of the Parliamentarians had a more substantial existence. They had various London connections especially with the Inns of Court that would have kept them in the city long after the dissolution of Parliament.

On the assumption that *The Elements* was read in the spring of 1640, it is easy to understand why it angered people. Some of what it said bore directly on the events surrounding the failure of the Short Parliament. Charles I wanted Parliament to vote him money, and it refused. Hobbes thought that the refusal was unjustified. In joining a commonwealth, each person, according to Hobbes, had "to resign his strength and means to him whom he covenants to obey; and hereby he that is to command may by the use of all their means and strength be able by the terror thereof" unite them.[3] The application of this principle to Charles's collection of ship money, distraint of knighthood, and forced quartering of soldiers on citizens would have been obvious to his readers. Hobbes also recommended "severe punishments for such as shall by reprehension of public actions, affect popularity and applause among the multitude by which they may be enabled to have a faction in the commonwealth at their devotion."[4] And Charles in fact after the dissolution of Parliament had several members arrested, some of whom had to be released when a search of their belongings produced nothing incriminating. (One of these latter was Robert Rich, the earl of Warwick and Devonshire's brother-in-law.) Strafford told the king, "Unless you hang up some of them [opponents of the king], you will do no good with them."[5] Hobbes's views in *The Elements* put him on Strafford's side.

So far I have mentioned attitudes that Hobbes expressed that bore upon quotidian problems. The more serious objections would have arisen from the political theory in *The Elements*. It contained almost all of the doctrines characteristic of *Leviathan*.

The Structure of *The Elements of Law, Natural and Politic*

As its name suggests, *The Elements* consists of two parts. The natural laws consist of both the descriptive laws of human psychology and the normative laws of nature that provide the foundation for civil government. The political laws are the laws of civil government, and this topic includes a discussion of political philosophy in general.

Psychology: The Background to Reason and Passion

In his dedication to Newcastle, Hobbes says that human nature consists of two parts, reason and passion. This way of dividing human nature is the modern transformation of the classic division of the soul into intellect and will. For Aristotelians and Thomists, intellect was considered superior to will. Will moved the human body to do what intellect had decided. Intellect proposes, the will disposes. In contrast, for Augustinians and Ockhamists, will was considered superior to intellect. The will commands the intellect. Hobbes's view was a descendant of this latter tradition. For him, passion has a kind of superiority to reason. Passions move people to action. The will, which most people wrongly consider a substance-like part of a person, is in fact merely the last passion or desire that a person has before acting, according to Hobbes.[6] A voluntary action, then, is any action caused by a desire. Although people usually think that only desires for an object cause voluntary acts, Hobbes maintains that fears, that is, desires to avoid some harm, also cause them. Pace Aristotle, Hobbes thinks that a sailor who jettisons his valuables in a storm in order to save his ship and hence himself is acting voluntarily since his act is caused by the desire for self-preservation. The jettisoning was not compelled, because the sailor had the option of drowning.

The action (or more precisely the person), not the desire, is voluntary. Desires are not under the control of the person. They are the effects of various external stimuli and involuntary biological processes. For example, the desire to eat some bread that is visible is a combination of the bodily motions that count as hunger and the appearance of the bread. This desire is not chosen. Indeed, Hobbes thinks that the idea of choosing a desire is logically absurd: If one could desire a desire, then one could desire to desire a desire, ad infinitum. Desires are not proposed by reason either. Rather than proposing anything, reason calculates the means to satisfy the ends that passions have. Reason does not say, "Eat the bread"; it says, "If you want to satisfy your hunger, reach out your hand, grasp the bread, bite, chew, and swallow it." It is up to the person himself to add the proposition that expresses his desire: "I want to satisfy my hunger." Hobbes's notion of reason as mere calculation was offensive to almost all seventeenth-century people (and still is to many contemporary people). Nonetheless, it is the one that guides research in cognitive science. His view of reason is one of his best claims to historical distinction.

Hobbes's objection to maintaining that people have free will was metaphysical. He thought that nature was a closed system and that every event must have a cause. But proponents of free will standardly think that a person's will somehow is outside the chain of natural causes and that acts of will are events that are not caused by previous events.

Because of their obsession with the importance of intellect and will, both the Aristotelian and Augustinian traditions were disposed to talk about the intellect acting or the will acting, and, worse, sometimes about the 'intellect intellecting'. Hobbes hated such stilted and, he claimed, literally nonsensical language. Even if there were such things as intellect and will, it would be the human being that thinks and acts, not those scholastic will-o'-the-wisps, just as it is the human being that sees, not the eye. This point, which is logically independent of the rest of his psychology, strikes me as eminently good sense.

Hobbes had a special reason for wanting to do away with or at least radically reinterpret psychology. Intellect and will were essentially tied up with a commitment to an immaterial soul, and the idea of soul has little to no role to play in Hobbes's philosophy. To the extent that he would be willing to admit to the existence of a soul, it would be some key bit of matter that is necessary for life. The soul would be material, not immaterial. Hobbes was adamant that the only substances that exist are bodies. Thus, the soul, in whatever sense it exists, is a body. Angels are bodies. Even God, according to Hobbes, is a body. Although he did not make all of this explicit in *The Elements*, it is there implicitly.

Reason and Passion

Hobbes, like almost all philosophers, often suggested that reason should guide passions and that passions unregulated by reason spell disaster. Reason is disinterested and thus "free from controversy and dispute." In *The Elements*, Hobbes said that reason "consists in comparing figures and motion only" and in "making of syllogisms."[7] Later, he would come to hold that reason is merely computation, that is, addition and subtraction. In pure calculation, "truth and the interest of men"[8] do not compete with each other. Passions, however, are in perpetual competition, not just within each individual, but between individuals. (In addition to waging war with reason, passions are engaged in a civil war.) And no one wants his desires frustrated. This has the consequence that "as often as reason goes against a man, so often will the man go against reason." Hobbes's strategy for short-circuiting this conflict is to use reason alone to set down the principles of "justice and policy." One can then deduce how specific issues ought to be handled, so that the whole edifice of law will be "inexpugnable."[9] At that point, the passions of people will be unable to topple the edifice. Hobbes adopted this very strategy two years later in *De Cive*, which he represented as a geometrical demonstration of politics.

Quentin Skinner has argued that in *The Elements* Hobbes professes to favor reason over passion and logic over rhetoric and that Hobbes did not use rhetorical elements in that book. I am dubious. First, it does not follow that if an author professes to eschew rhetoric, he does eschew it. (The most eloquent speech I ever witnessed in a contentious departmental meeting began with the speaker rising from his chair, draping his sport coat over his left shoulder as if it were the cape of a Roman senator, and saying, "I am not as eloquent as my learned colleagues; I cannot speak well in public," and so on. I don't remember the issue, but I remember the magnificent way in which it was delivered.) Indeed, denying that someone will do something as a preface to doing it is one of the grandest rhetorical devices: pretermission. Space does not permit a detailed discussion of the problem, but the evidence for Hobbes's rhetorical devices begins in his dedication to Newcastle, in which Hobbes satisfies two of the most important conditions for good rhetorical practice. First, he ingratiates himself to the reader by professing his obedience to his lordship and by claiming neutrality – Hobbes refuses to discuss any current political issue. Second, Hobbes promises to provide the reader with something new and important, namely, the fundamental principles for peace. Further, he does not deny that he employs rhetoric in his book, but says only that logic predominates. Even though it cannot match *Leviathan, The Elements* is still an impressive piece of prose. Granted that Hobbes's attitude toward rhetoric changed – it was out of favor in *The Elements* and enjoyed a limited amount of respect in *Leviathan* – it is not true that *The Elements* is devoid of rhetorical devices.

Hobbes probably later came to recognize that reason alone was incapable of disciplining the passions after seeing the effectiveness of the Parliamentarians in speaking against the king and his policies. In *Leviathan*, Hobbes consciously wrapped reason in eloquence and in that way hoped to have reason move people to behave correctly. (From this, it is fair to conclude that Hobbes was logically committed to the view that reason can influence passions.) At the very end of that book, he considers various tensions within human beings that have led some people to conclude that reason and passion are ultimately irreconcilable. Unfortunately, Hobbes does not lay out the problem neatly. He jumbles together tensions that exist within one individual between reason and passion, between one passion and another, and between principles of truth and opinion; and at one point he contrasts reason with the combination of opinion and passion. He also puts into the same mix the tensions that exist among many individuals that result from their having severally different passions, aspirations, and opinions. Sometimes he represents the problem as a conflict between "reason and eloquence."[10]

Hobbes's solution to the problem is largely unconvincing. After getting off to a good start by averring that "education and discipline"[11] are the keys to reconciling the contentious elements, he in effect gives up. Instead of showing how reason and emotion ("judgment and fantasy") can be integrated, he maintains that they have to alternate. They take turns in directing a person, "as the end which he aims at requires."[12] There are some gaping holes in this supposed solution. One is that reason was supposed to be wholly instrumental, not motivating. Another is that Hobbes's solution does not explain who or what is to determine when reason rules and when emotion does. Is reason going to make the decision or emotion? If the person himself makes the decision, the question recurs: Will he make it on the basis of reason or emotion? Still a third problem is that if on the one hand reason and fantasy (or passion) alternate, are both of them causing action? If they are, then often when reason puts someone on the right track, passion will knock the person off. That is a herky-jerky way of going through life. If on the other hand reason is not a cause of action, then what is it doing? If reason is the calculation of how to get what a person desires, then if the desires are bad, the consequences will be bad. So that is no prescription for good behavior.

Although Hobbes's solution is bankrupt, his conclusion is right (and his rhetoric stirring): "Nor is there any repugnancy between fearing the laws and not fearing a public enemy, nor between abstaining from injury and pardoning it in others. There is therefore no such inconsistence of human nature with civil duties as some think."[13] Hobbes is right, but for the wrong reasons. In fact, the received view that there is a conflict between reason and emotion is confused. It is rational to have certain emotions at some times and others at other times; there are rational and irrational fears, hopes, and desires. And the right emotions (such as the desire for truth and justice) move us to be rational.

Sensation

In scholastic philosophy, intellect and will were considered higher powers of the soul. Even when a scholastic maintained, as most did, that all knowledge begins with sensation, he thought that sensation became transmogrified by the time it got to the intellect. What had begun with one body acting on another body ended with an immaterial object, an idea. Parallel to the mind/body dichotomy is a reason/sensation dichotomy. Part and parcel of Hobbes's attack on scholasticism is his attack on the latter dichotomy. For him, not only does all knowledge begin with sensation, but knowledge is continuous with sensation.

The cognitive faculty in human beings makes conceptions possible. A sensation is a conception currently being caused. Imagination, then, is a conception that a person has when the object that originally caused the conception is no longer active. As this explanation suggests, Hobbes thinks that there is no difference between imagination and memory.

In addition to being reductive insofar as he reduces thinking to sensation, Hobbes's psychology is also mechanistic and materialistic. Sensation, as we said, is that motion in the brain caused by the action of an external object on a sense organ as long as that object is acting on the perceiver. The images of sensation are not true or iconic reproductions of any aspect of the sensed object. It is easy but false to believe that the experienced color and shape "are the very qualities themselves" of the object.[14] But colors and images do not exist outside the human mind. Although Descartes and Galileo had said or implied the same things, Hobbes's position was still novel and hardly credible to most of his readers. He tried to show the correctness of his counterintuitive position in several ways. One of the stronger considerations is the observation that an image of the sun seems to exist in water. Since there is only one sun, but two appearances of it – one in the heavens and one in the water, to speak loosely – the appearances must be different from the sun itself. Also, it is possible to have a double image of a candle's flame. There is no more reason to identify the flame with one of the images more than the other, so neither image must be identical with the flame. Another argument takes note of the fact that sense-images can be generated by jarring the brain, as expressed by the idiom 'seeing stars'. The upshot of all of these phenomena is that an image of something can be in a place where the thing itself is not. From this, Hobbes infers that images are nothing but motions in the brain.

The same conclusion could be reached by analogous premises for the other senses. Evidence that sound is not in the bodies that cause them is the existence of echoes. The clapper of a bell has only motion in it, not sound. Hobbes says, "The things that really are in the world without us are those motions by which these seemings are caused."[15] And it is not just in the external world that only motions exist. Because motion causes nothing but motion, the motions of light, sound waves, and odors cause nothing but motions inside the human being.

Imagination

Just as sensation is an internal motion occurring at the same time as the external object is causing it, imagination, as we said, is that same internal motion occurring after the external object is no longer affecting the sense organ. In the language of *Leviathan*, imagination is decaying sense. That this is the nature of imagination is made clear by an analogy:

As standing water put into motion by the stroke of a stone, or blast of wind does not presently give over moving as soon as the wind ceases or the stone settles, so neither does the effect cease which the object has wrought upon the brain so soon as ever by turning aside of the organ the object ceases to work; that is to say, though the sense be past, the image or conception remains, but more obscurely. . . . And this obscure conception is that we call PHANTASY or IMAGINATION.16

Imagination is to sensation as the rippling motion in water is to the motion caused by the wind or stone. The same principles of mechanics apply to each. This is a salient feature of Hobbes's psychology, just as it was for Descartes's. In *Leviathan*, Hobbes would adopt an analogy that was much more powerful and threatening to his audience than that of the rippling water. He asserted that it is not just sensation but human life that is strictly analogous to a machine:

For seeing life is but a motion of limbs, the beginning whereof is in some principal part within, why may we not say that all automata (engines that move themselves by springs and wheels as does a watch) have an artificial life? For what is the heart but a spring, and the nerves but so many strings and the joints but so many wheels, giving motion to the whole body, such as was intended by the artificer?17

Language

Ideas follow one another in our minds, sometimes in an orderly way and sometimes in a disorderly way. Without some special help, people would not be able to remember those ideas in either case. The special help are arbitrary "marks," that is, words, which are signs of the ideas. So the primary function of words and language is to aid a person's memory. Communication is the secondary function. To communicate is to use a word that will cause the hearer to think of the same idea as the speaker, and it presupposes the first; communication would not succeed if people did not remember what words meant. Hobbes's view is a paradigmatic case of the private-language theory, the view that the meaning of a word or sentence is an entity possessed only by the speaker. He does not stop to consider that since each person's ideas are private, there is no way to know whether the idea that the hearer thinks of when she hears a word is the same one as the speaker is thinking of. (Hobbes does not say why arbitrary marks would be easier to remember than the ideas themselves or what exactly makes a word, say, 'white', the name of white things, rather than black things or justice or oregano.) Often the same word is used for many things, as 'cat' is the word used for all cats. This use of one word for many things explains the belief in universals according to Hobbes. In fact, he maintains, "there is nothing universal but names."[18] This is a bald statement of his nominalism.

Reductivist Materialism

The contents of cognition are the phenomenal qualities of our ordinary experience, the appearances, sounds, smells, and tactile feelings. It may seem indubitable that these qualities are actually in the external world. But Hobbes says they are not. Persuaded by the researches of Galileo, Hobbes maintains that the content of a sense experience is in the person or animal having them and not in the object that causes them. Colors, noises, odors, and the felt texture of objects do not exist in the world itself. What exists there are bodies that are configured in such a way that when they act on us they either directly or indirectly cause certain motions in our body, especially our brain and heart, and we thereby have the experiences that we do.

This raises the question of the exact relationship between the motions of the brain and heart and the qualitative experiences. Sometimes Hobbes seems to suggest that the motions cause the experiences. But Hobbes's considered view seems to be that the experiences are identical with the motions: Motion causes nothing but motion. Since there is no way to get from motion to something of another kind, experiences themselves must be motions. But if this is his doctrine, and I think it is, then it would be appropriate for Hobbes to say something more about how motions can have the feel that they do. And yet he says nothing about it. He does not seem to marvel at or be puzzled by the fact.

Science

There are two kinds of knowledge, according to Hobbes: one is about sensation, the other is about propositions. Sense knowledge, which does not require language, is the foundation for propositional knowledge. The record of sense knowledge is history. By the time he wrote *The Elements*, Hobbes thought that history was intellectually inferior to science.[19]

Scientific knowledge consists of propositions. That is, it is essentially linguistic and depends on "the proper use of names in language."[20] In *The Elements*, Hobbes says that the propositions must be both true and evident. Thinking primarily of universal and affirmative propositions, Hobbes maintained that a proposition is true when the predicate expression names everything that the subject expression does. This view works nicely for universal affirmative propositions such as, 'All humans are mortal', but not for universal negative ones. What makes the sentence 'No humans are dogs' true is the fact that the predicate expression does not name anything that the subject expression does. There are ways of interpreting his theory and ways of tampering with it that forestall some objections; but ultimately it does not work. Although defining truth is difficult, it is unfortunate that Hobbes never saw the problems with his efforts. Fifteen years later in *De Corpore*, he would be maintaining fundamentally the same position.

The other component of scientific knowledge is "evidence." In current usage, there is a difference between something having evidence and something being evident. Uncertainty typically accompanies evidence; certainty accompanies what is evident. What Hobbes means by 'evidence' is that the propositions must be evident in the sense just described. The words that a scientist uses must be directly correlated with his ideas for those words. If the ideas were not required, then parrots could be scientists.

In line with his linguistic theory, which makes language private, Hobbes in effect makes science essentially private. In contrast, Robert Boyle and other members of the Royal Society, from which Hobbes would be excluded, emphasized the public and communal nature of science. Being a scientist in seventeenth-century England almost required being a member of a club that accepted only people of good repute. Ironically, Hobbes would turn the tables on the Royal Society and criticize them for not being genuinely public, as we shall see in Chapter 10.

Is Hobbes an empiricist or a rationalist? The answer depends on how those terms are defined. He is an empiricist in the sense that he maintains that all of the substantive terms of a proposition must be traceable to sensation. He is a rationalist in the sense that he maintains that all scientific knowledge is necessary. He is not an empiricist if that means maintaining that scientific propositions are statements of empirical fact. And he is not a rationalist if that means maintaining that some scientific propositions are nonanalytic.

Emotions

Philosophers tend to talk much more about rationality than emotions and typically assert the superiority of reason to emotion, probably because they think they have more of the former than the latter. They usually do, and that is too bad. If anything, Hobbes gives greater importance to emotion than to reason. What we would call emotions, Hobbes calls passions or affections, because he, like all classical philosophers, thought of emotions as ways in which an animal is affected by or responds to things, rather than to a way of orienting oneself to and experiencing the world. The seat of the emotions is the heart, according to Hobbes. The motions that originate in the senses and then proceed to the brain do not stop there. They continue to the heart, where they either help or interfere with the "vital" motion. The helpful motions are experienced as pleasure, the interfering ones are experienced as pain. In *Leviathan*, Hobbes would use these cardiac motions to account for belief in the external world. When the heart receives the motions coming from the head, it produces a countermotion outward; and it is this countermotion that gives people the idea that their sensations are caused by external objects.

Just as an idea is a motion in the brain, pleasures and pains are motions in and around the heart.[21] Pleasures are those motions that enhance life; pains are those that diminish it. On Hobbes's account, cocaine would be a life-enhancing substance.

His views about the basic emotions are simplistic because his physics is simplistic. In physics he maintains that all causes either push or pull an object. So, to speak a bit imprecisely, pleasure pushes an animal toward the object that causes it, and pain pulls the animal away from the object that causes it. These approaches and withdrawals are of themselves not visible, although when they are numerous and strong enough, they do result in visible behavior. But the basic units of pleasure and pain are invisibly small. The words 'pleasure' and 'pain' signify motions as experienced in a certain way. These motions, conceived of solely in terms of their direction of movement, either toward or away from an object, have different names, 'appetites' and 'aversions', respectively. This explains why he can also remark that "appetite is joy."[22] This would seem to be an obtusely cruel sentiment if one thinks about the suffering of starving children. What Hobbes could say is that the tiny joy that is identical with the appetite for food is overwhelmed by the intense pain caused by other things that accompanies that appetite.

Endeavors

Both appetites and aversions together are called 'endeavors'. The idea of endeavor was very important to Hobbes from 1640 onward in his physics as much as in his psychology. In *De Corpore*, Hobbes used endeavor to explain several other concepts. Resistance is the endeavor of one body against another body moving in an opposed direction.[23] Pressure on a body is the endeavor of another body against the first. Mutual pressure results from opposed endeavors.

We know that endeavors must exist in nature as a whole because any visible motion is divisible into a smaller part that is a motion; and this in turn can be divided again, ad infinitum. In *De Corpore*, Hobbes defines endeavor as a movement too small to be measured. This makes the concept of an endeavor relative. Suppose that one is not able to measure a distance smaller than an inch. Then a movement of half an inch would count as an endeavor within that system. If one were able to measure distances of a quarter inch, then a movement of half an inch would not be an endeavor. The concept of an endeavor also has a temporal application. Suppose that one is not able to measure less than one second of time. Then a motion that occurred in one-half second would be perceived as being instantaneous, even though Hobbes knows that every motion takes some amount of time. This result uncovers an inconsistency in Hobbes's views: He also holds that every cause precedes its effect, and so an instantaneous movement should be impossible, but he is logically committed to them by his conception of temporal endeavors.

Reductionistic Psychology

The whole thrust of Hobbes's psychology is reductionistic. In addition to wanting to reduce cognition and emotion to physics, he maintains that many of the words that seem to signify different things in fact signify the same thing, with perhaps a difference in connotation. In *The Elements*, he says that 'pleasure', 'appetite' and 'love' are "divers names for divers considerations of the same thing."[24] Each signifies an endeavor toward an object, but the first word connotes the sensation, the second the motion, and the third the possession of the object. The word 'fear' signifies the same thing as 'aversion', but it is used when the object of fear is expected rather than present.[25]

Already present in *The Elements* is the project of reducing diverse emotions to appetites and aversions, combined with certain types of objects or goals. But the project is carried out in a more thoroughgoing way in *Leviathan*. For example, according to Hobbes, pusillanimity is the appetite for an object that minimally serves one's goals. Anger is "sudden courage,"[26] and courage is an aversion for an object combined with the opinion that the object of aversion can be removed by resisting it. So anger is having a sudden aversion for an object combined with the opinion that the object of aversion can be removed by resisting it.

Although many of these analyses are unsuccessful as they stand, what is important is the general design of the project. Hobbes wants to show that things that appear to be very different from each other are at bottom very similar; and things that look as if they have to be categorized as nonphysical or nonmaterial in fact are physical and bodily. Hobbes's project is being pursued today by biochemists and brain physiologists. They replace psychological concepts with chemical and physical ones: Hunger is a certain state of certain brain cells and certain chemicals in the bloodstream. Although Hobbes's project is being fulfilled by contemporary scientists, his own analyses are old-fashioned because he presented not physiological but conceptual analyses of emotions. That is, he related the concepts of, say, fear and anger, to the concepts of appetite and aversion, not to chemicals or specific physical states.

Good and Evil

One of the most scandalous of Hobbes's doctrines concerns the nature of good and evil. In *The Elements*, he says, "Every man, for his own part, calls that which pleases and is delightful to himself, good, and that evil which displeases him."[27] This sentence is ambiguous because sometimes things are called something that they are not. Frank Sinatra was often called 'a great humanitarian', but he was not. So we have to ask, 'When people call their pleasures and pains "goods" and "evils" are they applying the words correctly or not?' The ambiguity is not resolved by the way Hobbes introduces the ideas of good and evil in *Leviathan*, because he uses the same language of 'calling'. Still, I think it is clear that Hobbes thinks that what we call 'good' is good for us, at least in the short term.

This is not to say that every immediate sensation of pleasure is a long-term good. Hobbes knows that the language of good and evil can be confused or confusing because pleasures and pains can succeed each other, and strings of pleasures and pains are often amalgamated as if they were one simple thing and called either 'good' or 'bad.' Being drunk may feel good, but a hangover feels bad. Is the conjunction of the drunkenness and hangover good or bad? Hobbes would say that the answer depends on the length and intensity of each aspect. If on balance there is more pleasure than pain, then it is good; if the opposite, then bad. People often get into trouble because they allow their desire for immediate and short-term pleasures to overcome their desire for long-term pleasures. Thus they are unhappy. Happiness, as it is used to describe a life, is not a state or condition, it is an activity or sequence of pleasurable or satisfying experiences: "Felicity . . . consists not in having prospered but in prospering."[28] In *Leviathan*, he puts this in a more provocative way. He denies that there is such a thing as the scholastics have been calling for a thousand years "a summum bonum,"[29] one object that is the goal for all human beings and that, when achieved, marks the end of striving.

The pursuit of immediate short-term pleasures is the natural inclination of human beings. What is needed to overcome nature is something artificial. In the first instance, a civil government is the thing. In the second instance, education and discipline provide the means of knowing how to achieve long-term pleasure and the strength to achieve it. There are two features of Hobbes's account of goodness and badness that are objectionable to many people. First, they are radically relativistic. There is nothing that is good or bad in itself but only to a particular person, and since people with different constitutions have different appetites, not all things are good or bad to all people.[30] The second objectionable feature is less often noticed. It is that Hobbes takes the concepts of goodness and badness out of the realm of morality and restricts it to human psychology. In fact, Hobbes is right in holding that 'good' and 'bad' are not essentially moral terms, as the phrases 'good plant', 'good thief', 'good painting', and 'good singer' should make evident. What is naturally good and bad is not to be prescribed but first to be discovered by observation and then to be described. Although people naturally seek what is good and avoid what is bad, goodness and badness are not essentially tied to obligation or morality on Hobbes's account. Goodness and evil are contingently tied to obligation when certain actions are commanded or prohibited, respectively, by the sovereign.

As a partial reply to the first objection (in order to defend Hobbes), it should be pointed out that there is nothing inherently wrong with making good and bad relative to people. Being a parent, being a lover, and being the God of Israel are examples of relative concepts that are not inherently objectionable. It is also not necessarily objectionable if tastes differ. Where is the harm in one person liking hamburgers and another person gardenburgers, one person liking Twinkies and someone else liking tofu? Further, Hobbes purports to be reporting the actual meanings of 'good' and 'bad', not recommending them. In fact, he recognizes that if everyone is allowed to pursue their immediate goods (that is, desires), then long-term misery is sure to follow. That is why he believes that people must replace their natural desires with the (artificial) desires of the sovereign. What the sovereign takes to be good serves as goodness for everyone, and hence within civil states there is something that is tantamount to objective goodness.

Concerning the second point, there should be nothing objectionable in removing 'good' and 'bad' from the vocabulary of morality as long as the work of morality – contributing to the happiness of people and regulating their interactions – is accomplished by something else. According to Hobbes, that something else is the law. To be moral is to be just; to be just is not to break one's covenants. To make a covenant requires that there be a law that obliges one to keep them. Therefore, to be moral requires that there be law. Whether his theory is successful or not, Hobbes thinks that his concept of law can be used to morally prescribe cooperation, kindness, gratitude, and all the other bourgeois or Christian virtues.

Passions of the Mind

Hobbes's cynical view of human beings is as evident in *The Elements* as in any of his later works: "Emulation is grief arising from seeing one's self exceeded or excelled by his concurrent [competitor], together with hope to be equal or exceed him in time to come, by his own ability. But envy is the same grief joined with pleasure conceived in the imagination of some ill fortune that may befall him."[31] In the preceding chapter, we saw how his cynicism is inherent in his view of laughter.

Lust and love are the same thing: a double desire to give and receive pleasure. And success is more likely to come to those who "care less than they that care more." Hobbes doubts that so-called Platonic love is not lustful. It smells of bad faith. He suspects that it is actually sensual "with an honorable pretense for the old to haunt the company of the young and beautiful."[32] This is a periphrastic description of Socrates as a dirty old man.

There is a certain delight that accompanies pity and inclines people to "be spectators of the misery of their friends." As regards adversity, better him than you, but better you than me. Life is like a race: "[it has] no other goal, nor no other garland, but being foremost. . . . Continually to be out-gone is misery. Continually to out-go the next before is felicity. And to forsake the course is to die."[33] These sentiments exude the stink of existential absurdity. This is not to say that they are false.

Religion

Some of Hobbes's religious views were introduced in Chapter 4 in the context of relating him to certain distinctive positions held by members of the Great Tew circle, positions that would eventually be picked up by various groups supporting either a more comprehensive Church of England or more toleration for Christians outside the institutional structure of the state church. These views are inherently liberal. Many of Hobbes's other views, such as those on biblical authorship and the correct under-standing of revelation, prophets, and miracles, are even more liberal, liberal to the point of inviting the accusation of being anti-Christian or antireligious, just as the views of Richard Simon, Julius Wellhausen, and other pioneers of biblical authorship were. These views will be discussed later. But some of Hobbes's religious views were in their foundations profoundly conservative and characteristic of Reformed Christianity.

Perhaps the most important of these conservative views concerns hu-man knowledge of God. Hobbes says that since "God Almighty is incom-prehensible, it follows that we can have no conception or image of the Deity."[34] This assertion, which has often been interpreted as an expres-sion of agnosticism or secret atheism, is standard Calvinist doctrine in the seventeenth century. It began with Calvin, who wrote that God is "in

himself incomprehensible."[35] Three distinguished puritan theologians of
the period said essentially the same thing. William Ames, in *The Marrow
of Theology*, wrote that God cannot be understood as he is in himself by
anyone except himself; John Preston, in *Life Eternall: or, A Treatise of the
Knowledge of the Divine Essence and Attributes*, wrote that God's nature "is
capable properly of no definition," and William Perkins wrote that nothing, not even "the virtues of reasonableness or justice, as human beings
conceived them, is literally true of God."[36] The idea of *deus absconditus*,
that God is hidden from human beings, is a standard Judeo-Christian
philosophical piety. Hobbes professes the piety. He also accepts that God
can be known only to the extent that he reveals himself supernaturally. So
he has no problem with accepting and using biblical language about God.
But it is also part of this view that God does not reveal his nature to
human beings. That is the force of his answer to Moses' question, "Who
are you?" God's answer, "Yahweh" ("I am what is"), is taken to have the
force: You cannot know who I am. Many other passages make the same
point, as when God says, "you shall see my back parts; but my face cannot
be seen" (Exodus 33:23). This is in effect a gloss on Calvin's statement
that when God "assumed a visible form," he was not showing himself "in
his essence but as the infirmity of the human mind could comprehend."[37]

Most of the sting of Hobbes's position is removed if one focuses on
those passages in which he says that people do not know anything about
the 'nature' of God.[38] This statement is weaker than the unvarnished
assertion about God's incomprehensibility and truer to his own intentions, for there are plenty of places when he asserts the literal truth of the
existence of God and also seems to assert that God is literally eternal and
omnipotent. Also, Hobbes says that it should not be surprising that
people do not know the nature of God, given that they do not even know
the nature of the smallest animal. In the *Institutes of the Christian Religion*,
Calvin made the same point in very similar terms: "For how can the infinite essence of God be defined by the capacity of the human mind . . . ?
Indeed, how can it, by its own efforts, penetrate into an examination of the
substance of God, when it is totally ignorant of its own?"[39]

In fact, it should not be astounding that Hobbes held that spirits, like
God, are of such a mysterious ("subtle") nature that they do not affect
human sense organs at all and hence do not directly produce an idea,
because he also believed that no human ideas are iconic; that is, none
resemble their objects. He made something like this point when he said in

reply to Descartes that a person "merely gives the name or label 'God' to the thing that he believes in or acknowledges to exist."[40] Human knowledge of God, he says, is like the kind of thought that blind men have of fire. They infer its existence from the heat that they feel.[41]

Proof of the Existence of God

Belief in the existence of God is inferential, not direct. It can be justified by one of the standard proofs for his existence. Many philosophers distinguish between proofs from motion and proofs from efficient causality. But since efficient causality is only motion for Hobbes, he combines the two. In *The Elements*, he says:

> For the effects we acknowledge naturally do necessarily include a power of their producing before they were produced; and that power presupposes something existent that has such power; and the thing so existing with power to produce, if it were not eternal, must needs have been produced by somewhat before it; and that again by something else before that: till we come to an eternal, that is to say, to the first power of all powers, and first cause of all causes. And this is it which all men call by the name of God.[42]

There are similar arguments in *De Cive* and *Leviathan*. Some scholars have taken these arguments to be clues to Hobbes's atheism, because they are short and defective. Neither reason should be the least bit persuasive. Anselm's ontological argument and Aquinas's Five Ways are as short and defective. To think that theological error is evidence of irreligion is to suffer from Torquemada syndrome.

I have referred to Hobbes's *proofs* for the existence of God and not his demonstrations, advisedly. 'Demonstration' had a technical meaning for him. A demonstration is a syllogism that has universal, necessary, and indubitable premises, and a universal and necessary conclusion. No proof for the existence of anything, a fortiori, no proof for the existence of God can be a demonstration, because the existence of every object is contingent, as Hobbes understood contingency.

The Nature of Religious Language

If God is incomprehensible, then it should be impossible to have any genuine conception of him. And from that it should follow that religious talk about God cannot be literally true, except for assertions of his existence, and perhaps his eternity and omnipotence. Most Christians did not draw the logical conclusion, and they were outraged that Hobbes had. (In this matter Hobbes was similar to Baruch Spinoza in beginning from conventional premises and drawing the logical but unwelcome conclusion.) How then does religious talk, which is so rich and elaborate, function? According to Hobbes, the purpose of religious language is to honor or worship God. When people say that God is omnipotent, omniscient, just, and merciful, they are expressing their reverence for him.[43] Hobbes's position was a brilliant anticipation of the insight of some followers of the later Ludwig Wittgenstein, especially Ian Ramsey, who was Nolloth Professor of the Philosophy of Christian Religion at Oxford.[44]

Hobbes's views about the nature of religious language came into full bloom in *Leviathan*. In that work, he produces a moving passage when he melds his views about the nature of God and the nature of religious language:

He that will attribute to God nothing but what is warranted by natural reason must either use such negative attributes as 'infinite', 'eternal', 'incomprehensible', or superlatives as 'most high', 'most great', and the like, or indefinite, as 'good' 'just' 'holy', 'creator', and in such sense as if he meant not to declare what he is (for that were to circumscribe him within the limits of our fancy) but how much we admire him, and how ready we would be to obey him, which is a sign of humility, and of a will to honor him as much as we can. For there is but one name to signify our conception of his nature, and that is, 'I am', and but one name of his relation to us, and that is God, in which is contained father, king, and lord.[45]

Because religious language is honorific and not descriptive, it is not the case that every property that is true of God will be appropriately applied to him. For example, although God is in motion (because he causes things) and every cause is in motion, it is not appropriate to say this because 'is in motion' is not considered an honorable predicate even though it is a true one. Pre–Vatican II Roman Catholic theology had a similar concept. Some true things were not to be asserted because they were 'offensive to pious ears'. It also follows that it is not the case that for every pair of contradictory properties, one or the other will apply to God. Assume that being in motion and being at rest are contradictory properties. We have already seen that it is inappropriate to say that God is in motion. But similarly since 'is at rest' is not an honorable predicate either, it is not to be applied. So God is neither said to be in motion nor at rest.[46]

Spirits

Since God exists and is a spirit, and since only bodies exist, it follows that all spirits are bodies. Hobbes no doubt held this view in 1640, but he was reluctant to assert it in public at that time. In *The Elements*, he asserts that spirits are subtle bodies and that the idea of "substance without dimension" is self-contradictory. He sidesteps the issue of whether God is a body by maintaining that when it is said that God is a spirit, the word is not being attributed literally, but only reverentially.[47] The implication that God is a body is clear, if not explicit. As late as 1651, Hobbes was only implying rather than asserting that God is a body. In *Leviathan*, he says that God is a substance and that the term 'incorporeal substance' is incoherent. It follows that God is a body.[48] It also follows from his assertions that God is a spirit and that spirits are bodies. But in neither case does he concatenate the words: God is a body.

In the Latin translation of *Leviathan*, published in 1668, Hobbes comes as close as possible to uttering the words. In that version, he includes an appendix that consists of a dialogue between two characters A and B. As John Wallis would say about similarly named characters in another of Hobbes's dialogues, they are Thomas and Hobbes in conversation. One of the characters says, "Affirmat quidem Deum esse corpus" ("He [Hobbes] asserts that God is a body"). Further, in his reply to Bishop John Bramhall's *The Catching of Leviathan*, written about 1668, though not published until after his death, Hobbes wrote, "I . . . maintain God's existence and that he is a most pure and most simple corporeal spirit."[49] There are similar assertions in *An Historical Narration concerning Heresy and the Punishment Thereof* and *Considerations upon the Reputation, Loyalty, Manners and Religion of Thomas Hobbes.*

Many of his critics maintained that the idea of a corporeal God is atheistic. Hobbes thought just the opposite was true. Only bodies are substances; only substances genuinely exist; God genuinely exists; therefore, God is a body. So Hobbes claimed, "to say that God is an incorporeal substance is to say in effect that there is no God at all."[50] Since one person's *modus ponens* is another person's *modus tollens,* some other criterion must be applied to settle the issue. Should it be the Bible? That was the one that Hobbes favored. He pointed out that far from asserting or implying that God is immaterial, the Bible implies that God is a body, as when Genesis says that the spirit of God moved upon the waters. (Only bodies move bodies.) Just to round out the presentation of his case, Hobbes points out several times that Tertullian maintained that God is a body and was never condemned for saying so. Hobbes may have been led to look into Tertullian through his connection with the Great Tew circle.

Created Spirits

The affirmation of a corporeal God makes the treatment of finite corporeal spirits easier in one way. They are obviously possible. The issue then concerns whether in fact there are any. In *The Elements*, Hobbes affirms the Christian belief in angels, based on revelation. But this is not the same as asserting that they know that angels exist, because knowledge requires evidence, evidence is rooted in sense experience, and spirits are "those substances which work not on the sense."[51]

On the supposition that spirits such as angels do exist, what should be said about their nature? If the Bible is our guide, then it is most probable, according to Hobbes, that they are corporeal. The Bible says that spirits abide and dwell in men, that they come and go, descend and ascend, and act as messengers. All of this language signifies that they both have a place in and move through space, and this kind of language applies only to bodies. Moreover, the Bible does not contain the word 'incorporeal'. In short, all the biblical evidence "favors them more who hold angels and spirits for corporeal." Against those who maintain that the existence of created spirits is a matter of knowledge, because many pagans have professed their existence, Hobbes points out correctly that this pagan belief is grounded in "ignorance of the causes of ghosts and phantasms"; it is superstition, not knowledge.[52] There is a further consideration. It would be very odd if Christians had to rely on revelation for their knowledge of spirits where pagans could do as well with reason. Why should Christians not have the same benefits of reason as pagans? Hobbes's rejection of the appeal to pagan philosophy is part of his staunch Protestantism. In the preceding chapter we quoted Luther as telling Christians not to "dabble too much in philosophy."

When Hobbes comes to settle the issue of the nature and existence of spirits and angels in *Leviathan*, he begins with a brief paragraph that in effect asserts that the meaning of a word is its use. Consequently, he surveys the uses of the words 'spirit' and 'angel' in the Bible. This gives him the data with which he will resolve the two issues. First, he maintains that if angels exist, they must be corporeal, because the term 'incorporeal substance' is self-contradictory. Second, they do exist. The candor in his statement of this latter point invites quotation:

> I was inclined to this opinion, that angels were nothing but supernatural apparitions of the fancy, raised by the special and extraordinary operation of God, thereby to make his presence and commandments known to mankind and chiefly to his own people. But the many places of the New Testament and our Savior's own words and in such texts wherein is no suspicion of corruption of the Scripture have extorted from my feeble reason an acknowledgment and belief that there be also angels substantial and permanent.[53]

To my mind the two most compelling features of this passage are his admission of a former skepticism concerning angels and then his reliance on the New Testament for his evidence. If he were teaching a secret doctrine of deism or atheism, then it would be sensible for him to consistently deconstruct the idea of angels and to treat the Old and New Testaments the same. In fact, like a good Christian, Hobbes favored the latter over the former and affirmed its historical reliability, as we shall see in Chapter 8.

This suffices as a sketch of the views Hobbes held about the nature of physical laws in *The Elements*. Let us now consider some of the political views.

Political Theory

Although he would sharpen the argumentation and improve the presentation in later works, Hobbes adhered for the rest of his life to the basic positions presented in his first political treatise. He begins with a description of what people are like in themselves. By this he means human beings unregulated by laws. Hobbes does not intend his description to capture the historically earliest or most primitive condition of human beings. He recognized that Adam had God as his sovereign. Rather, by beginning with the way human beings live in any society, he asks the reader to consider what life would be like if all laws were abolished. He is taking his readers through an intellectual exercise, a thought experiment, in order to get them to see the desirability of setting up a government. In *De Cive,* he explained his method in analogy with understanding the mechanism of a clock:

For everything is best understood by its constitutive causes. For as in a watch or some such small engine the matter, figure, and motion of the wheels cannot be well-known, except it be taken asunder and viewed in parts; so to make a more curious search into the rights of states and duties, it is necessary, I say, not to take them asunder, but yet that they be so considered as if they were dissolved; that is, that we rightly understand what the quality of human nature is, in what matters it is, in what not, fit to make up a civil government.[54]

People, he says, "considered in mere nature, ought to admit amongst themselves equality."[55] This proposition, which superficially looks like a law because of the word 'ought', is actually a factual description. The word 'ought' is functioning as it does in a sentence like, 'If you want to know the truth, you ought to see that people are equal by nature'. He calls people who "think one man's blood better than another's by nature" ignorant.[56] For him, differences of status are conventional; they depend on decisions made by the sovereign. For an employee of various noblemen for most of his life, this is a daring observation. The earl of Clarendon especially did not like it. In *A Brief View and Survey of the Dangerous and Pernicious Errors to Church and State . . . in Leviathan* (1676), he wrote: "In the meantime, he [Hobbes] must not take it ill that I observe [mention] his extreme malignity to the Nobility, by whose bread he has been always sustained, who must not expect any part, at least any precedence in his institution."

Hobbes's natural egalitarianism is not based on the dignity of man or any other high-sounding or sentimental principle. He is not talking about equal political rights or claims that each person has against every other person. What he sometimes seems to mean is that by averaging out physical and mental strength, everyone has roughly the same capacity for survival. This may suggest that he is implying that stupid people tend to be stronger than average and intelligent people tend to be weaker than average; but that is not what he really means. His point is that, except in the most extreme cases, no matter how stupid and weak a person may be, he still has enough wit and strength to kill another person, no matter how smart and strong. It is not equality in the ordinary sense that Hobbes is pointing to; rather it is human vulnerability:

[I]f we consider . . . with how great facility he that is the weaker in strength or in wit, or in both, may utterly destroy the power of the stronger, since there needs but little force to the taking away of a man's life, we may conclude that men considered in mere nature, ought to admit amongst themselves equality.[57]

Malmesbury market cross. (Photograph by the author.)

Church at Brokenborough, where Hobbes's father ministered. (Photograph by the author.)

Elizabeth Hardwick. (Photograph by John Bethell. Copyright The National Trust, Hardwick Hall. By permission.)

Ben Johnson. (Photograph by John Scanlan.)

Christian Cavendish. (By permission of The Harry Ransom Humanities Research Center, The University of Texas at Austin.)

Lady Anne Rich (née Cavendish). (Courtesy of Dr. Erik Larson and Luca Verlag.)

Francis Bacon. (Courtesy of Mrs. Elton M. Hyder Jr.)

William Cavendish, second earl of Devonshire. (Photograph: Courtauld Institute of Art, Somerset House, London. Copyright The National Trust, Hardwick Hall. By permission.)

William Cavendish, third earl of Devonshire. (From the painting by Sir Peter Lely. Photograph: Courtauld Institute of Art, Somerset House, London. By permission of The Chatsworth Settlement Trustees.)

William Cavendish, first duke of Newcastle. (Photograph by John Scanlan.)

Thomas Hobbes. (Photograph by John Scanlan.)

Charles II. (Courtesy of Mrs. Elton M. Hyder Jr.)

Kenelm Digby. (Photograph by John Scanlan.)

Thomas Hobbes at ninety. (Photograph: Courtauld Institute of Art, Somerset House, London. Copyright The National Trust, Hardwick Hall. By permission.)

Hardwick Hall

St. John the Baptist. (Pen-and-ink drawing by Elizabeth Criss.)

Even the strongest, most intelligent person has to sleep sometime; when he does, sneak up and bash his brains out. This is the "nature red in tooth and claw" argument. Natural equality contributes to universal warfare. A corollary of equal vulnerability is equal lethality.

Hobbes emphasizes the idea of human equality in the state of nature for rhetorical purposes. He wants the state of nature to be an unpleasant place; most of his audience would have thought of equality as socially and morally disastrous and wrong.

The causes of war are roughly the same as presented in *The Elements*, *De Cive*, and *Leviathan*: competition for the same things, diffidence (distrust toward one's fellowman) and the desire for glory. In *The Elements*, and *De Cive*, the different causes are not as sharply defined as they are in *Leviathan*. In *The Elements*, glory rather than competition or diffidence receives pride of place. Some people want more glory for themselves than they deserve. This causes other people, especially those who are in fact not 'inferior' to them, to resist them by force: Hence war.[58] Related to glory is the fact that each person wants to be thought well of by his fellows and yet hates that very attitude in other people.[59]

Competition, according to Hobbes, is inevitable. Here is one of his arguments: Everyone has a right to self-preservation. Whoever has a right to the end has a right to the means to that end. Anything might be useful at some time for self-preservation.[60] Therefore, everyone has a right to everything. This argument is fairly poor. From the premise that anything might be useful, all that follows is that a person might have a right to anything, not that he does. In *Leviathan*, Hobbes would argue more subtly. (See Chapter 8.)

Hobbes could have come up with a much simpler and more plausible argument for his position: Liberty is the right to act as one pleases. Only laws limit liberty. In the state of nature, there are no laws. Therefore, in the state of nature there is no limit on liberty and thus one has the right to everything. In short, if nothing is forbidden, then everything is permitted; and if everything is permitted, then everyone has a right to everything, even the body of another person.

Since the state of nature is insufferable, it is important to get out of it. The laws of nature instruct people about how that can be done. Before giving his own definition of them, Hobbes criticizes other standard ones. A law of nature cannot be whatever does not go against "the consent of all mankind" or against that of the "wisest and most civil."[61] His objection to the latter formula is that there is no criterion by which one can determine which nations are the wisest and most civil. His objection to the former formula is that every criminal by his very behavior nullifies what would otherwise be a law. That is, in breaking the law, the criminal shows that he does not consent to it.

In *The Elements*, he defines the law of nature as reason *simpliciter*.[62] In *De Cive*, he sensibly weakens the definition and says that the law of nature is a dictate of reason. In *Leviathan*, the definition becomes much more complicated and is the most sensible, as we shall see in Chapter 8. In general, his treatment of the laws of nature in *De Cive* and *Leviathan* is much more sophisticated than the one in his earliest political work. In *The Elements*, the injunction to seek peace seems to be the generic law of nature. In the two later works, "Seek peace" expresses only the first law of nature, from which others will be deduced. The second law of nature is "Lay down your right to all things."[63] This follows from the first because not laying down one's right to all things is inconsistent with the first law. While Hobbes does not try to prove the second law of nature in *The Elements*, he does provide one for the third. That third law, namely, to keep one's covenants, is derived from the second plus the ancient axiom 'Nature does nothing in vain'. In short, since it would be pointless for people to lay down their rights to all things unless people kept their covenants, and since nature does nothing in vain, it is a law of nature that people are obliged to keep their covenants.

There are at least two ways in which Hobbes's treatment in *Leviathan* of the second and third laws of nature, not to mention the others, is superior to that in *The Elements*. First, Hobbes does not use the anti-quated principle that nature does nothing in vain. Second, the concept of obligation is not part of either law. This second point may seem odd. Shouldn't obligation be a part of the content of every law? No. The content of a law expresses what is commanded or forbidden. The obliga-tion itself is a function of the authority of the person or thing that commands the law. As explained in Chapter 4, the structure of an explicit command is 'I command that p'. The proposition ('that p') expresses the content or the matter of the law. The phrase 'I command' expresses what may be understood as the form of the law. It is the authority of the speaker that makes it the case that the proposition that p is commanded rather than counseled or predicted or guessed at or something else. Authority entails obligation. In *Leviathan,* most of the laws of nature are in fact formulated without the use of the word 'obliged' or one of its cognates.

To return to the derivation of the second and third laws of nature in *Leviathan,* the implicit strategy in each case seems to be the use of reductio ad absurdum. Apropos the second law, suppose for the sake of the reductio that people do not lay down the right to all things. Then people do not seek peace. It follows that they do not make peace. But this proposition contradicts the first law of nature, that people do make peace. Thus, the supposition is false, and consequently people do lay down the right to all things. Q.E.D.

The derivation of the third law is similar. Suppose for the sake of the reductio that people do not keep their covenants. Then they do not seek peace. (Breaking a covenant leads to war.) So they do not seek peace. But this contradicts the first law of nature. Thus, the supposition is false, and, consequently, people do keep their covenants. Similar derivations could be produced for Hobbes's other laws of nature: Be gracious, be accommodating, be forgiving; punish only when some good comes of it; and so on.[64]

What is interesting about these laws of nature is their conventionality.[65] One of the oddities of this part of Hobbes's philosophy is that from his contentious starting point, namely, the state of nature, egoistic psychology, and the right of self-preservation, he derives a perfectly conventional normative system. Normally, philosophers try to proceed in the opposite way: from uncontroversial premises to shocking conclusions.

The fact that obligation is not part of the content of law raises the question 'By what authority are the laws of nature laws?' This is perhaps the most unsettled and fiercely debated question in Hobbes scholarship. The dominant interpretation is that reason commands the laws of nature. Because reason is not a person and only persons can genuinely command something, it follows that the laws of nature are not genuinely laws. In *Leviathan,* Hobbes says that "the dictates of reason" are not properly called laws, and this is often taken as tantamount to the assertion that the laws of nature are not properly called laws.[66]

Hobbes certainly held in *The Elements* and in *De Cive* that reason commands the laws of nature and that they are not, properly speaking, laws.[67] But there is a minority interpretation, to which I subscribe, according to which Hobbes changed his mind. In *Leviathan,* he came to maintain that the laws of nature are genuine laws and are made such by the command of God. One way to explain Hobbes's change is to pose the question that has worried most scholars whichever interpretation they favor. If the laws of nature are not genuine laws and if they are not commanded by any authority, how then do they oblige? As Hobbes said, the strength of obligation is power. And in the state of nature, no one has the power to give the laws of nature any strength, except God. So, if God does not command the laws of nature, then they are not laws; and if they are not laws, then nothing has the strength to provide the normative force needed to get people out of the state of nature.

Another way of putting this is that if the laws of nature are not genuine laws, then they are merely prudential maxims. As such, it would often be advisable to follow them, but not always. It would sometimes make sense to appear to follow them, but not really to do so. And at worse, a person who did not follow them would be imprudent, but not immoral or unjust. Within the general structure of Hobbes's principles, the most sensible solution to this problem is to make the laws of nature genuine laws, in virtue of being commanded by God. There are many places where Hobbes says that they are.

On the other hand, there are the exceptions and the complications. Hobbes says in one place (1) that "reason" commands the laws of nature and in another place (2) that the laws of nature are not really laws. How can the interpreters of the minority view reply? Briefly, they can say that the exceptions are really exceptions and do not carry as much weight as the large number of assertions that the laws of nature are genuine laws. Also, (2) occurs in a chapter that contains a lot of confusions. For example, in it Hobbes makes the indefensible claim that the laws of nature and the civil laws contain each other. This has to be false for a couple of reasons. One is that the relation of containing is asymmetrical: Two things cannot contain each other; the bucket contains the water or the water contains the bucket, but not both. Another is that because the laws of nature are operative when there is no civil government and hence no civil laws at all, they cannot mutually contain each other, so to speak. What Hobbes probably means by his absurd remark is that the civil laws are always consistent with the laws of nature. Concerning (2), what he possibly means is that the laws of nature are not as effective as the civil laws because the power behind them, though greater, is often ignored by humans. Earlier in *Leviathan*, he had said that the effectiveness of laws depends on the fear of being punished by something with power, and that although God is the stronger power, people are usually more afraid of their fellows.[68]

Laying Down a Right

The second law of nature is that people need to lay down their rights to everything, and Hobbes needs to explain how this is done. There are two ways. One can either renounce ("relinquish") or transfer them.[69] What he wants this distinction to amount to is this: To renounce a right is to give up that right without favoring the chances of anyone else to exercise his own right to that thing. For example, if a person renounces his right to the apples on a tree, then he indicates to other people that he will make no effort to get those apples. In contrast, to transfer a right is not only to give up that right but also to intend to help some other designated person or persons to exercise his or their rights to that thing. If a person transfers his right to the apples to Jones, then that person will help Jones get the apples either by warding off others or boosting Jones up or in some other way.

From his first introduction of it, Hobbes often had trouble correctly characterizing the distinction between renouncing and transferring. The problem is in his misdescription of the idea of transferring a right. In *The Elements*, he says:

> To relinquish it [a right] is by sufficient signs to declare that it is his will no more to do that action which of right he might have done before. To transfer right to another is by sufficient signs to declare to that other accepting thereof that it is his will not to resist or hinder him according to that right he had thereto before he transferred it."[70]

So described, renouncing ("relinquishment") and transfer amount to a distinction without a difference. Here's why. If Smith transfers his right to Jones, it is not enough for Smith to stay out of Jones's way. That much is required by relinquishment. Smith must also do something to help Jones exercise his right, because whoever wills the end wills the means. Hobbes himself sometimes seems to say or imply this: The institution of a government requires each person "to resign his strength and means to him whom he covenants to obey; and hereby he that is to command may by the use of all their means and strength be able by the terror thereof" to unite them.[71]

The importance of this point lies in the fact that Hobbes wants to explain the creation of sovereignty as the transfer of the right to govern oneself; and it would be impossible for a sovereign to do his job if all he received was the noninterference of his subjects. What the sovereign needs, and what Hobbes makes clear in other places that he gets, is the unrestricted cooperation of the subjects. In fact, Hobbes has no intrinsic interest in the idea of renouncing rights at all. He marks that term of the distinction only in order to focus on the nature of transferring a right. Consequently, it is unfortunate and odd that Hobbes's description of transfer is so often defective.

Covenants

The key to getting out of the state of nature is the ability to form a covenant with other people that will establish a sovereign, that is, a government. Hobbes insists that the agreement is a covenant, not a contract. A contract occurs when two or more people mutually transfer rights to certain things, with no further consideration required by either party, for example, when one person sells something to another. What distinguishes a covenant from a contract is the fact that a covenant imposes an obligation on a person to behave in a certain way in the future. In a sovereign-making covenant the future obligatory behavior is unwavering obedience to the government.

The word 'covenant' had strong theological connotations in the seventeenth century. The Hebrew Bible is full of covenants, such as God's promise to Noah not to destroy the world by flood and Abraham's promise to obey God as a condition for being the father of many people. Even the terms 'Old' and 'New Testament' are more precisely rendered as Old and New Covenant. The Old Covenant was the one by which the Israelites promised to have Yahweh as their only god. The New Covenant is God's promise to save human beings through the redemptive action of Jesus. The rebellious Scots exploited this theological concept in 1638 when they drafted the National Covenant in defiance of Charles's imposition of a Prayer Book on them. Hobbes was offended by their blasphemous audacity. In *The Elements*, he pointed out that "it is impossible for any man to make a covenant with God Almighty"[72] except through

God's representative, that is, the sovereign, because a covenant requires a sign of acceptance by the relevant party. And God's representative for Scotland, Charles, had not accepted it. The outrage is even more pronounced in *Leviathan*: "But this pretense of Covenant with God is so evident a lie, even in the pretenders' own consciences, that it is not only an act of an unjust, but also of a vile and unmanly disposition."[73] In *The Elements*, the motivating emotion for getting out of the state of nature is simply the fear that people have of death. In *Leviathan*, Hobbes had a more complex view of the psychological means that people use. It is a combination of some emotions and rationality: "The passions that incline men to peace are fear of death, desire of such things as are necessary to commodious living, and a hope by their industry to obtain them. And reason suggests convenient articles of peace upon which men may be drawn to agreement."[74] This is about as optimistic as Hobbes gets.

One obvious objection to Hobbes's view about the origin of a civil government is that covenants made under duress – and fear counts as duress – are typically considered not binding. To put the point a bit more precisely, an apparent covenant extorted by fear is not a genuine covenant. Hobbes disagrees. He simply could not see that coercion disables covenant making. He claims that an agreement extorted by fear is as voluntary as any other, because a voluntary act is simply one that is caused by a desire. The fact that an agreement is made out of the desire to escape death does not make it any less a desire. In reply to those who would object that the ordinary law of contracts voids agreements that are coerced, Hobbes would say that these contracts are voided, not because they were coerced, but because the sovereign made a law that dictates that they be voided. Even if Hobbes's argumentation is not persuasive, he simply cannot give up his point, because fear is a permanent condition in the state of nature and the only way to get out of it is to make a covenant.[75]

Absolute Sovereignty

Absolute sovereignty, as Hobbes understood it, has two components: the sovereign's possession of all the political force that exists in the government, and the right to control every external aspect of life (for the preservation of the lives of the subjects). As regards complete authority, this means that the sovereign has the authority to make war and peace, make and repeal laws, judge alleged criminal behavior, and administer every

other aspect of government. As regards pervasiveness, the sovereign even
has the right to command a subject to kill a parent. In *De Cive*, he would
use an expression that mimics Anselm's description of God as the greatest
conceivable being: Absolute sovereignty is "that than which a greater
cannot be transferred by men to a man" ("quo maius ab hominibus iure
conferri non potest").[76] From at least 1640 onward, Hobbes thought that
every sovereign was absolute. The idea of a limited sovereignty was
incoherent because if the sovereign were limited in either power or scope,
he would be deprived of the means to achieve the end for which he was
created.

Given his view about absolute sovereignty, what freedom does Hobbes
think is left to the subject? Only the freedom to act in those matters about
which the sovereign has not forbidden. In other words, freedom is a
leftover. Hobbes thinks that what will be served up the day after the
sovereign is established will be a heaping portion for everyone, because no
sovereign can make laws that cover everything. Hobbes could be extremely naive. He did not seem to notice that it is quite easy to formulate a
law that pronounces nothing legal or one that forbids everything except
eating, sleeping, and working, and not necessarily in the most welcome
proportions. He can be excused an incapacity to imagine governmental
intrusiveness through the use of sophisticated technology, but not his
forgetfulness of the madness of Caligula.

In *The Elements*, Hobbes thought that the concept of absolute sovereignty was established by the nature of the sovereign-making covenant.
He maintained that in making that covenant each subject gave up his right
of resistance to the sovereign: "no man in any commonwealth whatsoever
has right to resist him or them on whom they have conferred this power
coercive."[77] (The right to self-preservation is nowhere to be seen here.) In
1640, when this was written, people knew full well that refusing or being
reluctant to pay ship money, quarter soldiers, vote money to fight the
Scots, and so on, was resistance to the king. Hobbes maintained that the
sword of justice and the sword of war must be in the same hands. Since it
was uncontroversial that the king had the sole right to make war against
foreign enemies, it follows that the king has the sword of justice, and
parliamentary opposition to him is unwarranted. Further, having the
sword of war requires having the sole "judgment and discretion" of when
to apply it: "it follows that the power of judicature (in all controversies
wherein the sword of justice is to be used) and (in all deliberations

concerning war, wherein the use of that sword is required) the right of resolving and determining what is to be done belong to the same sovereign."[78]

One sign of sovereignty is the status of being above the law.[79] This fit the axiom of English constitutional law that the king could do no wrong. The king's opponents worried very much about this principle. At first, they could get around it by arresting or executing the king's chief ministers, such as Strafford and Laud. When that proved to be too little, they resorted to the legal fiction of attacking the man Charles Stuart, not the person of the king of England. Although Hobbes accepted the distinction between the natural person of Charles and the artificial person of the king of England, he also thought the distinction would not absolve the rebels and regicides of their crime since the death of the natural person was *eo ipso* the death of the second.

Another sign of sovereignty, according to Hobbes, is the ability to dissolve Parliament. The king of course had that power, until the Long Parliament coerced him into exempting it. Hobbes thought that the Act Against Dissolution (1642) was a sign of the demise of any government in England. Still a third sign of sovereignty is the authority to appoint "magistrates, judges, counselors, and ministers of state," all of which not coincidentally the king of England had.[80] Hobbes summarizes his view about absolute sovereignty in these words:

> The sum of these rights of sovereignty, namely the absolute use of the sword in peace and war, the making and abrogating of laws, supreme judicature and decision in all debates judicial and deliberative, the nomination of all magistrates and ministers, with other rights contained in the same, make the sovereign power . . . absolute in the commonwealth.[81]

Property Rights

Hobbes's views about absolute sovereignty had very strong consequences that worried and upset the king's opponents. His unswerving position is that there is no private property in the state of nature. If every one has a right to everything, then no one owns anything. Property originates within the civil state and ultimately belongs to the sovereign. In transferring all of their rights to the sovereign, he comes to own everything. If some property were not ultimately the sovereign's, then some property that could potentially help the sovereign maintain the peace and preservation of the state would not be available to him. Hobbes says that one of the biggest complaints that citizens raise against the government is the dependence of private property on the sovereign. But the complaint is illegitimate. Unless government has ultimate control over property, everyone would have a right to everything and no one could feel safe in the use of any physical object: "Therefore, this grievance for *meum* and *tuum* [mine and thine] is not real."[82]

Here are only some of Hobbes's powerful statements against private property:

There is no *meum* and *tuum* belonging to any of them [subjects] against the master himself, whom they are not to resist. . . . And seeing both the servant and all that is committed to him is the property of the master and every man may dispose of his own . . . the master may alienate his dominion over them . . . to whom he list. . . . Property therefore being derived from the sovereign power, is not to be pretended against the same, especially when by it every subject has his property against every other subject, which when sovereignty ceases, he has not. . . . those levies therefore which are made upon men's estates by the sovereign authority are no more but the price of that peace and defense which the sovereignty maintains for them.[83]

The practical consequence of Hobbes's position is that Englishmen had no right to complain about any of the king's taxes, in particular, no complaint about ship money. People are sadly mistaken and in fact contribute to rebellion "when they are commanded to contribute their persons or money to the public service and think they have a propriety [property] in the same distinct from the dominion of the sovereign power and that therefore they are not bound to contribute their goods and persons, not more than every man shall of himself think fit."[84]

Hobbes's position on both sovereignty and property rights put him at one extreme of the political spectrum. Most Parliamentarians thought that the English government was not absolute; and even those that thought it was, maintained that the king did not possess the entire sovereignty but shared it with Parliament. According to Hobbes, those who believe that subjects "allot unto them [sovereigns] a provision limited as of certain lands, taxes, penalties, and the like, than which (if misspent) they shall have no more, without a new consent of the same men that allowed the former, . . . deceive themselves."[85] He explicitly attacks the doctrine of "mixed monarchy," a doctrine to which Charles would eventually feel forced to give lip service as a desperate concession to Parliament on the eve of the Civil War.

Hobbes's One-Step Theory of Government

Let's distinguish between one-step and two-step theories. In a one-step theory, the origin of government does not involve any independently existing entity intermediate between the prepolitical and political states. Such theories may include a transitional entity in the explanation of the change from the prepolitical to the political state. In a two-step theory, there is an entity that exists on its own and is neither the government nor any purely natural object. Typically, two-step theories call the intermediate entity 'the society', 'the community,' or 'the people'. John Locke, for example, is a two-step theorist. His first step consists of the contract among people that establishes a society or community; the second step is the society's action of establishing a government. Two-step theories make civil war a less radical breakdown and hence more palatable: A civil war may destroy the government but not the society itself. They also bolster theories of limited sovereignty. The society has a political authority that can check abuses by the sovereign. Because Hobbes wanted to make civil war sound as unpalatable as possible and because he does not want there to be any check on the sovereign, he adopts a one-step theory: He has the state of nature and then the civil state.

However, a vestige of a second step is detectable in *The Elements*, in which Hobbes says that democracy is "first in order of time . . . and it must be so of necessity."[86] His reasoning is that before any man or group of men can be given sovereignty, everyone has to covenant to abide by the decision of a majority vote. And that is democracy. Once this first decision is made, the newly constituted civil state can either remain a democracy or it can covenant to make the sovereign one human being (monarchy) or more than one (aristocracy). The reason that this does not count as a two-step theory is that on Hobbes's account monarchy or aristocracy succeeds the democracy and does not build on it. In *De Cive*, he hedges the position taken in *The Elements* when he says that those who form a government are "almost in the very act of meeting a democracy."[87] In *Leviathan*, the vestige of the two-step theory is even more attenuated. Democracy is no longer said to be either the temporally or logically basic form of government. Every government arises in two phases: the coming together followed immediately by the election of a sovereign, which thereby determines the form of government. This is not a genuine two-step form of government because the first phase does not contain any independently existing entity. If for some reason the election does not come off, then the second phase is not completed and the people remain in the state of nature. Even if the second phase is completed, the elective body of the first phase does not exist independently of the sovereignty itself.

One practical reason that Hobbes wanted to abandon the view that every government begins as a democracy was to deprive the king's enemies of an argument. He did not want them to maintain that in Anglo-Saxon times England was a democracy and remained a democracy after it appointed or elected the king to be their representative, without alienating any rights to him.

Hobbes had already dispatched another argument of the king's opponents in *The Elements*. One standard view of political theory was that sovereignty was the result of a covenant or contract between the people and the sovereign. If this were true, then disgruntled subjects could argue that the sovereign had broken the terms of the contract and could be removed. Hobbes argues that such a position is logically incoherent. The sovereign cannot be a party to the covenant because he does not exist when the covenant is enacted. His existence is brought about and temporally follows the covenant that is entered into by people still in the state of nature.[88]

Because the subjects are parties to the covenant, they take on duties and obligations. Because the sovereign is not a party to the contract, he does not. This much may be defensible. What may seem much less so is his further claim that the subjects have their duties and obligations to the sovereign and not to each other. Typically, duties and obligations are directed to the parties to a contract or covenant itself, even though another entity may enforce them. The reason that Hobbes can maintain that the duties and obligations are owed to the sovereign is that for him a person acquires a duty or obligation to the person to whom he transfers a right and not necessarily to other covenanting parties. An important consequence of not having the sovereign be a party to the sovereign-making covenant is that he cannot injure anyone, where 'injury' is understood as harming a person without authority.

Sovereignty by Institution and Sovereignty by Acquisition

In *The Elements,* Hobbes draws a tentative distinction between governments that arise "by mutual agreement among many" and those that develop "naturally," that is, a "body politic by acquisition."[89] In *Leviathan* Hobbes would sharpen the terminology for this distinction and talk respectively of "commonwealth by institution" and "commonwealth by acquisition" to distinguish between (1) governments that arise when a group of people, fearing each other, see that it is in their best interest to transfer their rights to a sovereign and (2) governments that arise when a group of people, fearing some overwhelming power, see that it is in their best interest to transfer their rights to that object of fear.

Not too much should be made of the distinction. As my wording of (1) and (2) indicates, the only difference between them is in the fearsome object that motivates the institution of government. The nature of the sovereignty is the same for each. My guess is that the distinction serves a rhetorical function. The discussion of commonwealths by institution makes the logic of sovereignty clear, whereas the discussion of commonwealths by acquisition shows how the logical structure can be made to fit with the usual historical origins of governments. Some governments evolve out of families in which the father and, sometimes, the mother have authority over children because of their greater strength. Also, many governments arise from conquest. Hobbes was quite content to think of William I as the Conqueror although some of his contemporaries were squeamish about the title because they thought it implied a lack of legitimacy. (I won't even mention that William had been known as "the Bastard.")

Women, Children, and Patriarchy

As in so many things, Hobbes's treatment of women is logically ambivalent. On the one hand, he seems quite in advance of his time. Since all human beings are naturally equal, women are naturally equal to men. Moreover, mothers have a superior claim to men in the governance of their children, because everyone has the right to their own body and children begin as part of their mothers' bodies.[90] Hobbes does not consider the counterconsideration that, by his own view, in the natural state everyone has a right to everything. On the other hand, the natural condition of human beings is wretched and should be eliminated as soon as possible. So perhaps in an oblique way, Hobbes is indicating that the natural equality of women is one more defect in nature.

Because mothers have at least as much natural right to govern their children as fathers, the term 'patriarchy' is a misnomer. Also, the word wrongly suggests that the right of fathers (or parents) to govern their children is due to the fact that they generated or gave birth to them. But that is not at all the foundation of their authority. Rather, it is their power to keep or to kill the children. If she should choose, a mother could "abandon or expose" her child to death.[91] By the time Hobbes was fifty, the former tutor was completely unsentimental about children. He wrote that a parent has the right of "selling or giving them [children] in adoption or servitude to others"; alternatively, the parent may "pawn them for hostages, kill them for rebellion, or sacrifice them for peace, by the law of nature, when he or she, in his or her conscience, think it to be necessary."[92] Unlike Jonathan Swift, Hobbes was not satirizing anything. A few years later in *De Cive*, he would write, "Unless you give children all they ask for, they are peevish and cry, aye, and strike their parents sometimes."[93] If the children are not killed first, then their safety is assured by the acquired sovereignty of the mother: "By nurturing her children, a mother acquires in due course an implicit covenant from them to acknowledge her as their sovereign, as long as a male does not intervene, subdue the mother, and thereby acquire sovereignty over her and all of her possessions, human and otherwise."[94]

The Advantages of Monarchy

Following Aristotle, Hobbes admits that there are three forms of government: democracy, aristocracy, and monarchy. Each is legitimate, and each has its advantages and disadvantages, but overall, democracy, which is tantamount to "the government of a few orators," is worst and monarchy is best. If it is not, why is there only one God, who created and governs the world? Anyone who resents monarchy must resent being "ruled by Almighty God." Even the ancients, whose opinion Hobbes knew his fellow intellectuals would revere even if he did not, preferred monarchy. The first government, under Adam, was paternal, and paternal government is monarchy. And in most lands the oldest governments are monarchies.[95]

(This last reason seems to be inconsistent with his earlier claim that all governments begin as democracies.)

One reason that monarchy is more stable than the other forms of government is that the more people there are deciding matters, the more emotional are the deliberations about what should be done. That is because everyone always acts with an eye to "some good to himself"; not to have one's own plan accepted is to fail in achieving that good. With the least chance for emotions to run amok in decision-making assemblies, monarchies are the governments least likely to suffer civil war.[96] Although Hobbes preferred monarchy, he recognized the legitimacy of other forms of government and after 1650 was willing to live in England under the Commonwealth, which he called an aristocracy.

When there is a problem with monarchy, Hobbes says, it is because of the emotions that each human being has. For this reason, being ruled by an aristocracy is even worse because of the conflicting emotions of many men: "even as a great many coals, though but warm asunder, being put together inflame one another." If a monarchy is expensive to maintain, an aristocracy is much more expensive, because each aristocrat spends like a monarch. These defenses of monarchy are not very strong, being based on false analogies and false claims. At bottom, Hobbes probably preferred monarchies because he thought that they were the least likely "to dissolve into civil war," and civil war is "the greatest inconvenience that can happen to a commonwealth."[97]

The Causes of Civil War

All human creations dissolve. All civil governments are human creations. Therefore, all civil governments dissolve. In *The Elements*, Hobbes lists three necessary and sufficient conditions for civil war. The first is "discontent," the belief that one is unhappy because of the circumstances one is in. The second is the belief that one is right to be discontented. The third is the belief that one has a chance to change circumstances and to make oneself happy. When these conditions are present, civil war breaks out as soon as "a man of credit [steps forward] to set up the standard and to blow the trumpet."[98]

Hobbes in effect calls rebels cowards and glory seekers because when he explicates the first condition, he says that it is not discontent exactly, but fear of pain, that is a cause of civil war, and a desire for more recog-

nition from one's fellows. He also thinks that rebels are not very bright.
Like Catiline, the paradigmatic Roman rebel, all rebels have eloquence
without wisdom. If they were smarter, rebels would know that insurrec-
tions usually fail. But they are merely eloquent. Like Medea, who persuaded the daughters of Pelias to chop their old father into pieces in order
to rejuvenate him, a rebel may persuade subjects to rebel and in that way
chop their sovereign into pieces with the absurd hope that sovereignty
will be reinvigorated.[99]

Even worse, some of the Parliamentarians might have inferred that
Hobbes was accusing them of plotting the execution of the king. The
opposition in the Short Parliament wanted their "grievances" satisfied
before they would vote Charles the money he wanted. Many of the
members were left over from the Parliament of 1628. Hobbes wrote,
"when the commands are grievous, . . . they account him that commands
grievous things a tyrant, and tyrannicide, . . . not only lawful, but also
laudable."[100] Eventually, Hobbes's words would prove to be true, but
there is no good reason to think that in May 1640, he foresaw the events of
January 1649.

6

A Decade of Exile, 1641–1651 (I)

After consulting with three or four men from the parliament during its first days, he [Hobbes] realized that civil war was upon them; and almost sensing its presence, he again went to France. In Paris, he was free to devote all of his time to studying science with Mersenne, Gassendi, and other men who were well known for their knowledge and power in reasoning. ("Prose Life")

The Long Parliament and Exile, November 1640

It was clear by the fall of 1640 that Charles would have to call another Parliament. Hobbes arrived in London in late September, probably ready to assist Devonshire, who was a member of the House of Lords. There was little for him to do when he first arrived and even less when he was quarantined for visiting the house of a man dying of the plague. If he spent the full forty days in isolation, then he was not free to conduct his business until after the new Parliament began on November 3. Early on, two members gave speeches in which they complained about books and sermons in support of monarchy that cause dissension between "king and state." Hobbes did not like what he was hearing. He feared that he was at risk since the defense of absolute sovereignty had been one of his hobbyhorses in *Elements of Law, Natural and Politic*. He had no reason to think that he would be immune to prosecution. William Beale, master of St. John's College, Cambridge, who had preached that the king was an absolute monarch, had charges brought against him the next year.[1] But Hobbes's fears did not have to rely on speculation or foresight. The king's chief ministers came under attack as soon as Parliament opened. Strafford was soon arrested. The first charge against him was that he had "traitorously endeavored to subvert the fundamental laws and government of the realms of England and Ireland, and instead thereof to introduce an arbitrary and tyrannical government against law."[2] Hadn't Hobbes done the same thing in his writings? Then the archbishop of Canterbury was arrested. If the king's chief counselor and the highest-ranking clergyman were not safe from Parliament, why should Hobbes think that he was? Some have said that Hobbes was too obscure to be a target. These same people might have told Strafford not to worry about the charges against him. They were all trivial offenses, and no number of misdemeanors can add up to a felony. The logic was good, but Parliament wasn't logical; it convicted Strafford of treason. Parliament may have had larger fish to fry, but Hobbes would have made a nice appetizer.

Shortly after Strafford's arrest, Hobbes sensibly anticipated that other arrests would follow. Having quickly made his decision to leave England, he informed Devonshire of his intentions and left three days later. He did not even wait for his luggage to be packed; it was to be sent on later. Since he would eventually brag that he was the "first of those that fled," and Francis Windebank fled on December 10, it is plausible that Hobbes was on his way to France before that date. He was probably gone by November 23, the day that Parliament passed the Grand Remonstrance, a litany of complaints against Charles. In a letter to Lord Scudamore, a friend of the archbishop of Canterbury, Hobbes explained his departure in this way:

The reason I came away was that I saw [that] words that tended to advance the prerogative of the king began to be examined in Parliament. And I knew some that had a good will to have had me troubled, and might for anything I saw in their honesties make both the words and the witnesses. Besides I thought if I went not then, there was nevertheless a disorder coming on that would make it worse being there than here.[3]

Hobbes has been criticized for leaving, even being called a 'poltroon', on the grounds that he could have served the royalist forces in some noncombative role, as William Harvey and other soldiers over the age of fifty had. 'Could have', no doubt. But he had no military training and was under no obligation to get some. Leaving was a perfectly sensible act, and others would do the same. At first only a few in December, but later, many.

Some of the leaders of the Long Parliament were stuffy and self-righteous. They would have outlawed laughing if they could have gotten away with it. In the breach, they passed an ordinance requiring a monthly fast. In December 1644, people realized that the fast day would fall on Christmas and thus petitioned to have the requirement canceled for that month. The House of Commons refused and made the fast more onerous "for the better observance of the Monthly Fast, and most especially . . . [what is] commonly called the Feast of the Nativity of Christ." Commons criticized the celebration of Christmas by people who "took liberty to carnal and sensual delights contrary to the life which Christ himself led on earth." Commons later completely abolished the celebration of Christmas and Easter, among other feasts. The requirements for receiving communion were also tightened. Whereas communion previously had been permitted to anyone who did not live a scandalous life, the reformers of the Long Parliament required people "to present themselves for examination by the minister and elders on specific days immediately before the celebration." Those who passed muster were given a slip of paper that was to be presented at communion time. No one gets to heaven without a ticket.

Doubts about Descartes

Although Hobbes cared about the affairs of his country, scientific investigations occupied most of his time. An untitled manuscript, which must have been written some time between late 1637 and 1640, survives. Ferdinand Tönnies named it 'Tractatus Opticus', but since Mersenne published a different treatise by Hobbes under the same title, it makes sense to call the earlier manuscript by the name that Richard Tuck has coined for it, *Secunda Sectio*, because it is apparently an early draft of what two decades later would be published as *De Homine*, the "second section" of *Elementa Philosophiae*.[4]

In October 1637, Hobbes received a copy of Descartes's *Discours de la méthode* (*Discourse of the Method*) from Kenelm Digby. Hobbes became immersed in the problems Descartes discussed. But he did not reveal his opinion about Descartes's *Discours* in writing until November 1640, when he sent to Mersenne a fifty-six-page manuscript commenting on it and one of its appendixes, the *Dioptrique*. The timing of Hobbes's correspondence with Mersenne may have been part of a plan to have somewhere to go and something to do after he left England since he was gone before the month was up.

Descartes received at least part of Hobbes's manuscript through Mersenne. It ruined his day: "I was very surprised by the fact that, although the style in which it is written makes its author look clever and learned, he seems to stray from the truth in every single claim which he advances as his own."[5] In addition to criticizing Descartes's views, Hobbes had associated some of his own controversial views with those of Descartes. Hobbes identified his own concept of "internal spirit," according to which both God and the human soul were material, with Descartes's concept of "subtle matter." Descartes was not going to have any of that. He was even more cowardly than Hobbes, and he wanted to be accepted by the religious establishment. He had stopped publication of *Le Monde* for fear that the Inquisition would do to him what it had done to Galileo. He wrote dismissively about Hobbes's work: "I shall leave aside the initial section on his 'internal spirit', and on his corporeal soul and corporeal God, and other things that do not concern me."[6]

Like Descartes, Hobbes replied through Mersenne. He was bewildered at how a man as intelligent as Descartes could be so wrong about philosophy. In fact, Hobbes thought that he had not made any mistakes at all; and in reply to Descartes's remark that "he does not see how" a certain proof could be cogent, Hobbes pointed out that that is not an objection but "a reason why he [Descartes] should consider the matter more carefully."[7] But Hobbes was still conciliatory at this stage. He told Mersenne that he would be happy to have Descartes see more of his mathematical work: "For I have the highest admiration for his powers of judgment. I just wish that he would read more carefully what I have written; and if you could make him do that, there is no one to whose criticism I would rather submit." But Hobbes's respect for Descartes was fading fast. He told Newcastle's brother Charles that the obscure Florimond de Beaune was just as good a mathematician as Descartes and a better philosopher.[8]

Objections to the Meditations

Hobbes was one of the first people to receive a copy of the *Meditations on First Philosophy*. Mersenne had sent prepublication copies to various distinguished philosophers and theologians with the purpose of receiving comments to which Descartes would reply. In August 1641, *Meditations* was published, along with six sets of objections and Descartes's replies to them. Hobbes's objections and Descartes's replies constitute one of the great episodes of talking-past-one-another in the history of philosophy. Descartes was a mentalistic dualist; Hobbes was a materialistic monist. Descartes was obsessed with skepticism and thought it could be overcome only if certainty about the foundations of knowledge could be well grounded. Hobbes was sanguine about skepticism and thought that stipulative definitions either defeated or sidestepped the problem.

For Descartes, the key to certainty is captured in the formula "Cogito, ergo sum" ("I think, therefore I am"). How does that work? Like the demons in the Galilean pig, its interpretations are legion. I think that Descartes's *cogito* has two facets. First, it shows that skepticism is self-defeating. Doubting is a kind of thinking, and any kind of thinking presupposes the existence of the thinker. Thus, whether one begins with doubt or the more general mental action of thinking, a person can be certain that he exists. Second, the *cogito* has the advantage of being existential; it is an experience, not an abstraction or a tautology or some verbal trick. Skeptics typically made their case by showing how the contents of experiences are always dubious: Is the tower in the distance square or round? Is the stick in the water bent or straight? Descartes undermines the skeptic's strategy by pointing out that even if the content of an experience is dubious, the existence of the experience is not. In short, the power of "I think/doubt, therefore I am" lies in the fact that unlike most refutations of self-defeating positions that expose some purely verbal self-contradiction, it defeats skepticism in part by getting the person to experience the self-refuting character of skepticism. If you can get yourself to doubt, you know that skepticism cannot be right. Doubting provides a foundation for certainty.

Hobbes had no feeling for the angst of philosophical doubt. He seems to caricature Descartes's *cogito* by saying that one might just as well argue, "I walk, therefore I am." His pedestrian argument does not seem to take Descartes's problem seriously, so it adds insult to an intended injury. But there is good reason to think that Hobbes's objection to the *cogito* is not cogent. What Hobbes chooses to ignore is that Descartes is not concerned simply with getting a premise that happens to be true but one about which one can be absolutely certain. Hobbes has not responded at all to the Cartesian considerations that are supposed to justify uncertainty about the truth of a premise like 'I walk' and certainty about a premise like 'I think'.

Hobbes's own account of the certainty of the *cogito* is also weak. He thinks it derives from the fact that people cannot conceive of an instance of thinking without it being connected with a substance: How can you know the dancer apart from the dance? He seems to be implying that it is merely a curious limitation of human beings that they cannot conceive of the possibility of a thinking without a thinker. In fact, this line of argument was not logically available to Hobbes since he thought that bodies were the only kind of things that exist; a pure thinking is as much an impossibility as an immaterial substance. There cannot be free-floating properties or events. What is relevant here is not the epistemological point that one cannot *know* the dancer apart from the dance, but the metaphysical one that there *is* no dance apart from the dancer. There is not and cannot be a walking without a walker or a thinking without a thinker.

For Hobbes, Descartes's attempt to separate the thinking from the existing was part of his disastrous dualistic thinking. It led him to the view that thinking is the essence of a human being. For Hobbes, thinking is no more the essence of a human being than walking is. This is the underlying serious aspect of Hobbes's example. Just as a person who is walking does not consist of two things, a person and his walking, but only one thing (namely, a person with a certain kind of motion), a person who is thinking does not consist of himself and his thinking but again only himself with a certain kind of motion. Different thoughts are just different motions in the brain. Descartes thought that Hobbes's view was crazy. His response was that Hobbes "might just as well conclude that the earth is the sky or anything else he likes."9

Hobbes thought that what Descartes should have inferred from the *cogito* was that "a thinking thing is something corporeal." For Hobbes, human thought essentially involved manipulating images. Images are motions "occurring in various parts of the body." So thought is bodily. Descartes was astounded that anyone should believe such a thing: What did thinking have to do with matter? In the seventeenth century, to conceive of "thinking matter" was almost impossible. Perhaps every property needs to be part of a substance, "but it does not follow that it must be understood in terms of a body," says Descartes. Hobbes and Descartes were at loggerheads. For Descartes, mental and material substances were completely different things. For Hobbes, only bodies were substances.

If we return to Descartes's concerns, the next thing to worry about is how to extend the set of things that we can be certain about beyond our own doubts, thoughts, and existence. The solution, according to Descartes, was to find an epistemic criterion that would distinguish veridical from nonveridical experiences, for example, the difference between dreaming and waking. He thought that he had found it in the ideas of clarity and distinctness. Whatever is clear and distinct is certain. In contrast, Hobbes did not think that the solution to skepticism could involve an epistemological criterion. No matter what criterion one proposed, nothing could bar the skeptic from asking how one *knew* that that criterion would give the right result. But if one had to know that the criterion was correct before it could be used, then its possible use as a criterion for knowledge was self-defeating.

Hobbes realized that the solution to the epistemic problem of skepticism was not to be found within epistemology, for no criterion could be justified and no experience was privileged. What was needed was something that did not permit there to be any gap between the words used to say something and the thing that made it true. Stipulative definitions fit the bill. They are true in virtue of being asserted. To say stipulatively, 'A human is a rational, animate body', or 'A square is a plane figure with four equal sides and four right angles', is *ipso dicto* to say what is true.

By the halfway mark in their respective objections and replies, Hobbes and Descartes are giving each other's arguments short shrift. Concerning Descartes's proof for the existence of God, based on the idea of God, Hobbes says that because "we do not have an idea of God, . . . the whole of this [Descartes's] argument collapses." Period. Descartes responds in kind: Because "we do have an idea of God . . . , this whole objection [of Hobbes] collapses." Period. After being told by Hobbes for the umpteenth time that humans have no idea of God, Descartes says in exasperation, "As for how we can have an idea of God, I have gone over this *ad nauseam*. There is absolutely nothing in this objection to invalidate my demonstrations."[10]

Hobbes had a very different way of reasoning to the existence of God. Just as all mathematical explanation must be traced back to a definition or basic principle, all explanations of natural phenomena must end at "the immediate hand of God."[11] With respect to belief in God, human beings are like the blind, as we saw in the preceding chapter. A blind person believes in fire because he feels the heat of fire, even though he lacks the appropriate sense organ to see the fire itself; he reasons from the effect to the cause. Similarly, human beings believe in God because they see the effects of God in nature even though they lack any sense organ that would permit them to experience him directly. Thus, they are able to believe in him without having an idea of him, just as they believe in infinitely small bodies without having any of idea of them either.

Although Hobbes never wavered from his position that humans have no idea of God, his argument for it is very odd: (1) People have ideas or images of shapes and colors; and they "can doubt whether this image is the likeness of a man or not." (2) They can also have an image of an angel as a flame or beautiful child, but they cannot believe that this image has any likeness to an angel; therefore, humans have no idea of an angel. Hobbes then says, (3) "In the same way we have no idea or image corresponding to the sacred name of God." For that matter, human beings do not have an idea of a soul or substance either. Concerning (1), Hobbes thinks that no human ideas are iconic; so why should it be important that there is no idea or image of God? Also, Hobbes seems to use 'idea' and 'image' interchangeably; but in (2), he mentions only an image of an angel. Why shouldn't a flame be either an idea or an image of an angel? Further, many people believe that their images of angels do bear a likeness to them. That they are in fact mistaken is not relevant. Concerning (3), analogous things can be said. People do have images of God and believe that those images bear a likeness to God. Again, even though those images bear no likeness to God, they are no different as images from any other ideas. They are different in a different way. What I think that Hobbes is getting at but does not convey is that God is a body so subtle that he does not causally affect our gross sense organs. So the images that people have of God are not causally related to him in the way that their images of gross bodies are. This position is sensible, and all or most scholastic, Aristotelian philosophers would have agreed.

Hobbes defended his position that humans have no idea of God by saying that "the Christian religion obliges us to believe that God cannot be conceived of." He is referring in part to the many creedal formulas that describe God as "incomprehensible." Descartes was unimpressed: "it is manifest that we do" have an idea of God. What the Christian religion teaches is that human ideas of God are not "fully adequate," not that they are nonexistent.[12] What divides Hobbes and Descartes on this point is a shared criterion for *being an idea of something*. They were engaged in the same debate as Anselm of Canterbury and Gaunilo, a monk of Marmoutier. Anselm and Descartes, both of whom had ontological arguments for the existence of God, maintained that people do have an idea of God, whereas Gaunilo and Hobbes denied it. Neither group was less religious than the other, just philosophically different.

The Source of the Animosity

Much of what Hobbes and Descartes said to each other has little to do with the philosophical issues. Each was maneuvering to discredit the other. They thought that the fight for glory was a zero-sum game, and originality was a necessary condition for winning. That is why Hobbes began his objections with the observation that Descartes's skeptical worries were a rehash of what the ancients had said. What underlay this animosity?

The existence of deep philosophical differences between Hobbes and Descartes provides a superficial explanation. Descartes thought that rationality and free choice depended on a kind of substance that would not be subject to the laws of physics. So he believed in immaterial human minds. Hobbes thought that rationality was nothing but computation and that free will was in fact an impossibility. More than simply thinking that he did not need immaterial substances, Hobbes thought the very idea of them was incoherent. The philosophers also differed concerning the idea of certainty. Descartes was gripped by skepticism. Hobbes was not. Descartes used God to solve the problem. God's goodness guaranteed certainty. Hobbes relied on definitions via man's will. To will that a word x means y is to make it true that x means y.

Nonetheless, I think that a more important explanation for their differences relates to this principle: Similarity breeds contempt. Both wanted to give materialistic and mechanistic explanations to the physical world. Both wanted the physical laws of the universe to be formulated mathematically. Both believed that sensations are noniconic; ideas are not similar to the features of the physical objects that cause them. Colors, sounds, tastes, and odors, as they are experienced, exist only in being perceived and not in bodies. On a personal level, both were vain, glory-seeking, self-absorbed, self-proclaimed geniuses. This statement is purely descriptive. Hobbes, like Descartes, was obsessed with being first.

Descartes suspected that Hobbes's allegation that their views were similar was a gambit to establish Hobbes's priority. Hobbes had told Mersenne that he had first explained his ideas to Newcastle and his brother in 1630. Descartes called the report "childish and laughable." He issued a challenge: "If his philosophical system is such that he is afraid of other people stealing it from him, let him publish it; for my own part, I promise him that I shall not try to publish mine a moment sooner on his account."[13] Descartes may have felt confident in challenging Hobbes if he thought that the slightly published fiftyish Hobbes suffered from writer's block.

Hobbes's enemies who knew about his obsession to be first used it to get his goat. This comes out clearly in an exchange between John Wallis and Hobbes in the mid-1650s. Wallis wrote in *Elenchus Geometria Hobbianae* that Hobbes's work was derivative. Hobbes responded not merely by trying to distinguish between his views and those of Descartes, but in vaunting his achievement over that of his dear friend Gassendi and the accommodating Digby:

But let any man read Descartes, he shall find, that he attributes no motion at all to the object of sense, but an inclination to action, which inclination no man can imagine what it means. And for Gassendus and Sir Kenelm Digby, it is manifest by their writings that their opinions are not different from that of Epicurus, which is very different from mine. Or if these two or any of those I conversed with at Paris had prevented me in publishing my own doctrine, yet since it was there known and declared for mine by Mersennus in the preface to his *Ballistica* (of which the three first leaves are employed wholly in the setting forth of my opinion concerning sense, and the rest of the faculties of the soul) they ought not therefore to be said to have found it out before me.[14]

But Hobbes's published work on physics, which amounted to part of a preface in Mersenne's *Ballistica* (1644), did not measure up to Descartes's.

Descartes's mentalism has been overemphasized by contemporary scholars. It is central to the *Meditations*, but the ordeal of assiduously reading that work is supposed to be a one-time-only exercise; it exorcises the demon of skepticism. Once purged, one is supposed to get on with one's life. Much the same can be said about Descartes's use of God. God is needed to guarantee certainty. This is foundationally important, but God does not have a day-to-day role to play in scientific explanation. For working scientists, God is a useless hypothesis.

In the early 1640s, Hobbes was much more inclined than Descartes to emphasize a similarity between the two philosophies. This may have been his way of establishing his credentials. In the spring of 1641, Hobbes suggested that Descartes was silent about most of Hobbes's theory because he agreed with it. Descartes gave a different reason for the silence:

"[I] did not take that part of his [Hobbes's] writings seriously enough to think I was obliged to spend my time refuting it."[15] As early as February 1641, Descartes asked Mersenne to insulate him from Hobbes.

I think it best if I have nothing to do with him [Hobbes] and therefore refrain from replying to him. For if his character is as I suspect, we could scarcely communicate without becoming enemies. So it is better for us, him and me, to leave it there. I also beg you to communicate as little as possible to him of those of my opinions which you know, and which have not appeared in print. For unless I am very much mistaken, he is aiming to make his reputation at my expense, and by devious means.[16]

Hobbes came to be equally averse to Descartes. He refused to see him in 1644 during one of Descartes's rare visits to Paris. In a letter of March 1646, John Pell wrote to Charles Cavendish, "I durst make no mention" of what Descartes said about Hobbes.[17] They finally met in 1648 through the efforts of Mersenne. But they quarreled and never met again. Hobbes needed to read only a bit of *Principia Philosophiae* to know that it was not to his liking.

Just as praise is worth only as much as the person giving it, so is criticism. Thus, it is not surprising that having failed to win the admiration of Descartes, Hobbes discredited him. He told Aubrey that if the Frenchman had "kept himself to Geometry he had been the best geometer in the world but that his head did not lie for philosophy."

Hobbes had nasty things to say about Descartes even in the 1660s. Describing the latter's view that air particles are like "tree branches," Hobbes says that the view is "scarcely that of a sane man."[18] His attitude toward Descartes may have softened in his last years. In *Decameron Physiologicum,* published the year before Hobbes died, he referred to Descartes as "a very ingenious man."[19] Perhaps Hobbes was moved by the maxim not to speak ill of the dead and hoped that his critics would be similarly moved when he died.

The Root and Branch Petition, 1641

While he was in exile, Hobbes continued to monitor events in his native country. He read and commented on the Nottingham petition of April 1641 to abolish the episcopacy. (This was one of numerous petitions following in the wake of the London petition to get rid of episcopacy "root and branch.") Hobbes knew that he could not defend the behavior of individual clerics, many of whom were corrupt. There was widespread disgust with the bishops. One member of Parliament said that "our bishops had well near ruined all religion amongst us."[20] But the abuse of episcopacy did not show that episcopacy itself was at fault. Hobbes distinguished, like many others of the time, between the bishops and the episcopacy. He wrote that the "abundance of abuses committed by ecclesiastical persons and their officers . . . can neither be denied nor excused. But that they proceed from episcopacy itself is not so evidently proved."[21] Some Bedfordshire men acting against the root and branch petition said that it was a "dangerous inference from personal abuses to conclude the eradication of the function."[22] Episcopacy itself could not be the cause of them since Christianity was regulated by many forms of government. Hobbes wrote, "Experience teaches . . . that the dispute for [precedence] between the spiritual and civil power has of late more than any other thing in the world been the cause of civil wars in all places of Christendom."[23] In fact, he preferred the episcopal form of government to all the others. Writing in about 1668, he would say, "all that know me know also it is my opinion that the best government is by episcopacy."[24] Like James I, he thought that it was the most likely to preserve the monarchy. Episcopal systems are strongly hierarchical, just as monarchies are. James may have exaggerated when he said, "No bishop, no king," but the spirit was right.

One problem with many of the Anglican clerics in the 1630s, as far as Hobbes was concerned, was that they thought the episcopacy was *iure divino*, that is, established by Christ and prescribed by God for all times. Hobbes, like many others, thought that the theory of *iure divino* was self-serving and historically unfounded. Although it emerged early, the episcopacy did not exist from the very earliest stage of Christianity. So other forms were acceptable in certain circumstances, and in 1641 and 1651 Hobbes was willing to accept another form of church government, though not presbyterianism. He never had a good opinion of that Scottish, subversive institution. He suspected that the support of the root and branch petitions by Presbyterians was hypocritical and self-serving. They wanted the bishops out so that they could get in. And he expected that they would be very upset if Parliament approved the plan being debated in July 1641, which would put all ecclesiastical matters under the control of nine laymen.[25]

Hobbes's position was either similar to or more conservative than those of many members of the Church of England. Falkland argued vigorously for the abolition of episcopacy. Clarendon would have been willing to change the ecclesiology of the church if it would have prevented the Civil War, though he did not think it would. He thought that the expulsion of the bishops from the House of Lords was "a violation of justice," not an offense against religion. In part of his autobiography, he wrote that episcopacy had been "part of the Government of England," not that it had a foundation *iure divino*.[26] As discussed in Chapter 4, in *Leviathan* Hobbes would concede that given the circumstances, namely, the abolition of the episcopacy and only the skeleton of a national church, "the Independency of the primitive Christians to follow Paul or Cephas or Apollos, every man as he likes best . . . is perhaps the best"[27] form as long as it does not cause bickering. He is punning on the word 'Independency'. In addition to referring to everyone going his own way, 'Independents' was the name of the ruling sect in England in 1651. Hobbes's use of the word is also ironic. Paul had complained about different factions claiming "Paul, Cephas, or Apollos" as their leader. Paul preached the unity of all Christians in Jesus. Hobbes certainly expected his readers to recognize the irony.

Elementa Philosophiae

Also explained in Chapter 4 was Hobbes's plan initiated sometime in the 1630s to publish his grand scheme of philosophy under the title *Elementa Philosophiae* (*The Elements of Philosophy*). It was supposed to consist of three "sections" as Hobbes preferred to call them: *De Corpore* (*Of Body*), *De Homine* (*Of Human Beings*), and *De Cive* (*Of the Citizen*). The main doctrines of sections two and three had been sketched out in *Elements of Law*. So it would have made sense to begin with the first section. In fact, the first section would not be published until 1655, the second not until 1658.

The standard view about Hobbes's scientific development is that he came up with the general idea of materialism and mechanism in the early 1630s but did not work out the details until much later, perhaps the early 1650s. Recently, Richard Tuck has contradicted both parts of this. He maintains that Hobbes had "no consistent natural philosophy before 1637,"[28] that is, before reading Descartes's *Discourse*, but had "an elaborate and sophisticated" theory in the 1640s. It is beyond the scope of this book to weigh the evidence for each interpretation, but I think the truth lies somewhere in the middle. One problem that makes defending an answer to this difficult is that it is not clear how much detail is necessary to have a well-worked-out science. Here is some of the hard evidence concerning this issue.

In 1644, two items that are directly related to Hobbes's scientific work were published. One was his short treatise, *Tractatus Opticus* (published through the good graces of Mersenne), in which Hobbes presented his view of vision and light. It begins with a statement of his general scientific view: "Every action is the local motion of an agent [that is, the movement of a body through space], just as every passion is the local motion of a passive object. By the name 'agent' I understand a body, by the motion of which an effect is produced in another body; by 'passive object', I understand a body in which some motion is generated by another body."[29] At about the same time, Mersenne published his own *Ballistica*. Part of proposition 24 of that work was indebted to Hobbes's research. Mersenne acknowledged this in his preface and also provided there a summary of Hobbes's philosophy. According to it, everything can be explained in terms of "local motion," that is, the movement of bodies through space. Things happen when one moving body strikes another. One of the startling corollaries of this view is that sensation is nothing but a certain motion within animal bodies that is caused by external objects striking a sense organ. Vision, for example, is the result of a motion of a "lucid body propagated through a diaphanous medium."[30] In *Tractatus Opticus*, vision is defined as a passion (*passio*) produced in a seeing thing through the action of a lucid or illuminated object: "In vision, neither the object nor any part of it travels from its own place to the eye."[31] These two publications indicate that Hobbes had a project and was making some progress, but not enough to assert that he had his whole science well thought out.

What about progress specifically on *De Corpore*? Hobbes said that he was up to Chapter 13 of it in the spring of 1645. He reports slow progress in the summer of 1646, and in November of that year Charles Cavendish wrote to John Pell that "it will be long before Mr. Hobbes publishes anything."[32] In 1648, Hobbes wrote that he had resumed work on *De Corpore*. Publication was still years away.

Hobbes's problems with putting *De Corpore* into a finished form was part of his more general problem in tackling the project of *The Elements of Philosophy*. His dithering with *De Corpore* overlapped with his fiddling with the prospective second section, *De Homine;* their contents also overlapped. Hobbes composed a large part of the material destined for *De Homine* in a manuscript written in English with the title *A Minute or First Draught of the Optiques* (1646). As he did with *De Cive*, he dedicated this work to Devonshire. He said he was quite satisfied with it and wanted "to publish it in Latin at the first opportunity." He must have been referring to his projected *De Homine*, which was written in Latin. But only the first eight chapters (out of fifteen) of *De Homine* were finished by 1649,[33] and that book was not published until 1658.

A Minute or First Draught of the Optiques was never published and lies in the British Library little read. The manuscript consists of two parts. The first deals with such things as the nature of light, transparency, and reflection. (A different treatment of this same material would eventually be included in *De Corpore*.) The second part consists of nine chapters that deal with vision. The content of these nine chapters forms eight chapters of *De Homine*. The difference in the numbering is explained by the fact that two chapters of *A Minute or First Draught* are combined into one of *De Homine*. In general, the treatment of vision in *A Minute or First Draught* is about twice as long and sometimes substantially different from the versions eventually published in *De Homine*.[34] In short, Hobbes did not yet have a settled idea about central parts of his general philosophy in the 1640s.

In a letter in which he was making arrangements for the publication of the new edition of *De Cive*, he says that he expected *De Corpore* to be finished within a year and attributes the long delay partially to laziness but mostly to his desire that it be incontrovertible. These reasons are not plausible. Given the plethora of manuscripts that he produced between 1642 and 1646 related to *De Corpore*, not to mention his ability to expand *De Cive*, laziness was not a factor. Furthermore, in that same letter, he asked Sorbière to change the title of the first edition from *Elementorum Philosophiae Sectio Tertia De Cive* to more simply *Elementa Philosophica De Cive*. The official explanation for the simplified title is that it would increase sales. But if Hobbes really had the other parts of his manuscript near completion and able to be printed within the year, the longer title would have been a good advertisement for them.

Another sign of Hobbes's procrastination is his decision to accept the position of mathematics tutor to the Prince of Wales in the early summer of 1646. A month or two earlier he was confident that *De Corpore* would be completed by the end of the year; and in order to help ensure that he would make his self-imposed deadline, he decided to go to the estate of his friend, de Martel, in southern France. The supposedly single obstacle to finishing his project, Hobbes thought, was simple exposition. He knew what he wanted to say but not precisely how to say it. He wanted his presentation to be so compelling and complete that there would be "no place left for a critic." These are the words of a procrastinator; he sets his standard impossibly high in order to rationalize away his failure to produce. He predicted that it would be finished by the end of the year, "provided I am alive and healthy." Instead of finishing his book, Hobbes began tutoring the Prince of Wales and perhaps one or two others. (We know, for example, that he tutored Edmund Waller's son during this period.) So *De Corpore* was not finished by the end of 1646, contrary to his prediction; and his health did not hold up. He was gravely ill in late 1647. Was it partially brought on by the mental strain of self-disappointment? In 1649, he again predicted that it would be finished by the end of the summer.[35] It was not. Progress on the book would continue to be slow. It would first be published in 1655.

It was not writer's block, but intellectual block, it seems to me, that kept *De Corpore* and *De Homine* from completion and publication. But Hobbes could not very well tell his readers that. Rather, in the "Preface to the Reader," prepared for the second edition, Hobbes explains that the reason that the third section of *De Cive* appeared before the other two was that the turmoil of the events leading up to the Civil War moved him to work on political theory, presumably to support the king's cause. All of this is well and good and explains the publication of *De Cive* in 1642. It does not explain why the first two sections had not yet appeared by 1647. Richard Tuck has pointed out that the English translation of *De Cive*, published in 1651 as *Philosophical Rudiments*, has Hobbes saying: "Wherefore the first Section *would* have contained the first philosophy and certain elements of physic. . . . In the second, we *would* have been conversant about [psychology]" (my emphasis). Tuck rightly points out that the proper translation of the Latin is this: "So Section One contains Metaphysics and some elements of Physics . . . Section Two deals with [psychology]. . . . What Section Three deals with, I have already said."[36] Tuck attributes the discrepancy between the Latin and English to a mistake on the part of the translator. I am not convinced. It is unlikely that a translator would have mistaken the present tenses (*continet/occupatur*) for the future ones (*continebit/occupabitur*). Another explanation, especially in light of his decision to simplify the title of *De Cive*, is that Hobbes asked the translator to change the tense, because he then knew that the first and second sections of *Elementa Philosophiae* were years away from publication.

De Cive, 1642, 1647

Hobbes said that he devoted two years to writing *De Cive*. Given that it was published in April 1642, he must have meant the period when Charles began his struggle with the Long Parliament. He probably thought of *The Elements of Law, Natural and Politic* as a good first draft. As I indicated earlier, he explained the circumstances of his writing *De Cive* in the preface added in 1647 as follows:

> [It] so happened . . . that my country, some few years before the civil wars did rage, was boiling hot with questions concerning the rights of dominion and obedience due from subjects, the true forerunners of an approaching war; and was the cause which, all those other matters deferred, ripened and plucked from me this third part. Therefore it happens that what was last in order is yet come forth first in time.[37]

Hobbes's revulsion for the men who perpetrated the Civil War also comes out when he says that it is much better to put up with the irritations of government than to allow "private men" to "wade through the streams of your blood"[38] as they establish themselves in power. He also displays some sad prescience:

> How many kings, and those good men too, have by this one error, that a tyrant king might lawfully be put to death, been the slaughter of! How many throats has this false position cut, that a prince for some causes may by some men be deposed! And what bloodshed has erroneous doctrine caused, that kings are not superior to, but administrators of the multitude. Lastly, how many rebellions has this opinion been the cause of, which teaches that the knowledge whether the commands of kings be just or unjust, belongs to private men; and that before they yield obedience, they not only may, but ought to dispute them![39]

Unlike Locke, who took the more sober view that political philosophies do not cause civil wars and cannot provide stability to a tyrannical government, Hobbes thought that ideas had direct consequences. He thought that his doctrine would prevent bloodshed:

[I]f anyone will now dissipate those clouds [of bad political philosophy], and show by the strongest reasons that there are no authentic doctrines about right and wrong, good and evil, other than the constituted laws in each realm and government . . . certainly he will not only show us the highway to peace, but will also teach us how to avoid the close, dark, and dangerous by-paths of faction and sedition; and it is impossible to think of anything more useful than that.[40]

Those same beliefs would lead him later to urge that the doctrine of *Leviathan* be taught in the universities, and why in *Behemoth* he cited as one of the causes of the Civil War the corrupting political philosophy taught in them.

De Cive was first published in Paris in a very small print run, probably not more than one hundred copies, and financed by Sir Kenelm Digby. It was intended for some of his "friends," as he put it.[41] Hobbes would later say that the book made him famous. And it did, but not immediately. Those who did read *De Cive* were impressed. But the small number of copies gave him only something of an underground reputation. His fame spread among the major intellectuals through word of mouth. In *Anti-White*, written the next year, Hobbes represented himself as not being disturbed about his public obscurity:

The reason that I and others are without honor is either that we are neither craftsmen nor outstanding; or if we are, we are not known to be. However, one must not expect those civil honors that attach to public affairs to be conferred on philosophers. Indeed, it would be unjust to the human race to interfere, for the sake of public responsibility, with the study of those minds that strive for the good and the honor not only of one country alone but of the entire human species.[42]

Hobbes's sentiments are clear and laudible. Although they do important work, philosophers are no better than other people. At least everyone can agree about this:

Must one be a philosopher in order to keep the laws? Rulers will say 'no'; the ignorant will say 'no'; the very philosophers will say 'no' as they squabble among themselves. Finally, it will be denied by the practices of many philosophers who cut one another about with abuse and do all the things the rabble do – the more disgracefully, because they set themselves above the common herd.[43]

His big break would come in 1647, when *De Cive* appeared in a second edition and a larger print run. He had added some footnotes designed to clarify certain points. Ironically, his reputation as a political philosopher was also helped by the defeat at Marston Moor. Many royalists saw it as a deathblow to the king's fortunes, and thus they fled to the Continent, where they were able to become acquainted with Hobbes and his doctrine. That absolutist doctrine was also attractive to many of the Roman Catholic French. France was in fact an absolute monarchy. Further, unlike *Leviathan, De Cive* did not contain anti-Catholic diatribes.

In the dedication, Hobbes ostensibly discusses the ignorant attitudes of the ancient Romans toward their kings and the seditiousness of private people publicly talking about politics; in fact, it is a thinly veiled reference to the English and the leading Parliamentarians. Hobbes concedes that man to man is a wolf ("homo homini lupus"), but only as regards the relations of one state to another where there is no government that can make laws to control their behavior. In contrast, man to man is a god ("homo homini deus") under the protection of a government. The sovereign institutes "justice and charity." In holding that the sovereign is God, Hobbes is echoing the sentiments of James I, who, as we have seen, often compared kings to gods.

According to Hobbes, politics had never been given any kind of scientific treatment by any philosopher from Plato onward until his own work on the subject was published. The principal problem had been that the subject lacked foundations. Hobbes reported that he happened on the foundations when he devised the following sequence of reasoning: Justice is giving every person what is owed to him. Ownership arises from the consent of people. It cannot arise from nature, in which all things are held in common. Rather, the natural condition motivates the institution of ownership. The only way to forestall the fighting that results from things being held in common is for everyone to agree to divide the objects. This consensual division of objects is ownership. In short, Hobbes arrived at two maxims of human nature: People want to take for themselves things that other people also have an interest in; and people do not want to die a violent death.

Hobbes's jaundiced view of human nature has often been interpreted as implying that he thought that human nature was sinful or wicked in itself. He did not. Appealing to the Bible, he conceded that all human beings are in fact wicked because everyone breaks God's laws, but he denied that they were wicked by nature. In the pure state of nature, where there are no

laws, wickedness is impossible since a person may do whatever he thinks
best to preserve his life. His doctrine was Calvinism without original sin.

The English Translation of *De Cive*

De Cive, which was written in Latin, was intended for an international
audience. But because it was inspired by the political upheavals in England and because it won admiration from many people, including officials of the Church of England, there was a demand for an English
edition. In 1645, the exiled poet Edmund Waller was thinking about
translating *De Cive* into English. He decided against it, according to
Aubrey, when he saw Hobbes's sample translation of the first part of it.
Waller thought that he could not measure up to Hobbes's own work and
abandoned the project. This story is the firmest basis for thinking that
Hobbes himself was the translator of the English edition of *De Cive*,
which appeared in 1651 under the title *Philosophical Rudiments concerning
Government and Society*.

Three main considerations count against the hypothesis of Hobbes as
translator. First, since Hobbes would have been working hard on *Leviathan*, it is unlikely that he would have found it profitable or relaxing to be
translating an earlier work. This is confirmed by an exchange between
Hobbes and Robert Payne. When Payne suggested that Hobbes do a
translation of *De Cive*, Hobbes said that he was already at work on another
treatise, namely, *Leviathan*. Second, if Hobbes were translating *De Cive* as
he was writing *Leviathan*, the stylistic similarities ought to be more
pronounced than they are. One would expect telling phrases from the one
to be echoed in the other. But they often are not. For example, the phrase
"state of nature" occurs in *De Cive* but not in *Leviathan*. Third, there are
some odd divergences between the translation and the English version of
Leviathan, for example, the use of 'compact' rather than 'covenant'.
There are also several errors of translation that Hobbes would not have
been likely to have made. For example, *Philosophical Rudiments* sometimes
translates *arbitrium* as 'free will' instead of 'choice' and *praecepisse* as
'commanded' instead of 'advised', where these differences would have
been very important to Hobbes. It is plausible that Hobbes would have
permitted someone else to translate *De Cive* while he was working on
Leviathan, and although he would have read it over, he may not have been

as careful as he otherwise would have been. He never criticized the translation, but he also never claimed it as his own.

Kenelm Digby, Thomas White, and the Critique of *De Mundo*

With *De Cive* published, Hobbes could turn his thoughts back to the first section of his philosophy, the part that would deal with geometry and physics. He approached the project obliquely. He wrote a commentary on Thomas White's book, *De Mundo Dialogi Tres* (1642), which seems to have been modeled on Galileo's *Dialogue concerning the Two Chief World Systems*. White, alias Albius, alias Blacklo, and alias Anglus, was an exiled English Roman Catholic priest and self-admitted eccentric.

White was a political and intellectual renegade, something of a Roman Catholic version of Hobbes. He had left England in March 1640, even earlier than Hobbes, although there is not enough information to claim that he left for political reasons. Each was a philosophical late bloomer. They became famous at an age when most of their contemporaries were dead. Hobbes was in his early fifties when *De Cive* appeared and White in his late forties when *De Mundo Dialogi* was published. Both were part of Mersenne's circle. The scientific work of both White and Hobbes was mentioned in the same letter of March 10, 1640, by Mersenne: "I should like very much for Mr. Hobbes, of whom you speak, to give some hint of his philosophy, because assuredly he is excellent, and also that Sr. [*sic*] White or Blaclow [*sic*] give his thoughts on light and refraction, but there is no great hope of obtaining these."[44] Parliament men also linked Hobbes and White. Some bigots in the Commonwealth instigated an investigation into atheism. Hobbes and White were two of the usual suspects, but the action did not even get so far as to have them rounded up. Nothing at all came of the inquiry. In the early 1640s, however, Hobbes and White were more concerned about physics. Where Hobbes's specific goal would be to reconcile modern physics to orthodox Christian doctrine, White's own slant was to reconcile Aristotle and atomism.

White was a protégé of Kenelm Digby, who was variously a Roman Catholic and an Anglican, a friend of everyone from Henrietta Maria and Archbishop Laud to Hobbes and Descartes. Hobbes and Digby probably had met either at Welbeck Abbey or at Great Tew during the 1630s. Digby, White, and Hobbes were all connected to Great Tew at least through their association with William Chillingworth. Hobbes certainly would have known about the debate in the late 1630s between Falkland and White on papal infallibility. Hobbes and Digby were on good terms in Paris in 1636. Much of Digby's success has to be attributed to his ingratiating behavior. He expressed the highest regard for both Descartes and Hobbes. To Hobbes, whom he referred to as "you that know more than all men living," he wrote, "I confess I exceedingly value all that comes from you; for you join solid and mature reason together: whereas many others that are accounted learned beget Chimeras and build castles in the air."[45] But Hobbes was not inclined to have his admirers champion Descartes, with the possible exception of Mersenne. Digby, perhaps with the support of Newcastle and his brother, had invited Descartes in 1641 to settle in England; this act and his unmitigated support for White helped to alienate him from Hobbes. *De Mundo* was published in early 1642 and praised by Digby in his *Observations upon Religio Medici*.

It is possible that Digby brought Thomas Browne's *Religio Medici* (first published in 1642) to Hobbes's attention. Hobbes echoes Browne's opinions on several issues. Where Browne wrote "Miracles now cease," Hobbes would later write, "Seeing miracles now cease." Both Browne and Hobbes thought that miracles were consistent with the laws of nature. Also, Brown wrote that "all things are artificial, for nature is the art of God," while Hobbes wrote, "Nature, the art whereby God makes and governs the world."[46]

Soon after *De Mundo* was published, Hobbes resolved to refute the book point by point. The resulting five-hundred-page manuscript was written for Mersenne, who sent parts of it to a few friends. But Descartes, who said that he agreed with much of the metaphysics in *De Mundo*, refused to read any part of Hobbes's critique. Hobbes's manuscript is neat enough to have been presented to a printer. But whatever favorable reaction it might have received from those who read it in the 1640s, it was forgotten soon enough until it was rediscovered by the great French scholar Cornelis de Waard.

At the beginning of his critique, Hobbes defines philosophy as "the science of general theorems or of all the universals, the truth of which can be demonstrated by natural reason, to do with material of any kind." 'First philosophy', which is another name for metaphysics, concerns "essence, matter, form, quantity, the finite, the infinite, quality, cause, effect, motion, space, time, place, vacuum, unity, number, and all the other notions which Aristotle discusses," partly in his *Physics* and partly in

Metaphysics. The rest of philosophy concerns "natural effects in natural bodies" and is called 'physics'. Aristotle deals with these topics in *Of the Heavens, On Generation and Corruption, De Anima,* and several other works. Hobbes also mentions that philosophy treats the passions, manners, and the purposes of men, in short, ethics, and also society, civil laws, justice, and other virtues – in short, political philosophy. But it is not exactly clear how they fit into the general scheme. Concerning communication, he says that there are "four legitimate goals": teaching the truth, narrating facts, persuading an audience, and celebrating the acts of someone. Philosophical prose belongs to the first category. It begins with definitions and then deduces consequences, "just as mathematicians do." Hobbes has adapted the method of geometers to philosophy. He says that "geometry has always held sway over all the other branches of philosophy" because it always begins with unambiguous definitions.[47] When he explicates his idea of these demonstrations, he asserts that they are "syllogisms" consisting of either definitions or propositions that have been deduced from other syllogisms. Hobbes never seems to have understood that there could be scientific arguments of more than two premises.

As important as valid syllogistic reasoning is, the definitions are even more so. Hobbes never quite resolved a tension between a conventionalist view of definitions, according to which any definition of a word is true because the meanings of words are stipulated, and a nonconventionalist view, according to which there are better and worse definitions depending on how well they enable people to deal with reality. Usually, his explicit view is the conventionalist one, but it is accompanied by assertions that imply the nonconventionalist view. In *Anti-White,* he says that it is important to get "the correct meaning" of the word 'motion', otherwise "nothing certain" can be known about the phenomenon. But if definitions are stipulated, they cannot be wrong.

Hobbes insists that philosophical propositions be strictly literal. They should not include figures of speech, especially not metaphors, because they are inherently ambiguous. Rhetorical flourishes are appropriate when persuasion is the point. In such cases, metaphors and other figures of speech are justified.[48] It should be evident, even from these initial remarks, that Hobbes is using White as a foil. He is trying to clarify his own views about the very topics with which White is struggling.

White's intention was to construct a synthesis of Epicurus and Aristotle. It led him, for example, to assert with Epicurus that there were atoms but with Aristotle that matter was infinitely divisible. Traditionally, people believed one could not have it both ways. Atoms by definition were indivisible. The religious objection to atoms was that, because they were indivisible, they were immutable and hence eternal, perfect, and uncreated. Hobbes's way of avoiding the clash between atoms and divisibility was to assert that the smallest units of matter were "corpuscles" (not atoms) and that they were potentially infinitely divisible. These corpuscles are too small to be perceived. But it is certain that they exist, as the following argument shows. Consider two quantities x and y, where x is twice as much as y and y is the smallest perceivable size. Since proportions are applicable universally, y must itself be twice as large as some other quantity z, and, because y is the smallest perceivable size, z must be imperceptibly small and hence unimaginable.[49]

Although there are infinitely small quantities, there are no infinitely large ones. Whatever quantity is added to another quantity is always another determinate quantity. Yet, we sometimes say that something is infinite. What is meant in these cases? According to Hobbes, what is meant is that, due to human ignorance, a quantity cannot be assigned to infinity. And to say that the world is infinite is to say that no body can be added to it. Reason cannot decide whether this is true or not. It is a matter of Christian doctrine that the world is finite.[50] Hobbes's position is a conventional one that he shares with such theologians as Thomas Aquinas. White takes the unconventional position that he can prove that the world is finite. On the different issue of the existence of incorporeal beings, that is, spirits, White takes the conventional view that their existence can be proved and Hobbes the unconventional one that they cannot. After criticizing White's arguments on both points, Hobbes moralizes, as Aquinas did, about the danger of trying to prove "supernatural dogmas" in philosophy. The arguments "necessarily fall into . . . absurdities."[51] This leads to the danger that a person will mistakenly think that since all the attempted proofs of a dogma are not cogent, the dogma is false. Human arrogance then can lead to bad results for religion.[52]

In general, White was a victim of his own project. He wanted to reconcile as much of Aristotle (whom he considered the philosopher of the Catholic Church) and the Bible (which he considered the revealed word of God) with the results of modern science. Another example of this is his attempt to get the Copernican and the biblical view of the cosmos to jibe. Because he accepted the Copernican view as scientifically established, he needed a way to justify the Bible's view that the world stood still and the sun moved. His solution was to adopt a theory of relativity. Any moving object is moving relative to another object, and so it is arbitrary which object is taken to be fixed and which moving. Thus, it is just as true that the sun moves (as the Bible says it does) as that the earth moves (as Copernicus says). Hobbes declares White "quite confused." He attributes the source of the confusion to White's double allegiance to science and Christianity. He says that this is like "Odysseus's yoking two draught-beasts" together that might pull in opposite directions.[53] Many scholars have interpreted Hobbes's analysis of White's problems as committing himself to the irreconcilablity of science and religion; and further, that since Hobbes was obviously a proponent of modern science, he must not have been religious, that his professions of belief are insincere, and that most of his discussions of religious concepts are secretly designed to undermine religion. I think this interpretation is mistaken. If Hobbes's words had the implication just attributed to him, why would he have written them for the eyes of Mersenne, who has never been accused of atheism? The correct interpretation, I think, is this: White's project was the same as that of Mersenne, Gassendi, and Hobbes. Each wanted to reconcile something old (Christian beliefs) with something new (modern science). Each had a different way of doing it. White wanted to keep both the Bible and Aristotle. Gassendi gave up Aristotle altogether and hitched his wagon to Epicurus; Hobbes rejected all the ancients, radically rein-terpreted the Bible, and separated theology from science. (Mersenne engendered the work of all of these people, and others, so that he could benefit from the eventual winner.) White's mistake was to hitch science and religion to the same plow. Hobbes's view was that they worked in different fields. Religion therefore does not compete with science. Hobbes separated the two to safeguard religious belief. His separation was a form of fideism and no more irreligiously motivated than Søren Kierkegaard's. That is the force of his comments that by trying to prove what cannot be proved, White was unwittingly undermining the very thing that both he and Hobbes were trying to save. Hobbes thought that a certain myste-riousness was built into the universe:

[I]t is worth observing how serious the errors are that philosophers must fall into when they are ashamed to admit that there is any body or any act that they do not understand or properties that they themselves cannot demonstrate. I believe, however, that those who worship only the god that they understand are not Christians, and those who think they can demonstrate an attribute of something they do not comprehend are not philosophers.[54]

This attitude was widespread in Hobbes's day. Many who opposed the establishment of the Royal Society, such as the Cambridge divine and future bishop Peter Gunning, did so because of their fear that scientific investigations might intrude on religious belief. My interpretation makes sense of the fact that Hobbes was able to identify the source of White's confusion and the fact that Hobbes should invest so much effort in a scientific work that was so obviously oriented to religion.[55]

There is a related misinterpretation of Hobbes's position as regards the possibility of "demonstrating" the existence of God. Hobbes says it is not possible, and this had been taken as indicative of at least agnosticism and more likely atheism, since without a demonstration there would be no reason to think that God does exist and there would be reasons, such as the extent and intensity of evil, for thinking that he does not exist. The proper understanding of Hobbes's position depends on the meaning of 'demonstration'. As mentioned in Chapter 5, 'demonstration' is a technical term of Aristotelian philosophy that Hobbes adopted as his own. A demonstration is a syllogism consisting of propositions that are necessary and certain. Certainty is an epistemological requirement. One must know that the premise is true. Their necessity – and necessity is the crucial concept here – is a logical or metaphysical requirement. (Informally, a proposition is necessary if it must be true and cannot be false.) Hobbes puts this in a linguistic way: "the meaning of the subject must be included within the meaning of the predicate."[56] Now according to Hobbes, the proposition 'All humans beings are animals' is true because everything that 'human being' names is also named by 'animal'. That is the sense in which the meaning of the subject is included in that of the predicate.

Because necessary propositions are semantic truths, they are not made true by facts in the world; another way to put this is that they do not hook up with the world as propositions but only indirectly through the meanings of their terms. One consequence of this is that every necessary proposition is really 'hypothetical' or conditional in form; they are never genuinely categorical or existential. The adverbs, 'really' and 'genuinely', which are often weasel words, are justified here, because, like Bertrand Russell and Anselm of Canterbury before him, Hobbes thought that ordinary language could be misleading as to its form. And that is precisely the position he takes here. The genuine form of 'All human beings are animals', according to Hobbes (and later Russell), is 'If something is a human being, then it is an animal'. Hypothetical or conditional propositions never assert the existence of anything: "demonstrable truth lies in logical inferences; and in every demonstration the term that forms the subject of the conclusion demonstrated is taken as the name, not of a thing that exists but of one supposed to exist."[57] A proof that a triangle has a certain property is not a proof that there is such a triangle, but only that if there exists a triangle with the properties assumed in the premises, then there is a triangle with the property asserted in the conclusion. In short, demonstrations do not prove the existence of any object.

A necessary condition for proving the existence of anything is sense experience. But it is not sufficient. What a person asserts on the basis of sense experience is fallible in just the ways explored by the ancient skeptics. A person who claims to have seen Jones may have seen only Jones's twin; or perhaps he was dreaming. As we saw when we discussed *Elements of Law, Natural and Politic*, the justification for believing in the existence of God is no worse than the justification for believing in the existence of bodies (and Hobbes was not a phenomenalist). Again, Hobbes draws the moral that philosophers who try to prove unprovable religious propositions do a disservice to religion. He then goes on to make a point about faith and reason:

When a demonstration persuades us of the truth of any proposition, that is no longer faith, but is natural knowledge. Just as knowledge is being convinced through reasons arising from what is under discussion, so faith is being persuaded by the reasons derived from the authority of the person who speaks. Therefore as soon as any proposition is demonstrated, it is no longer an article of faith but a theorem of philosophy.

He believes that philosophers inevitably run up against the limits of intelligibility. If a philosopher reasons correctly, then he will conclude, "I do not understand under what meaning of terms that proposition is true." That attitude, Hobbes says, is the mark of a "balanced mind."[58]

Space and Time

Let's now return to some of the specifically scientific doctrines of *Anti-White*. One consequence of Hobbes's metaphysics is that all objects are within space and time. Every substance is a body, and every body is in some place. Hobbes considered the idea of a substance having no place or being outside of space to be unintelligible. Similarly, every object is in time because no movement is instantaneous. Eternity is simply time without end; the idea of eternity as an everlasting 'now' is unintelligible, nothing more than a bit of scholastic fraud.

This statement of the nature of space and time gives the impression that space and time are objective realities. In fact, Hobbes was ambivalent about this point. In *Anti-White*, he distinguishes between imaginary and real space. Real space is "corporeity itself," that is, "the essence of a body, insofar as it is a body." Imaginary space is the image of a body, abstracted from all qualitative modifications, such as color. In *De Corpore* (1655), which grew out of *Anti-White*, Hobbes maintained that space is the phantasm of a body, thought of as a thing merely existing and independent of the mind.[59]

Granted that there are two kinds of space, how are they related? Hobbes thinks that they sometimes coincide. The coincidence of these two is "place," according to him. He uses this view to explain what a vacuum is: the failure of an imaginary space to coincide with a real one. Unfortunately for Hobbes, the idea of a coincidence between real and imaginary space does not make sense within his philosophy. This was already noticed in 1656 by his admirer François Peleau: "You say in your metaphysics or first philosophy that space is 'the phantasm of an existing body considering it simply insofar as it exists'; but Sir, you will admit that everything is 'in space', and that it is not 'in a phantasm'. Therefore, space is not a phantasm, etc."[60]

Hobbes's considered view in *De Corpore* seems to be that there is no such thing as real space, even though his language sometimes commits him to it. His discomfort with the position that space exists independently of bodies is the doctrine that only bodies are real. So, if space were real, it would be a body. But if space were a body, then there would be no room for anything else, because a body, by definition, is something that fills up a space. One alternative to Hobbes's view is the Cartesian one: to identify body with space. But Hobbes did not want to hold that position, partially because it was Descartes's. Another seemingly possible maneuver for Hobbes would be to make space a nothingness, which bodies would then fill up. But Hobbes could not accept such a tactic because it really is nothing more than verbal legerdemain. If space were nothingness, then nothing would be something, and that is absurd. Also, if Hobbes could come to admit that nothingness existed, then he might as well admit that vacuums exist; but by the mid-1650s, his opposition to vacuums had hardened.

Hobbes had always been uncomfortable with the idea of a vacuum because it seemed to compromise one of his basic positions: All action occurs through the contact of one body with another. If there were a vacuum, then no action could occur across that space. Of course, action could still occur around a vacuum. So Hobbes was sometimes willing to admit to the existence of empty places. But he was never convinced that anyone, including Boyle, had shown that there were actual vacuums.

Conatus

Some of the actions of one body against another are basic motions. Hobbes calls them *conatus*. As defined in *Anti-White*, *conatus* – the Latin plural is the same as the singular – is the principle of motion, and for him that means that it is a motion. When Hobbes had perfected his view of it, he defined *conatus* as a motion too small to be measured. Although it is logically not the same thing, he also described it as a motion too small to be perceived. That there must be *conatus* can be proved as follows. Every motion can be divided in half. Every part of a motion is a motion. One-half of the smallest measurable (or the smallest perceivable) motion is a motion that is too small to be measured (or too small to be perceived). Hobbes appeals to *conatus* to explain resistance and certain gravitational phenomena. The resistance of an object is the object's *conatus*, that is, the unseen internal motions of the object that push other objects away, until an object with greater *conatus* overcomes that of the resisting object. Concerning gravitation, the reason that a ball on a table falls to the floor when the table is removed is that the object that had been resisting its *conatus* has then been eliminated, and that allows the *conatus* of the ball to move to the floor. So although the ball taken as a whole is at rest, its internal parts are not.[61]

The Nature of Being

One of the marks of Hobbes's modernist metaphysics is his denial that there are degrees of being. For him, all beings are on the same level. In contrast, Plato, Aristotle, and almost all of the scholastic philosophers distinguished between levels or grades of being. For them, some things were more real than others. They distinguished between infinite substance and finite substance. Infinite substance, which is the most real, exists *per se* (through itself), while finite substance exists *ab alio* (from something else). Infinite being is independent; finite being is dependent.

Aristotelians had still another kind of being: accidents. These were the qualities that they believed inhered in substances, such as weight, shape, color, sound, tastes, and odors. The essence of a finite substance was specified by an accident. Thus, in the definition of a human being as a rational animal, rationality is the accident (an essential accident) that specifies the kind of substance that a human being is. The hierarchy of being, then, is infinite substance, finite substance, accidents, or ideas. Following Aristotle and the scholastics, Descartes distinguished between infinite and finite substance and formal and objective reality. So in this respect, he was less modern than Hobbes.

For Hobbes, there is only one kind of being (*ens*): bodies or perhaps bodies in motion. In *Anti-White*, he was not quite ready to assert unequivocally that God is a body. So he begins by distinguishing beings into those that leave us with an image after having sensed them and those that do not. This distinction allows him to put the issue of God and the angels on the sidelines. Philosophy deals only with what is within man's ability to think about. 'Being' Hobbes then defines as anything that occupies space. From this it follows that all being is body. (But space, he cautions, is not a body.) Mirror images and dreams are not bodies and hence not beings because they do not occupy space. If there are spirits that can be perceived, like air or humors, then they are bodies. But he does not assert that there are or are not such spirits.[62]

With the definition and hence the nature of being settled, Hobbes is able to explain what *esse* or accidents are without positing a different level of being. His view is that accidents are names of bodies moving in ways that cause sentient beings to perceive them variously. When Socrates is walking, there is no difference between Socrates and Socrates walking. The walking itself is not detachable from him. In contrast, within Aristotelian physics, accidents are logically detachable (metaphysically distinguishable) from substances. To be walking and to be sitting are accidents of a substance, say, Socrates. They are different from him in some way such that they inhere in him. (Whatever is in x is not the same as x.)

Socrates' accidents are also dependent on him. The sitting Socrates loses that accident when he walks, and the walking Socrates loses that accident when he sits. Most accidents have a short life.

One reason for comparing Hobbes's views with Aristotle's is that that is how Hobbes presents his own view in *Anti-White*. It contains no anti-Aristotelian diatribes but rather a respectful comparison of the merits of the two views, although his view always comes out on top. There may be several reasons why he proceeded like this. One is that he was interested in the same issues as that ancient Greek. Another is that since White was an Aristotelian and Mersenne knew Aristotelianism, it would make sense for Hobbes to explain his own view in terms familiar to them. Also, since Hobbes intended his view to supersede Aristotle's, it would be important for him to show that his theory could explain all of the things that Aristotle's could. Finally, Hobbes shows that his view is philosophically more economical than Aristotle's. Whereas Aristotle needs essence, form, nature, subject, and matter, Hobbes does it all with body.[63]

Causality and Motion

Hobbes similarly reduces Aristotle's four causes to one. All causality consists of an agent moving a patient. Aristotle's efficient cause is nothing but the agent; his material cause is nothing but the patient. The final cause, when one exists, is nothing but the efficient cause. For example, the piece of candy causes a thought of enjoying it; this thought causes the idea of reaching out one's hand to get it; this causes one to reach out and eat it. Aristotle's formal cause is not a genuine cause at all. According to Aristotle, the form of a human being is what makes the animal to be a human being. A formal cause exists simultaneously with its effect; an object is a human being only when and no longer than it has the form of a human being. In contrast, Hobbes adopts the modern view that every cause precedes its effect; so the so-called formal cause cannot be a cause at all. According to Hobbes, what Aristotle calls 'form' in fact relates to the way human beings understand things, not to what makes an object move or exist.[64]

Hobbes takes over the Aristotelian principle that everything in motion is moved by something other than itself. His proof of the principle is a rather clever reductio ad absurdum. Here is a simplified version of it. Suppose that body B causes its own motion M at t_2. Then (according to

White) B has within itself at t_1, a time earlier than t_2, the cause of M at t_2. From this it follows that B causes M at t_1. But this contradicts the supposition.[65]

Hobbes applies his principle of motion uncompromisingly, in contrast with Aristotelians, including White, who occasionally made an exception of God or the soul. Hobbes points out that White's views are inconsistent because after first asserting the principle, he then goes on to maintain that the soul is a self-mover.[66] Like any good modern scientist, Hobbes will have none of these exceptions. Laws apply universally.

Hobbes agrees with the conventional philosophical view that because everything that is in motion is moved by something other than itself and because the world is in motion, something other than it moves it, namely, God. What Hobbes cannot explain is what moves God. But since he consistently maintains that God is incomprehensible, he is sanguine about the problem. What he is not willing to maintain is that God is external to the world. Since all causality, even divine causality, happens by contact (either pushing or pulling), God must be in contact with other bodies. There is no action at a distance. God cannot be physically detached from the universe, that is, the aggregate of all comprehensible bodies.[67]

Since the possibility of anything happening depends on motion, if there were a question as to whether motion or rest is better, then the correct answer would be 'motion' because rest does not cause anything. But Hobbes will have no truck with assigning value terms to (nonintentional) physical phenomena. Whether rest is nobler than motion is "a ridiculous question." Nobility is an invention of human beings.[68]

Hobbes believes in both inertia and the conservation of motion. A body in motion remains in motion until acted on by some other body. The belief that motion runs down results from anthropomorphizing it. People think that because they get tired after moving for a long time, it must be natural for motion to run down after some period. But just as a body at rest will stay at rest until something acts on it, Hobbes argues, the same reasoning applies to motion. And the totality of motion does "not diminish or disappear" unless it is acted on by an external agent.[69]

The General Character of *Anti-White*

From our discussion to this point, I hope it is obvious that some of *Anti-White* is very interesting. But most of it is as tiresome as *De Mundo.* The scientific speculations of Hobbes and White strike most of us today as absurd. Often the refutations are just as fantastic. Although it is not worth going into them here, they can teach us a general lesson: Good and lasting scientific theories are difficult to devise. At any particular time, there might be several equally plausible models or hypotheses that might be right. Different scientists latch onto different models. Those who happen to latch onto the right model are celebrated as geniuses while equally talented scientists are soon forgotten. Hobbes and White were among the most brilliant people of their day, and yet most of their scientific hypotheses about such things as the causes of wind, tides, ocean currents, the motion of the moon, gravitation, the position of the earth's axis, interaction between the sun and moon, and the rotation of the earth and moon would strike us as ludicrous today. They did not happen to fix on what proved to be the right course. Scientific greatness is partially a matter of luck.

7

A Decade of Exile,
1641–1651 (II)

I decided to write down my book *De Corpore*, of which all the material had been prepared. But I was forced to put it aside; *I am unwilling to allow so many and such great crimes to be attributed to the commands of God*. I decided to vindicate the divine laws and I acted as soon as possible. I worked at this little by little and was mentally anguished for a long time. While I was helping the Prince with his mathematical studies I was not always able to help myself with my own. Then I fell sick for six months, and prepared myself for approaching death. I did not depart, but death did. I finished my book in my native language, so that it could be read by my fellow Englishmen often and usefully. ("Vita Carmina Expressa")

Dissections with William Petty, 1645

William Petty, destined to become one of the founders of economics, left England at the beginning of the Civil War, probably because he sympathized with the king's opponents. Through the good graces of Dr. John Pell, who was then a professor of mathematics at Amsterdam, Petty was introduced to Hobbes in 1645.[1] They immediately liked each other. Their difference in age – Petty about twenty and Hobbes in his late fifties – did not pose a problem. Petty, who was a medical student, was happy to read the works of Andreas Vesalius, the famous Belgian anatomist, with Hobbes. Hobbes's interest in anatomy was dictated by his goal of presenting a complete scientific account of the world. He needed to figure out the mechanics of sensation, and this included finding their precise location in the brain or heart. When simple book anatomy proved to be insufficient, Hobbes attended dissections carried out by Petty.

Hobbes was also working intensively on his optics at this time. Petty drew some of the diagrams that were destined for publication in *De Homine*. Through Hobbes, Petty was introduced to Newcastle, Newcastle's brother Charles, Mersenne, and others. Although Petty returned to

England in 1646 and received his medical degree from Oxford, he never forgot Hobbes. In 1685, he drew up a short list of great men that included Hobbes in company with Bacon, Donne, Descartes, Galileo, Molière, and Francisco Suarez.

John Bramhall, Free Will, and Necessity, 1645

John Bramhall was educated at Cambridge and was an ally of Strafford and Laud. In 1633, he went to Ireland, where he prospered in the church; he became bishop of Londonderry the following year. As convention dictated for those times and alliances, he was occasionally accused of popery, which was sometimes a code word for Arminianism. His enemies forced him to flee Ireland for England in the spring of 1641. Out of the frying pan, into the fire. There he became an adviser to Newcastle, with whom he fled to Hamburg after the battle of Marston Moor. He returned to Ireland in 1648 and went to London at the Restoration. He was made archbishop of Armagh, primate and metropolitan of all Ireland in January 1661.

Bramhall met Hobbes in Paris in 1645. In August, they debated the question of free will in the presence of Newcastle. (The year that is often given for the debate, 1646, is wrong.) Bramhall, good Arminian that he was, took the affirmative; Hobbes, good English Calvinist that he was, took the negative. The debate, which seems to have been amicable,[2] impressed Newcastle enough to ask Bramhall to write up his views and for Hobbes to respond to them. Bramhall's manuscript, "A Discourse of Liberty and Necessity," was sent on to Hobbes. From Rouen, Hobbes wrote to Newcastle in August with his reply. Bramhall got around to replying to Hobbes's reply some months later. In the first published version, Hobbes's letter to Newcastle is dated August 20, 1652, but that is obviously impossible. A subsequent edition changed the date to 1646, and Hobbes later wrote that the debate had occurred in 1646; but 1645 seems to be the correct date because he was in Rouen in August 1645 but not in August 1646.

Hobbes and Bramhall agreed not to publish their manuscripts. Hobbes worried that the truth about predestination was socially dangerous: If people thought that their eternal fate was unrelated to their behavior in this world, then they would very likely engage in worse debauchery than they otherwise would.

[I]f we consider the greatest part of mankind, not as they should be, but as they are, that is, as men, whom either the study of acquiring wealth, or preferment, or whom hate, appetite of sensual delights, or the impatience of meditating, . . . have made unapt to discuss the truth of things: I must, I say, confess that the dispute of this question will rather hurt than help their piety; and therefore if his Lordship had not desired this answer, I should not have written it, nor do I write it but in hopes your Lordship and his will keep it private.[3]

Hobbes's attitude was widespread among Reformed theologians. Many theologians, especially in biblical scholarship during the nineteenth century (like some today), did not want their results disseminated for fear of causing their congregations to stampede to atheism or to scuttle to despair. Hobbes accepted in his own fashion the seminary aphorism: Teach predestination from the podium and preach Pelagianism from the pulpit.

One might think that there is no need to worry about what people would do if they were to learn about predestination if they are predestined to do whatever they will do anyway. But this belief is confused. As Hobbes would point out to Bramhall, this sentiment is either a misleading tautology (people will do what they will do) or a gross error (people will do what they will do no matter what precedes it). Hobbes's view is that what will happen is determined by what precedes it; so there is a very good reason not to promulgate the doctrine of predestination if that will determine that people will run amok. Of course, Hobbes had to think that.

In fact, Hobbes and Bramhall sidestep the issue of predestination almost completely. The most substantive comment about the matter in the debate itself is Hobbes's admonition:

If God be omnipotent, he is irresistible; if so, just in all his actions, though we, who have as much capacity to measure the justice of God's actions as a man born blind to judge of colors, haply may not discern it. What then need any man trouble his head, whether he be predestinated or not? Let him live justly and honestly according to the religion of his country, and refer himself to God for the rest, since he is the potter, and may do what he please with the vessel.[4]

Earlier, in *The Elements of Law, Natural and Politic,* Hobbes had urged people not to worry about the fact of predestination because human reason is incapable of knowing "the manner of God's predestination." The doctrine is also not an essential article of faith, of which there is only one: Jesus is the Christ.[5] What was the precise issue of the debate? Bramhall at one point put it this way:

Whether all events, natural, civil, moral (for we speak not now of the conversion of a sinner, that concerns not this question), be predetermined extrinsically and inevitably, without their own concurrence; so as all the actions and events which either are or shall be, cannot but be, nor can be otherwise after any other manner or in any other place, time, number, measure, order, nor to any other than they are. And all this in respect of the supreme cause, or a concourse of extrinsical causes, determining them to one.[6]

Hobbes said he was willing to accept this statement, which was drawn up with "as much caution as he [Bramhall] would do a lease, yet excepting that which is not intelligible."[7] Hobbes then goes to work showing that most of it is not intelligible.

A fair summary of Bramhall's position may be gotten by paraphrasing his opening argument: (1) Either I am free to write this discourse for free will and against determinism, or I am not. (2) If I am free, then I have won the debate and should not be punished for holding my position. (3) If I am not free, then I still should not be punished for holding my position since my actions in the debate were predestined and thus not within my control. Therefore, I should not be punished for holding my position. Furthermore, if I should not be punished for holding my position, then my position is justified.

Hobbes attacks both premises (2) and (3). Consider (2) first. The debate is about free will and not blame, so the premise is irrelevant. Also, Hobbes agrees with Bramhall that when people are not free, they should not be blamed for their actions. Next, Hobbes does not deny that people are free; what he denies is that wills are free. What he and Bramhall disagree about is the relationship between being free and having free will. This brings us to premise (3). Hobbes maintains that a person is free (or acts freely) when the cause of the person's action is a desire. This desire is properly termed 'a will', but from that it does not follow that the will is free or that the person has free will. The desire (will) is itself caused by some earlier event (perhaps another desire or a bit of reasoning), which in turn was caused by some earlier event, and so on to some unimaginable starting point. And there is and need be nothing in this account that mentions free will. Bramhall of course disagrees. He thinks that the concept of an action requires that an action be free in the sense of being undetermined by any cause external to the human being.

When are people not free? According to Hobbes, it is when their motions are caused by external events that violently move them. A person blown by a strong wind in a direction she does not want to go is acting under compulsion, but a person throwing her cargo overboard in order to prevent a ship from sinking is not. Her action is free because she is doing what she wants and will is the last want (desire) a person has before acting. The source of her action is the normal internal mechanism that humans have. She had a choice. She might have not thrown the cargo over and gone down with the ship. Hobbes would give the same kind of analysis to a situation in which a person hands over her money to an armed robber in order to avoid being shot. The person is acting not under compulsion but out of a fear for her own life; and that fear is a causative desire and hence a will. The robbery victim had a choice. She might have not handed over her money and gotten shot.

These analyses rankle, but Hobbes had no choice in the matter. One reason that he needed to maintain that coerced actions or actions motivated by fear are free actions is that the sovereign-making covenants are always motivated by fear; so he could not allow such actions to annul agreements.

Hobbes thinks that the doctrine of free will is not only false but incoherent. Many proponents of free will think that if people are free, then they do not act with necessity. Hobbes disagrees. Freedom and necessity are compatible. Hobbes was simply giving a philosophical defense of the Christian view championed by Calvin, who wrote in the *Institutes:* "we posited a distinction between compulsion and necessity from which it appears that man, while he sins of necessity, yet sins no less voluntarily."[8] Hobbes wrote, "It may be his Lordship thinks it all one to say, '*I was free* to write it', and, '*It was not necessary* I should write it'. But I think otherwise."[9] According to Hobbes, a person is free to do something if she can do it if she wants to and free not to do something if she can choose not do it if she does not want to. Yet if she does it, then the antecedent circumstances were such that it was necessary that she would want to do it; and if she does not do it, then the antecedent circumstances were such that it was necessary that she would not want to do it.

Hobbes had already sketched out his views about necessity in *Anti-White*. There he asserted that what is necessary is "what is not able not to be,"[10] and a necessary event is an event that was not able not to happen. Now, when all of the necessary circumstances for an event are present, then the event necessarily occurs. For actions, a will or desire is one of these circumstances that necessarily leads to an action. So all events are necessary. Defenders of free will try to remove the will or desire from the chain of physical causality, but this move is illegitimate, according to Hobbes.

Bramhall was not persuaded by Hobbes's compatibilism of freedom and necessity. He says that Hobbes's liberty is not true liberty because true liberty is incompatible with "determined" necessity. Bramhall is willing to concede that certain preceding circumstances make some subsequent act necessary, but when this is the case, at least one of the circumstances is a free action that is not itself determined. For example, the circumstances of someone being in good health, having unimpeded access to a cup, and being willing to pick up the cup necessitate the picking up of the cup. He calls such preceding circumstances "determining," as opposed to "determined," necessity. He makes numerous other distinctions, similarly scholastic and dubious. They infuriated Hobbes, who thought they were nothing but nonsensical cant: "And with these distinctions his Lordship says he clears the coast, whereas in truth he darkens his own meaning and the question not only with the jargon of 'exercise only', 'specification also', 'contradiction', 'contrariety', but also with pretending distinction where none is."[11]

Hobbes was hopelessly mistaken about some features of necessary and contingent propositions. In *Anti-White* he argued that since 'It will rain tomorrow or it will not rain tomorrow' is necessarily true, and is made true by the truth of one of the component sentences, that component sentence must also be necessarily true.[12] If necessity did not come from the true component proposition, there would no place for it to come from, according to Hobbes. His reasoning is a textbook example of the fallacy of division. He argues that because the whole proposition has the property P, it follows that one of the component propositions has the property P. That is like arguing that because the whole proposition consists of ten (token) words, it follows that one of the component propositions has ten (token) words. Hobbes never saw the error of his modal argument and repeated it in *De Corpore* (1655). He could be stubbornly obtuse.

Because every event is necessary, nothing happens by chance. The reason that people think that events are not necessary or contingent is that they do not know all of the causes of any event.[13] Since Hobbes had already argued for this position in *Anti-White,* perhaps some discussion of White's book caused the debate between Hobbes and Bramhall.

One of the reasons that the philosophical problem of free will and determinism grips people is that it seems to have practical consequences. If free will does not exist and every action is necessitated by previous events not under the control of the agent, how can the practice of praising or blaming some actions be justified and how can people genuinely plan out their lives? Hobbes replies that to praise an action is simply to declare that action good and to blame an action is to declare it bad. And people need to plan their lives because certain causal sequences will allow them to achieve their goals and others will not. To say that an event is necessitated does not mean that it will happen no matter what one does.[14] Rather, it means that it will happen because of what will happen and nothing other than that could happen.

For people in the Judeo-Christian tradition, sin is being held responsible for a bad action, and being held responsible for an action implies that it was done by free will. All humans are sinners, and all deserve punishment because of their sin. But how can God justly punish them if they could not have done otherwise? The repulsiveness of this doctrine comes across in Bramhall's rejection of it:

Though I honor T.H. for his person and for his learning, yet I must confess ingenuously, I hate this doctrine from my heart. And I believe both I have reason so to do, and all others who shall seriously ponder the horrid consequences which flow from it. . . . It makes the first cause, that is God Almighty, to be the introducer of all evil and sin into the world, as much as man, yea, more than man, by as much as the motion of the watch is more from the artificer, who did make it and wind it up, than either from the spring or the wheel or the thread, if God, by his special influence into the second causes, did necessitate them to operate as they did. And if they, being thus determined, did necessitate Adam inevitably, irresistibly, not by an accidental, but by an essential subordination of causes to whatsoever he did, then . . . God is more guilty of it [the sin] and more the cause of evil than man.[15]

Hobbes has an answer though not a sweet-sounding one. He holds that two things are required for a sin: a law of God and an action, caused by a will, that breaks that law. It does not matter whether an action is necessitated or not: "if the action be forbidden, he that does it willingly may justly be punished. . . . men are justly killed, not for that their actions are not necessitated, but because they are noxious, and they are spared and preserved whose actions are not noxious." He goes on to say, "A judge in judging whether it be sin or no, which is done against the law, looks at no higher cause of the action than the will of the doer."[16] Hobbes believed in strict liability.

Doesn't Hobbes's position directly implicate God in every sin that ever has been or ever will be committed, just as Bramhall had claimed? The literally true answer is this question is 'Yes'. Given some standard Judeo-Christian beliefs, it is logically impossible for God not to be implicated: God is the cause of everything; sin is something; therefore, God is the cause of sin.

Many theologians from Augustine to Thomas Aquinas, down to the last cleric to preach on this topic, have tried to block this argument either by claiming that sin is in fact nothing ('nonbeing') or that God causes everything except sin. Neither tactic is very good. If sin were nothing, then people would no more be the cause of it than God: Only things have causes; nonthings do not. Alternatively, if sin is nothing and if sinners were punished for sin, then they would be punished for nothing; and that does not seem right. Some, like Bramhall, want to distinguish between, say, the sin of unjustifiably killing an innocent person and the event of unjustifiably killing an innocent. But Hobbes maintains that this is a distinction without a difference.[17] The unjustifiable killing is the sin. Others maintain that God permits the sin but does not will it. Hobbes correctly objects that he sees "no difference between the will to have a thing done and the permission to do it, when he that permits can hinder it and knows that it will be done unless he hinders it."[18] Concerning the other tactic, namely, to maintain that God causes everything except sin, is to be one step away from Manichaeanism. If God is not the cause of absolutely everything, then he is not the absolute principle of all reality. There is something, sin, that requires an independent principle of explanation.

In fact, in order to avoid Manichaeanism and perhaps some other heresies, theologians for centuries had said often enough that God is the cause of everything. Hobbes would take up Bramhall on this point in *Liberty, Necessity and Chance:* "Perhaps he will say, that this opinion makes God the cause of sin, but does not the Bishop think Him the cause of all actions? And are not sins of commission actions? Is murder no action? And does not God Himself say, *Non est malum in civitate quod Ego non feci* ["There is no evil in the state that I do not do"] and was not murder one of those evils?"[19]

As a matter of fact, Hobbes is right to maintain that being the cause of a bad action does not entail that the cause is culpable for the bad action. Suppose that some act of charity on Alice's part, such as helping an AIDS patient or counseling at a family planning center, causes Bob, an ardent opponent of that behavior, to do something evil. Alice is not thereby culpable for the wicked action. This example, however, does not solve the problem, because there is a difference between the role that Alice plays in causing Bob's bad behavior and the role that God plays. God has control over Bob in a way that Alice does not. It is the conjunction of God's absoluteness as understood by the Judeo-Christian tradition (omnipotence, omniscience, and omnibenevolence), combined with the reality of suffering and evil, broad and deep, that makes the classic Judeo-Christian view a tough problem for any intelligent and honest theist. A coherent account of it requires no less than some very hard pronouncements, if any coherent account is possible at all.

I think that Hobbes's solution is no worse than any other. He explains that to sin is to break a law, not merely to cause an action that breaks a law. He appeals to Paul for support. In Romans 9:20–21, Paul says that there is no injustice in God even though he hardened Pharaoh's heart. God caused Pharaoh to act as he did. Because Pharaoh willed his action and was subject to God's law, he sinned. But God did not. Calvin goes even farther. He concedes that God, Satan, and human beings are all in the same causal chain: "we see no inconsistency in assigning the same deed to God, Satan, and man; but the distinction in purpose and manner causes God's righteousness to shine forth blameless there, while the wickedness of Satan and of man betrays itself by its own disgrace."[20]

At one point Hobbes tries to ameliorate the harshness of saying that God is the cause of sin by saying that God is the cause of sin but not its author. In taking this line, he was availing himself of Theodorus Beza's supposed solution:

We conclude therefore that this fall of Adam did so proceed out of the motion of his will that notwithstanding it happened with the will of God, whom it pleases by a marvelous and incomprehensible means, that what he forbids (since it is sin) nonetheless happens with his will.[21]

The deficiency here is that the appeal to an "incomprehensible means" shows that no solution is given at all.

Hobbes chose the solution that seemed the best to him, given his philosophical principles and religious upbringing. And it is not one bit worse than that of other Calvinists. In the end, he sounds a note of pious resignation: "This I know; God cannot sin, because his doing a thing makes it just, and consequently no sin; as also because whatsoever can sin is subject to another's law, which God is not. And therefore it is blasphemy to say, God can sin; but to say, that God can so order the world, as a sin may be necessarily caused thereby in a man, I do not see how it is any dishonor to him."[22] It is the stubborn certainty of the phrase "This I know," which reminds me of Luther's "Here I stand," combined with the affirmation that whatever God does is just that leads me to believe that Hobbes is sincere and not sarcastic. Admittedly, it is sometimes difficult to tell the difference. I have heard the motto "Fiat iustitia, ruat caelum" ("Let there be justice, even if it causes the heavens to fall down") used sincerely and sarcastically about an equal number of times.

Hobbes's replies to the objections already discussed have a set pattern that makes it easy to see, if not to swallow, his answers to others. For example, to the objection that if all actions are necessary, then prayers are in vain, he says, "Not so." God blesses those who pray even though the prayers do not cause God, whose will is unchangeable, to do anything: "prayer is the gift of God," and is preordained like everything else.[23]

Job and the Problem of Evil

Related to God's omnipotence, sin, and punishment is the problem of evil. The problem may take various forms, but the most difficult to solve is that presented in the book of Job, roughly, 'Why do innocent people suffer?' or more precisely 'Why do people suffer disproportionately to the evil they do?' The conventional wisdom, professed by Job's friends, that all and only the good prosper and all and only the wicked suffer, is falsified by experience. Hobbes has two basic solutions. One is the callous solution that he had presented in *Anti-White:*

Everyone thinks himself good. And if he suffers some evil, then he thinks that this shows that there is no providence or (if providence does govern things), it does not do so rationally. And everyone thinks that the world is administered rationally when everything happens to the advantage of good men, that is, himself. But [in

my opinion] it should not be said that the good suffer or the bad do well universally or even for the most part. The contrary is the case. Even in this life, the good
do better than the bad and there is no skill better for gaining wealth or honors (or
anything else more pleasant than these in this life) than integrity. No doubt the
complaint is universal; but the cause is that no one is willing to admit to their own
depravity and because of jealousy a person calls the virtues of the person he envies
'wickedness'.[24]

Hobbes's other solution to the problem of evil can be called 'The God
above Justice Solution'. God is neither literally just nor literally unjust.
The reason has already been explained. Being unjust is breaking a law; no
lawgiver can break a law because he makes the law. God is a lawgiver and
therefore cannot break the law. Hobbes sometimes makes his point in
biblical, nonlegalistic language: The relationship of God to human beings
is the same as a potter to his clay. A potter cannot injure his clay. At
bottom, what justifies God's behavior toward Job is his absolute power:

[T]he power of God alone without other helps is sufficient justification of any
action he does. . . . That which he does, is made just by his doing it. . . . Power
irresistible justifies all actions, really and properly, in whomsoever it be found; less
power does not, and because such power is in God only, he must needs be just in
all actions.[25]

As omnipotent, God makes laws but is subject to none; hence, he cannot
break any or be culpable for anything.

Within the context of his times, Hobbes's views are not outrageous.
Compare them with what Cromwell said after the massacre at Wexford,
which included many noncombatants:

Indeed, it has not without cause been deeply set upon our hearts that we, intend-
ing the better to this place than so great a ruin, hoping the two might be of more
use to you and your army, yet God would not have it so; but by an unexpected
providence in His righteous justice brought a just judgment upon them, causing
them to become a prey to the soldiers who in their piracies have made preys of so
many families, and now with their bloods to answer the cruelties which they
exercised upon the lives of divers poor Protestants.[26]

Cromwell's remark helps to explain why it is plausible that Andrew
Marvell was not being sarcastic when he wrote after the slaughters at
Drogheda and Wexford:

They [the Irish] can affirm his praises best,

And have, though overcome, confessed
How good he is, how just,
And fit for highest trust.

The Second Edition of *De Cive,* 1647

In 1646, the second, expanded edition of *De Cive* was being prepared for publication by the Dutch publishing firm Elzevier. It was eagerly awaited. Sorbière mentions William Boswell, Samson Johnson, Henricus Regius, and Adrian Heereboord, all men of distinction, as being especially interested in it.[27] Unlike the first edition, which had a very small print run, the second edition would be available to many people. Hobbes was happy to have the congratulatory prefaces that Gassendi and Mersenne had written even though their first appearance would be in the third edition. But for the most part he was paranoid. In a letter of 1646, he wrote:

The following things may, I think, hinder the publication of the book. First, if the people who hold sway in the universities learn that a book of this sort is in the press. For their public reputation demands that in the subject which they teach no one should have discovered anything which they have not already discovered. So you must proceed quietly and not ask for testimonials except when you are sure that you can get them. Nor, accordingly, if it can be prevented, should the printer be allowed to get judgments on the book's importance from people who, in his own opinion, he considers to be learned men. Then you must beware of those who approve of most of it but disapprove of the rest. Such people will treat me as if I were their pupil; they will expect me to be content with the praise they give me in private, and will begrudge me public praise. Furthermore, if M. Descartes hears or suspects that a book of mine (this or any other) is being assessed for publication, I know for certain that he will stop it if he can. Please believe me on this one thing, for I do know. I leave all other precautions to you, as I am fully aware of both your prudence and your goodwill towards me.[28]

Descartes's disdain for Hobbes was great,[29] but he had better things to do than interfere with Hobbes's career.

The second edition of *De Cive* was a long time at the printer. After various delays, it finally appeared in January 1647. A great success, it had sold out by August, with hundreds of requests for the book. Two more printings followed within a short time. Many of the royalists in exile approved of *De Cive.* It was an uncompromising defense of absolute sovereignty and it did not threaten the independence of the church.

Clarendon, who had read Hobbes's translation of Thucydides and *The Elements of Law, Natural and Politic*, asked Hobbes to send him *De Cive*. Clarendon respected Hobbes's work even though he disagreed with important parts of it. In contrast with Hobbes, he did not accept the legitimacy of absolute sovereignty and thought that property rights did not depend on the monarch.

The most important addition to the second edition is the Preface to the Reader. It contains what is in my opinion Hobbes's single greatest argument, which I have called 'The Great Ignorance and Fear Argument': Only a few people are evil, but because we do not know how to distinguish them from the good, "there is a necessity of suspecting, heeding, anticipating, subjugating, self-defending, ever incident to the most honest and fairest conditioned."[30]

What makes this argument so impressive, in addition to the fact that the premises are plausible, is that its applications are wide-ranging. Schoolchildren are taught that they need to fear all strangers because some strangers are dangerous. Many women fear all men because they know that some men are rapists. Police officers fear every person they stop for a traffic offense because they know that some of the people they stop are dangerous. Many whites fear all African Americans because they know that a disproportionate percentage of certain crimes are committed by them. Many African Americans anticipate racist behavior from all whites because they know that some whites are racists.

The Great Ignorance and Fear Argument has another impressive feature: It can be ramified. In addition to every person being suspicious of every other person, every person is made even more suspicious by the knowledge that he is suspected by everyone else. Honest citizens, males, African Americans, and whites resent the cautious behavior of police, women, whites, and African Americans, respectively. They become not only resentful but more standoffish in their own behavior, knowing that even well-intentioned movements may be misinterpreted as threatening. These new suspicions themselves get ramified. When males, African Americans, and whites see that females, whites, and African Americans are standoffish, they interpret the behavior as unfriendly, which upsets them and confirms their initial suspicions. Given this line of argument, Hobbes's repeated assertion that the state of nature is a war "of all men against all men"[31] does not sound hyperbolic.

What strikes me as odd is that Hobbes never used the Great Ignorance and Fear Argument again. It would have been especially helpful to him in *Leviathan*, where it is replaced by a much less plausible argument. For his empirical proof that all men are dangerous, he says:

[W]hen taking a journey, he [every person] arms himself and seeks to go well accompanied; when going to sleep, he locks his doors; when even in his own house he locks his chest; and this when he knows there be laws and public officers armed to revenge all injuries shall be done to him; what opinion he has of his fellow subjects when he rides armed, . . . [and] locks his doors, and of his children and servants when he locks his chest. Does he not there as much accuse mankind by his actions as I do by my words? [32]

When travelers lock their doors, it is not all mankind that they accuse but only some unknown ones. Sometimes Hobbes's later thoughts were worse than his earlier ones.

Work on *De Corpore*, 1645–47

In Chapter 6, we discussed Hobbes's slow progress on *De Corpore*. Although he was confident in May 1646 that it would be finished by the end of the year, it was not. Instead of going to de Martel's estate, he accepted the position of tutor to the Prince of Wales at the English court in exile at Saint-Germain.[33] He seems to have been recommended by Henry Jerman (Jermyn), who would later call Hobbes one of the strangest men he ever met. Hobbes stayed in Saint-Germain for about two years. He associated with Edmund Waller, Abraham Cowley, William Davenant, and others. Hobbes tutored Waller's son, Cowley would later write a nice poem in honor of Hobbes, and Davenant conferred daily with Hobbes about his poem *Gondibert*.

Crisis Theology, the Illness of 1647

In August and part of September 1647, Hobbes was seriously ill. At times he was delirious and unable to recognize anyone. But he was lucid when Mersenne came to visit and tried to get him to convert to Roman Catholicism. Hobbes declined to abandon the church into which he had been born and told Mersenne that he had considered the differences between the Protestant and Roman Catholic churches very carefully and was comfortable with his belief in the Church of England. He asked if Mersenne had any news about Gassendi. A few days later, John Cosin, a

protégé of William Laud and a future bishop of Durham, visited in order
to pray with him. He asked Hobbes whether he wanted to receive communion. Hobbes was grateful for the offer. "Yes," he said, "if you will do it
according to the rites of the Church of England." For the care of his soul,
so to speak, Hobbes also confessed to John Pierson. Later, he would write
that he was more religious when he thought he was dying than when he
was healthy. Some have inferred from this that Hobbes was not religious.
That seems to be to be exactly the wrong inference to draw. The whole
premise of crisis theology is that people find God in extreme situations.

After recovering from his illness, Hobbes was in fine fettle and back at
disputation.

The Vacuum, 1648

Hobbes read a criticism of Evangelista Torricelli's experiments concerning the vacuum in February 1648. The critic was the Jesuit Etienne Noel,
who claimed that purified air (ether) was able to penetrate and fill the
glass tube where the vacuum allegedly was. Less than a decade later,
Hobbes used a very similar explanation in order to counter Boyle's hypothesis about the vacuum. But in February 1648, Hobbes did not like
that sort of objection to Torricelli's results. At that time he thought that
"there are certain minimal spaces here and there, in which there is no
body."[34] But Hobbes was never a great fan of the vacuum. He believed
that all motion and a fortiori all action takes place by immediate contact of
one body with another. So vision, which requires a continuous motion of
light reflected off the object seen to the observer, could not occur through
a vacuum. What might seem to be looking through a vacuum would have
to be explained by having light transmitted through bodies that sur-
rounded the vacuum. Just a few months later, in May 1648, Hobbes told
Mersenne that the latter's experiments had failed to prove the existence of
a vacuum because "subtle matter" can pass through mercury and any
fluid body, "just as smoke passes through water."[35]

The Execution of Charles I

Charles I was executed on January 30, 1649. Hobbes must have been as
shocked by it as most Englishmen and Europeans were. Unfortunately,
there is no record of his specific reactions until 1651, when he represented

Charles I as a Christ figure, as many Englishmen did. Defying Parliament's order against discussing the execution, Hobbes wrote about it in *Leviathan:*

[I]n a discourse of our present civil war, what could seem more impertinent, than to ask (as one did) what was the value of a Roman penny? Yet the coherence to me was manifest enough. For the thought of the war, introduced the thought of the delivering up the king to his enemies. The thought of that brought in the thought of the delivering up of Christ; and that again the thought of the 30 pence, which was the price of that treason: and thence easily followed that malicious question.[36]

We have already seen that Hobbes decided to leave England for his own safety. His intention had always been to return to England when circumstances permitted. He did not want to do anything to jeopardize that eventuality. He was upset when he saw that the inscription under his portrait in the second edition of *De Cive* read "Academic Tutor to His Serene Highness the Prince of Wales." He wrote to Sorbière to protest the mistake. First, the inscription was untrue; he taught only mathematics. Second, he did not want to compromise the standing of the prince by having him associated with "a political theory which offends the opinions of almost everyone," namely, Hobbes's own. Third, any bad consequences of this, Hobbes says, "will all be blamed on my carelessness and vanity, to my great dishonour." Finally, and most important, Hobbes did not want being identified as the tutor of the Prince of Wales to wreck his chances of returning to England. Hobbes professes his complete innocence: "Nothing in this whole business can be blamed on me; I hardly knew what was going on."[37] Since his correspondent, Sorbière, knew this, Hobbes's motive for writing this sentence may have been self-serving. He could use it if necessary as evidence of his innocence. He repeated his desire to be in England in May 1648, but feared for his safety because of the continued uncertainty there.[38] In September 1649, he told Gassendi that he was keeping himself fit because he hoped to return to England. His residence on the Continent was dictated by necessity, not choice. He was first and always an Englishman even though his fame was greater on the Continent.

What prevented his return was the absence of a stable government. The continuing struggle between Parliament and its army in 1649 and 1650 meant that England did not meet his criterion of stability. He loosened that criterion when he began to fear that he might be arrested or murdered in France. Royalists had assassinated Anthony Ascham, who defended the Engagement, and Isaac Dorislaus, an Anglo-Dutch lawyer who had helped write the charge of high treason against Charles. Hobbes also feared that the French Roman Catholic clergy might persecute him. The publication of *Leviathan* is especially pertinent here. Almost all of Part IV, "The Kingdom of Darkness," is strongly anti-Catholic. A large part of the longest chapter of the book, Chapter 42, is a detailed refutation of the defense of the papacy presented by Robert Bellarmine, the patron saint of the Counter-Reformation and one of the two cardinals who had impressed Hobbes in Rome.

William Davenant and the Preface before *Gondibert*, January 1650

William Davenant had succeeded Ben Jonson as poet laureate in 1638 on the strength of his wide output: plays, masques, and poems. Like Hobbes, he was low born and worked hard to become a formidable intellectual. Unlike Hobbes, he was dissolute. Syphilis caused his nose to fall off at a relatively early age. He covered the hole with a patch. He was a favorite of Henrietta Maria and was more closely connected with her court than with Charles's. In 1641, he participated in the bungled First Army Plot with Newcastle and others. Having supported Charles during the Civil War, he fled to the exiled court of the queen. He may have converted to Roman Catholicism in 1646. Around 1649, he began writing an innovative epic poem, *Gondibert*. It was designed to incorporate all the major genres of literature. Each day Davenant gave Hobbes the work to critique, and in gratitude he addressed his preface to Hobbes. He was in effect dedicating the work to him. Hobbes's comments moved Davenant to discuss his aesthetic ideas in this preface. Hobbes then responded with "A Reply before the Preface of Gondibert." These companion pieces were published together in France in early 1650, without the poem, which was published the next year.

Hobbes's short essay came to have a substantial effect on literary criticism and literature in the late seventeenth century. He presents an elaborate and, in a loose sense, metaphysical, taxonomy of poetry. Just as the universe consists of three regions, celestial, aerial, and terrestrial, so poets imitate these three regions and produce poems about court, city, and country. A monarch's court is like heaven, the city is like the aerial region, and rural areas are like the terrestrial sphere. Each of these topics can be treated in one of two ways: in narrative (in which the poet is a narrator) and in drama (in which characters "speak and act their own parts").[39]

These two dimensions yield exactly six kinds of poetry: heroic poetry, tragedy, satire, comedy, pastoral poetry, and dramatic pastoral poetry. Since this taxonomy leaves out such genres as sonnets, epigrams, and eclogues, Hobbes rationalizes that these are simply parts of one of the six types just enumerated. Hobbes's theory also entails that the works of Empedocles, Lucretius, and Lucan are not poetry but either philosophy or history. He stipulates that the subject matter of poetry must be the manners of men, not the nature of the universe. This makes the works of Empedocles and Lucretius merely verse, not poetry. That leaves Lucan. His work is ruled out as poetry on the grounds that the story line of a poem must be invention, not reportage. Finally, in order for verse to qualify as poetry the manners of men have to be described, not prescribed (so as to distinguish poetry from ethics). Conversely, the subject matter of poetry cannot be handled by prose, because prose lacks the delightfulness of poetry. Take that, Jane Austen and George Eliot.

These views, which may strike us as perversely revisionist, should be understood as part of a tradition of literary criticism that goes back to Aristotle, who wrote in *Poetics* that the work of Herodotus would remain history and would not be poetry even if it were written in verse: "poetry tends to express the universal, history the particular." These ideas were revived during the Italian Renaissance. For example, Daniello in his *Poetica* paraphrased Aristotle when he wrote that Livy's works would still be histories even if they were written in verse. Conversely, as Robortelli pointed out, certain prose works would be poetry even if they were not written in verse.

When Hobbes turns to consider the poetic possibilities of individual languages, he judges that Greek epics had to be in hexameter and English epics had to be in rhyming pentameter. Not surprisingly, *Gondibert* has the latter form. Hobbes asserts that poetry is older than prose because poets took over verse from the Greek prophets and oracles, who spoke in verse. Also, poets wanted their works sung, and only poetry has the regularity to allow for singing. Alluding to some of the work of George Herbert, a brother of Lord Herbert of Cherbury, he castigates poems that take the shape of an egg, an altar, or a pair of wings.

Hobbes notes that Davenant's refusal to invoke a muse or a god at the beginning of his poem is a sign of good Christian practice. There is nothing pious in the custom, followed by supposedly Christian poets, of calling on pagan beings for inspiration. To do so is "either to profane the true God or to invoke a false one."[40] When he came to translate Homer's poems late in life, he often left out references to the Greek gods. He has been criticized for this, but I think it was consonant with his Christianizing poetic theory.

Fancy and Judgment

Hobbes distinguishes between fancy, which is the primary tool of poets, and judgment, which is the primary tool of philosophers. Yet the distinction is not absolute. An epic poet can have some share of the philosopher's judgment and needs it when he paints a picture of "heroic virtue."[41] Hobbes had already come to this distinction in *The Elements of Law, Natural and Politic.* Fancy sees similarities in dissimilar things. It is the talent of the poet. (Hobbes is thinking of the use of metaphor and simile: My love is a red rose.) Judgment sees dissimilarity in similar things.[42] It is the talent of the scientist. Sometime around the publication of his reply to Davenant's preface, Hobbes was working on *Leviathan,* in which he talked about the distinction at greater length. Fancy comes in for some rough handling. Fancy alone is not a virtue, he says, but judgment alone is. Judgment is the same as discretion and is necessary to keep fancy in check; without "steadiness and direction to some end, a great fancy is one kind of madness."[43]

Someone apparently had argued that it was impossible for any one person to be a complete citizen because people of judgment are supposedly censorious, unforgiving, and vengeful whereas people of fancy are unpredictable, undiscriminating, and cowardly. Hobbes admits the difficulty of incorporating both dispositions in the same person but believes that it can be overcome through "education and discipline"[44] as explained in Chapter 5. Then follows an eloquent testimony to the man to whom he dedicated his book: "I have known clearness of judgment and largeness of fancy, strength of reason and graceful elocution, a courage for the war and a fear for the laws, and all eminently in one man, and that was my most noble and honored friend Mr Sidney Godolphin."[45]

The Writing and Publication of *Leviathan*, 1650–51

At the same time that Hobbes was commenting on *Gondibert*, he was probably writing *Leviathan*. One scholar sensibly guesses that Hobbes started it in January 1649, just about the time that Charles I was on his way up the steps of the scaffold on Execution Hill, and near the beginning of the French rebellion called the Fronde. All the evidence points to a very quick composition. By May 1650, he was up to Chapter 37, about two-thirds of the way through the book. Hobbes reported his method of writing it to Aubrey:

He walked much and contemplated, and he had in the head of his staff a pen and ink horn, carried always a notebook in his pocket, and as soon as a thought darted, he presently entered it into his book or otherwise he might have lost it. He had drawn the design of his book into chapters, etc. so he knew whereabouts it would come in. Thus that book was made.

The printer in London must have begun setting the type for *Leviathan* around the beginning of 1650. Part of it would be set, then sent to Hobbes for corrections, then returned to London for resetting and printing. It was a slow and expensive way to produce a book. It was bound and available for purchase at 8 shillings 6 pence by the end of April or the very beginning of May.

There are three editions bearing the date 1651 and listing Andrew Crooke as the publisher. Each edition is named for the printer's ornament that appears on the title page. The so-called Bear and twenty-five-ornaments editions are later than the so-called Head edition, the "head" being the head of a column. The Head edition itself appeared in two versions: a standard folio and a deluxe version with margins edged in red. Among the printed versions, the red-edged versions are the most accurate because they were printed last and the printer would occasionally correct mistakes in the type during the process of printing each sheet. There is another version that competes with the red-edged one for pride of place: a manuscript written on vellum and presented to Charles II. It probably was prepared shortly before the printed editions and on a couple of occasions takes swipes at the Presbyterians and Independents that are omitted from the printed ones. But some of its changes, those in Hobbes's handwriting, may be later than the printed version.

It is plausible that Hobbes hoped that *Leviathan* would enhance his position in the court. If that is right, then the later slanderous explanations such as Clarendon's, that Hobbes wrote *Leviathan* because he had a mind to go home, are obviously false. As Hobbes said later, there is hardly a page that does not support monarchy and condemn rebellion.

Hobbes gave away a fair number of copies of *Leviathan*. In addition to the one to Francis Godolphin, he sent two copies to Ralph Bathurst, who had written a commendatory poem in Latin for *Humane Nature*. Bathurst had been a scholar and fellow of Trinity College, Oxford, and turned to medicine when the royalist cause failed. He was back in Oxford in 1654. He practiced medicine with Hobbes's young friend William Petty and also was a friend of John Evelyn, Richard Allestree, Boyle, and Christopher Wren. One of Bathurst's copies may have been for Seth Ward, who had written the "recommendatory address" for *Humane Nature*. Before *Leviathan* appeared, Bathurst and Ward strongly supported Hobbes because his published teaching in *De Cive* defended the moderate Anglican position that the church is subject to the secular power in matters of order and discipline, but independent of it in matters of doctrine. They could not very well defend the new teaching in *Leviathan* that the sovereign was the ultimate authority in every matter. Even worse was Hobbes's view that the sovereign was the high priest of the church and could administer any of the sacraments if he chose to and merely chose not to.

Charles probably received the presentation copy in December 1651. He had been away from France since 1648. After being defeated at Worcester, he arrived in Paris on October 30, 1651. Clarendon arrived in mid-December. He and other members of the court, especially the Anglican clergy, were turning Charles against Hobbes. Hobbes had at least as much reason to fear the French Roman Catholic clergy, who had even more reason to hate him. Throughout *Leviathan*, he represented Roman Catholicism as one of the two greatest dangers to true religion and stable government (presbyterianism being the other). So he knew it would be better not to be in a Catholic country once it was published. England now looked safer to him than France. In general, the Continent was not safe for people perceived to be enemies of royalism. As mentioned earlier, Anthony Ascham, who justified obedience to the Commonwealth and quoted *De Cive* approvingly, had been assassinated by royalists in Spain, and Isaac Dorislaus, one of the regicides, was assassinated in The Hague. Perhaps Hobbes would not have felt comfortable in the Netherlands because of Dorislaus's mortal experience there, but otherwise, it is a mystery to me why Hobbes never took advantage of the relatively tolerant policy of the Netherlands and settled there. In any case, just as Hobbes felt the hounds of Parliament at his heels when he fled England in late 1640, he felt the same dogged pursuit in early 1652, according to Clarendon's report: "He was compelled secretly to fly out of Paris, the Justice having endeavored to apprehend him."[46] Hobbes was back in England by February 1652.

8

Leviathan and the Engagement Controversy, 1651–1653

I returned to my homeland, not quite sure of my safety. But in no other place could I have been safer. It was cold; there was deep snow; I was an old man; and the wind was bitter. My bucking horse and the rough road gave me trouble. ("Vita Carmina Expressa")

The Return of the Prodigal Son

Hobbes returned to England about February 1652. A cold coming he had of it. But his life would soon warm up. With three books published in two years (*Humane Nature, Philosophical Rudiments,* and *Leviathan*), and prominent participation in Mersenne's circle, he was something of a celebrity. Decades later in his autobiography, he downplayed his public persona. He explained that he went to London "in order to avoid the appearance of having arrived secretly." He then says, "[I] retired in utter peace, and I devoted myself to my studies as before." His explanation is unconvincing. He could have just as easily passed through London and then resided in the country as Devonshire did. My guess is that he lived in London for two reasons: He wanted to enjoy his fame and to be where the action was. He was quite full of himself, and at age sixty-three he had no good reason to think that he had many years left to live. So he probably thought that he would make the most of them. He would volunteer his presence to any gathering of London intelligentsia that would have him.

John Selden and William Harvey

Some of his time was spent with John Selden, the famous jurist, and William Harvey, who discovered how blood pumps through the heart and arteries. According to Aubrey, Hobbes first became acquainted with Selden when he sent him a copy of *Leviathan* as a gift. I think it is plausible that they at least met earlier. Selden was a member of Great Tew and a close friend of Ben Jonson; Jonson was often at Newcastle's estates and at Great Tew, and Hobbes very probably visited Great Tew. Also, Hobbes had expressed his admiration for Selden's *Mare Clausum* in the 1630s. With all of these interconnections, I think they probably met before 1652, although their close association extended from 1652 until 1654, the year that Selden died. Selden admired *Leviathan,* and there are interesting similarities between doctrines in that book and those expressed by Selden in his *Table Talk.* Like Hobbes (on one interpretation), Selden thought that the laws of nature have to be the commands of God. About witches, neither Selden nor Hobbes thought they existed, but both thought that people who pretend to be witches ought to be punished. As Selden put it,

The law against witches does not prove there be any; but it punishes the malice of those people that use such means to take away men's lives. If one should profess that by turning his hat thrice and crying 'Buz', he could take away a man's life (though in truth he could do no such thing) yet this were a just law made by the state, that whosoever should turn his hat thrice and cry 'Buz' with an intention to take away a man's life shall be put to death.[1]

Hobbes expressed the same view in *Leviathan:* "For as for witches, I think not that their witchcraft is any real power, but yet that they are justly punished for the false belief they have, [namely] that they can do such mischief, joined with their purpose to do it if they can."[2]

Aubrey reported secondhand that Hobbes was present at Selden's last illness: "When he [Selden] was near death, the minister was coming to him to assoile [absolve] him: Mr. Hobbes happened to be there; said he, 'What, will you that have wrote like a man, now die like a woman?' So the minister was not let in." This story is sometimes used as evidence of Hobbes's alleged atheism. Even if the story were true – and there are others that contradict it – it is no evidence of atheism. Hobbes was giving Selden advice about what Selden ought to do, given his, not Hobbes's own, principles of living. Also, Protestants are generally suspicious of deathbed conversions and absolutions, because they give the false impression that a ritual has the magical power of getting someone into heaven. Finally, when Hobbes thought he was near death in 1647 he had two Anglican clergymen in attendance, and would have another near him when he actually died.

Concerning Harvey, Hobbes could have met him during the 1620s since both were associated with Bacon at the time. It is possible that a shared dislike for Bacon may have planted the friendship. Harvey said that Bacon wrote philosophy "like a Lord Chancellor." His poor opinion of Bacon's philosophy could have found a sympathetic ear in Hobbes since it is hard to reconcile Bacon's extreme empiricism with Hobbes's rationalism. Harvey never mentions Bacon in his published works; Hobbes's sole mention of Bacon occurs in *Decameron Physiologicum*, published the year before he died.

Hobbes was more generous to Harvey in his public praise than to almost anyone else. In *De Corpore*, he puts Harvey in the small class of great scientists that includes Copernicus, Johannes Kepler, Mersenne, and Gassendi.[3] Perhaps more impressively, in *Six Lessons*,[4] Hobbes compares Harvey favorably to himself: Just as Harvey was insubordinately treated by Moranus, Hobbes was insubordinately treated by Seth Ward. Hobbes and Harvey also shared the honor of being criticized by Alexander Ross. And, in *Dialogus Physicus*, speaking in the voice of one of his alphabetic characters, B, he praised Harvey's great discovery. Of course, he also uses that compliment as the foundation for praising himself. Speaking of himself in the voice of one of his characters, he wrote, "Now however, the same people both confess that Harvey's opinion is true and they are also beginning to accept your beliefs."[5]

Hobbes and Harvey must have been together occasionally during the 1630s when Harvey was doing autopsies on the king's deer. Near the end of his life, Hobbes mentioned these activities: "At the breaking up of a deer, I have seen it plainly in his bowels as long as they were warm. And it is called peristalique motion, and in the heart of a beast newly taken out of his body; and this motion is called systole and diastole. But they are both of them this compounded motion, whereof the former causes the food to wind up and down through the guts, and the later makes the circulation of the blood."[6] (Recall that Hobbes would study human anatomy and be present at dissections conducted by William Petty in the 1640s.) Harvey's biographer speculates that Harvey treated Hobbes in the 1650s. When Harvey died in 1657, he left ten pounds "to my good friend Mr Thomas Hobbes to buy something to keep in remembrance of me."[7]

Hobbes, Selden, and Harvey may have gathered at the salon of Harvey's protégé, Dr. Charles Scarborough (Scarburgh). Hobbes was a welcomed, but not always genial, guest. Here is one report of his behavior:

This Mr. Hobbs, I say, was just come from Paris, in order to print his *Leviathan* at London, to curry favor with the government. He had a good conceit of himself, and was impatient of contradiction. As he was older than any of that convention, he also thought himself wiser; if any one objected against his dictates, he would leave the company in a passion, saying, his business was to teach, not dispute.[8]

The Engagement Controversy

Hobbes's return to England engendered different feelings in different people. Some thought that he was a turncoat who had twisted his political doctrine in *Leviathan* in order to ingratiate himself with the powers that be. According to Edward Nicholas, writing to Lord Hatton, "Mr. Hobbes is at London much caressed, as one that has by his writings justified the reasonableness and righteousness of their [the rebels'] arms and actions."[9] This view is unfair at best but also absurd. Let's begin with the absurdity. On this view, when Hobbes presented Charles II with a handwritten copy of *Leviathan*, he was giving his king a treatise that defended the behavior of the men who had executed his father; and he gave the gift with the hope of promoting his career! Concerning its unfairness, *Leviathan* is filled, as I mentioned before, with promonarchical and antirebellious sentiments, which would not have endeared him to the victorious Parliamentarians. Near the end of that book, Hobbes said that he should have included among his laws of nature this one: "That every man is bound by Nature, as much as in him lies, to protect in war, the authority by which he is himself protected in time of peace."[10] This is tantamount to a defense of the royalists and a declaration that he felt no need to apologize for or retract his support for the king during the Civil War. More important, Hobbes's doctrine in both *The Elements of Law, Natural and Politic* and *De Cive* is consonant with the position that a citizen of a defeated sovereign may submit himself to the conqueror.

Parts of *Leviathan* make the legitimacy of this position even clearer, and it led many people, including royalists stuck in England and wanting to act with integrity, to be grateful for Hobbes's views. In 1656 Hobbes bragged that the doctrine of *Leviathan* "has framed the minds of a thousand gentlemen to a conscientious obedience to present government, which otherwise would have wavered in that point."[11] Weak and politically motivated minds used that statement against him after the Restoration. From a logical point of view, Hobbes should not have suffered for it. Its truth is consistent with everything taught in his political works, and it is not legitimately used as an argument against his loyalty to the king. As he would eventually explain, his argument for loyalty to a conquering army is addressed "only to the king's faithful party and not to any that fought against him." Only those "faithful servants and subjects of his Majesty that had taken his part in the war or otherwise done their utmost endeavor to defend his Majesty's right and person against the rebels" needed some moral and philosophical counseling about how they could in good conscience submit to the king's enemies when, "having no other means of protection, nor for the most part subsistence, they were forced to compound with your [Wallis's] masters and to promise obedience for the saving of their lives and fortunes."[12]

The execution of Charles traumatized Englishmen much more than the assassination of John Kennedy affected Americans or that of Anwar Sadat affected Egyptians. Charles had been killed by the people's representatives, not a private assassin. Also, many Englishmen thought that the king was divinely appointed and that his execution was as much an act of rebellion against God as man. Some grieved over the destruction of an institution that had stood for almost six hundred years. Few were as sanguine as Andrew Marvell when he wrote about the execution in "An Horatian Ode on Cromwell's Return from Scotland:"

> Tis madness to resist or blame
> The force of angry heaven's flame:
> . . . .
> Though justice against fate complain,
> And plead the ancient rights in vain.

Great authors are often not representative authors. On a more mundane level, the execution of the king was patently illegal. Most Englishmen felt, if they did not explicitly know, that the action was against their constitution, according to which the king was above the law. It may have been right for the king to be killed, but no court or Parliament had the right to do it.

Those who suffered the worst pangs of conscience were those who had taken the Solemn League and Covenant (1643), by which they swore to preserve "the honor and happiness of the king's Majesty and his posterity." They were grieved to the bottoms of their souls. Their agony was exacerbated by Parliament's heavy-handed attempt to bring all Englishman into line. In 1649, Parliament required all officeholders to take an "engagement," which was an acknowledgment of the legitimacy of the Commonwealth and a pledge of allegiance to it. At the beginning of 1650, the engagement was extended to all men over the age of eighteen. Women did not count. The prescribed formula was as follows: "I do declare and promise that I will be true and faithful to the Commonwealth of England as it is now established without a king or House of Lords." Technically, a man could avoid the engagement; but if he did, he would have no standing in the courts. He could neither sue nor defend himself against a suit.

The practical problem of deciding whether to engage was dealt with in different ways. Those who were steadfast and refused to engage were typically more upright but less interesting than those who did. Among those who took the engagement, some, like one Dr. Minshen, professed in public that they would not engage and then "crept at night . . . and put [their] hand to the parchment." Many took refuge in casuistry. Some royalists devised an aphorism: "He is a fool that will not take it [the Engagement], and he is a knave that will not break it."[13] One of the more sensible of the casuistic lines of reasoning maintained that people could take the Engagement and be bound "negatively" but not "positively." That is, they would act in conformity with the commands of the Rump Parliament but not endorse it. If they could not in good conscience obey a certain law, then they would accept their punishment without opposition. This is similar to the theory of civil disobedience adopted by the Civil Rights movement in the United States.

It did not take a great deal of integrity, only a reasonable belief in the divine backing of oaths, for those who swore to the covenant to be tortured in conscience. Even many of those who had not sworn the Solemn League and Covenant had bad consciences. Given the illegality of the execution of the king and his very alive son who had asserted his right of kingship, the legality of the Commonwealth was very much in doubt. Nonetheless, to the extent that anything in England looked like it was a government, it was not a king but either the Rump Parliament or its Council of State or the parliamentary army or some conjunction of these. The situation was very confused, and rationalization, if not justification, of the de facto government was sorely needed.

Necessity is the mother of invention, and it is often necessary to invent a moral or political theory when the foundations of government are threatened. Moral and political inventions do not even have to be true; they just have to be reassuring. And often all that is required to make them work is the pretense of belief. Americans, for example, have no problem with, on the one hand, proclaiming that life, liberty, and the pursuit of happiness are inalienable rights, and, on the other hand, supporting capital punishment and incarceration.

Political theorists of several different persuasions, notably Presbyterian and royalist, contributed to the political invention that would fix conflicted consciences. Historically, the most important theory to emerge between 1649 and 1652 is known as the de facto theory. In its simplest form, it is the view that "the power of the sword gives title to government," as expressed by Marchamont Nedham, who was always a good barometer of the political weather.[14] One of the more important versions of what is usually called de factoism, though it strictly is not, focuses on what citizens are morally permitted to do when their previous government has been overthrown. According to this view, people are permitted to obey those commands of the dominant power that would be laws if the government were legitimate. One of the advantages of this theory is that it is silent about what constitutes a legitimate government. It addresses only what is morally permissible. Supporters of the Rump Parliament were not happy with this theory because it implied, without actually asserting, that the Rump was not legitimate.

The forerunner of the de facto literature was Anthony Ascham's *A Discourse: Wherein is Examined, What is Particularly Lawfull during the Confusions and Revolutions of Government*, published in July 1648. Ascham, who had taken the Solemn League and Covenant, was somewhat intellectually daring in maintaining that the parliamentary forces were a usurping power. Nonetheless, he argued, "a man may lawfully submit to and obey . . . unjust force [that] has possessed himself of another's right."[15] Inspired by the work of Hugo Grotius, Ascham argued that obedience was justified by the right to self-preservation. The connection with the foundations of Hobbes's views is obvious; moreover, Ascham had quoted Hobbes's views approvingly. Ascham, whose views were moderate, was nonetheless assassinated by royalists. It is no wonder that Hobbes was concerned about his own welfare on the Continent.

The staunch royalist and proponent of absolute sovereignty, Robert Filmer, also devised a theory to justify obedience to the Commonwealth. In *Directions for Obedience to Governours in Dangerous and Doubtful Times* (1652), he granted that "protection and obedience are reciprocal, so that where the first fails the latter ceases."[16] The inability of the Stuarts to protect Englishmen released the latter from obedience. This raised the question of what government succeeded the Stuarts. Filmer's answer is that the people can obey the usurping power if they do not know of anyone with a "better title to authority."[17] This in effect legitimated obedience to the Rump Parliament or its agents. It rests upon the skeptical proposition: We do not know of any other entity that may be more legitimate.

Filmer's views are relevant to Hobbes's for at least two reasons. First, he cites Hobbes, along with Ascham, Grotius, and John Selden, as people who accept the foundations of his patriarchal theory of sovereignty. Second, he was one of the earliest commentators on *Leviathan*. (He will be discussed in this connection below.) In *Observations Concerning the Original of Government, Upon Mr Hobs Leviathan, Mr Milton Against Salmatius, H. Grotius De Jure Belli* (1652), he said that he thinks that no one else had "so amply and judiciously handled . . . the rights of sovereignty" as Hobbes did. It is worth remarking that Hobbes's law of nature was echoed by Filmer, who pointed out that although it was acceptable to pledge allegiance to a usurper after his victory, prior to it subjects of the defeated sovereign had an obligation to defend him.

One other possible contribution to the Engagement controversy needs to be mentioned before we discuss the role of *Leviathan* directly. In *The Grounds of Obedience and Government*, Thomas White argued in a way that smacked of Hobbism: All men are created equal; government originates from their needs; and the authority of a government terminates when its ability to protect its citizens terminates. This position could be used to provide solace to the Covenanters: Their obligation to protect the king ended with his inability to protect them. One of White's Catholic enemies called him "a patriot even *ultras aras* beyond justice and without due regard to right."[18] Some have maintained that White's book was first published in 1649, that is, before *Leviathan*. But it is more likely that it was first published in 1655 and that Hobbes's political views influenced it. At least, there are no surviving copies of a 1649 edition nor any mention of the book until after 1655. Rather than stealing Hobbes's views, White probably intended to tailor them for a Roman Catholic audience.

This brings us to Hobbes's contribution to the Engagement controversy. Although *Leviathan* is a classic of political theory because it has timeless importance, it was equally a tract of the time. During the Engagement controversy, the catchphrase was "the relation between obedience and government" or some variation of it. Near the end of *Leviathan*, Hobbes says that his goal is nothing other than "what is necessary to the doctrine of Government and Obedience."[19] And at the very end, he states clearly his solution to the controversy: "And because I find diverse English Books lately printed that the Civil Wars have not yet sufficiently taught men in what point of time it is that a subject becomes obliged to the conqueror, . . . [therefore] I say the point of time, wherein a man becomes subject to a conqueror is that point wherein having liberty to submit to him he consents either by express words or by other sufficient sign to be his subject."[20] Hobbes has sometimes been called a de facto theorist because he holds that a person formerly obligated to one sovereign may pledge allegiance to a different sovereign when the former ceases to protect the person. But that fact does not qualify Hobbes as a de facto theorist at all. He actually is concerned with what makes an apparent government legitimate, and his answer is that two things are required: (1) the power to protect people and (2) the consent of the people protected to have that power be its government. As their name implies, de facto theorists did not require (2).

What Hobbes shows is that what may look like a betrayal of one's sovereign is not. Charles II in 1650 and for a decade after was not the sovereign of England because he did not satisfy condition (1). Consequently, ardent, former subjects of the king of England can engage with the Rump Parliament and its minions without scruple. Not only do these erstwhile royalists not violate their consciences or obligations, but they also in effect promote the cause of royalism to the extent feasible, given their situation. Erstwhile royalists who did not take the engagement had all of their estates forfeited to the Rump Parliament. They were therefore in a much weaker position to help the king if he should ever try to return to England than those who had engaged, and submission was the more subversive royalist tactic. Ironically, Hobbes could not have baldly asserted such a thing because his theory excludes every justification of rebellion. Although his rationalization for taking the engagement applied to a large number of royalists, it may have had special significance for his patron Devonshire, who had made peace with Parliament even before the death of the king and thereby saved his estates from confiscation.

In addition to the ones mentioned earlier, there are other passages in *Leviathan* that make clear Hobbes's royalist sympathies. Early in the book, he compares the execution of Charles to the crucifixion of Jesus.

The implication is that the two deaths were equally unjustified. More important than this anecdotal evidence is the simple fact that Hobbes's doctrine in *Leviathan* is the same as that in *De Cive* on the matter of when a conquering power becomes a sovereign.[21]

Leviathan: A Bible for Modern Man

All or almost all of the central points of *Leviathan* had been made by Hobbes in early books and manuscripts. The materialism, mechanism, and absolutism are all there in *The Elements of Law, Anti-White*, and *De Cive*. Still, it is *Leviathan* that deserves to be called 'A Bible for Modern Man' because no other work of his or any of his contemporaries presents such a forceful, eloquent, and comprehensive statement of the doctrine that expresses the spirit of modern thought. It adumbrates a physics, physiology, psychology, morality, politics, and critical theology.

Consonant with good rhetorical practice, the author makes the reader immediately aware that something important and startlingly original is awaiting him. The very first phrase of the Introduction, "Nature (the Art whereby God hath made and governs the world)," may be imitating, if only subconsciously, the opening clause of Genesis: "In the beginning God created the heavens and the earth." If so, then the reader should notice that rhetorically Hobbes has promoted nature above God, because nature is mentioned first. Another startling aspect of the opening phrase is that nature is actually artificial, because art is whatever is made by a person and God made nature. This opening may be seen as deconstructive. The distinction between what is natural and artificial is deeply embedded in our thought, both philosophical and nonphilosophical. But Hobbes in effect denies that the distinction is a proper one. The paradigmatic case of nature, creation, is actually an artifice. So the distinction breaks down.

Also, what is natural typically is supposed to be superior to what is artificial. Our breakfast cereals proclaim, "All natural flavors, no artificial colors or sweeteners," as selling points. Hobbes inverts the value of what is natural and artificial in many places throughout the book. The state of nature is a wretched condition; but the civil state, an artificial construct, is the only redeemer for man on earth (until Jesus returns). In the natural state, human beings are equal. Social and political differentiation arises only with the creation of civil government. In the natural state, everyone is the judge of what is good and evil for himself. That is the state of anarchy. Orderly and decent living requires that there be one standard of good and evil, and Hobbes maintains that only the sovereign can fit the bill. Furthermore, in the state of nature, women are equal to men, and mothers have a better claim to authority over their children than fathers do.

Hobbes's point is not to make his audience's blood boil, or at least not his only point. He wants the recognition of these truths to move his audience to accept his political theory, which will justify all of the socially approved sorts of inequality: monarchs over subjects, males over females, fathers over mothers, parents over children.

The deconstruction continues. The distinction between what is alive and what is a machine is bogus: "For seeing life is but a motion of limbs, the beginning whereof is in some principal part within, why may we not say that all automata (engines that move themselves by springs as does a watch) have an artificial life?"[22] Further, the heart is a pump; the nerves are strings, and the joints are wheels. The outrageousness of characterizing life as nothing but motion and machines as living things should be obvious. Even today, only the most intellectually daring believe that. Sportswriters, talking about an athlete's injured leg, sometimes refer to it as "a bad wheel," but that is just colorful talk.

Hobbes knew what he was doing. He gloried in outraging people with his position. Writing to a friend in 1645, he said this:

My odd opinions are baited. But I am contented with it as believing I have still the better, when a new man is set upon me that knows not my paradoxes but is full of his own doctrine, there is something in the disputation not unpleasant. He thinks he has driven me upon an absurdity when t'is upon some other of my tenets and so from one to another till he wonder and exclaim and at last finds I am of the antipodes of the schools.[23]

Hobbes never lost an adolescent delight of shocking the intellectual establishment.

Another one of the doctrines of the Introduction that would have been offensive to some readers was his claim that human beings imitate God's creation of the world when they create a civil government. Just as God said, "Let there be man," and there was man, humans in effect say, "Let there be a government," and there is a government. This doctrine would not offend his audience in the way it might offend contemporary people. His audience had the thought that God made people in his own image and likeness firmly in mind; so people have some godlike characteristics. Also, Psalm 82 was translated to say that kings were gods, Jesus repeated it (John 10:34), and two respectable books with the title *Men are Gods* were published in 1660. What would be offensive is the idea that within the political sphere, it was the subjects that exercised the divine activity of creating. For those who would accept some analogy between human government and the divine, the standard view was that the sovereign was a kind of god. In several of his speeches and writings, James I professed this view eloquently, even if Parliament was not persuaded:

The state of monarchy is the supremest thing upon earth. For kings are not only God's lieutenants upon earth, and sit upon God's throne, but even by God himself they are called gods. . . . Kings are justly called gods for that they exercise a manner or resemblance of divine power upon earth. For if you will consider the attributes to God, you shall see how they agree in the person of a king. God has power to create, or destroy, make, or unmake at his pleasure, to give life or send death, to judge all and to be judged nor accountable to none; to raise low things and to make high things low at his pleasure, and to God are both soul and body due. And the like power have kings: they make and unmake their subjects; they have power of raising and casting down, of life and of death; judges over all their subjects, and in all cases, and yet accountable to none but God only.[24]

Hobbes's view about the quasi-divine properties of the sovereign is the same as James's. When he says that Leviathan, that is, the government, is "a mortal god to which we owe (under the immortal God) our peace and defense,"[25] he is not saying something unprecedented or blasphemous. The difference between Hobbes and James does not concern the absoluteness of sovereign authority but the political theory that justifies it. James subscribed to the top-down theory of the divine right of kings. Hobbes subscribed to the bottom-up theory of democracy or popular sovereignty. What makes Hobbes odd is not his absolutism but the way he gets to that position. The great royalist and defender of patriarchy, Robert Filmer, praised Hobbes for his treatment of "the rights of sovereignty" in both *De Cive* and *Leviathan*: "no man that I know, has so amply and judiciously handled [this topic]. I consent with him [Hobbes] about the rights of exercising government, but I cannot agree to his means of acquiring it."[26]

Since the basics of Hobbes's political theory have already been discussed, it is appropriate here only to call attention to certain important refinements that appear in *Leviathan*.

The State of Nature

Hobbes had already explained the wretchedness of the natural condition of human beings in *The Elements of Law*. But he sings the sweetest song of that misery in *Leviathan*:

In such condition, there is no place for Industry, because the fruit thereof is uncertain, and consequently no culture of the earth, no navigation, nor use of the commodities that may be imported by sea, no commodious building, no instruments of moving, and removing such things as require much force, no knowledge of the face of the earth, no account of time, no arts, no letters, no society, and which is worst of all, continual fear and danger of violent death; and the life of man is solitary, poor, nasty, brutish and short.

There does not seem to be just one reason why the state of nature is so miserable. It is the result of three elements. First, people will be in competition for the same things. This idea presupposes that the earth is not as bountiful as the island of Tonga, where there are so many coconuts, bananas, and fish easily available that no one needs to fight over food, and the climate is so mild that a grass hut is sufficient protection against the weather. It also presupposes that the population is dense enough that avoiding human contact is not easy. But these are modest assumptions. The second element leading to a conflict of all against all is more interesting. Each person knows that other people may attack him and believes that the best defense is a good offense; that is, he believes that the best strategy for survival is to launch preemptive attacks on anyone who may pose a threat. The operative principle is Do unto others as they are likely to do unto you; but do it first. The result of these mutual suspicions is "diffidence," distrust of everyone for everyone. Because the diffidence is pandemic, even people who would otherwise have no aggressive tendencies are forced by the logic of diffidence to become opportunistic aggressors. Each person must distrust everyone else because everyone else distrusts him. The third element contributing to the war of all against all in the state of nature is the desire that some people have for glory.

According to Hobbes, everyone wants respect: "And upon all signs of contempt or undervaluing naturally endeavors, as far as he dares (which among them that have no common power to keep them in quiet, is far enough to make them destroy each other), to extort a greater value from his contemners by dommage [harm], and from others by the example."[27]

In general, Hobbes wants to show how wretched human life would be without laws. Oddly enough, he never says this straight out. Instead, he makes much of the consequences of the absence of laws. The first is that since nothing would be forbidden, everything would be permitted. From this it follows that a person has a right to all things.

Hobbes's analysis of the state of nature may apply more obviously to international relations than to individuals. Nations compete with each other for scarce resources; they distrust each other because they are distrusted, and most want to be better thought of than they are. The logic of the cold war between the United States and the former Soviet Union illustrates the second element brilliantly. Each feared and was suspicious of the other in large part because each knew that the other was afraid of and suspicious of it. If it were relevant, we could also derive along Hobbesian lines the strategy pursued by the United States of MAD (mutually assured destruction).

The Principle of Self-Preservation

Almost everyone immediately recognizes the right to self-defense, but people are slower to see that this right presupposes the right to self-preservation. One argument that seventeenth-century thinkers might have put forth for the right of self-preservation is this: Nature does nothing in vain. If there is a natural desire for something, then there is a right to fulfill that desire. There is a natural desire for self-preservation. Therefore, there is a right to self-preservation. One might also have argued that it is obvious that since God creates people, he wants them to live; so everyone has a right to preserve himself.

Hobbes prefers a more controversial line. According to him, everyone has a desire for self-preservation; if a person desires something and there is no law against acting to satisfy that desire, then the person has a right to satisfy it. Whoever has a right to an end has a right to the means to that end. Therefore, anyone who has the right to self-preservation has the right to the means of achieving self-preservation. If that requires killing another person, possibly even eating him, then so be it.

The Right of Nature

Everyone in the state of nature has the right of nature, that is, either the right to everything or alternatively the right to at least everything she needs to survive. There is apparently a difference between these alternatives. Hobbes sometimes slides from one to the other because he thinks that in the state of nature the one entails the other. If Beth is accumulating what strikes Alan as an excessive amount of stuff, and Alan challenges Beth's claim to it on the grounds that she does not need it to survive, she can respond that she does need it. The matter is thus in dispute. Now, who is there to decide the issue in the state of nature? No one. Since there are no mutually agreed upon judges, everyone is his or her own judge about what is necessary for survival. So the difference between the right to everything needed for survival and the right to everything collapses. Hobbes has a clever refutation of Alan's challenge. He says that if Alan can challenge Beth's judgment, then, since turnabout is fair play, she can challenge his judgment that her judgment is mistaken. Thus, if his challenge has any merit, then it does not have any merit.

There are two basic ways of establishing that people in the state of nature have a right to everything. One depends on the definition of rights as liberties to act and of laws as constraints on action. Because there are no laws in the state of nature, there are no constraints on action and hence one has every liberty to act; that is, one has the right to all things.

The second begins with the proposition that whoever has a right to the end has a right to the means to that end. Everyone has the right to self-preservation, and thus everyone has the right to the means to that end. Since anything in nature may be necessary for survival, a person has the right to everything in nature. The preceding sentence of this argument is obviously fallacious. Neither the shift from 'anything' to 'everything' nor from 'possibly' to 'is' will wash. Given that a person has permission to choose *anything* from a box, it does not follow that he can choose *everything* in the box. And given that Smith is possibly at home, it does not follow that Smith is at home. I think that underlying Hobbes's argument here is the one explored above. If each individual is the judge of what he needs for survival, then his judgment that he needs everything cannot be gainsaid. And if a person may need something for survival, then he can judge that he does need that thing for survival.

The Law of Nature

Part of contemporary ideology is that the more liberty, the better. Hobbes had to contend with the origin of that view. His goal was to show that having complete liberty is a horrible state to be in. Safety, happiness, and all the comforts of civilization depend on the restriction of liberty by laws.

He divides laws into two types: natural and civil. The civil laws depend for their existence on the natural ones. These laws of nature are eternal; the civil laws come into and go out of existence as the sovereign changes his commands. Sometimes Hobbes equates the natural and civil laws with divine and human laws, respectively. This alternative nomenclature has caused problems for interpreters. If the laws of nature are identical with the divine laws, then the laws of nature must be commands of God. This seems to be his reflective view in *Leviathan* – or so I and some other scholars have argued – but it is not the view that he held in his earlier two political works. There, his considered view was that the laws of nature are nothing but "the dictates of reason" and would exist even if God did not exist.[28] In *Elements of Law*, he had said, "There can therefore be no other law of nature than reason." This is a rather unsophisticated view, which he would abandon in *Leviathan:* Human beings find out what the law of nature is by reason, but reason is not literally the law. Hobbes probably adopted this early position from Grotius, who was widely admired and discussed at Great Tew. I think that Hobbes moved away from the Grotian position in *Leviathan* because he came to see that the laws of nature construed solely as dictates of reason would not have the force they need to constrain human behavior. If the laws of nature were merely dictates of reason, people would not follow them. The emotions to depend on are fear and hope: "The passions that incline men to peace are fear of death, desire of such things as are necessary to commodious living, and a hope by their industry to obtain them."[29] Most scholars disagree with my interpretation of *Leviathan*. They think that Hobbes did not really believe that the laws of nature were necessarily commands of God, but only said so as a sop to theists or in order to garner a measure of respectability.

The First Law of Nature

The list of the laws of nature in *Leviathan* is substantially the same as that in *De Cive*. However, there is an interesting difference between the first law of nature in *De Cive* compared with what it becomes in *Leviathan*, namely, "the Fundamental Precept of Reason." This fundamental precept consists of the first law of nature and the right of nature. What Hobbes may have wanted this distinction to do was to make the choices open to people more stark: peace or war; law or rights (liberties). Many Parliamentarians had used the rhetoric of rights, as in "The Petition of Right." This rhetoric had landed England and Scotland into a decade of Civil War, followed by a decade of unpopular and unstable governments.

Laying Down the Right to All Things

Since everyone has a right to everything in the state of nature, conflict is inevitable, as we have seen. Anything consumable that one person wants to use for his own benefit conflicts with another person's desire to use that same thing for his benefit. It follows that peace requires that people lay down their right to all things. In other words, in the end of liberty you will find the beginning of peace.

The clause "people lay down their right to all things" is ambiguous. It can mean either (1) that a person gives up some of his rights, so that he no longer has a right to everything, or (2) that a person gives up every right he has, so that he is left with no rights. Hobbes waffles between which sense he means depending on what he wants or needs to prove. Sense (1) is perfectly reasonable, so Hobbes tends to trade on it when he wants to persuade people of the wisdom of his system. But (1) will never get one to absolute sovereignty. To the extent that a subject keeps some rights the sovereign's authority is limited. Consequently, when Hobbes wants to prove the necessity of absolute sovereignty, he gives the impression that the reader has committed himself to (2). It is plausible that Hobbes preferred sense (2) in *The Elements of Law* because he was trying to make resistance to the king's policies indefensible. Of course, (2) is unacceptable to everyone except totalitarians and martinets, and it is not even consistent with Hobbes's basic principle that the universal desire and right of self-preservation is the foundation of political theory. So, even as he is using (2) for his purposes, he will sometimes throw in a disclaimer to the effect of denying that (2) means what it says: "And therefore there be some rights which no man can be understood by any words or other signs to have abandoned or transferred."[30] Instead, (2) means that a person gives up every right he has except the right to self-preservation. This exception may sound innocent, but it is not, because, by Hobbes's own reasoning, a person never can be sure of what he may need for his self-preservation, and that is one reason why he has a right to all things. The one thousand dollars I pay in income taxes may not appear to be necessary to my survival now, but who knows what the future will bring? Next year I may need exactly that one thousand dollars to survive. It is no good for the defender of Hobbes to reply that one should only think about what is necessary for survival now, because Hobbes often rightly points out that much human misery is caused by satisfying immediate desires and not thinking long term. I think that the line of reasoning I have been exploring reveals a basic incoherence in Hobbes's theory. But let's not worry about that. I am here to praise Hobbes, not to bury his theory.

Egoism and Altruism

More than anything else, Hobbes has a reputation as a philosophical egoist. It comes from statements such as this remark from *The Elements of Law:* "every man's end being some good to himself."[31] This astounded his contemporaries as much as it enraged them. The Reverend Jasper Mayne once saw Hobbes give some money to a beggar. He suggested that Hobbes's charity contradicted his theory:

> He [Hobbes], beholding him [a beggar] with eyes of pity and compassion, put his hand in his pocket and gave him 6d. Said a divine (scil. Dr. Jasper Mayne) that stood by, 'Would you have done this if it had not been Christ's command?' 'Yes', he [Hobbes] replied. 'Why?' quoteth the other. 'Because,' said he, 'I was in pain to consider the miserable condition of the old man, and now my alms, giving him some relief, does also ease me.'

Possible but not plausible.

What Hobbes said on other occasions about his own behavior and the character of other people is even harder to square with his theory. In a letter of October 1646, he assured Sorbière that he would act only in the best interests of his friends. No egoism is expressed there. And in the dedication to *Leviathan* he said that Sidney Godolphin's sociability was "inherent" and part of his "generous constitution."[32]

There is no way to eliminate the contradiction between egoistic and nonegoistic statements completely. But some things can be said to soften it. One is that a distinction should be drawn between tautological egoism and selfish egoism. Tautological egoism is the view that every act is caused by some desire of the agent, and everyone acts in order to satisfy that desire. This is interesting, harmless, and true. Mother Teresa's charity was caused by her desire to help other people. Selfish egoism is the view that everyone acts only with the desire to benefit himself. This doctrine is interesting, dangerous, and false. At various times, Hobbes says things that sound like one or the other. How he phrases his egoism usually depends on the point he is trying to make. The formulation of tautological egoism comes in handy when he is trying to persuade his audience of the truth of egoism. How can it be false? Selfish egoism comes in handy when he is trying to persuade his audience of the necessity of absolute sovereignty. If people are as self-centered as selfish egoism suggests, having the strongest government seems a prudent policy.

Rhetorically, then, it makes sense for Hobbes to argue for tautological egoism and then pretend that selfish egoism was proved when he argues for absolute sovereignty. But Hobbes does not always proceed in that way. Sometimes, he starts right in with selfish egoism. In those cases, his philosophy sounds daring and dangerous. Whichever way he proceeds, equivocating on 'egoism' is logically objectionable.

The Wealth of a Sovereign and His Subjects

James I had been a spendthrift. All the while he was crying to Parliament for more money, he was spending enormous amounts on private entertainment. Charles I was not a spendthrift, but he did not manage his money well, and his resources would not have been sufficient to get the job done even if he had been a better manager. The ancient English ideal that a king must "live of his own," that is, live on his private wealth, was already a thing of the past, though most people did not recognize it.

The knowledge that the people had of Stuart profligacy explains to a large degree their resentment of various taxes. It was obvious to almost everyone that there is a clear difference between the wealth of a nation and the wealth that the king and his court control and spend. Yet Hobbes could not see the difference. In *The Elements of Law*, he argues that the wealth of sovereign and subject is symbiotic:

[S]uperfluous riches . . . so belong to the sovereign, as they must also be in the subject; and so to the subject, as they must also be in the sovereign. For the riches and treasures of the sovereign is the dominion he has over the riches of his subjects. . . . That distinction therefore of government, that *there is one government for the good of him that governs, and another for the good of them that be governed,* . . . is not right.[33]

This claim would convince no one not inclined to believe it. He was preaching to the court.

To the objection that a monarch takes from his subjects in order to enrich his own "children, kindred, and favorites," Hobbes's response is that there are even more of these in aristocracies, so the expense is even greater. An aristocracy is like "twenty monarchs."[34] And democracies are the worst because everyone is squandering the state's wealth on everyone else. Presumably, Hobbes expects someone to believe this.

The Burden of Being a Sovereign

In a commonwealth, only the sovereign has liberty, and his liberty is absolute; only the sovereign has authority, and his authority is unlimited; only the sovereign ultimately owns property, and he owns everything he controls. Although these features would make the benefits section of a job description for a sovereign sound very attractive, Hobbes makes the case that a sovereign is terribly burdened and deserves both the sympathy and unbounded assistance of his subjects. The first burden of a sovereign is that he has the "continual care and trouble about the business of other men, that are his subjects." As if that were not enough, his life is in continual danger. He is the head of the commonwealth, and that is the body part "against which the stroke of the enemy most commonly is directed." How prescient he was! He might have mentioned that the sovereign is vulnerable because he is in the state of nature with respect to every other sovereign. His liberty comes at the price of not being in a covenantal relation with other people. In contrast with the sovereign, subjects, he says in *The Elements of Law*, suffer from no "inconveniences of government."[35]

Theological Views

Already in *The Elements of Law*, Hobbes had proclaimed the essence of Christianity to be the belief that Jesus is the Christ. In Chapter 4, we saw this as his solution to the problem that vexed the Great Tew circle: Given the varying interpretations of the Bible, is there anything that can be considered the constant and indispensable teaching of Christianity? Even if some disagreed with his answer, it was not generally offensive. In *De Cive*, Hobbes said more about religion. He asserted the supremacy of the secular sovereign in matters of religion but kept a place for the authority of religious experts, possibly independent of the sovereign. This was good Anglicanism. By the Act of Supremacy, the monarch was the head of the church, but the clergy had an honored role. So *De Cive* was generally well received by court clergy.

Like the serpent that slithered onto the scene after the bucolic description of Adam and Eve in the garden, Hobbes's *Leviathan* slithered and seemed to choke off Christianity. Some of his most objectionable religious doctrines concerned the nature of religion; the nature of revelation; the nature and reliability of prophets; the nature and credibility of miracles; the offices of Jesus Christ; the authority of the Bible; the composition of the Bible; the geography of heaven and the kingdom of God; hell; and the dangers of the Roman Catholic Church. These topics will be discussed now seriatim.

The Nature of Religion. In *Leviathan*, religion and true religion are appropriately defined. Religion is "fear of power invisible, feigned by the mind or imagined from tales publicly allowed." True religion is "fear of power invisible . . . when the power imagined is truly such as we imagine."[36] His supposed definition of 'superstition' however, was inflammatory: Superstition is "fear of invisible power . . . imagined from tales . . . not allowed." It follows from this definition that Christianity was superstition in ancient Roman for two hundred years and that Islam is not a superstition in Turkey. The standard interpretation of his passage is that Hobbes was trying to subvert revealed religion in general by it. I find that view implausible. How could a definition, especially an obviously defective one, refute a substantive position? A defective definition raises questions about the competence of the author, not suspicions about what is defined. Also, Hobbes knew what the correct definition of superstition was. In *De Cive*, he had defined it as "fear of invisible things when it is severed from right reason."[37] I think that Hobbes was being sardonic in *Leviathan*. He knew that he was not giving a genuine definition of 'superstition', but had a rhetorical purpose in describing the usage of the word.

People used the word as if it meant any religious doctrine that disagreed with the speaker. He had seen how people had used the word 'superstition' and how much destruction such use had brought on in both the Thirty Years War and the English Civil War. He could control himself during the former war since it barely affected England, but he could not after the latter one, which destroyed his country. He was indirectly trying to get people to reflect on their usage.

In Chapter 12 of *Leviathan*, Hobbes claims that religion, like language, is distinctive of human beings. Nonhuman animals are wholly absorbed in quotidian pursuits. In contrast, human beings look at causal chains that extend indefinitely into the past and future. There are two main elements relating to the human preoccupation with causation to consider here. First, people are curious about the causes of past events, especially those related to their own lives. They want to know why something happened exactly at the time it did and not earlier or later. Second, believing that every event has a cause, people posit or invent invisible causes when they cannot find a visible one. The first element makes people anxious. They worry about what is going to happen to them and when it will happen. Because the past is a good, though not infallible, indicator of the future, they often look to past events to predict and anticipate future ones. The second element influences the kind of causal explanations they come up with. When these two elements are allowed to direct human musings, they invariably generate false religions. People invent the oddest kinds of invisible causes to explain events and then worship them as gods in order to enhance their future prospects. Their minds darkened by their fears, these people are led to affirm such contradictory things as that God or the gods are "incorporeal spirits." In contrast, the correct way to come to believe in "one God eternal, infinite, and omnipotent" is to detach oneself from one's own self-interests and passions and to reason according to the principles of cause and effect. Given that each event has a cause, and each cause is an event that itself needs a cause, "there must be . . . one First Mover, that is, a first and an eternal cause of all things, which is that which men mean by the name of God."[38] Further, since humans cannot figure out what the nature of this first cause is, one rightly concludes that he is incomprehensible.

There are two kinds of true religions: natural and revealed. Although humans are capable of discovering and practicing in accord with true,

natural religion, in fact almost every human being, left to his own resources, would end up superstitious. Hobbes was following Calvin, who
put the point more acerbically:

[S]carcely one man in a hundred is met with who fosters [true religion]. . . .
Religion is thus the beginning of all superstitions, not in its own nature, but
through the darkness which has settled down upon the minds of men, and which
prevents them from distinguishing between idols and the true God. . . . What
happens except that religion degenerates into a thousand chimeras of superstition; and consciences pervert every act of judgment.[39]

The firm path to correct religion, according to Hobbes, comes through
revelation. There was only one correct revelation, the one that goes from
Moses (or Abraham) to Jesus.

The Nature of Revelation. Corresponding to natural and revealed religion, there is a distinction between two ways in which God talks to
humans. First, he talks to humans naturally through reason, "the natural
word of God."[40] By using reason, people can deduce the laws of natural
religion, namely, the laws of nature. Second, God talks to humans in
revealed religion through divine revelation. It is not difficult to define
"revelation." It is the message that God gives to individual human beings.
What is difficult is figuring out whether a purported revelation is genuine.

Revelations might be divided into those that are immediate and those
that are mediate. Immediate revelations are those in which God speaks
directly to some human being. Only the most privileged prophets, such as
Moses and Jesus, ever had such an experience. Mediate revelations are
those in which God speaks to people through some other human being.
The privileged prophets excepted, everyone relies on mediate revelations.
Anyone who believes in the Bible relies on mediate revelation because the
Bible records the words of human beings who purported to have immediate revelations from God.

For any purported mediate revelation, a person is free not to accept it
as a genuine revelation. To do so never amounts to rejecting God, but only
the purported prophet:

For if I should not believe all that is written by historians of the glorious acts of
Alexander or Caesar, I do not think the ghosts of Alexander or Caesar had any just
cause to be offended, or anybody else but the historian. If Livy say the Gods made
once a cow speak, and we believe it not, we distrust not God therein, but Livy. So

that it is evident that whatsoever we believe upon no other reason than what is drawn from authority of men only and their writings, whether they be sent from God or not, is faith in men only.[41]

What about immediate revelation? As a matter of fact, God usually revealed himself supernaturally to people in visions and dreams. But from that one cannot conclude that if a person has a vision of God or dreams of God, that God is in fact revealing anything to that person. Hobbes astutely points out that to say 'God appeared to me in a dream' means the same thing as 'I dreamed that God appeared to me'. This latter statement obviously has no evidential value whatsoever any more than 'I dreamed that Napoleon appeared to me' does. To someone who claims that God sometimes appears to people who are awake, Hobbes would respond that people who are asleep sometimes think that they are awake. And which is more probable, that a person who is asleep thinks that God is appearing to him or that God is genuinely appearing to the person? Obviously the former. It seems to follow that no one can ever know that God really appeared to him. Yet Hobbes never denies that revelation has occurred and says, "How God speaks to a man immediately may be understood by those well enough to whom he has spoken."[42]

Sometimes Hobbes maintains that God communicated to Moses in some unspecified but unique way and thus his revelations are not subject to the skeptical worries just explained. In other places, however, he seems to take this back and says that God appeared to Moses in "a more clear vision than was given to other prophets." One thing is clear: No one, not even Moses, could have seen God's nature, because to say this "is to deny His infiniteness, invisibility, and incomprehensibility."[43]

The Bible uses various locutions to convey God's direct communication with people, but these cannot be taken literally. If God literally spoke to human beings, then he would have a mouth, teeth, and a tongue. And since God made man in his image, someone might argue that he had a body similar to human beings and that he made the same use of the parts. This is objectionable because "many of them [are] so uncomely, as it would be the greatest contumely in the world to ascribe to them."[44] Instead, the proper way to interpret talk about God's vision and speech is honorifically.

We have been using the notion of a prophet in exploring the logic of revelation. Now something should be said about prophets themselves.

Prophets. Hobbes's treatment of prophets is by and large deflating. One way of diminishing the importance of prophets is to show that the concept is so broad that prophets are all over the place and consequently have no special significance. Every high priest was a prophet. Anyone who praises God "in psalms and holy songs," women included, is a prophet. Any spokesman is a prophet. And Hobbes is happy to concede that even his opponent Bramhall is a prophet, just like the high priest, Caiaphas, who "prophesied that one man [Jesus] should die for his nation."[45]

Prophets who foretell the future usually are only part-time prophets, like the witch of Endor, and such soothsayers do not even have to be truth sayers to be prophets. Hobbes likes to tell the story of the four hundred prophets who predicted that the king of Israel would win a battle against his enemies; only one prophet, Michaiah, and he reluctantly, predicted that the king would be killed. And the king was killed. So prophets are unreliable, and majority rule obviously is not a good method for winnowing the reliable from the unreliable ones. But if that is not a good method, what is? In fact, there is none. Hoping to rely on prophets is even worse than it looks. The four hundred mistaken prophets may have been well intentioned but inept. Often, prophets are liars. We know this because God himself says it: "The prophets, says the Lord by Jeremy, chapter 14, verse 14, prophesy lies in my name. I sent them not, neither have I commanded them, nor spake unto them, they prophesy to you a false vision, a thing of naught, and the deceit of their heart."[46] God goes on to tell people not to obey prophets.

The idea of a reliable prophet is a backward-looking concept. People only know who the reliable prophets are after the fact, and then it is too late. None of this entails that there is no such thing as true and reliable prophets. Indeed, Jews, Christians, and Muslims now believe that Moses, Isaiah, Elijah, and Jeremiah, to name a few, were. The problem is epistemological, not ontological. The reliable prophets often predict doom, are not heeded by their audiences, and then become celebrated when the people are destroyed and have nothing left but bitter memories. In *De Cive*, Hobbes said, "the Israelites were commanded not to account any man for a true prophet but him whose prophecies were answered by the events. And hence peradventure it is that the Jews esteemed the writings of those whom they slew when they prophesied for prophetic afterwards; that is to say, for the word of God."[47]

If it is impossible to know the difference between a true and a false prophet, must people be completely agnostic about them? No. Now, just as in biblical times, a person is

bound to make use of his natural reason, to apply to all prophecy those rules which God has given use to discern the true from the false. Of which rules, in the Old Testament, one was conformable doctrine to that which Moses the sovereign prophet had taught them; and the other the miraculous power of foretelling what God would bring to pass. . . . And in the New Testament there was but one only mark, and that was the preaching of this doctrine, that Jesus is the Christ, that is, the king of the Jews, promised in the Old Testament.[48]

There are three main elements in this advice. First, reason in effect becomes superior to prophecy because reason judges it. Second, Hobbes affirms what he takes to be the essence of Christianity, the confession that Jesus is the Messiah. Third, as Hobbes makes explicit because it may not be immediately evident, "every man therefore ought to consider who is the sovereign prophet, that is to say, who it is, that is God's vicegerent on earth and has next under God the authority of governing Christian men, and to observe for a rule that doctrine, which in the name of God, he commands to be taught." In short, obey your local sovereign. Failing to do so leads to "destroying all laws, both divine and human, reduc[ing] all order, government, and society to the first chaos of violence and civil war."[49]

Miracles. During the Reformation and Counter-Reformation, Protestants were very suspicious of miracles, whereas Roman Catholics championed them in certain circumstances. The Roman Catholic Church was not happy with miraculous claims made by people who wanted to initiate some new practice or doctrine into the church or to exercise some authority independently of the church. These people were always a threat and were invariably condemned. Even today the Roman Church is reluctant to declare anything a miracle, and when they do, there is always some institutional control over it. The greatest miracle recognized by the Roman Church and one fully under its control was that of the Mass. According to the Roman Church, a miracle occurs when ordinary bread and wine are consecrated during the worship service; it becomes completely transformed into the body and blood of Christ, through the agency of the priest. Since the office of the priest depends on the church, the performance of miracles, at least the greatest miracle, is under its jurisdiction. No individual person and no secular authority can compete with that power, even if the power to forgive sins were left out. It was in the interests then of both Protestant reformers and secular leaders to deny or otherwise undermine the claim of the Roman Church.

One way to do this was to affirm that miracles had ceased centuries before. Martin Luther and John Calvin each did this in his own way, and both denied the Roman Catholic theory of bread and wine transubstantiated into the body and blood of Christ. The view that revelation had ceased with the death of the last apostle was well established, and it was natural to extend that view to include the claim that miracles ended with the death of the last apostle. What point could there be in having miracles once revelation was complete, not to mention the salvific action of Jesus? And so Hobbes, along with Thomas Browne and other Protestants, maintained that miracles no longer occurred, or at least very rarely. In 1668, Hobbes investigated the case of a woman who supposedly had not eaten anything for more than eight months. He describes the situation matter of factly and withholds a definitive opinion: "I cannot therefore deliver any judgment in the case. The examining whether such a thing as this be a miracle belongs (I think) to the Church."[50]

Deciding whether an event is a miracle is within the competence of the religious authorities. But giving a definition and explaining how miracles might fit into a scientific view of the world are jobs for a philosopher. Hobbes defines a miracle as an "admirable work of God, for the benefit of the elect, usually done to reveal the mission of a prophet for their salvation."[51] A work is admirable if it is unprecedented or rarely occurs and one cannot imagine what natural events might have caused it. Since the consecration of bread and wine in Christian services regularly occurs, it cannot involve a miracle. Unique events, of course, are not thereby miraculous. The first gymnast to perform a standing backward flip did not do anything miraculous, because it was easy enough to see what natural causes were involved. Hobbes's reflective view is that only God performs miracles. His intention is to keep the pride of human beings in check. They might be God's instruments in performing miracles, but they are not the doers of them. Hobbes sometimes verbally slips and says that Pharaoh's priest performed miracles, but the slip is not significant. The biblical language itself often gives the impression that the priests are performing the miracles, and it is normal conversational practice to abbreviate, 'The X seemed to do Y' as 'The X did Y'.

Miracles are not for everyone and are not magic tricks, according to Hobbes. They are for the elect only and usually have a divine purpose. Usually it is to give people evidence that a particular person is a true prophet.[52] Occasionally, a miracle has neither purpose, for example, the first rainbow, which was a sign that the world would never again be destroyed by flood.

Only the first rainbow was a miracle.[53] Subsequent ones lacked the requisite novelty. The example of the first rainbow is important for several reasons. First, it shows how the concept of a miracle can be incorporated into a scientific view of the world. Noah's rainbow was miraculous because no one at the time could imagine what natural phenomena might have caused this. But this is not to say that it had no natural causes. In fact, the physical laws explaining the rainbow had only recently been discovered when Hobbes used this as an example. Many contemporary biblical scholars have attempted to give naturalistic explanations for strange biblical events, which they continue to view as miraculous: Dry land in the Red Sea was caused by an unusually strong dry wind; the multiplication of loaves and fishes was caused by people sharing food that they had hidden in their clothing; and so on. What is required for a miracle is not that there is no natural explanation for it, but that its witnesses not have one.

To witness a miracle is to admit to ignorance. The more one knows about the world, the less apt one is to construe something as one: "And thence it is that ignorant and superstitious men make great wonders of those works which other men, knowing to proceed from nature (which is not the immediate but the ordinary work of God) admire none at all."[54] Hobbes is exploiting what he takes the pride of human beings to be: Few people will be willing to proclaim that they have seen a miracle if the upshot is that they are declaring their own ignorance.

As in his treatment of so many theological concepts, Hobbes manages to have things both ways. It is important for religion that there were revelations, true prophets, and miracles, and according to Hobbes there were. But it is important for political and religious stability that allegedly new revelations, prophets, and miracles not intrude. Hobbes accommodates both. One might suspect him of being disingenuous. But that is worse than unfair to him; it is implausible. One goal of a sincere religious philosopher is to reconcile science and religion. And the simplest explanation for Hobbes's behavior is that that was what he was trying to do, just as he said he was. He failed, but I do not know of anyone who has succeeded. It is the project that dooms the efforts.

The Offices of Jesus Christ. Medieval theologians recognized three offices of Jesus. Aquinas lists them as lawgiver, king, and priest. But Calvin made the threefold distinction into an important theological theme; he lists the offices as priest, prophet, and king. Following Calvin, Hobbes made the three offices a theological theme, but his list is different: redeemer or savior; pastor, counselor, or teacher; and king. As redeemer, Jesus "ransomed" human beings held captive by their sins. In adopting the terminology of the ransom theory of redemption, Hobbes is doing three things. First, he is rejecting the Roman Catholic theory of 'satisfaction', according to which human beings needed to repay a debt owed to God. This theory was offensive to Hobbes because it suggested that sin was a commodity that could be bought or sold, something "vendible," as he says.[55] In effect, the theory holds that humans bought sin on credit and only needed to pay for it in order to be back in the divine storekeeper's good graces. Second, unlike earlier ransom theories, Hobbes does not make Satan the person to whom the ransom is due. Such theories are Manichaean, and Hobbes was strongly anti-Manichaean. God simply requires a ransom. Third, the work of redemption is completely attributed to God's mercy, in contrast with the Roman Catholic view that found a place for God's justice. According to the standard Catholic view, once Jesus paid a fair price for human sin, justice obliged God to let humans into heaven.

Since Jesus was the redeemer, he could not have been king when he was on earth. He will become king and reign eternally when he returns to earth. (This point will be explained more fully below.) But if Jesus is not yet king and was not king while he walked the earth, what was his status on earth, other than being the redeemer? He was a pastor, in the sense of being a teacher, according to Hobbes. And what Jesus taught was obedience to the sovereign: "He taught all men to obey . . . them that sat in Moses seat: He allowed them to give Caesar his tribute and refused to take upon himself to be a judge. How then could his words or actions be seditious or tend to the overthrow of their then civil government?"[56] Implicit in these remarks is a rhetorical question: Why do Christian citizens think it is good for them to overthrow a Christian government when Jesus did not even try to overthrow a pagan one?

The Authority of the Bible. Hobbes's appeal to the Bible to settle various matters about religion invites the question, "How do we know that Scripture deserves as much respect as the voice of God?" To put the question another way, "How do we know the Scriptures to be the word of God?" Hobbes's answer in *The Elements of Law* is that both forms of the question have a false presupposition. It is not a matter of knowledge at all. It is a matter of faith.[57] If it were not a matter of faith, then the Bible would be wrong when it says that faith will cease when people get to heaven.

In *Leviathan*, Hobbes's attack on the appropriateness of the two questions about knowledge and the Bible become sharper. Only the person to whom God immediately revealed a part of the Bible can know that God is its author. Since none of us received this revelation, the questions are beside the point. It is a matter of belief, not knowledge. But even here there is a confusion. To ask why people believe something is to ask for the causes of their belief. And to expect there to be one cause of belief for everyone is ridiculous. One person believes because his minister or parents told him to believe, another because the liturgy is beautiful, another because the doctrine is comforting, still another because she finds it plausible.

The crucial issue, according to Hobbes, is the authority by which the Bible is made law. Those parts of the Bible that are identical with the laws of nature obviously have their authority from God.[58] The remaining parts have their authority from the only other entity that has authority, namely, the secular sovereign. Just as a commonwealth is given unity by the person of the sovereign, so also is a church. A Christian commonwealth, such as England, is a commonwealth in which the secular and religious heads are the same. If the church were not united in one person, it would not have any authority at all, because human authority is given and created by the people. And without authority, the church could neither command nor act. Up to this point Hobbes's doctrine was the conventional English one, as codified in the Act of Supremacy.

When Hobbes goes on to deny that there is a "universal church," he would begin to pick up some significant opposition, because the idea of a "catholic church" had been a truism for almost fifteen hundred years. But even here his explanation of what he meant would have kept most Englishmen on his side. Christian churches are national churches. This was the position endorsed by various Protestant nations, sometimes by French kings, and the city of Venice (during its fight against Rome).

Hobbes lost a significant amount of support when he declared the
secular sovereign to be a priest. This was an innovation of *Leviathan*. In
his earlier works, *The Elements of Law* and *De Cive*, Hobbes allowed the
clergy enough independence from the sovereign to satisfy the bishops of
the Church of England. In these works, Hobbes argued that since the
Bible depends on faith, and faith is trust, Christians need to put their
trust in "the holy men of God's church succeeding one another from the
time of those that saw the wondrous works of God Almighty in the flesh."
Furthermore, these same men are the proper authority to resolve any
dispute that may arise over the correct interpretation of the Bible, as long
as they do not deny the fundamental point of Christianity, namely, that
"Jesus Christ is come in the flesh."[59] This view would raise hosannas
from any bishop.

And not to leave any doubt about the divine element in all of this,
Hobbes goes on to say:

[N]or does this imply that God is not the worker and efficient cause of faith or
that faith is begotten in man without the spirit of God; for all those good opinions
which we admit and believe, though they proceed from hearing; and hearing from
teaching, both which are natural, yet they are the work of God. For all the works
of nature are his and they are attributed to the Spirit of God.[60]

In *De Cive*, he acknowledges in religious leaders a special competence:

But for the deciding of questions of faith, that is to say, concerning God, which
transcend human capacity, we stand in need of a divine blessing (that we may not
be deceived at least in necessary points), to be derived from Christ himself by the
imposition of hands. For, seeing to the end we may attain to eternal salvation we
are obliged to a supernatural doctrine, and which therefore it is impossible for us
to understand; to be left so destitute as that we can be deceived in necessary
points, is repugnant to equity. This infallibility our Savior Christ promised (in
those things which are necessary to salvation) to his apostles until the day of
judgment; that is to say, to the apostles and pastors succeeding the apostles, who
were to be consecrated by the imposition of hands. He therefore who has the
sovereign power in the city is obliged as a Christian where there is any question
concerning the mysteries of faith to interpret the Holy Scriptures by clergymen
lawfully ordained.[61]

Why did Hobbes change his view in *Leviathan* and deny the special
competence and partial independence of the clergy? A large part of it, I
think, is the simple reason that he came to believe that it was true. Some

think that the larger part of the explanation is that he was trying to conciliate Oliver Cromwell and the Rump Parliament. To the extent that this explanation makes sense, it shows Hobbes to be accommodating his doctrine to the reality of the national church that survived in a reduced state. The church was as subordinate to Parliament as it had ever been to the king, as the Westminster Assembly had learned to its consternation. When the assembly had proposed a confession to be the standard of orthodoxy, Parliament thanked them for their interest and told them to mind their own business. In other words, Hobbes's view, far from looking like the novel doctrine of a fifth-column atheist, was an ideological defense of the status quo.

The alternative to thinking that the public authority must be the only religious authority is to think that there could be a private authority grounded in a revelation from God. But this view is absurd, according to Hobbes, because human beings "out of pride and ignorance take their own dreams and extravagant fancies and madness for testimonies of God's spirit, or out of ambition pretend to such divine testimonies falsely and contrary to their own consciences."[62] Acceptance of alleged private revelations as normative is the road to anarchy.

The Composition of the Bible. Hobbes was the first person to argue in print that Moses was not the author of most of the Pentateuch. His argument relied on premises of internal criticism; that is, he was able to show that features of the biblical text itself indicate that much of the Pentateuch was written long after the death of Moses. For example, Moses could not have written the last chapter of Deuteronomy, because it records his death and burial. If one objects that details of his death could have been revealed by God to Moses before his death, Hobbes has the response that if that were the case, then the biblical text should read that Moses 'would' die when he was one hundred and twenty years old and there 'would' not arise a prophet in Israel like Moses. In fact, the biblical text uses the past tense as well as phrases that are appropriate only if the author was writing a long time after the death of Moses, such as 'to this day' and 'never since': "He was buried in the valley in the land of Moab . . . but no one knows his burial place to this day. Moses was one hundred twenty years old when he died. . . . Never since has there arisen a prophet in Israel like Moses" (Deuteronomy 34:5–7, 10). Another example of Hobbes's sensitive textual analysis relates to Genesis 12:6. The text says, "Abraham passed through the land to the place of Sichem . . . and the

Canaanite was then in the land." The use of the word 'then' shows that the passage was written when the Canaanites were no longer in the land. This had to be at a time after the death of Moses.

There are other considerations that point to an author other than Moses. The text talks about Moses in the third person; it describes him in terms inappropriate for a man of God to apply to himself (e.g., "he was unequaled for all the signs and wonders that the Lord sent him"), and it indicates reliance on other written sources, such as "The Book of the Wars of the Lord," a lost and otherwise unknown book that is quoted at Numbers 21:14–15.

Hobbes did not maintain that Moses did not write any of the Pentateuch. On the contrary, he maintained that Moses wrote that part of it that the Bible says he did, namely, Deuteronomy 11–26.

Using considerations similar to those employed to analyze Genesis, Hobbes went on to show that the books of Joshua, Judges, Samuel, Kings, Chronicles, and others were written long after the occurrence of the events that they describe. Using the Apocrypha as evidence, Hobbes judged that the Old Testament was put into its final form by Ezra after the Babylonian Captivity.

His opinion of the composition of the New Testament stands in stark contrast to that of the Old. The authors of the New Testament, Hobbes judged, "lived all in less than an age after Christ's Ascension and had all of them seen our Savior or been his Disciples, except St. Paul and St. Luke, and consequently whatsoever was written by them is as ancient as the time of the Apostles."[63]

Hobbes's instincts about the Bible were excellent. But it was difficult for most people of the seventeenth century to appreciate his arguments. Alexander Ross completely missed Hobbes's point about the use of the word 'then' and affirmed, correctly but irrelevantly, that the Canaanites lived in Canaan when Moses lived. Charles Wolseley did not reason badly but rather hitched his wagon to falsehood in order to discount Hobbes's point about "The Book of the Wars of the Lord." Wolseley claimed that Moses was prophesying the writing of those books in the future, and, in any case, 'books' did not have to be books but any verbal report.[64]

Although there was enormous resistance to Hobbes's discoveries, other persecuted geniuses of biblical criticism, such as Spinoza and Richard Simon in the seventeenth century, elaborated on and extended Hobbes's discoveries. It took more than two and a half centuries for his results to become commonly accepted among biblical scholars, but now they are accepted as commonplace. In his own day, he was vilified for his work in this area, just as most true prophets are for their unpopular truths.

Heaven and the Kingdom of God. The standard view of heaven in the seventeenth century was that it was somwhere in outer space. While many people today continue to hold the same view, many theologians now think that heaven will be on earth. The latter are the theological descendants of Hobbes. He pointed out that God will rule "on Mt. Zion"; John has a vision of the New Jerusalem coming down from the heavens; and Jesus will return to earth to rule. Also, the Bible never says that "the place wherein men are to live eternally after the resurrection is the heavens, meaning by heaven, those parts of the world, which are the most remote from the earth."[65] Realizing that his proof that "the kingdom of God is to be on earth" is novel, Hobbes says that he merely proposes it for consideration,

maintaining nothing in this or any other paradox of religion, but attending the end of that dispute of the sword concerning the authority . . . by which all sorts of doctrine are to be approved or rejected, and whose commands, both in speech and writing (whatsoever be the opinions of private men), must by all men that mean to be protected by their laws be obeyed.[66]

Given that heaven will be on earth, it is easy to see that it, that is, "the kingdom of God," as the New Testament calls it, is a real kingdom. The phrase 'the kingdom of God' refers to earthly kingdoms in its other uses. So God has both natural and prophetic kingdoms. In addition to the whole world, which is his natural kingdom in virtue of his omnipotence, God had two natural kingdoms that were created through his commands to particular people. The first involved Adam and Eve. God directly commanded them not to eat of the fruit of the tree of the knowledge of good and evil. By disobeying, they decided to make their own judgments of good and evil, independently of God. Hobbes in effect explains that Adam and Eve must have had the power of judging good and evil from the beginning of their existence, otherwise they could not have sinned. So having their eyes opened must mean something else. His interpretation, namely, that they chose to judge according to their own lights and not according to the laws of God, the supreme authority, makes sense of the Bible story while complementing his philosophy.[67] The next kingdom established by God involved a covenant with Abraham and his descendants: "This is which is called the 'Old Covenant' or 'Testament'."[68] Unfortunately, Hobbes's description of the covenant does not fit with his general theory about sovereign-making covenants. Because God becomes sovereign over Abraham and his descendants, he should not be a party to the covenant; yet Hobbes says that the covenant "includes a contract between God and Abraham."[69] It is unfortunate that Hobbes did not have the benefit of twentieth-century biblical criticism, for then he could have used the concept of suzerainty covenants to explain that God sets the terms of the covenant for Abraham and announces what he will do for Abraham without thereby obligating himself to Abraham and thus not giving up any rights to Abraham. This is tantamount to God's not being a party to the covenant in Hobbes's understanding of sovereign-making covenants.

Since God was the sovereign of the Israelites, Israel was actually a theocracy. Neither Moses nor the succeeding high priests were sovereigns but rather were God's lieutenants or representatives. Eventually, the Israelites rebelled against God and set up Saul as their king because they wanted to be "like the nations." Thus God no longer had a kingship over any particular people and will not have one until Jesus returns to earth at the Second Coming. Hobbes proves all of this with appropriate biblical quotations.

In short, Hobbes divides human history into four stages: (1) From Adam to Abraham, God was not the king of any particular people. (The brief time that God had a special sovereignty over Adam is not counted.) (2) From Abraham until Saul, God was the king of the Israelites. (3) From Saul until the end of this age, God is not the king of any particular people. (4) After the Second Coming, Jesus will be king over all the elect. This is a neat scheme that is true to the biblical story and also fits Hobbes's political views. Hobbes is able to accommodate two important religio-political points: He affirms the kingship of Jesus, and he makes that kingship irrelevant to current political events. Until Jesus returns to earth, the only legitimate sovereigns are ones constituted by subjects, and they at the same time have ultimate religious authority. It is clear that Jesus cannot be a king now; otherwise it would make no sense to pray that "thy kingdom come" or to say that his "kingdom is at hand."[70]

Hell. Like heaven, hell will be on earth. In his usual careful way with the Bible, Hobbes surveys the talk about hell and the place of punishment. Sometimes the Bible says that the wicked are under water, sometimes that they are destroyed by fire, and sometimes cast into the darkness. The word 'hell' is the usual translation of 'Gehenna' or 'the Valley of Hinnon', which is the name of a garbage dump, outside Jerusalem, where fires often burned. Weighing all the evidence, Hobbes concludes that the wicked will be resurrected and then "suffer such bodily pains and calamities as are incident to those who not only live under evil and cruel governors but have also for enemy the eternal king of the saints, God Almighty."[71] Later he makes it clear that these pains will be caused at least in part by eternal fires, which will also cause the wicked to suffer a "second death." What does not count as part of the evidence are the absurd stories of the pagan poets, such as Virgil, who maintains that hell is twice as deep as the heavens are high.

Hobbes's insistence on a second and final death for the wicked is certainly biblically based, but it is motivated by his desire to reconcile punishment with divine mercy:

[I]t seems hard to say that God, who is the father of mercies, that does in heaven and earth all that he will, that has the hearts of all men in his disposing, that works in men both to do and to will, and without whose free gift a man has neither inclination to good nor repentance of evil, should punish a man's transgressions without any end of time, and with all the extremity of torture that men can imagine and more.[72]

Some will object that since the flames of hell are eternal, the punishment of the wicked must be eternal as well. That is simply a non sequitur. Further, Hobbes correctly points out that the Bible never says that "any man shall live in torments everlastingly."[73] The flames are eternal because the wicked, unlike the elect, would continue to have sex. Their offspring, Hobbes implies, would be as wicked as the parents and thus keep the fires stoked with their bodies. This was undoubtedly an unfortunate view. What started off as a humane reinterpretation of hellfire went seriously wrong. There is not enough difference between the eternal suffering of some people and the finite but intense suffering of an infinite number of people. Hobbes eventually came to see that his views about eternal flames were not acceptable. In the Latin version, published in 1668, he left out the part about the sexuality of the wicked.

Bramhall was not satisfied that Hobbes's version of hell was anywhere near terrible enough; in fact, the situation of the damned had its attractions, according to the bishop:

It is to be presumed that in those their second lives, knowing certainly from T. H. that there is no hope of redemption for them from corporal death upon their well doing, nor fear of any torments after death for their ill doing, they will pass their times here as pleasantly as they can.[74]

That is a simple misrepresentation of Hobbes's view. Although finite pain is preferable relative to eternal pain, it is not preferable in itself nor is it preferable relative to eternal happiness.

The Dangers of the Roman Catholic Church. The ruler of hell is the Antichrist. Most Protestants identified him with either the pope or the Roman Catholic Church in general. Hobbes did not. The pope cannot be the Antichrist because he does not deny Christ; and his church is a legitimate church, but of Rome, not England. This does not mean that Hobbes liked the Roman Catholic Church. It was the largest landowner in the kingdom of darkness, which he construed broadly to be "a confederacy of deceivers that to obtain dominion over men in this present world, endeavor by dark and erroneous doctrines, to extinguish in them the light, both of nature and of the gospel and so to disprepare them for the kingdom of God to come."[75] A large part of the corruption of the Roman Catholic Church is the result of its superficial assimilation of pagan customs and beliefs. No wonder; the papacy is "the ghost of the deceased Roman Empire, sitting crowned upon the grave thereof; for so did the papacy start up on a sudden out of the ruins of that heathen power." Being a ghostly empire, it is appropriately compared to that creation of the old wives' fables, the kingdom of fairies: Both speak a foreign language; both have one king that reigns over the whole world; both have ghostly or spiritual men as their leaders; both have their own legal system and practice enchantments; both take children and make fools of them. Finally, fairies do not marry, although they "have copulation with flesh and blood" under the name 'incubi'.[76] Priests also do not marry.

≈

Leviathan plays a relatively small role in this biography. The major reason for this is that we want to get an accurate perspective on Hobbes's entire life, and, while *Leviathan* bulks large in the history of philosophy, it did not dominate his life. He spent more time on other things; he published most of its doctrines in earlier works; he was famous before he published that work and famous afterward for things unconnected with it; some of his most conspicuous and long-lasting battles are only tangentially related to its doctrines. I have concentrated on the 1651 English version of that book. Some maintain that there are significant changes between that version and the Latin version of 1668. But such an argument would require a long, detailed, and scholarly treatment, which is beyond the scope and purpose of this book.

9

Demonstrations and
Disputations, 1652–1659

I received . . . your rich present [*De Corpore*] (for so I value it and have good
reason so to value any thing of yours) you were pleased to send me, which I shall
carefully keep as a monument of your (undeserved) kindness and civility. You
have done me a great honor. . . . I concur in what you say of Scotch Divines. . . .
they challenge a transcendent power, which has no foundation in Scripture or
antiquity. And it infinitely concerns the civil magistrate to be jealous of any power
superior to his own, for whatsoever makes him less than supreme puts him in the
capacity of a subject and so liable to the punishments of that power which
pretends itself to be greater. . . . I have read your books constantly as they come
out and do thankfully acknowledge to you . . . that I have learned much by them
in many particulars. I confess (at present) I do not concur with your judgment in
everything, yet I have (as I think all sober men should) according to the principles
of natural reason and Christianity, learned this much civility as to be thankful for
those discoveries of truth which any man makes to me and where I doubt or differ,
to suspend my censure till more mature consideration. (Thomas Barlow to
Hobbes, December 23, 1656)

During the 1650s, Hobbes published several major works on a variety of
topics. These sometimes initiated or were the outcome of acrimonious
debates with well-placed people at Oxford and the larger intellectual
community. The decade was thus filled with purported demonstrations
and real disputations. From our perspective, these disputes, which included politics, religion, metaphysics, education, and geometry, seem
unrelated. For Hobbes and his opponents, they were often intertwined.
Some could have said, "Politics, religion, geometry, education! What's the
difference?" This chapter is devoted to making this odd equation easier to
understand.

The preceding excerpts from the letter by Barlow, keeper of the
Bodleian Library, nicely summarize Hobbes's situation in the 1650s. He

was respected by many, including respectable people, although quite a few of those disagreed with his views. Several years later, Barlow decided that Hobbes's views were seriously mistaken and he criticized them. But he made the locus of his dislike clear: "It is the positions of that author which I severely, (may be) but truly confute, not his person. . . . So say I, of Mr Hobbes and truth; I love both, but truth better."[1] In the letter of December 1656 above, Barlow had written "I neither do nor ever did like your fierce censurers, who are (against all reason) more apt to censure an author for a supposed error, than commend him for many certain truths evidently discovered. . . . I know you have many admirers."[2]

Several of Hobbes's admirers wrote poems in honor of him. The best is "To Mr Hobbes" by Abraham Cowley, who described Hobbes in this way:

> Nor can the Snow which now cold Age does shed
> Upon they reverend Head,
> Quench or allay the noble Fires within,
> But all which thou has been,
> And all that Youth can be, thou 'rt yet,
> So fully still dost thou
> Enjoy the Manhood and the Bloom of Wit,
> And all the Natural Heat, but not the Fever too.
> . . . .
> To Things Immortal Time can do no Wrong,
> And that which never is to die, for ever must be Young.

He designated Hobbes the "great Columbus of the Golden Lands of new Philosophies." Cowley claimed that Hobbes was greater than Aristotle for the following poetic reason:

> Thy Task was harder much than his,
> For thy learned America is
> Not only found out first by thee,
> And rudely left to future Industry,
> But thy Eloquence and thy Wit
> Has planted, peopled, built, and civilized it.

(This comparison offended many people, and a witless satire of Cowley's poem appeared in 1680.)

The Early Reaction to *Leviathan*, 1652–59

It is important not to oversimplify the reaction to *Leviathan*. Many people liked it. And many hated it. Some were ambivalent. Since it contained numerous doctrines and numerous arguments, it was easy for a reader to like some of the doctrines and to dislike others, to agree with the premises of some of the arguments and to disagree with the conclusions, and vice versa. Some and maybe most of the adverse reaction to *Leviathan* was generated by those who either did not read it or did not understand it. It was a fad book, one that many people bought and talked about but did not read. Henry Hammond called *Leviathan* "a farrago of Christian atheism." This fine phrase is literally contradictory and figuratively unclear. My guess is that Hammond meant that Hobbes's apparent attempt to defend Christianity has the logical consequence of undermining it. Richard Baxter, an enemy of the Anglican bishops, nonetheless agreed with them in hating *Leviathan*. He recommended to Parliament that it be burned. It was not. But Baxter received his comeuppance when his own opinions were coupled with Hobbes's and condemned by Oxford University in 1683.

Because almost all of the books written about Hobbes's *Leviathan* in the seventeenth-century were critical, the mistaken impression arose that it was universally condemned and that Hobbes did not have any followers. In fact, his followers typically did not feel the need to write in defense of the doctrine. They knew that Hobbes could take care of himself. Often later seventeenth-century thinkers simply incorporated Hobbesian features into their own theories without acknowledgment. Evidence of Hobbes's good reputation is the concession that many of his critics make at the beginning of their criticisms. Clarendon wrote that Hobbes was "a man of excellent parts, of great wit, . . . has long had the reputation of a great philosopher and mathematician. . . . In a word, Mr Hobbes is one . . . of whom I have always had a great esteem. . . . his person is by many received with respect, and his books continue still to be esteemed, as well abroad as at home."[3] Seth Ward said that he had "a very great respect and a very high esteem" for Hobbes and trusted that his philosophical (that is, physical) and mathematical works would be valuable.[4] Alexander Ross respectfully bowed before Hobbes: "I quarrel not with Mr. Hobbes, but with his book. . . . I find him a man of excellent parts, and in this book

[*Leviathan*] much gold and without much dross."[5] James Harrington, the author of *Oceana*, was perceptive enough to see the brilliance of Hobbes's work even as he rejected it: "I firmly believe that Mr. Hobbs is, and will in future ages be accounted the best writer, at this day, in the world: And for his treatises of *Humane Nature* and *Of Liberty and Necessity*, they are the greatest of new lights, and those which I have followed and shall follow."[6]

Hobbes's place in seventeenth-century political theory can be gleaned from the titles of some of the works critical of him. Philip Scot's book, for example, joins Hobbes with Matthew Hale. (In the text itself, William Chillingworth is criticized more than Hale.) Filmer's *Observations concerning the Original of Government, Upon Mr Hobs Leviathan, Mr Milton against Salmatius, H. Grotius De Jure Belli* (1652) puts Hobbes in some odd company. Hobbes defended absolute sovereignty and the king; John Milton defended popular sovereignty and the regicides; and Hugo Grotius believed in an unequivocally effective moral law before the establishment of government. Marchamont Nedham's "Appendix Added out of Salmasius and Mr. Hobbes," joined to *The Case of the Commonwealth of England, Stated*, is different. Nedham criticizes Claudius Salmasius's view, which was an attack on the regicides from the perspective of Continental Protestant political theory but endorses Hobbes's position. He quotes select passages from Hobbes's *De Corpore Politico* (part of *Elements of Law, Natural and Politic*), published in 1650, in order to bolster his own case that the Commonwealth should be obeyed. Nedham concludes: "I once again recommend [Hobbes's book] to all nonsubscribers, whether Royal or Presbyterian. God give them impartial hearts to weigh the particulars."[7] In short, Hobbes was treated along with other theorists, most of whom have become over the centuries more respectable than he, but not more deservedly so. Sometimes he was criticized, but also sometimes endorsed. We shall see more of this below.

It is important to note, as Richard Tuck has shown, that *De Cive* was read happily by many Anglican royalists. Its English translation, *Philosophical Rudiments concerning Government and Society*, was put out by R. Royston, a royalist publisher. This may partially explain why strong and widespread opposition to *Leviathan* did not occur until about 1658, after Hobbes had accumulated numerous mathematical and scientific enemies, such as Robert Boyle, Seth Ward, and John Wallis. Before then, the criticisms were for the most part either limited or indirect.

Some Early Critics

Some of the early opposition to Hobbes's political views came from Roman Catholics. In *A Treatise of the Schism of England. Wherein particularly Mr. Hales and Mr. Hobbs are Modestly Accosted* (1650), Scot attacked Hobbes's Erastianism. The Jesuit Guy Holland attacked Hobbes in *Grand Prerogative of Human Nature. Namely, the Soules Natural or Native Immortality, and Freedom from Corruption, etc.* (1653). And *De Cive* was put on Rome's Index of Forbidden Books in 1654.

But most of the criticism came from fellow Protestants. Ross, who specialized in writing potboilers, had a knack for identifying and criticizing authors whom history would recognize as being greater and more important than he. Among the targets of his insipid criticisms were Thomas Browne, Kenelm Digby, and Thomas White. He also authored *New Planet, No Planet; or, The Earth No Wandring Planet, Except in the Wandring Heads of Galileans* (1646), a defense of the Ptolemaic system. In 1654, Hobbes's young friend John Davies (Davys) justifiably spoke of Ross as "perpetually barking at the works of the most learned." Ross had a shotgun approach to criticism. He said that Hobbes "vomited up the condemned opinions of the old heretics, and chiefly the Antropomorphites, Sabellians, Nestorians, Arabaens, Tacians or Eucratits, Manichies, Mahamutans and others." And that is not all. He is an "Audean, Montanist, Aetian, and Priscillianist, Luciferian, Originist, and Socinian, and a Jew."[8] These accusations, which came trippingly off Ross's tongue, are supported with superficial reasoning.

Ward, who had written a commendatory preface to *Humane Nature*, started to backpedal after the publication of *Leviathan*. He criticized Hobbes's doctrine of mortalism in *A Philosophicall Essay Towards an Eviction of the Being and Attributes of God. Immortality of the Souls of Men. Truth and Authority of Scripture. Together With an Index of the Heads of Every Particular Part* (1652). The criticism in fact was mild. But a little criticism was too much for Hobbes. He was so angry with Ward that he refused to be in his presence. When Hobbes went to Dr. Charles Scarborough's salon, he "would enquire if Dr. Ward was there." If Ward was, Hobbes would not enter; and if Ward came later, Hobbes immediately left: "So that Dr. Ward, though he much desired it, never had any conversation with Mr. Hobbs."[9] Hobbes's attitude, as much as his writings, turned Ward against him.

One of the oddities of the early criticisms of *Leviathan* is that some of them unwittingly used Hobbes's own doctrines with the intention of criticizing him. Robert Vilvain, a superannuated physician from Salisbury, wrote: "Where none can answer or satisfy that word's sense in Scripture, it falls not under human understanding, and faith consists not in our opinion but submission: specially where God is said to be a spirit or where by spirit is meant God. For his nature is incomprehensible; and we know not what he is, but that he is."[10] Vilvain was in fact expressing the views of Hobbes himself.

Robert Filmer

One of Hobbes's most important early critics, Robert Filmer, is best known as the author of *Patriarcha*, first published in 1680 but written decades earlier. Several of his other political treatises were published during the late 1640s and early 1650s, before his death in 1653, and it is one of these that contains his criticism of Hobbes. Until recently Filmer's reputation was low, but reconsiderations of what he actually said have revealed a mind that could be astute in criticism. He began *Observations Concerning the Originall of Government* (1652) by saying, "With no small content I read Mr Hobbes' book *De Cive* and his *Leviathan* about the rights of sovereignty, which no man that I know has so amply and judiciously handled. I consent with him about the rights of exercising government, but I cannot agree to his means of acquiring it. It may seem strange I should praise his building and yet mislike his foundation, but so it is."[11] This passage explains why it is appropriate to call Hobbes "a radical in the service of reaction," as John Tulloch did.[12] Hobbes's democratic premises were radical, but his absolutist conclusion was reactionary.

In some ways it is convenient to contrast the theories of Filmer and Hobbes. Filmer subscribed to the top-down theory of patriarchalism; Hobbes subscribed to a bottom-up theory of democracy. Filmer was old-fashioned; Hobbes was innovative. But there are similarities between them that add up to being almost as important as their differences. Both defended absolute sovereignty. Both preferred monarchy. Both thought that Roman Catholic political theory, especially as espoused by Robert Bellarmine and Francisco Suarez, was subversive. Both were able to justify obedience to the Commonwealth government. Both started publishing their important works after the age of fifty, and both became rather prolific once they did. And both were born in 1588. I think this last fact, which made both of them 'older than average' theorists, partially explains some of the other similarities. They were products of late Elizabethan and Jacobean England.

Filmer is particularly unhappy with two of Hobbes's concepts: *ius naturae* (the right of nature) and *regnum institutivum* (sovereignty by institution). Filmer thinks that if Hobbes had started with the idea of patriarchal government, which Hobbes does admit is a form of government, then the inapplicability of these two concepts would be obvious. Here is why. Under a patriarchy, children have no rights at all; so there cannot be any rights of nature. Further, if people have no rights, then in particular they do not have the right to institute a sovereign. Filmer's observation has merit in that it points out the brute fact that people are born into subjection. Talk about the right of nature therefore seems unrealistic. Filmer's criticism has some force. People are born into a world that is already filled with obligations that restrict the freedom of their lives. In the colorful language of Martin Heidegger, people are thrown into the world; it is already there with an elaborate network of chains. Another objection, raised by François Peleau, is that Hobbes had said that primogeniture, that is, the convention of bestowing all of one's property on the firstborn male offspring, was a law of nature. But if that is so, then it cannot be the case that everyone has a natural right to everything; consequently, there is no right of nature.

Hobbes does have replies to these objection, but they are best presented in the context of his views about the state of nature. (Whether Hobbes's replies are cogent or not is difficult to say.)

The State of Nature Again

Filmer thinks that by 'the state of nature' Hobbes is referring to the historically earliest condition of mankind. And this, he says, denies "the truth of the history of creation."[13] In fact, Hobbes does not think of the state of nature in that way. He recognizes that the state of nature never existed throughout the entire world and says that Adam was subject to the law of God. Hobbes uses the concept of the law of nature to clarify the human condition and to explain how the institution of governments is possible. In other words, the state of nature is part of a thought experiment. Hobbes is asking his readers to imagine what things would be like if there were no laws. Such conceptual exploration is untouched by the possible historical fact that patriarchal governments were historically the earliest ones.

The state of nature is any condition in which people are not subject to law. This definition is vague because it is not clear whether the laws of nature exist in the state of nature. Hobbes's text does not provide decisive evidence. Some passages of the text suggest that the laws of nature are operative, and others that they are not. This has led me to distinguish for expository purposes between a primary and a secondary state of nature. In the primary state of nature, there are no laws of any kind whatsoever. Since only laws restrict rights and there are no laws in the primary state of nature, everything is permitted. Everyone has a right to everything else, even to another person's body. The secondary state of nature is the condition of humans when there is no civil government, but the laws of nature are added to the conceptual mix.

In short, Filmer has confused the historical fact of patriarchy with the theoretical grounds or nature of government. This is not necessarily a sign of superficiality in Filmer. This confusion was common in seventeenth-century readers (and it still is today among first-time readers). Hobbes's admirer Peleau reports that he is "hounded with syllogisms designed to prove to me that the state of nature in the strict sense . . . has never existed in the world. . . . [Your critics] say that there have always been families in the world and that since families are little kingdoms, they exclude the state of nature." Peleau tried to defend Hobbes by citing the condition of the American Indians, Noah and his sons after the flood, and all savages against all other savages, to no avail.[14]

We can now suggest what Hobbes could say to the preceding objections about the right of nature. First, the right of nature follows from the state of nature, because where there are no laws, there are no restrictions on liberty. The right of nature, like the state of nature, should be understood as part of a thought experiment. Second, primogeniture, as part of the law of nature, operates in the secondary state of nature and not the primary one.

Covenants

Filmer, like many other critics, also has objections to Hobbes's description of the covenant that creates the sovereign. On the one hand, Hobbes says that the sovereign is not a party to the contract and, on the other, that the covenant involves "every man with every man," as Filmer describes it. This criticism is even weaker than his earlier one. All that Hobbes needs to say in order to evade it is that every person who is to be a subject covenants with every other person who is to be a subject. The not yet existent sovereign entities, which are brought into existence by the covenant, obviously are not parties to the covenant. This handles monarchical and oligarchical governments easily enough. It might seem that democracies still pose a problem because the people themselves are the sovereign. What Hobbes would say is that the people who covenant are not identical with the democratic sovereign. The people who covenant are individuals acting as individuals. They do not have any unity. In contrast, the democratic sovereign comes into existence through the covenant and has a unity that is not the same as the collection of people who covenant. To use a mathematical analogy, the members of a set are not identical with the set, even though those members constitute the set. Another way to come to see the difference between the subjects and the democratic sovereign is to realize that even as the subjects of a democracy change by dying or being added, the sovereign does not change. Also, when subjects break the law, no part of the sovereign, who is completely above the law, breaks it to any degree.

Filmer has a criticism of aristocracy that in fact seems to apply more strongly against monarchy. He says that the individuals who are part of the aristocratic sovereign must, according to Hobbes's view, remain in the state of nature and hence have the right to kill others with impunity. It might seem that Hobbes could evade this objection by maintaining that the aristocrats as individuals are subjects and thus subject to the law. This reply fits the facts. Aristocracies prosecute individual members, as individuals, even though the aristocracy as a whole never prosecutes itself because it, as a whole, is not subject to the law.

What about monarchy? Isn't there a distinction between the private person who is the king and the public person of the king? And if there is, would it not be possible in theory for the public person to put the private person on trial? This is an interesting problem. There was a long tradition of distinguishing between the king's two bodies. In *Leviathan*, Hobbes himself makes the analogous distinction between the public and private person of the king. And the enemies of Charles sometimes made this very distinction and maintained that they were not attacking the king of England but Charles Stuart. The distinction seems to work against Hobbes's theory. In *Behemoth*, Hobbes would angrily reject the distinction as metaphysical nonsense. To pretend to differentiate between the man Charles and the king Charles is to make a distinction without a difference. Hobbes's response is not adequate. It has as much cogency as the sermon of the learned minister who wrote numerous syllogisms in the margins of his Bible next to the passages about which he was going to preach. He was confident that he could prove each point. However, next to one text he wrote, "Raise voice and strike pulpit firmly: argument weak." Fortunately, a better reply is open to Hobbes. He could accept the distinction between the private and public persons of the king and point out that since only the king can judge the actions of the private person who may be the king, the private person would never be judged as breaking the law unless the king were a perfect lunatic; and if the king were a perfect lunatic, then sovereignty would be dissolved anyway, because with such diminished capacity the king could not guarantee the safety of the people.

Filmer also objects to the idea of sovereignty by acquisition. He sees two impossibilities involved in the concept of a conquered group of people covenanting with the conqueror. First, because conquered people have no rights at all, they can hardly transfer rights to the conqueror. Second, by Hobbes's own theory, the conqueror, who is sovereign, cannot be a party to the covenant. Hobbes has replies to both objections. It is simply not true that conquered people have no rights. They may not have the physical power to exercise their rights effectively, but they still have enough power to covenant. Also, it is not the conquering sovereign that is a party to the covenant. Rather, the conquered people either covenant with and among themselves and designate the conqueror as their sovereign, or they covenant with the subjects of the conquering sovereign and thus simply become incorporated into that government.

Authorization and Alienation

Filmer identifies a genuine problem when he points out two contradictions near the center of Hobbes's political theory. Essential to getting out of the state of nature is the making of a covenant. But what is the nature of that covenant? Hobbes tries to explain it when he specifies an ideal wording for it: "I authorize and give up my right of governing myself to this man or to this assembly of men on this condition that thou give up thy right to him and authorize all his actions in like manner."[15] Filmer points out an inconsistency in this formula. In order for one person *A* to authorize another person *B* to act for or represent *A*, *A* has to have the right to act in those matters himself. For example, Smith can have Jones represent him in selling a piece of property only if Smith owns that property. If Smith has previously sold or given away the property, then he has no right to have anyone represent him with respect to it. And Hobbes makes clear in the sovereign-making formula itself that the people taking the covenant are giving away that right ("I . . . give up my right of governing myself").

Hobbes cannot have it both ways. He needs to choose between authorization of the sovereign or alienation to the sovereign. But he refuses to make that choice. He wants authorization in order to make his theory palatable and to insulate the sovereign from criticism – when things go wrong the sovereign can point out that the people are the authors of his actions. And he needs alienation in order to establish the incontestable rights of an absolute sovereign.

Another contradiction exposed by Filmer (although he does not get it exactly right) applies to Hobbes's position that people can never give up their right to self-defense and that they do give up all of their rights to the sovereign. If Hobbes were to reply that he also said that there are some rights that a person can never lay down, no matter what his words seem to indicate, then Filmer could reply that Hobbes's theory is severely deficient until he specifies exactly what the limits of the right of self-defense are, and that is not an easy thing to do.

The Debate over the Universities, 1654–57

Hobbes was sometimes grouped with certain antiacademic Commonwealth men. In 1653, the short-lived Barebones Parliament discussed "suppressing universities and all Schools for learning as heathenish and unnecessary."[16] Cromwell's dissolution of that Parliament ended the threat that the universities would actually be suppressed. But the attack on them continued. Two of the leaders of the attack on universities were former army chaplains, John Dell and John Webster. Dell, master of Gonville and Caius College, Cambridge, believed that because religion did not depend on secular learning, it was not necessary for ministers to be produced in universities. He wanted universities to be turned into technical schools teaching arithmetic, geometry, and geography, because those studies are "very useful to human society"; and he wanted new universities founded throughout England to dilute the influence of Oxford and Cambridge.

Webster was not quite anti-intellectual, but he aligned himself with the mystical chemistry of Robert Fludd, Jan van Helmont, and the Paracelsians over the mechanical philosophy of Galileo, Ward, and Wilkins. In *Academiarum Examen,* he promoted the study of mystical symbolism in nature. He was optimistic that natural reason can discover important truths about God. He thought that the scholastic curriculum led students into atheism. The "atomical" doctrines of Descartes, Hobbes, White, and Digby were better. Indeed, he thought that Hobbes was a better political philosopher than Aristotle.[17] Ironically, Webster could parade under the banner of Baconism because he interpreted Bacon's inductive method as a commonsense approach to reality: Follow your experience, not abstract theory.[18] What united Hobbes, Dell, and Webster was their dislike for clerical domination of the university.

Presbyterians, Independents, and Episcopalists joined together to defend the universities against their critics. Hobbes had criticized the universities in *Leviathan,* and he was for that reason lumped together with Dell and Webster in Ward's defense of the universities, *Vindiciae Academiarum.*[19] Scholars today want to draw a sharp distinction between Hobbes on the one hand and Dell and Webster on the other. As a logical point, they are correct, but as a record of how they were perceived in the 1650s, it tends to give the wrong impression.

However, one difference between Hobbes and the other critics is that his concerns about the universities were directly self-interested. Wallis, Ward, and Bramhall all complained that Hobbes wanted his book "taught in the universities" because it contained nothing "contrary either to the Word of God or to good manners or to the disturbance of the public tranquillity," as Hobbes put it. They were offended by the apparent arrogance of recommending one's own book to be required reading.[20] Hobbes's response to Bramhall is disingenuous. He claims that he said nothing more than that he wanted his doctrine taught, not the book itself. Although his text can bear that reading, it is not the plausible one. Here is what he had written in *Leviathan:* "Therefore I think it [*Leviathan*] may be profitably printed and more profitably taught in the Universities." To Wallis and Ward, Hobbes replied that he thought his doctrine was true; otherwise he would not have written it. And having written it, it would be absurd not to recommend it.[21] Bramhall also thought Hobbes's recommendation contradicted Hobbes's ban against taking to oneself "the knowledge of good and evil."[22] Hobbes's reply to this objection is cogent. He was merely expressing his opinion and never represented it as more than that.

A vigorous defense of the universities against Webster, Dell, and Hobbes was presented by Seth Ward in *Vindiciae Academiarum* (1654). In the preface, written by John Wilkins, Hobbes is accused of trying to advance "the reputation of his own skill." Worse, he is accused of plagiarizing from the scientific works of Walter Warner. The same charge appears again in the appendix. In any case, the scientific work was superfluous, Wilkins observes, given that Descartes, Gassendi, and Digby had published their findings earlier than Hobbes did. We already saw in Chapter 4 that Hobbes cared a lot about his originality and was particularly stung to be compared unfavorably to Warner. In *Six Lessons to the Professors of the Mathematicks, etc.* (1656), he commented on his originality:

But let any man read Descartes; he shall find that he attributes no motion at all to the object of sense, but an inclination to action, which inclination no man can imagine what it means. And for Gassendus and Sir Kenelm Digby, it is manifest by their writings that their opinions are not different from that of Epicurus, which is very different from mine.[23]

Ward claimed that Hobbes did not know what the Oxford curriculum was. He maintained that scientific discussion in Oxford and Cambridge was open and nondogmatic, that only the Copernican system was taught by specialists in astronomy, and that the latest results and techniques in mathematics were taught. Webster and Hobbes really did not know what they were talking about. Ward's harsh assessment that Hobbes's views were like those of "the seven sleepers, who after many years awaking, in vain addressed themselves to act according to the state of things when they lay down" was probably right.[24] It is unlikely that Hobbes had ever visited Oxford after 1637.

The Free Will Controversy, 1654–56

Hobbes's problems with Ward and Wilkins over the state of the universities were complicated by the resurrection of the controversy he had had with Bramhall over free will the decade before. John Davies of Kidwelly asked Hobbes to lend him the manuscript on liberty and necessity on the pretext of translating it into French for another friend.[25] (Davies became a prolific translator of French works into English and became well known in London circles.) Hobbes obliged, not suspecting Davies of any ulterior motive. Without Hobbes's knowledge or permission, Davies copied the manuscript for himself, wrote a prefatory letter that denounced priests, and had the whole thing published in 1655 as *Of Liberty and Necessity; a Treatise Wherein all Controversy concerning Predestination, Election, Free Will, Grace, Merit, Reprobation, &c. is fully Decided and Cleared: in Answer to a Treatise Written by the Bishop of Londonderry on the Same Subject.* The full title seems to be Davies's creation.

When Bramhall discovered that *Of Liberty and Necessity* had been published, and worse, without his own manuscript or reply to Hobbes included, he was furious. Consequently, he published a book, *A Vindication [sometimes: Defence] of True Liberty from Antecedent and Extrinsecal Necessity*, that consisted of the complete text of his original manuscript, Hobbes's reply, and his reply to that. But the three works are chopped up into relatively brief passages and interlaced as if they were the interchanges of the original debate. Bramhall gave Davies's letter short shrift. According to him, Davies would "lick up the spittle of Dionysius by himself, as his servile flatterers did, and protest that it is more sweet than nectar." Hobbes he accused of having broken his promise not to publish on the subject.

Hobbes defended himself in *The Questions concerning Liberty, Necessity, and Chance* (hereafter *Liberty, Necessity, and Chance;* 1656) specifically against Bramhall, but he mentioned some of his other enemies as being of the same ilk. The issue of free will was not an isolated metaphysical or theological issue. Bramhall's book attacked one of Hobbes's flanks; Seth Ward's *Vindiciae Academiarum* (1654), *A Philosophicall Essay* (1655), and *In Thomae Hobbii Philosophiam Exercitatio Epistolica* (1656) attacked another.

Liberty, Necessity, and Chance, which occupies an entire volume of Molesworth's edition, is generally tedious. Building on Bramhall's *Vindication*, it consists of alternating segments of text from his original essay, followed by a segment of *Of Liberty and Necessity*, followed by a segment of Bramhall's reply, followed by a new reply by Hobbes. It is a confirming instance of the law of diminishing returns. Neither Hobbes nor Bramhall was willing to learn from the other. At this stage, scoring points against each other was the chief goal. Each criticism is met with a reply that is motivated by this thought: "What do I have to say in order to show that my original position was right and that my opponent is an idiot?" Bramhall claims that *Leviathan* is "*Monstrum horrendum, informe, ingens, cui lumen ademptum.*" The line comes from Virgil's description of the cyclops Polyphemus in the *Aeneid.* Hobbes does not give any indication that he is aware of this, but answers the charge epithet by epithet. He says that of course *Leviathan* is "monstrum horrendum" given that Bramhall takes Leviathan to be a big fish, but as a big fish, it cannot be "informe" (shapeless); and it is not "ingens" (huge) because it is not a big book, and it is false to call it "cui lumen adeptum" (blind/obscure) because it is much more clearly written than Bramhall's own "scholastic jargon." Sparks were flying from the pens of both men, but they did not give off much light.

Still, there are some notable features of the debate that come out best in *Liberty, Necessity, and Chance.* In "To the Reader" Hobbes sharply lays out his position as being "that men are free to *do* as they *will* and to *forbear* as they *will;* . . . that it is not in a man's power now to choose the will he shall have anon; that chance produces nothing; that the will of God makes the necessity of all things." The view espoused here is Christian determinism, and more specifically Calvinist determinism, because it entails double predestination. Hobbes appealed to the authority of Paul, Luther, Calvin, and others of "the reformed church" to support his view.[26]

Some mid-seventeenth-century English Calvinists explicitly dissociated themselves from Hobbes because he was so odious to so many people. William Barlee said that he would rather "own the devil for his master, as Mr. Hobbes." But anti-Calvinists were not willing to let the Calvinists off the hook merely with an asseveration. Thomas Pierce, in *Heauton-timoroumenos; or, The Self-Revenger Exemplified in Mr. William Barlee* (1658), said that Barlee wrote like one of Hobbes's disciples and that *Leviathan* supported Calvinist doctrine.[27] Pierce understood both Hobbes and Calvinism correctly. And some Calvinists were happy enough to admit it. Philip Tanny (Tandy) said that Hobbes's books on liberty and necessity led him to believe that Hobbes was "a good man" and that the books themselves contain "certain high mysterious speculations, . . . the best opened by you [Hobbes], of any man living that I ever yet saw."[28] Although a certain kind of Calvinism enjoyed some favor in England at the time, determinism and predestination are hard doctrines, and even Calvin preferred not to talk about them. So Hobbes was defending a position that at least made people uncomfortable. Hobbes himself thought that his problems with Bramhall, Ward, and Wilkins had less to do with the idea of free will or the condition of the universities and more to do with his view that "the supremacy in matters of religion . . . reside in the civil sovereign."[29]

God the Author of Sin

Hobbes maintained that since God is the cause of everything (as Christianity always taught), he was the cause of sin also. Many readers thought that this view implied that God is culpable for all the sin in the world. Alexander Ross wrote that Hobbes's view is "the heresy of the Libertines, who made God the author of sin; or of the Manichees and Valentinians, who held that God made sin."[30] Hobbes did his best to explain that being the cause of sin does not entail being either the author of sin or being culpable for it. He was certainly right to hold that in general being the cause of x does not entail that one is the author of x.

Bramhall was particularly concerned that Hobbes's doctrine made "God Almighty to be the introducer of all evil and sin into the world." He went on, "Excuse me if I hate this doctrine with a perfect hatred, which is so dishonorable to God and man."[31] Bramhall was not just attacking Hobbes; he was attacking John Calvin, who said that he had no trouble saying that sin was God's action. If God were not the cause of everything, sin included, then one would open oneself to the heresy of Manichaeanism. To some extent, Bramhall does not care. He said that it is "better to be a Manichee, to believe in two gods, a God of good and a God of evil . . . than thus to charge the true God to be the proper cause and the true author of all the sins and evils which are in the world."[32] This is revealing. Bramhall would prefer to be a heretic than to assert categorically the absoluteness of God's creative power. His position sounds like blasphemy because it demeans the power of God. Why should Hobbes be blamed for eschewing that heresy and steadfastly asserting what had been a basic formula of God's sovereignty?

In fact, the complaint that Hobbes made God the author of sin was not directed solely or even first at him. It was a standard complaint made by Arminians against Calvinists. Years before, Peter Heylyn had attacked both Calvin and Theodorus Beza for holding the same position: "The odious inferences which are raised out of these opinions I forbear to press and shall add only at the present that if we grant this doctrine to be true and orthodox, we may do well to put an *Index expurgatorius* upon the Creed and quite expunge the Article of Christ's coming to judgment."[33]

Aside from its unpleasant consequences, one barrier to accepting predestination is the fact that it denies free will. What a defender of determinism needs to show is that the intuitive belief in free will is understandable but false. He needs a persuasive analogy that might get a person to see the source of his illusion about free will. Hobbes came up with one:

A wooden top that is lashed by the boys and runs about sometimes to one wall, sometimes to another, sometimes spinning, sometimes hitting men on the shins, if it were sensible of its own motion, would think it proceeded from its own will, unless it felt what lashed it. And is a man any wiser, when he runs to one place for a benefice, to another for a bargain . . . because he thinks he does it without other cause than his own will, and sees not what are the lashings that cause his will?[34]

Bramhall replied to Hobbes's book with *Castigations of Mr. Hobbes, His Last Animadversions, in the Case Concerning Liberty and Universal Necessity* in 1657. Another edition put out the next year included *The Catching of Leviathan, or the Great Whale; Demonstrating out of Mr. Hobs his own Works that no Man who is thoroughly a Hobbist, can be a Good Christian, or a Good Commonweath's Man, or Reconcile Himself to Himself, Because his Principles are not only Destructive of All Religion, but to all Societies; Extinguishing the Relation between Prince and Subject, Husband and Wife; and abound with palpable contradictions.* With this, the debate between Hobbes and Bramhall over free will ended.

Others picked it up. But not all of Hobbes's opponents were happy with Bramhall's line of attack. Bramhall was an Aristotelian scholastic, and the Cambridge Platonists thought that there were serious problems with that view. Ralph Cudworth claimed that Bramhall failed to see that the crucial point was Hobbes's materialism. For Cudworth, it was essential to establish the existence of an immaterial, self-moving spirit. Hobbes, who never knew of Cudworth's objections, would have found them pointless. He had often enough argued that the ideas of an immaterial spirit and of a self-mover are incoherent. Even if Hobbes were not right about this, he would be right in asserting that Cudworth's view was unintelligible:

"[The will is] the whole soul redoubled upon it Self, which being as it were with in it Self, and comprehending it Self . . . has a *sui potestas* over it Self, and can command it Self or turn it Self this way and that way."[35] But then Cudworth's philosophy was considered suspect by many conventional intellectuals also. The Cambridge Platonists have acquired a respectability that they did not possess in the third quarter of the seventeenth century.

De Corpore, 1655

Hobbes had figured out the main lines of his physics and metaphysics by the late 1630s. A sketch of his views occupied a large part of the manuscript of *The Elements of Law*. The complete published statement of his view appeared in 1655, more than a decade after it had been expected. Although much of *De Corpore* is interesting, it is nowhere near as successful as *De Cive*. The leading idea of *De Corpore* is that the only things (substances) that exist are bodies. The term 'immaterial substance' is self-contradictory. Either spirits do not exist or they are a special type of body. Accidents or properties, such as being red, having a pungent odor, or sounding tinny, are to be understood as certain types of motions in bodies. Although macroscopic bodies are sometimes at rest, most bodies are usually in motion, either causing other bodies to move in a certain way by striking them or being caused to move in a certain way by being struck by other bodies in motion. Nothing moves itself. The total amount of motion remains constant. And all motion occurs by contact; there is no motion at a distance. All the motions are determined by eternal laws, devised presumably by God. In short, Hobbes's physics or metaphysics is uncompromisingly materialistic, mechanistic, and deterministic.

Philosophy and Science

For Hobbes and almost everyone else before the eighteenth century, philosophy and science are the same thing. The locus classicus for Hobbes's explanation of the nature of philosophy is in the first chapter of *De Corpore*, although the essentials of his view were already stated in *Leviathan*. Philosophy, he says, is knowledge acquired by correct reasoning either (a) of effects by thinking of how those effects were caused or (b) of causes that could produce effects. Hobbes's word for knowledge (*cognitio*) is used with a general meaning. Sense experience and memory are also *cognitiones* but do not count as scientific knowledge because they do not involve reasoning. Sense experience and memory come directly from the objects that stimulate the sense organs. Not even large clusters of sensations or memories count as scientific knowledge, again because they are not the result of reasoning.

Reasoning, according to Hobbes, is computation, and all computation is either addition or subtraction. Multiplication is simply the addition of numerous equal objects; division is simply the subtraction of numerous equal objects. The objects of reasoning are ideas. His first example of additive reasoning is the idea that results from seeing a distant object. The idea is of a body. When the object gets closer, the idea of animate is added to body. This yields the sum of the idea of an animal. When the object draws even closer and one hears it talking (which is a sign of rationality), the idea of rationality is added to that of animal, and the sum is the idea of a human being.[36] The process of subtraction is illustrated by reversing the procedure just described. When the man standing close by begins to depart, the idea of rationality is removed from the idea of a human being and the remainder is the idea of an animal, and so on.

One of the points of Hobbes's example is to emphasize that computation is not restricted to numbers: "magnitude can be added or subtracted to magnitude, body to body, motion to motion, degree to degree (of quality), action to action, conception to conception, proportion to proportion, speech to speech, name to name."[37] As long as the addition and subtraction takes place with the same kinds of things, reasoning will not go awry. A problem with analytic geometry, to be discussed later, is that its practitioners unwittingly add and subtract things of different kinds.

The view that reasoning is nothing but computation was deflating and objectionable in the seventeenth century. Most philosophers of the time, following the classical Greek and medieval Latin traditions, considered rationality to be the highest thing in human beings, and sometimes identified reason with God. If reasoning is nothing more exalted than mechanical addition and subtraction, both human beings and God seem to be demeaned. Notwithstanding its broadly objectionable character, Hobbes's position that reasoning is computation is one of his great contributions to philosophy, and it is the dominant and indispensable idea of artificial intelligence. This is not to say that Hobbes had an adequate or even consistent idea of computation. He thinks that adding the ideas of *rational* and *animal* is the same as joining words to form a sentence or inferring a conclusion from premises. But they obviously are not.

The next element in Hobbes's definition of philosophy to consider is his insistence that scientific knowledge is generative knowledge. Causes generate effects; effects are generated by causes. To know something is to know how it came to be. It is easy not to see this point in the examples that have already been given. It is either false or not obvious how (the ideas of) body, animateness, and rationality generate (the idea of) a human being in a sentence like 'All humans are animals'. A rational, animate body just is a human being. It is also odd to think of conclusions as caused by premises. In a valid argument, the conclusion has to be true if the premises are true, but the premises do not make the conclusion true.

Hobbes illustrates the generative aspect of science with a different kind of example. If a person sees a geometrical figure constructed with a compass (by fixing the distance between the two arms, keeping one arm on a point, and moving the other arm in the only fashion it can in order to draw a line), then one knows that the resulting line is a circle. This is fair enough, but how such generative knowledge fits with the view that reasoning is computation is mysterious. What is crucial in the case of the generated circle is the sense experience; addition seems to play no role at all. Certainly seeing the circle drawn involves a sequence of sense impressions (ideas), but succession is not addition. The purpose of raising this problem is not so much to object to Hobbes's view as to let the reader know that she is not misunderstanding Hobbes if she detects this problem and also to indicate that Hobbes's views were counterintuitive or even incoherent in some cases. The presence of incoherence is not an indicator of insincerity.

Hobbes thinks that there are two kinds of generative knowledge, and these are indicated by the clauses labeled '(a)' and '(b)' in the definition given at the beginning of this section. The first clause expresses what is known as synthetic knowledge, and is the result of the synthetic method. That method begins with causes and computes effects. The example of the constructed circle is an instance of synthetic knowledge because the cause is observed in action. The other kind of knowledge (and methodology) is analytic. It begins with an effect and reasons to a cause. Suppose that an already constructed plane figure is observed. It has the appearance of a circle. This leads one to guess that it is a circle; and one way it could have been generated is by the procedure described already. One might thus be led to use a compass to trace over the given figure. If the traced line coincides at every point with the given figure, then one can conclude that the figure is a circle. But one cannot conclude that the figure was actually generated using a compass. Perhaps it was stamped out with a cookie cutter. There is thus a kind of asymmetry between synthetic and analytic scientific knowledge.

What is the nature of this asymmetry, and is it an especially important element in Hobbes's scientific views? I don't think so. (Scholars heatedly disagree about the intepretation of the analytic and synthetic methods in Hobbes's thought.) The nature of the asymmetry concerns certainty. If a person sees the cause generate an effect, then there is no doubt about what the cause is and she is certain about the cause and the effect. If a person sees only the effect and must conjecture about the cause, then she can never be certain what the actual cause was and there is always some doubt. A logically related difference between synthetic reasoning and analytic reasoning is that synthetic reasoning does not use conjectures, whereas analytic reasoning does.

Since science often reasons from effects to causes, it may seem that science for Hobbes is largely conjectural and probabilistic in the modern sense. I think that this interpretation of Hobbes's position is wrong for several reasons. First, for Hobbes, like all philosophers in the classical tradition, scientific propositions are universal and necessary. As universal, they do not directly apply to any particular instance and do not speak directly about any particular instance. The proposition 'If a compass with arms at a fixed length has one arm fixed on a point and the other arm moved, etc.', does not talk about any particular circle. That proposition is true even if nothing is a circle. Applying the scientific proposition to a particular figure is not strictly speaking a part of science for Hobbes, and one of his objections to the program of the Royal Society was that they were mucking around with particular things instead of drawing inferences from general propositions.

One way to come to realize that scientific propositions are not directly related to particular objects is to understand their genuine logical form. A proposition like 'All animals are bodies' looks like the paradigmatic scientific proposition. But according to Hobbes, it is not. Scientific propositions are not categorical, subject-predicate propositions, but conditional or hypothetical ones. Hypothetical propositions are those that have an 'if . . . , then . . .' structure. So the correct way to understand 'All animals are bodies' is like this: 'If something is animal, then it is bodily'. This form of proposition makes it clear that the existence of no object is being asserted. It would be true even if there were no animals. Hobbes's analysis of universal propositions is very close to the one that became generally accepted only in the twentieth century. It is significantly different from standard Aristotelian logic, according to which universal propositions presuppose that the subject term denotes existing objects.

Because scientific propositions are necessary, according to Hobbes, they must be true. What makes them necessary, according to Hobbes, is their meaning; they are definitions or consequences of definitions. They are precising or stipulative definitions, which consequently are made true by fiat and not by anything in the world. Scientific propositions are necessary and universal whether they are used for synthetic or analytic methods. They are never probably true or probably false. Probability only enters discussions within broadly scientific discourse when one wants to know whether some effect was actually generated by some given cause. But such broadly scientific discourse is not part of science strictly considered. Hobbes uses the word 'probability' in *De Corpore* several times, but never in connection with the nature of science.

Having said all of this, I have to note that there are places where Hobbes says something inconsistent with the view I have just ascribed to him. At the beginning of Part IV of *De Corpore*, "Of Physics; or, The Phenomena of Nature," he reiterates the definition of philosophy that he had given in the first chapter. He says that his work up to this point has used the synthetic method in philosophy, that is, in his treatment of language, logic, motion, and magnitude. He then declares that he will use the analytic method. And he calls attention to a great asymmetry between them. The synthetic method employs definitions as causes and depends on stipulations that cannot be false. But the analytic method begins from individual observed effects and produces conjectures about how they may have been generated – "I do not say that they actually are." Further, the analytic method uses particular propositions in its inferences and general propositions, that are not, however, "necessary."[38] That is what he says. But I am at a loss to make it consistent with what he says in most other places. Also, his actual reasoning in this and the following chapters looks exactly like that of the earlier parts of *De Corpore*. He does not reason to causes from particular effects, and he does just as much defining as he had earlier; for example, "Sensation is a phantasm made from the reaction by the outward endeavor of a sensory organ, which [endeavor] is generated by an inward endeavor from an object remaining for some time."[39]

His definition of philosophy may give the impression that he thinks of philosophy as every bit as theoretical as did Plato and Aristotle. From one perspective that is right. But from another, it is not. Although the propositions of science themselves are detached from immediate experience, the goal of philosophy is practical. It is supposed to produce effects for the benefit of human beings: "For I do not think that the great effort that must be expended in philosophy is worthwhile in order for someone to rejoice and exult silently to himself alone over some difficulty regarding doubtful matters that has been conquered or the detection of extremely hidden truths." Paraphrasing Bacon, Hobbes says, "Knowledge is for the sake of power."[40] Again, one of his criticisms of the Royal Society was that it spent enormous sums of money on experiments that seemed to benefit no one. Charles II shared Hobbes's sentiments. He thought of experimental equipment as toys for big boys.

Hobbes's view of the appropriate benefits of science are not completely mundane: "of measuring bodies as well as their motion; of moving heavy weight; of building; of navigating; of making instruments for every use; of calculating the celestial motions, the appearance of the stars, and the moments of time; of mapping the face of the earth." These benefits belong only to natural philosophy, however. The chief benefit of civil or political philosophy is not what they give but what they prevent: "civil war, . . . massacres, loneliness, and shortages of all things."[41]

The Parts of Philosophy

Since all science is about bodies and only bodies exist, all science is unified. Nevertheless, science is divided into types, and it is not necessary to learn the types in any particular order. The basic division of philosophy is into natural science and political ("civil") science. Natural science studies bodies as they operate in nature, that is, without a certain distinctive intervention by human beings. Political science is the study of those bodies that are created by human will in contracts and agreements, especially, governments. This basic division is a bit odd because Hobbes's complete system, *Elementa Philosophiae,* is a trilogy. The initial oddity is relieved by the information that the second part of his overall system, the one that is to treated in *De Homine,* is a subpart of one of the two basic sciences. But which one? In *De Corpore*, Hobbes makes it a part of civil philosophy and calls it 'ethics' ('ethica').[42] This is a change from the taxonomy in *Leviathan*, which begins with the very same division of two basic sciences, that is, natural philosophy (knowledge of "consequences from the accidents of bodies natural") and political philosophy (knowledge of "consequences from the accidents of politic bodies"). The difference comes in the subdivisions of natural philosophy. Natural philosophy is divided into knowledge about "accidents common to all bodies natural" (and those accidents are "quantity and motion") and knowledge about "physics or consequences from qualities."[43] These two subdivisions of natural philosophy are then each subdivided several more times to yield a panoply of sciences, including "philosophia prima" (first philosophy or metaphysics), geometry, arithmetic, astronomy, geography, astrology, optics, music, ethics, poetry, rhetoric, and logic.

The last of the subsciences is "the science of just and unjust." There are at least three interesting aspects of this part of the taxonomy. First, ethics and the science of justice and injustice are no more privileged than geography and astrology. Second, the subject of *De Homine* is a cluster of subsciences that properly includes poetry and rhetoric as much as ethics. Third, either ethics and the science of justice and injustice are not normative sciences, or normative sciences are part of the natural sciences. Either alternative would be odd, measured against the classical tradition. There are other consequences that are only a little less interesting. Logic, which should belong to the subject of *De Homine*, is treated in *De Corpore*, and rhetoric, which again belongs in *De Homine*, is not treated in any section of the trilogy, probably because Hobbes usually thought it caused more harm than good and partially because it was typically classified as an art, not a science. Finally, Hobbes's standard view in *Leviathan* is that justice and injustice are possible only after covenants are made, and covenants presuppose the science of politics, which is logically posterior to the others.

Given all of these problems, one might want to scrap or ignore the taxonomy in *Leviathan*. But that would be ill advised because the elaborate taxonomy is intrinsically interesting. It is problematic primarily because it does not square with the explicit taxonomy in *De Corpore*. Is there a way of resolving the problem by looking at the taxonomies in *De Cive* and *De Homine*? No. In *De Cive*, the basic sciences are simply divided into three, each of which is assigned to a section of *Elementa Philosophiae*. *De*

Homine compounds the problem by saying that its subject matter consists partly of natural philosophy and partly of political philosophy. This makes it hybrid. In fact, much of its material had already or could have been treated explicitly in one of the earlier two sections. The first nine chapters, which are devoted to optics, could easily have been treated in *De Corpore*, and in fact are not appropriate in a section that is supposed to be on topics distinctive to human beings. The next four chapters, devoted to speech, appetite, and emotions, had been treated in *De Corpore*. Finally, the last two chapters, devoted to religion and government, had been treated in *De Cive*. So the topics of *De Homine* do not fit neatly into Hobbes's descriptive taxonomies and should have been doled out between natural and civil philosophy. *De Homine* thus became little more than his second thoughts about the issues already discussed in the two sections of *Elementa Philosophiae* already published.

Mathematical and Theological Disputations, 1656–59

Long before Hobbes acquired his reputation as a political theorist, he was recognized as a mathematician of some distinction.[44] During the winter of 1642–43, he produced a proof "for the equality of a parabola and an 'Archimedean' spiral"[45] in the presence of Mersenne, Gilles Personne de Roberval, and possibly another mathematician. As it turned out, the proof was defective. This failed proof did not discredit Hobbes as a mathematician. It inspired Roberval to work on and solve the problem the next day.[46] In 1644, John Pell asked Hobbes among other mathematicians, including Francesco Cavalieri, Descartes, Mersenne, and Roberval to submit proofs of a lemma he needed to refute a position of Longomontanus (Christian Severin). (The contributions were published in *Controversiae de Vera Circuli Mensura . . . Prima Pars* in 1647.) Even into the early 1650s, some of the best mathematicians of the time counted him as one of their own. In 1654, Christiaan Huygens sent Hobbes a copy of his *De Circuli Magnitude*. Although his reputation began to decline shortly after he published *De Corpore*, which included several invalid geometric proofs, he was still referred to as a mathematician without sarcasm even in the 1670s.

The downfall of his reputation was caused by the very public debate that Hobbes waged with John Wallis for two decades. The debate began when Wallis published in 1655 a refutation of Hobbes's attempt to square the circle in *De Corpore*. Hobbes responded to Wallis the next year in an appendix to the English translation of *De Corpore* (*The Elements of Philosophy, The First Section, Concerning Body*). The title of the appendix – *Six Lessons to the Professors of Mathematics of the Institution of Sr. Henry Savile, in the University of Oxford* (1656) – indicates its supercilious tone. Wallis then published *Due Correction For Mr. Hobbes, or School Discipline, For Not Saying His Lessons Right* (1656). Hobbes duly followed with *Stigmai Ageometrias, Agroikias Etc.; or, Marks of the Absurd Geometry, Rural Language, Scottish Church Politics and Barbarisms of John Wallis Professor of Geometry and Doctor of Divinity* (1657). Some sense of the fury and tedium of this ongoing debate can be given by perusing the short titles of Hobbes's contributions – to use the term loosely – to it during the 1660s and 1670s: *Examinatio & Emendatio Mathematicae Hodiernae. Etc.* (1660), *Problemata Physica . . . Adjunctae sunt etiam Propositiones duae de Duplicatione Circuli* (1662), *Rosetum Geometricum . . . Cum Censura brevi Doctrinae Wallisianae de Motu* (1671), *Lux Mathematica. Exussa Collisionibus Johannis Wallisii Theol. Doctoris, Geometrica in celeberrima Academia Oxoniensi Professoris Publici . . .* (1672), *Principia et Problemata Aliquot Geometrica Ante Desperata, Nunc Breviter Explicata & Demonstrata* (1674). These books have been virtually unread for the past three centuries.

Wallis was a first-class Presbyterian mathematician. It may seem odd to modify 'mathematician' with a denominational term, but it would have made some sense in the seventeenth century, because part of the invective between Hobbes and Wallis was caused by their ecclesiologies and because both men thought that whoever won their mathematical war would also win a theological victory. Writing to Huygens in 1659, Wallis said, "Our Leviathan is furiously attacking and destroying our universities . . . and especially ministers and clergy and all religion . . . as though men could not understand religion if they did not understand mathematics. Hence it seemed necessary that some mathematician should show him . . . how little he understands the mathematics from which he takes his courage."[47] This sentiment would find its way into print three years later. In *Hobbius Heauton-timorumeno; or, A Consideration of Mr Hobbes his Dialogues* (1662), Wallis wrote, "Jeering upon every turn at immaterial substances: But, nowhere proving either the impossibility, or the nonexistence of them. . . . His [Hobbes's] new divinity was to be flankered by his philosophy. . . . His philosophy is to be relieved by his mathematics. . . .

But now 'tis so happily fallen out that geometry, which he thought his greatest sanctuary, has most failed him."[48] The mixed marriage of mathematics and theology was also blessed by Thomas Tenison, future archbishop of Canterbury, who will have some prominence in the next chapter. In *The Creed of Mr. Hobbes Examined,* he covers a wide area of disagreement. Following on his complaints that Hobbes "subjected the canon of Scripture to the Civil Power" and "injected . . . uncertain novelties in doctrine" is the one that he "affronted geometry itself, who so well deserves the name of science."[49]

Hobbes accepted the theologico–mathematical rules of his debate with Wallis. The conflation of mathematics and theology, not to mention politics, is evident from the title of Hobbes's *Stigmai Etc.; or, Marks of the Absurd Geometry, Rural Language, Scottish Church Politics and Barbarisms of John Wallis Professor of Geometry and Doctor of Divinity* (1657). He wanted to associate Wallis with Scottish presbyterianism because he knew that that politico–religious combination was out of favor with the Commonwealth government. The English presbyterians had lost substantial power after Pride's Purge in late 1648; the Scots had then supported Charles II after the execution of his father in 1649, and Cromwell invaded Scotland and conquered the independent-minded Scots in 1651. (There is a contemporary example of fusing religion with something very different. The narrator of Norman Maclean's *A River Runs through It* says that in his family "there was no clear line between religion and fly fishing." The father is a Presbyterian minister of Scottish ancestry.)

Hobbes's *Six Lessons to the Professors of the Mathematicks, etc.* contains, in addition to a discussion of geometrical methods, a lesson on "manners," in which he defends his religious views.[50] In the same work, Hobbes shows that the correct understanding of what a geometrical point is – that is, his own understanding of it – is relevant to several theological issues. One concerns the relationship between the correct definition of a figure (as a "quantity every way determined") and the existence of God. Hobbes's opponents use a bogus distinction between something being at a place "definitively" and "circumscriptively." They do this to "save themselves from being accused of saying he [God] is nowhere; for that which is nowhere is nothing."[51] That is, they assert that although God is nowhere (circumscriptively), he is everywhere (definitively). Hobbes thinks this involves a distinction without a difference. On his view, because they maintain that God is nowhere, they are logically committed to the view that God does not exist: geometrical atheism.

Another connection between geometry and theology involves the nature of souls and angels:

[A point is] a mark . . . of which there is no part. Which definition, not only to a candid but also to a rigid construer, is sound and useful. But to one that neither will interpret candidly, nor can interpret accurately, is neither useful nor true. Theologers say the soul has no part and that an angel has no part, yet do not think that soul or angel is a point. A mark or as some put instead of it, στιγμη, which is a mark with a hot iron, is visible; if visible, then it has quantity, and consequently may be divided into parts innumerable. That which is indivisible is no quantity; and if a point but not quantity, seeing it is neither a substance nor a quality, it is nothing.[52]

While Hobbes's debate with Wallis may be termed the external cause of his downfall, the internal cause was Hobbes's philosophy of mathematics. His mathematics suffered because of his conception of the relationship between physics and geometry. He thought of geometry as the premier science because it accurately represented physical reality, namely, matter in motion. In other words, geometry is the science of bodies in motion "when we consider nothing in [them] besides [their] motion."[53] One consequence of this is that since every body has some quantity, every point and line has a quantity.

The Logical Priority of Geometry over Arithmetic

One further aspect of the priority of geometry should be mentioned. It implicitly denigrated arithmetic. The dominant view since ancient times had been that mathematics had two branches, arithmetic and geometry, neither of which had priority over the other. Arithmetic was the science of discrete quantity or multitude. Geometry was the science of continuous quantity or magnitude.

In the seventeenth century, some mathematicians began to claim that one had priority over the other. Descartes and Wallis, for example, thought that arithmetic was more basic than geometry. In *Mathesis Universalis*, a book that explores the foundations of mathematics, Wallis promoted arithmetic in this way: "But in truth the objects of arithmetic are higher and more abstract in nature than geometrical ones. For example, it is not because a *two-foot line added to a two-foot line makes a four-foot line,* that *two and two make four;* instead, because the latter is true, the former follows."[54]

Isaac Barrow, the first Lucasian Professor of Mathematics at Cambridge, and Hobbes disagreed. In *Mathematicae Lectiones* (1664–66), Barrow argued that the priority of geometry could be seen from the fact that numbers can be added to numbers only if the underlying matter, that is, the underlying geometric entity, is the same. Not only is it improper to compare apples and oranges, they cannot be counted as such. (They of course can be counted as fruit, but then the underlying matter is considered to be the same.) If numbers could be abstractly added together, then a line of two feet added to two apples would be four of something, either a line of four feet or four apples or something else. But it does not: "from whence I [Barrow] infer that 2 + 2 makes 4, not from the abstract Reason of the Numbers but from the Condition of the Matter to which they are applied." Hobbes was making the same point when he asserted this: "For though an arithmetical calculation be true in numbers, yet the same may be, or rather must be false, if the units be not constantly the same."[55] In short, as Barrow says, "a Mathematical Number has no existence proper to itself, and really distinct from the magnitude it denominates, but is only a kind of note or sign of magnitude considered after a certain manner."[56]

Hobbes has a criticism of Wallis that is in the same spirit as Barrow's. He claims that algebraic or analytic geometry confuses lines with geometric figures; it applies numbers to each indiscriminately. In *Seven Philosophical Problems* (1657), Hobbes says, "I see the calculation [done by Wallis] in numbers is right, though false in lines. The reason whereof can be no other than some difference between multiplying numbers into lines or planes, and multiplying lines into the same lines or planes." The problem with applying arithmetic to geometry, from Hobbes's perspective, is that while in geometry there are "three dimensions," in arithmetic, there is only one and "that is number or length which you will."[57] Confusion is the result: "when they reckon by arithmetic in geometry, there a unit is sometimes part of a line, sometimes a part of a square, and sometimes part of a cube."[58] For algebraists, according to Hobbes, "the same number is sometimes so many lines, sometimes so many planes, and sometimes so many solids."[59] For him, a square root is always a line.[60] He says, "Consequently they [his opponents] have ignorantly applied a rule of algebra, which is a purely arithmetical rule, to geometry, and having supposed the most ingenious things they have deduced the most absurd, by promiscuously taking a line, a square and a cube for a unit."[61] Although Hobbes wanted to keep arithmetic separate from geometry, in order to keep geometry pristine, it seems to me that he thought that arithmetic depends on geometry.[62] Arithmetic is made possible by the fact that bodies can be divided, if only mentally, into an infinite number of equal parts. It is this possibility of equal division that gives rise to numbers. Numbers, then, are derivative. Since algebraic or analytic geometry founded by Descartes and advanced by Wallis was a kind of arithmetization of geometry, Hobbes was very much against it.

At the very least, he thought that geometry was more basic than arithmetic for two general reasons. The first is that since only matter is real, geometry, which is the measure of matter, is foundational mathematics. The second is that the method of geometry, which begins with definitions and axioms, is superior to that of algebra, which does not. In addition, he has some specific arguments and objections. One argument is that algebra depends on certain results in geometry, such as the Pythagorean theorem, and hence cannot be more basic.

Algebraic Anxiety

Hobbes's complaints about algebra may well have a psychological cause; he suffered from symbol anxiety. He had a hard time understanding algebraic equations and thought of algebraists as symbolmongers. In his *Six Lessons to the Professors of the Mathematicks etc.*, he wrote:

[Wallis] mistook the study of symbols for the study of geometry, and thought symbolical writing to be a new kind of method, and other men's demonstrations set down in symbols new demonstrations. . . . I never saw anything added thereby to the science of geometry, as being a way wherein men go round from the equality of rectangled planes to the equality of proportion, and then again to the equality of rectangled planes, wherein the symbols serve only to make men go faster about, as greater wind to a windmill.[63]

About Wallis's *Treatise of Conic Sections*, Hobbes wrote that it was "so covered with a scab of symbols that I had not the patience to examine whether it be well or ill demonstrated."[64] For him, algebraic symbols were merely abbreviatory devices at best. But instead of adding calculative power, they obfuscate reasoning:

I shall also add that symbols, though they shorten the writing, yet they do not make the reader understand it sooner than if it were written in words. For the conception of the lines and figures (without which a man learns nothing) must proceed from words either spoken or thought upon. So that there is a double labor of the mind, one to reduce your symbols to words, which are also symbols, another to attend to the ideas which they signify.[65]

So algebra could yield brevity in the writing of a proof but not brevity of thought because the objects of thought are not the words we use to express thoughts but the things themselves; and these things cannot be abbreviated.[66] This is an odd line to take for the man who claimed that reasoning is nothing but the addition and subtraction of words, which are merely symbols. But, to paraphrase what he said in another context, a mathematician will be for symbols as long as symbols are for him.[67] Earlier in the same work, he had written that such symbols are obscene and "ought no more to appear in public than the most deformed necessary business which you do in your chambers."[68] Many high school students feel the same way.

Numbers

One of the consequences of the denigration of arithmetic vis-à-vis geometry is a certain dubiousness that Hobbes assigns to numbers and to certain operations involving them. Number relates to noncontinuous or "discrete quantity," while motion, the primary phenomenon, and all quantity "designed by motion" is continual.[69] So number contains within itself a certain deflection from reality. It is possible that Hobbes's views about numbers dovetailed with his views about the vacuum. The belief that numbers connected with discrete bodies might foster the idea that there was a vacuum or void between bodies, when in fact, according to Hobbes, matter is continuous and there is no vacuum or void.

Hobbes is not even quite certain what numbers are. He gives two explanations ("expositions") of them. One is that numbers are the names of points. The number one is the name of one point; the number two is the name of two points, and so on. What makes numbers less than perfectly representational is that while every point has a quantity, no number expresses it. The names 'one', 'two', and so on make no mention of any quantitative dimension of the points they name. Hobbes's other explanation of what numbers are is that they are names ('one', 'two', 'three') "recited by heart and in order." Merely saying "one, one, one" does not allow a person to know where she is numerically as soon as she gets beyond two or three.[70] It seems that Hobbes thought that what is important about cardinal numbers was their ordinality.

For Hobbes numbers greater than one are not independent entities. The number 'two' designates two occurrences of a unit; 'three' designates three occurrences of a unit. The unit (oneness) remains the foundational numerical entity. My guess is that most nonmathematicians think of natural numbers in the same way that Hobbes did. They think that because $4 = 1 + 1 + 1 + 1$, there are really only ones and that 'four' is an abbreviation for something reducible to ones. In fact, the natural numbers, like other types, are infinite and not unitary. Two, three, four, and so on are different from one, however it is construed.

Mathematics and Epistemology

Concerning the relation of epistemology to mathematics, Hobbes maintains that knowledge must ultimately be reducible to sensations. That is one reason why he wants to explain numbers in terms of Hobbesian points, which, unlike Euclidean points, are observable. When 2 and then 3 are subtracted from 5, the result is 'nothing', and 'nothing' is not a name of anything. (The use of the word 'zero' did not come into common mathematical usage until the late eighteenth century. Latin has no word for it, 'nihil' ['nothing'] being the closest approximator to 'zero'.) If 6 is subtracted from 5, then the result is "less than nothing," which is not a thing but only "feigned" or invented by the mind.[71] For Hobbes, there are no negative numbers, much less imaginary ones, such as the square root of −2.

In contrast to these feigned entities that result from arithmetical operations performed on numbers, geometrical entities can never yield a feigned entity, because all of them, according to Hobbes, are constructible. They are real observable entities: "the lines and figures from which we reason are drawn and described by ourselves."[72] So, mathematics ought to begin, not with numbers, but with points.

A nice summary of Hobbes's views about the relationship between causality, geometry, and knowledge occurs in his *De Principiis et Ratiocinatione Geometrarum* (1666):

"But," you will ask, "why is it necessary for demonstrations of purely geometric theorems to appeal to motion?" I respond first: All demonstrations are flawed, unless they are scientific; and they are not scientific unless they proceed from causes. Secondly, demonstrations are flawed unless their conclusions are demonstrated by construction, that is, by description of figures, that is, by the drawing of lines. For every drawing of a line is a motion; so every demonstration whose first principles are not contained in the definitions of motions by which the figures are described is flawed.[73]

Points, Lines, and Figures

In addition to opposing the standard view that arithmetic and geometry were equal and independent, Hobbes challenged the idea that geometry was abstract. Triangles and squares, for example, are usually considered ideal entities that approximate to but are not genuinely realized in the physical world. The objects studied by geometry are supposedly not physically existing shapes and figures, but ideal or mental ones. That is a central reason why Plato had such a high opinion of geometry. It was part of his view that what is nonphysical is 'really real' and what is physical is not. Although Descartes did not think that the material world was unreal, he did think that mathematics was abstract and did not depend on sensation or imagination. Hobbes loathed such abstractionist and nonmaterialistic interpretations of reality and mathematics. So, if he was going to persuade people of the truth of his philosophy, he would have to explain geometry in materialistic terms. This required a redefinition of its basic concepts: points, lines, and figures.

Euclid had defined a point as "that which has no parts." The correct understanding of this definition, according to Hobbes, is that a point is undivided, not indivisible; and the quantity of a point is not to be considered in any demonstration. The incorrect understanding of Euclid's definition, the understanding in favor with modern mathematicians, is that a point actually has no parts. Impossible, Hobbes maintained. What has no parts is *nothing:* Every quantity has parts. If a point is not a quantity, then "it is neither substance nor quality, it is nothing."[74]

A similar problem infects Euclid's definition of a line as "breadthless length," if it is taken in the wrong, that is, the modern, way.[75] In contrast, Hobbes maintains that Euclid's words are correctly understood as meaning that a line is a body, the width of which is ignored in demonstrations. A line is "a body whose length is considered without its breadth," and this of course means that the line has a breadth. Otherwise, it would not make sense not to consider it.[76] There could theoretically be points without motion, but there cannot be lines without motion, according to Hobbes. Thus, the complete definition of line is "the path traced by a moving body, the quantity of which is not considered in a definition."[77]

All other geometrical objects can be generated and hence defined in terms of derivative motions. A surface is generated by the motion of "a line so moved that each of its points describes a right [straight] line." A solid is the motion of a surface "drawn into another right line equal to the first two and orthogonal to them."[78] Hobbes asserts in effect that there cannot be more than three-dimensional figures. His target is Descartes and other proponents of analytic geometry, who were able to describe figures of n-dimensions through their methods.

Even ratios, which intuitively seem to be static relations between numbers or some sort of abstract object, are treated by Hobbes as relations between bodies that result from certain motions. Equal ratios such as $1:1$ are the result of two bodies generated by lines in equal times moving at equal speeds. Unequal ratios are the result of two bodies generated by lines moving either for unequal times or at unequal speeds. Hobbes admired his novel treatment of ratios precisely because he expressed them in terms of bodies and motions, in other words, in terms of causes and effects.

To know something is to know how to construct it. Consequently, if a certain figure could not be constructed in a certain way, then knowledge of those things would be limited. Knowledge and construction are tied to each other because, for Hobbes, science is the knowledge of causes, and the motions that construct an object are the cause of that object. Hobbes thought that if a person knew how to define all the basic terms of geometry – point, line, plane, ratio, and so on – in terms of how they can be generated, then one knows in theory how to generate all the figures that can be generated from them. In particular, it should be possible to generate those figures that formed the recalcitrant problems of traditional geometry: squaring the circle, constructing a cube with twice the volume as a given cube, and trisecting a given angle. Unfortunately, Hobbes presupposed something that was not justified. He thought that all geometrical constructions could be accomplished using compass and straightedge. In fact, that is not true. Since that result was not proved until the nineteenth century, Hobbes has some excuse for believing it –

some excuse, but not exculpation. He greatly underestimated the power of the analytic geometry that was invented by his rival Descartes and extended by his enemy John Wallis. It is impossible to say whether his personal feelings for these people colored his view of their mathematics or whether his view of their mathematics intensified his disdain for them. It does not matter which is the case, because the result is the same. He blazed a new path for geometry that led nowhere.

For all of the novelty and innovation in his theories, Hobbes also had a deeply conservative strain. It led him to want to retain the traditional method of constructing geometrical objects using compass and straightedge, just as it led him to want to preserve the traditional Christian doctrines formulated in the creeds.

Squaring the Circle

The squaring of the circle is the problem of constructing a square equal in area to a given circle using only a straightedge and a compass. There were only three rules or ways of constructing a figure. (1) A straight line could be extended (using the straightedge alone). (2) A new line could be drawn from a point on a given line to another given point (using the straightedge and compass). (3) A circle could be drawn (using the compass alone). These are obviously very restricted means, and one of the interesting and powerful features of Euclidean geometry is how much one can prove with them.

The problem of squaring the circle is related to the problem of the rectification of the cube, which is the problem of constructing a straight line equal to the circumference of a circle. If this construction could be completed, then the other problem would be solved, because Archimedes had proved that the area of a circle is equal to the area of the right triangle consisting of the radius as the height and the circumference as the base. If such a triangle could be constructed, then a square having the same area could easily be constructed and the problem of squaring the circle would be solved. Consequently, in addition to trying to square the circle directly, Hobbes tried to rectify the circle.

Our discussion of Hobbes's views about the relationship between physics, epistemology, and geometry should make his optimism about squaring the circle more intelligible. If geometry deals with real, physical bodies, and if the method of geometry essentially involves constructing various figures of bodies, and if an actual circle or cube is given, why shouldn't it be possible to construct a square of exactly the same area or a cube of twice the volume? It seems plausible. (But it is impossible all the same.)

Another Circle Squarer

While Hobbes was defending his attempts to square the circle against Wallis, a complicated subplot was being spun out. At the first level – and there are several others – Thomas White held the same view as Hobbes and yet Wallis supported him. In 1659, White was preparing a book called *Tutela Geometrica* under the pseudonym 'Chrysaspis'. When he discovered a flaw in his proof to square the circle, he withdrew the manuscript from publication. However, an antagonist, writing under the pseudonym 'Querula', published a pirated edition of part of the work along with an abusive commentary. (A similar thing had happened to Hobbes: Wallis had gotten hold of an early version of Hobbes's attempt to square the circle. Hobbes withheld the manuscript from publication. But Wallis got a copy of it and criticized the defective proof. Hobbes execrated Wallis: "And seeing you knew I had rejected that proposition, it was but a poor ambition to take wing as you thought to do, like beetles from my egestions.")[79] To return to White and Querula, when White had been identified as the author of the defective proof, he had to defend himself, just as Hobbes did. White argued that Querula was actually a secret Jesuit and not really interested in geometry at all. He went on to claim that Jesuits regularly confuse themselves with the Catholic Church and consequently take every attack on one of their members as an attack on the church itself. He thought that the ecclesiastical egoism of the Jesuits was bizarre enough, but worse was their novelty in identifying Jesuits with geometry, as revealed in the title of his opponent's work: *Querula Geometrica; or, Geometry's Complaint of the Injuries Lately received from Mr. Thomas White in his Late Tract, Entituled "Tutula Geometrica."* Since Querula was really the person complaining and since he said in his book title that "Geometry" was complaining, White rationated that Querula arrogantly and nonsensically identified himself with geometry: This "is the first time I ever heard them style themselves *Geometry* and aver what is written against one of them is written against Geometry."[80] Admittedly, this debate, which confused parochial Roman Catholic bickering with mathematics, was bizarre. But it helps put the debate between Hobbes and Wallis, the nonstandard Anglican geometer versus the Presbyterian algebraist, into the appropriate historical perspective.

One irony of the debate between White and Querula is the fact that Wallis was friendly with White. It seems that Wallis and White, along with White's friend and champion Digby, allied themselves because they were all alienated from Hobbes at the time. The source of Wallis's complaint is clear enough; in White's case, he may have felt he had an unsettled score with Hobbes left over from Hobbes's sharp critique of *De Mundo*. Digby reported to Wallis that White was promoting Wallis's reputation. Wallis, who never mentioned White's problems with circle squaring, answered, "we must all acknowledge ourselves deeply indebted to Mr. White, who is pleased not only to judge so favorably of us, but to represent us to you in such a character as has given us so advantageous a place in your opinion."[81] In fact, Digby had an extensive correspondence with Wallis and published it in 1658 as part of a plan to promote religious tolerance of Roman Catholics in England. What Digby and White really cared about in the 1650s was an alliance with friends of the Protectorate that would help the cause of Roman Catholics. White's generally antipapal stance, combined with his skepticism about purgatory, endeared him to the Calvinistic Independents that controlled the Commonwealth. A series of papal condemnations against him in the late 1650s tended to establish his credentials. The efforts of Digby and White succeeded to some degree, to the disgust of many other Protestants. Because of their courting of Cromwell, one writer referred to White and Digby as "Rump-like Anarchical" Catholics.[82]

Politics, religion, mathematics. What's the difference?

Geometry, Latin, and Scatology

What stands out in the debate between Hobbes and Wallis is the irrationality of it. In the context of settling geometrical issues, they argued about what counted as correct Latin and Greek. In *Six Lessons*, Hobbes wrote, "Before I proceed, I must put you in mind that these words of yours, '*adducis malleum, ut occidas muscam*' are not good Latin, *malleum affers malleum adhibes, malleo uteris*, are good."[83] Wallis accused Hobbes of confusing στιγμα with στιγμη. Hobbes defended himself by quoting various ancient poets. He then accused Wallis of misusing the Latin verb 'adducere'. Hobbes buttressed his case by scoring points about the correct translation of 1 Timothy 2:15, and contrasting it with the text of 1 Peter 3:20.[84]

Hobbes did not need to defend himself against other grammatical objections raised by Wallis, because Henry Stubbe came to Hobbes's aid. At the end of *Stigmai,* Hobbes included a twenty-six-page "extract" from a letter that Stubbe had written to him. The letter is a detailed vindication of Hobbes's Latin and Greek grammar. Stubbe, who was deputy keeper of the Bodleian Library at the time, was still a respectable figure. But his unpredictable attacks on various groups, one of which would be the Royal Society, eventually marginalized him. Wood, in *Athenae Oxoniensis,* described Stubbe in this way: "He had a hot and restless head (his hair being carrot-colored) and was ever ready to undergo any enterprise, which was the chief reason that macerated his body almost to a skeleton. He was also a person of no fixed principles and whether he believed those things which every Christian doth, 'tis not for me to resolve."[85]

To give some taste, or perhaps, odor, of the dispute between Hobbes and Wallis, I will mention that one of the supposedly key issues concerned the meaning and etymology of the word 'Empusa'.[86] In *De Corpore,* Hobbes had said that "school divinity" is like the Empusa, a ghost that changes shapes, that has one good leg but limps because its other leg is rotten. The good leg is Scripture; the rotten leg is the "pernicious philosophy" of Aristotle.[87] Wallis claimed that an Empusa was a hobgoblin that hopped on one leg, and he punned on 'Hobbes' and 'hobgoblin'. Stubbe helped out by telling Hobbes about the etymology of 'hobgoblin'. It is partially French and partially Saxon. The 'hob' part comes not from 'Hobbes' but from 'Robert', "just as Richard, Richardson, Rixon; Dick, Dickinson, Dixon; Robert, Robinson, Robson; Hobbinall, Hobson, Hob."[88] (In fact, the word 'Empusa' is ambiguous; both Hobbes and Wallis were describing different meanings of it.)

These grammatical and mythological issues had no bearing on geometry. Still, both men found it hard to let any possible criticism go. There is some irony in this because Hobbes bragged about how nice he was to everyone:

Truly I remember not an angry word that ever I uttered in all my life to any man that came to see me, though some of them have troubled me with very impertinent discourse; and with those that argued with me, how impertinently soever, I always thought it more civility to be somewhat earnest in the defense of my opinion, than by obstinate and affected silence to let them see I contemned them or hearkened not to what they said.[89]

He was nice even in the face of impertinence:

When vain and ignorant young scholars, unknown to him before, come to him on purpose to argue with him and to extort applause for their foolish opinions, and missing of their end, fall into indiscreet and uncivil expressions, and he then appear not very well contented, it is not his morosity but their vanity that should be blamed.[90]

Of course, Hobbes realized that the invective had to be explained away. He said that behavior that would count as abusive if unprovoked is not abusive when it is done in response to another person's abuse. He appealed for support to the emperor Vespasian, who acquitted a knight who had insulted a senator: "Since the senator did not have to bad mouth you, it was right and civil for you to bad mouth him back."[91]

Both Hobbes and Wallis went over the edge with their vitriol. Some of it is literally scatological abuse. Hobbes ends *Six Lessons* with this: "So go your ways you *Uncivil Ecclesiastics, Inhuman Divines, Dedoctors of morality, Unasinous Colleagues, Egregious pair of Issachars, most wretched Vindices and Indices Academiarum.*" But Wallis was probably worse for calling Hobbes's work "a shitten piece."[92] Hobbes also quotes Wallis as writing, "and now he [Hobbes] is left to learn his lurry." It is not quite clear what Wallis meant, but Hobbes puts the worst interpretation on it:

I [Hobbes] understand not the word 'lurry'. I never read it before nor heard it, as I remember, but once, and that was when a clown threatening another clown said he would give him "such a lurry come poop &c." Such words as these do not become a learned mouth, much less are fit to be registered in the public writings of a doctor of divinity.[93]

I think that Hobbes won these exchanges because he pretended to stand on the high ground of gentility, and Wallis, being a clergyman, was more easily dirtied by his own filth. Hobbes relished citing the un-Christian behavior of clerics like Wallis and Ward. In the next chapter, however, we shall see Hobbes emitting his own vulgarities.

10

Baiting the Bear, 1660–1669

The wits at court were wont to bait him. But he feared none of them, and would make his part good. The king would call him 'the bear'. "Here comes the bear to be baited!" (Aubrey, *Brief Lives*)

The decade of the 1660s was a thorough mix of joy and controversy for Hobbes. Because "Man bites dog" is news and "Dog bites man" is not, we know much more about Hobbes's fights than about his enjoyments. He was embroiled in disputes with John Wallis over mathematics, with Robert Boyle over experimental philosophy, and with numerous Anglican bishops over religion. He was supposed to be investigated by a parliamentary committee for atheism and was shut out of the Royal Society. Perhaps worst of all, he was old and losing friends to death. Mersenne had long been dead. Selden died in 1654, Gassendi in 1655, Harvey in 1657, Charles du Bosc in late 1659. Already in his seventies, Hobbes thought that he did not have long to live. Grieving for du Bosc, he wrote stoically that "we should not mourn too long over one death; otherwise we should have too little time to mourn for others."[1] Two months later, he learned of the death of Abraham du Prat.

But the 1660s were also good to Hobbes. He reconciled with the king, Digby, and White, and he continued to enjoy some fame and respect, especially on the Continent. His self-satisfaction showed on his face. Here is Aubrey's description:

[A]mple forehead; whiskers yellowish-reddish, which naturally turned up – which is a sign of a brisk wit. . . . Below he was shaved close except a little tip under his lip. Not but that nature could have afforded a venerable beard . . . but being naturally of a cheerful and pleasant humor, he affected not at all austerity and gravity and to look severe. . . . He desired not the reputation of his wisdom to be taken from the cut of his beard but from his reason. . . .

He had a good eye and that of a hazel color, which was full of life and spirit, even to the last. When he was earnest in discourse, there shone (as it were) a bright live-coal within it. He had two kind of looks: when he laughed, was witty, and in a merry humor, one could scarce see his eyes; by and by, when he was serious and positive, he opened his eyes round (i.e. his eyelids). He had middling eyes, not very big nor very little.

He lived life at a leisurely pace. Although he said he was drunk fewer than one hundred times in his life, a very moderate number given the culture and his years, he gave up drinking wine at the age of sixty. He also gave up meat and ate fish daily. He awoke at about 7:00 A.M., had a breakfast of bread and butter, and walked as he meditated until about 10:00. He wrote up his thoughts on a lapboard about sixteen inches square that had paper pasted on it. He had lunch at about 11:00, smoked a pipe, and then took a nap. He sang popular songs for his health. As Aubrey describes it:

He had always books of prick-song lying on his table . . . which at night, when he was abed and the doors made fast, and was sure nobody heard him, he sang aloud (not that he had a very good voice) but for his health's sake: he did believe it did his lungs good and conduced much to prolong his life.

In matters of personal hygiene and care, he thought his biggest problem was "to keep flies from pitching on the baldness." But he also had intestinal worms.

In the rest of this chapter, we will begin with one of the bright spots, spend a long time on his troubles, introduce some relief due to his friends, and then return to his troubles.

The Restoration, 1660

Perhaps the single brightest spot of the decade for Hobbes was his reconciliation with Charles II. Aubrey reported the event:

It happened about two or three days after his majesty's happy return that, as he was passing in his coach through the Strand, Mr. Hobbes was standing at Little Salisbury House gate (where his Lord [Devonshire] then lived.) The king espied him, put off his hat very kindly to him and asked him how he did. About a week after, he had oral conference with his majesty at Mr. S. Cowper's [Samuel Cooper], where, as he sat for his picture, he was diverted by Mr. Hobbes's pleasant discourse. Here his majesty's favors were redintegrated to him and order was given that he should have free access to his majesty, who was always much delighted in his wit and smart repartees.

Sometime later Charles gave Hobbes a pension. It may not have been regularly paid, however, sometimes as a result of the interference of Hobbes's enemies at court and sometimes as part of a tactic for economizing. Charles also bought a portrait of Hobbes from Samuel Cooper. It may be the unfinished miniature that is owned but not currently displayed by the Cleveland Museum of Art.

The year of the Restoration was generally a happy one for Englishmen. In anticipation of the king's arrival, people had been rollickingly joyous in February. They lit bonfires and rang the bells in all the churches. Blaming much of their miseries on the Rump Parliament, people began to replace the expression "Kiss my arse" with "Kiss my rump." People bought rumps of meat to burn in effigy. The English had grown weary of the governments that had succeeded one another after the execution of Charles I: Councils of State, the Barebones Parliament, and the Protectors Cromwell. The return of Charles II was a return to the good old days that superseded 'The Good Old Cause'. The large and enthusiastic crowds that greeted the king gave the false impression that the English were united in what they understood the character of the restored monarchy to be and what they expected from the monarch. Some understood the king to be an absolute monarch in the sense that he was the only authority in England. Some of these thought that his right to rule was divinely justified; others thought that it was derived from the people. Some thought that the king was absolute over the Church of England in that the institution of bishops depended on him. Others thought that the king's authority over the church extended only to matters of discipline, that the episcopacy was divinely instituted (*iure divino*) and was not dependent on the monarchy.

The tens of thousands of Englishmen who had either fought against the royalist forces or had sympathized with the parliamentary cause had not gone away or changed their views very much. They had to accommodate themselves to the new regime just as the royalists had had to do in 1649. There were Presbyterians and Independents who variously wanted to be included in the established Church of England as part of some policy of 'comprehension' or not persecuted as part of a policy of 'toleration'. It was not to be.

As part of the maneuvering to make his return to England as desirable as possible, Charles issued a declaration at Breda in which he declared his willingness to let bygones be bygones: "And to the end that fear of punishment may not engage any, . . . we do, by these presents, declare that we do grant a free and general pardon, which we are ready, upon demand, to pass under our Great Seal of England, to all our subjects, excepting only such persons as shall hereafter be excepted by Parliament."[2] The exception cited was a reasonable one given that there was no reason for him to oppose the wishes of parliament on this issue.

This first genuine Parliament of the Restoration, nicknamed 'the Cavalier Parliament' because of its royalist leanings, was not as forgiving as Charles. Stocked with bitter Anglicans, it passed four religiously repressive bills, known as the Clarendon Code, between 1661 and 1665. The first, the Corporation Act, required all municipal officials to be communicants in the Church of England. The Act of Conformity required the same for church officials. The Conventicles Act made it illegal for four or more dissenting Protestants (not of the same family) to worship together. The Five Mile Act forbade dissenting ministers to come within five miles of any town in which they had held a position. These laws were in effect for the rest of the Stuart era. Everyone except conventional Anglicans was officially suspect.

Hobbes was not conventional. His troubles with the clergy connected with the royal courts had started in France in 1650, as we have seen. It escalated at the Restoration. Although his clerical enemies could not persecute him under any of the provisions of the Clarendon Code or even in an ecclesiastical court, they were not about to make life easy for him. His first difficulties with clerics in the 1660s came in the guise of scientific disputes. As we saw in the preceding chapter, science and religion, not to mention politics, were intertwined enough to be confused with each other. Many inferences from science to religion, and vice versa, that would be easily recognized as invalid today were not at all obvious to many educated people of the Restoration. The separation of church and state, which is now a commonplace in the United States, was then still a generally scandalous idea in England.

Troubles with the Royal Society

The Royal Society of London for the Improving of Natural Knowledge, chartered by Charles II early in the Restoration, was the institutionalized successor to groups of scientists who had met informally in London and Oxford since the 1640s. Early members of the society included John

Wilkins, John Wallis, Seth Ward, Elias Ashmole, Henry Oldenburg, Jonathan Goddard, George Ent, John Eveyln, Kenelm Digby, Matthew and Christopher Wren, F. Glisson, Christopher Merret, Theodore Haak, Robert Moray, William Petty, Lawrence Rooke, Charles Scarborough, Ralph Bathurst, William Brereton, and Robert Boyle. As this list indicates, Anglicans, Presbyterians, Independents, and even Roman Catholics interacted comfortably with each other. By the end of 1663, there were 137 regular members – in short, almost everybody of scientific note except Hobbes and White. And some members were not even scientists. Many of the members liked and respected Hobbes. Lord Bruce, Devonshire, Digby, Evelyn, Petty, Scarborough, and Waller have to be counted as friends or friendly to him. He was also on at least civil terms with John Pell, Ralph Austen, Brereton, Oldenburg, and Matthew Wren in the early 1660s. Why wasn't Hobbes a member? He wanted to be, and his international reputation should have made him attractive to the fledgling institution. The explanation is complicated and somewhat speculative.

Of course he had enemies in the society: Boyle, Ward, Wallis, and Wilkins. These were powerful opponents, but they did not have the power to veto or blackball his candidacy if it had ever been brought to a vote. It never was.

Part of his problem stems from the purpose of the society to advance "natural knowledge by experiment." As Robert Hooke described it, the purpose was

to improve the knowledge of natural things and all useful arts, manufactures, mechanic practices, engines and inventions by experiments – (not meddling with Divinity, Metaphysics, Morals, Politics, grammar, rhetoric or logic).

. . . [T]his Society will not own any hypothesis, system or doctrine of the principles of natural philosophy, proposed or mentioned by any philosopher ancient or modern, nor the explication of any phenomena whose recourse must be had to original cause . . . ; nor dogmatically define nor fix axioms of scientifical things, but will question and canvass all opinions, adopting nor adhering to none, till by mature debate and clear arguments, chiefly such as are deduced from legitimate experiments, the truth of such experiments be demonstrated invincibly.

This is wittingly or unwittingly an anti-Hobbesian statement. He had meddled in divinity, metaphysics, morals, politics, grammar and logic. Also Hobbes thought that experimentation was overrated and experiments manufactured within a laboratory setting almost always useless.

Nature itself in the form of tides, eclipses, falling objects, and the motions of the heavenly bodies provided sufficient data on which to reflect and by which to measure one's theories. Perhaps worst of all, as I have discussed earlier, Hobbes thought that science had to be axiomatic in the sense of being founded on principles that were stipulative definitions. This typically amounted to redefinition, and many members of the society rejected such semantic imperialism. John Wallis mocked it:

For Mr. Hobs is very dexterous in confuting others by putting a new sense on their words rehearsed by himself: different from what the words signify with other men. And therefore if you [Boyle] shall have occasion to speak of chalk, he'll tell you that by 'chalk' he means cheese: and then if he can prove that what you say of chalk is not true of cheese, he reckons himself to have gotten a great victory. And in like manner, when that heterogeneous mixture (whatever it be) wherein we breath is commonly known by the name of air and this air wherein we live abounds, you say, with parts of such a nature, he tells you that by 'air' he understands such an ether as is among the stars and that in this air there be no such particles.[3]

Hobbes was convinced that his definitions were proper and thought that canvassing the opinions of others was a waste of time. The right procedure for the Royal Society, he maintained, would have been for it to pick up drawing deductive inferences at the point where he had left off in *De Corpore*. They need not bother themselves with the definitions and theorems in the book since he was certain that they were correct, and he told them so.

In *Dialogus Physicus* (1661), Hobbes criticized members of the Royal Society for their sophomoric and invalid reasoning. At the end of the dialogue, having demolished their views to his own satisfaction solely through the use of his own philosophical principles, Hobbes concludes that the Royal Society has not progressed beyond *De Corpore*. They have in fact wasted their time and money by constructing expensive experimental machinery. These gadgets could not be an aid to the advancement of science when they are used without a sound scientific method. In fact, they are a hindrance because they give the illusion of being helpful. Speaking in the character of A, Hobbes writes: "Why such apparatus and the expense of machines of difficult manufacture, just so as you could get as far as Hobbes had already progressed? Why did you not rather begin from where he left off? Why did you not use the principles he established?"[4] In *Considerations Upon the Reputation . . . of Mr. Hobbes*, he continued the same theme: "not everyone that brings from beyond the seas a new gin or other jaunty device is therefore a philosopher. For if you reckon that way, not only apothecaries and gardeners, but many other sorts of workmen, will put in for and get the prize."[5] In short, these gentlemen scientists were behaving beneath their station. The stated goal of the Royal Society, namely, to advance natural knowledge by experiment, was no part of Hobbes's agenda.

So part of his problem was that he did not share some of the goals and methods of the society. Ironically, another part of the problem was that his views were too similar to those of many of the members. One of these was the belief that the physical universe operates mechanistically. Joseph Glanvill, for example, accepted that "as far as the operation of nature reaches, it works by corporeal instruments" and that "sense is made by motion, caused by bodily impression on the organ and continued to the brain, and center of perception."[6] Another similarity was an excessive reliance on reason in matters of religion, and the idea that Christ had not dictated episcopacy as the only form of church government. This seemed to some people to imply that monarchy was not necessarily the only or best form of government. These were dangerous positions to hold early in the Restoration.

Some of Hobbes's supposedly offensive doctrines were espoused by other members of the society in words very similar to his own. Glanvill maintained that because "the divine nature is infinite and our conceptions very shallow and finite," people should not try "to pry into the secrets of [God's] being and actions" and in fact "do not know the essence and ways of acting of the most ordinary and obvious things of nature and therefore must not expect thoroughly to understand the deeper things of God."[7] This echoes Hobbes's remark that "the principles of natural science . . . are so far from teaching us anything of God's nature, as they cannot teach us our own nature nor the nature of the smallest creature living."[8] An echo of Hobbes's remark that the papacy is the ghost of the deceased Roman Empire sitting crowned upon the grave thereof can be heard in Glanvill's quip: "A schoolman is the Ghost of the Stagirite, in a body of condensed air: and Thomas but Aristotle sainted."[9] Seth Ward in *Against Resistance of Lawful Powers* in effect endorsed Hobbes's position about the sovereign's monopoly on religious authority: "If none have power to order matters of religion, there must be confusion; if any other beside the supreme magistrate, there will be division."[10] And Thomas Sprat in *The*

History of the Royal Society expressed the essence of Hobbes's view of religion: "Religion ought not to be the subject of Disputations; it should in this be like the temporal laws of all countries." Meric Casaubon, shocked by Sprat's assertion, could not believe his ears: "The sense [of the words] is obvious enough; but a sense so amazing that it is not credible."[11]

Even the society's literary ideals matched Hobbes's. Sprat condemned "this vicious abundance of Phrase, this trick of Metaphor, this volubility of Tongue, which makes so great a noise in the world." The society rejected "all amplification, digressions, and swellings of style." Their goal was "to return to the primitive purity and shortness, when men delivered so many things almost in an equal number of words." What was required of the members' prose is the following: "a close, naked, nature way of speaking, positive expressions, clear sense, a native easiness, bringing all things as near the mathematical plainness as they can, and preferring the language of Artisans, Countrymen, and Merchants before that of wits and scholars." In 1664, a committee that included John Dryden and John Evelyn was formed to consider how English prose style could be improved.[12]

Much is made of Hobbes's materialism, which is usually held to entail atheism. But Mormons believe in a material God. Moreover, materialism could have been attributed by implication to one of the foremost members of the Cambridge Platonists. Henry More held that all substances are extended (even spirits). From the commonplace that only matter is extended, it follows that More is committed to the view that God is material. So he was as logically committed to atheism as Hobbes was. But More was acceptable in a way that Hobbes was not. In short, as Noel Malcolm says, "the more disreputable Hobbes became, the more necessary it was for the other scientists to dissociate themselves from him by attacking him, precisely because he was in some ways embarrassingly close to their own position."[13]

The main opposition to the society came from two overlapping groups. One was composed of the conservative intellectuals who thought that if Aristotle had been good enough for Elizabethan scholars, it should be good enough for Restoration ones. The other was composed of religious conservatives who were afraid that corpuscular science led to atheism.[14] The dangers to the society were so great that, to quiet criticism, its history was published just five years after it had received its charter. As its author Sprat wrote, "The objections and cavils of the detractors of so noble an institution did make it necessary for me to write of it, not in the way of a plain history, but as an apology." Part III of that history is an extended argument to the effect that science is not a threat to government or religion. Because the project of the Royal Society was suspect to some people, it could not afford the luxury of embracing the controversial Hobbes.

Another reason for excluding Hobbes from the society is the embarrassingly simple but true one that he would have been a "club bore."[15] Hooke wanted the benefits of membership in the society to include "desirable acquaintance, delightful discourse, [and] pleasant entertainment by experiments." Hobbes would not have contributed to these goals. His arrogance is neatly conveyed in Hooke's description of the way Hobbes conducted himself:

I found him [Hobbes] to lard and settle every observation with a round oath, to undervalue all other men's opinions and judgments, to defend to the utmost what he asserted though never so absurd, to have an high conceit of his own abilities and performances though never so absurd and pitiful.[16]

So his attitude was a genuine problem, even though he could also be a witty and engaging conversationalist.

Although Hobbes's view of rational science did not fit neatly with the Society's experimentalism, he did not scorn observation. He reported to the society in 1668 that a young woman had not eaten anything for several months

but only wets her lips with a feather dipped in water. The were told also that her guts (she always keeps her bed) lie out by her at her fundament shrunken. . . . The woman is manifestly sick and 'tis thought she cannot last much longer. Her talk (as the gentlewoman that went from this house told me) is most heavenly. To know the certainty, there be many things necessary which cannot honestly be pried into by a man. First, whether her guts (as 'tis said) lie out. Secondly, whether any excrement pass that way or none at all. For if it pass, though in small quantity, yet it argues food proportionable, which may, being little, be given her secretly and pass through the shrunken intestine, which may easily be kept clean. Thirdly, whether no urine at all pass; for liquors also nourish as they go. I think it were somewhat inhumane to examine these things too nearly, when it so little concerns the commonwealth; nor do I know of any law that authorizes a justice of [the] peace or other subject to restrain the liberty of a sick person so far as were needful for a discovery of this nature. I cannot therefore deliver any judgment in the case. The examining whether such a thing as this be a miracle belongs, I think, to the Church. Besides, I myself in a sickness have been without all manner of sustenance for more than six weeks together; which is enough to make me think that six months would not have made it a miracle. Nor do I much wonder that a young woman of clear memory, hourly expecting death, should be more devout than at other times. 'Twas my own case. That which I wonder at most is how her piety without instruction should be so eloquent as 'tis reported.[17]

Some cynics think that Hobbes is being sarcastic. But the phenomenon of anorexia was unusual at the time; Hobbes's description is clinical; the questions he asks are appropriate. The simplest account of his letter is that Hobbes was being candid.

Troubles with Robert Boyle

In 1661, Hobbes published *Dialogus Physicus,* which was a joint attack on the work of Robert Boyle and the methods of the Royal Society.[18] More precisely, Boyle was being used as an example of what was wrong with the society. Hobbes begins with an attack on the society itself: "Those Fellows of Gresham who are most believed and are as masters of the rest dispute with me about physics. They display new machines to show their vacuum and trifling wonders in the way that they behave who deal in exotic animals which are not to be seen without payment." Hobbes was implying that some of the members of the Royal Society were mercenary and consequently not disinterested observers of nature.

Hobbes was particularly irritated that the reason that the society rejected his theories was precisely that they were his. He quotes John Owen as saying, "Whatever be Hobbes's doctrine, we will not accept it." In the 1668 edition of *Dialogus Physicus,* Hobbes added a sentence: "All of them are my enemies." The reference of "all of them" is a certain part of the clergy, all algebraists, and "Greshamites," that is, the members of the Royal Society. Wallis was a member of each category and a friend of Boyle. Boyle had cited Wallis's presence at some of his experiments as partial evidence of their reliability: "the principal fruit I promised myself from our engine [which was used in the presence of] those excellent and deservedly famous mathematic professors, Dr. Wallis, Dr. Ward, and Mr. Wren . . . whom I name, both as justly counting it an honor to be known to them and as being glad of such judicious and illustrious witnesses of our experiment." So, if Hobbes could discredit Boyle, he could kill two birds with one stone.

Dialogus Physicus takes the form of a discussion between A, Hobbes's literary persona, and B, a friend of the Royal Society. One of A's objections to the procedure of the society is that its experiments were closed to all except its members and their guests. When B explains that the society consists of about fifty men who meet at a fixed time once a week, A expresses surprise: "Why do you speak of fifty men? Cannot anyone who wishes come, since, as I suppose, they meet in a public place, and give his opinion on the experiments which are seen, as well as they?" B says, "No." A is struck by the arbitrariness of having such a small number of men constitute the official scientific community of England. Why should not the number be one hundred or something else? Hobbes of course wanted to be in that number however large or small it might be and probably would not have objected to the number if he had been included in it. But he was not, and he had an objection: The scientific activity of the society was not public. This criticism is barbed because some members of the society thought of it as conducting its experiments in public, in contrast with alchemists, who were secretive. As Steven Shapin and Simon Schaffer comment,

[T]he space in which it [the Royal Society] produced its experimental knowledge was stipulated to be a *public space*. It was public in a very precisely defined and very rigorously policed sense: not everybody could come in; not everybody's testimony was of equal worth; not everybody was equally able to influence the institutional consensus.[19]

Other important members, however, such as Robert Hooke wanted the society to be a closed and elitist group. Michael Hunter summarizes that position:

[Hooke] felt it essential that the Society's benefits should be exclusively limited to its Fellows, so that active membership would be obligatory for any with serious scientific interests: "there must be somewhat to be had by those that meet and are regular members which others must want." To achieve this he would even have overturned the Society's Baconian commitment to the free dissemination of knowledge, arguing that 'Nothing considerable in that kind can be obtained without secrecy because else others not qualified . . . will share of the benefit.' He even wanted to limit the circulation of the Society's 'azets' to Fellows and to allow no one else to see them for twelve months.[20]

Notwithstanding the legitimacy of Hobbes's complaint against secrecy, there is something odd about his making it. He himself had argued on many occasions that the prime goal of society is to forestall conflict and that the sovereign alone has the authority to decide how to do this. Since Charles II had chartered the society and seemed to have no objection to the limited membership, Hobbes should not have been complaining. Indeed, one reason why Hobbes could not get admitted to the society even though several of the members were his friends was that he was cantankerous and a troublemaker. His debates with Wallis, Ward, and Wilkins were ample proof of that.

Hobbes illustrated the failure of the experimental methods of the society by critiquing Boyle's use of the air pump. Put simply, the pump was a glass globe with a suction device at the bottom consisting of a piston in a cylinder. Boyle inferred that air was supposedly extracted from the globe when the piston was retracted. Hobbes thought the inference was unjustified for at least two reasons: First, since air is extremely liquid and subtle, it is plausible that any air drawn out by the piston would be replaced by air that leaks in where the cylinder is attached to the glass. Moreover, there have to be some small gaps where the glass meets the cylinder because nothing is "infinitely smooth." As a matter of fact, Boyle had a difficult time preserving the integrity of the device. Even he admitted that sometimes the glass cracked and some other part of the device leaked. Second, Hobbes objected, some extremely subtle air ("pure air") might be able to penetrate the glass itself. When the piston is extracted, it takes up space (outside the globe) that had been occupied by air; that air has to go somewhere; why not hypothesize that it slips back into the glass in one of the ways he suggested earlier?

Hobbes also critiqued the great experiment of Evangelista Torricelli, who had inverted a long tube, open at one end and filled with mercury, into a bowl of mercury. The mercury in the tube descended until it reached a level of about twenty-nine inches. From this, Torricelli and others inferred that a vacuum had been created in the open space at the top of the tube. Hobbes was not convinced. When the mercury in the tube leaked into the bowl, it displaced air near the top of the bowl and this air had to go somewhere. Since every other part of the world was full, Hobbes hypothesized, the air was forced up the tube, through the mercury (or perhaps where the mercury meets the glass tube), and came to rest at the top, exactly where Torricelli thought the vacuum was. Hobbes was also able to account for the differential in the height of the mercury when the experiment is performed on the top of a mountain. Mountain air has fewer earth particles mixed with it, so it exhibits less force.

For every Royal Society explanation of an experiment, Hobbes had an alternative, and often plausible, explanation. The only problem with them is that they were wrong. For example, a dog placed in the glass jar would die within two or three minutes, after the piston had been worked several times. As a counter to Boyle's explanation that the dog died from lack of oxygen, Hobbes argued the opposite. The dog died from in effect drowning in air that was circulating through the glass so rapidly ("violently") that it stopped the dog's circulation.

The Vacuum

Hobbes never liked the idea of a vacuum. He held that all motion or causation occurs by contact of one body against another, and therefore vacuums would be places free of causal action. They would be genuine gaps in reality. As he had said in *Leviathan*, "the universe . . . is corporeal, that is to say, body; . . . and consequently every part of the universe is body and that which is not body is not part of the universe: and because the universe is all, that which is no part of it is *nothing*, and consequently *no where*."[21] The idea of a Swiss cheese universe offended Hobbes's philosophical sense. Added to this general abhorrence for vacuums is the specific problem of explaining certain phenomena if vacuums were to exist. When a vacuum is allegedly caused by extracting air from a jar containing water, the water appears to boil. But how would it be possible to see what is happening in the jar, Hobbes points out, if vision requires a continuous motion from the observed object to the eye? The alleged vacuum should make the water invisible.

It has also been suggested that Hobbes opposed vacuums because it opened up a space that could be populated by immaterial spirits. This does not seem plausible to me because immaterial spirits do not need vacuums for their residence; they can occupy the very same space as material bodies, as the soul allegedly is in the body.

In a way, Hobbes should not have been as antagonistic to Boyle's claims as he was. Boyle eschewed what he thought of as the metaphysical issue of vacuums. When he pumped air out of his glass device, he claimed only to have produced an experimental vacuum, that is, "not a space wherein there is no body at all, but such as is either altogether, or almost totally devoid of air." This left open the possibility that the air was replaced with "some ethereal matter." In other words, Boyle wanted to use the word 'vacuum' in an operational sense. And in his "Examen of Hobbes," Boyle said, "the atmosphere or fluid body that surrounds the terraqueous globe may, besides the grosser and more solid corpuscles wherewith it abounds, consist of a thinner matter, which for distinction-sake I also now and then call ethereal." Other members of the society followed Boyle in their nonmetaphysical interpretation. Wallis wrote to Oldenburg: "therefore where I speak of 'vacuity' . . . I do expressly caution . . . not to be understood as affirming absolute vacuity (which whether or not there be, or can be, in nature, I list not to dispute)." This kind of qualification could have led to a compromise. Hobbes could have kept his absolute plenism if he would let the experimentalists have their relative vacuums. But Hobbes would not compromise. Since he thought that science was identical with philosophy, science could not ignore the metaphysical issue of whether a (metaphysical) vacuum had been created in Boyle's glass jar or not. Despite his antipathy for vacuums, Hobbes never asserted that there could not be one. Rather his claim was always that no one had proved their existence and that he could provide explanations of all phenomena without appealing to them.

Disputes with Some Mathematicians, 1662

Simultaneous with his disputes with Boyle about science, Hobbes was continuing his battle with Wallis about geometry. He was looking for allies wherever he could. He solicited the help of his old acquaintance John Pell. On March 31, 1662, the day after Easter, Hobbes ran into Pell in the Strand. He insisted on having Pell look at his latest mathematical proofs. They went to Hobbes's room in Salisbury House, where Hobbes showed Pell his manuscript on the doubling of the cube, which was to be sent to the printer the next day. Hobbes wanted to send copies to the Continent although he feared that it would not be well received. He also worried about its domestic reception. He believed that Viscount Brounker was writing a refutation of it, and he wanted Pell to endorse his proof. Pell begged off; he was busy and could not judge the matter without careful consideration. Time was no matter to Hobbes. He gave Pell some of his work and told him to take as long as he needed. Pell could hardly refuse the papers thrust into his hand. "Well," Pell said noncommittally, "if your work seem true to me, I shall not be afraid to tell the *world* so: but if I find it false, you will be content that I tell *you* so, but privately, seeing you have only thus privately desired my opinion of it." This was good enough for Hobbes: "Yes, I shall be content, and thank you too. But, I pray you, do not dispute against my construction, but shew me the fault of my demonstration, if you find any." With that Pell took his leave. Because Pell did not endorse Hobbes's mathematical work, he eventually became an enemy.

In August of 1662, Hobbes received a letter in which Christiaan Huygens explained several mistakes that Hobbes had made in his proofs to square the circle and to duplicate the cube. Hobbes was not convinced and responded to Huygens's objections via Sir Robert Moray. Huygens had not included any bile or negative evaluation of Hobbes's mathematical abilities in his first letter.[22] But he began to show his exasperation after Hobbes sent his reply. Huygens said that he would not have written the first letter at all if he had not been pressured by his friends. The second letter was also being coerced: "I am convinced that I am making this effort utterly in vain – given that, in my opinion, he [Hobbes] is incapable of being led thereby to admit his error." The only bright spot for Huygens was that he was confident that no one else would be convinced by Hobbes's supposed proofs ("absurd childish nonsense"). Hobbes's numerous mathematical errors were diminishing his reputation.

Hobbes refused to let the matter rest. The mathematician René-François de Sluse, who received a copy of Hobbes's attempted proof of duplicating the cube through Sorbière, pointed out Hobbes's errors and then ended with a combination caution and insult. He wrote that "this eminent man" should not criticize mathematicians when he apparently had not "sufficiently understood their thinking." He would be sorry if Hobbes's "deservedly great reputation" were to be damaged "as a result of this little work of his old age." Hobbes took umbrage at being called in effect a benighted old fool. He was shocked that de Sluse would make the very same objection that Laurence Rooke, the Gresham Professor of Geometry, had made, since in his opinion he had already refuted Rooke in *Problemata Physica* (1662).[23] De Sluse should have read it before making his objections, said Hobbes. As for his reputation, Hobbes would make it clear to everyone, except those "who think that ten times one stone equals ten square stones," that de Sluse and Huygens and Rooke were all wrong and that he was right.

The basis of Hobbes's rejection of the criticisms of Huygens, de Sluse, Wallis, and others was his belief, explained in the preceding chapter, that analytic geometers confused numbers with geometric figures. In particular, they mistakenly thought that the square root of a number is a side of a square.[24] In a letter of December 1663, he avers that this kind of mistake "shows how inadequate numbers are for confirming or refuting a geometrical demonstration."[25] Nonetheless, he does his best to be conciliatory. He says that he does not think any the less of de Sluse despite his confusions, because his mistakes were no worse than anyone else's: "I do not think that Archimedes himself could have used a better one [argument] since he too was mistaken in his application of numbers to geometry."[26] But by March 1664, he is tired of arguing:

I do not want to change, confirm, or argue any more about the demonstration which is in the press. It is correct; and if people burdened with prejudice fail to read it carefully enough, that is their fault, not mine. They are a boastful, backbiting sort of people; when they have built false constructions on other people's principles (which are either false or misunderstood), their minds become filled with vanity and will not admit any new truth.[27]

Hobbes Defends Himself

Hobbes's most effective weapon against Wallis was completely non-mathematical. It came in his small work, *Mr. Hobbes Considered in His Loyalty, Religion, Reputation, and Manners* (1662) (hereafter *Considerations*), a reply to *Hobbius Heauton-timorumenos* (1662), in which Wallis had criticized Hobbes for taking the title of tutor to the Prince of Wales in the second edition of *De Cive*. Hobbes was happy to put the record straight about what each of them had done during the Civil War. His attack on Wallis was so devastating that Wallis realized that prudence dictated retreat. He never attacked Hobbes's religion or politics in print again.

What had Wallis done during the Civil War? He had been deciphering "the letters of the king and his party and thereby delivered his Majesty's secrets to the enemy and his best friends to the scaffold and boasted of it in your book of arithmetic, written in Latin, to all the world, as a monument of your wit, worthy to be preserved in the university library." He had also taken the Solemn League and Covenant in order to wed himself to the Scottish rebels, "a very great crime and you [Wallis] guilty of it."[28] He had also been a member of the Assembly of Divines, which prepared the Directory of Church Worship, which changed the liturgy of the Church of England, without the approval of the king, the head of the church.

In contrast, Hobbes's behavior was impeccable. Referring to himself in the third person, he says that he was "the only man I know, except a few that had the same principles with him, that has . . . [nothing] to blush for."[29] He, "the first that had ventured to write in the king's defense," had authored *The Elements of Law, Natural and Politic* in April 1640, and thus needed to escape England in November because the Long Parliament "proceeded so fiercely in the very beginning against those that had written or preached in the defense of any part of that power." He had lost several thousand pounds as a result.[30] In exile he continued his intellectual war in behalf of the king's cause by writing both *De Cive* and *Leviathan*. Far from defending Cromwell, Hobbes had attacked "both him and you [Wallis] and others such as you with your abominable hypocrisy and villainy." *Leviathan* could hardly have been a defense of Cromwell's right to govern, because he did not become Protector until "two or three years" later.[31]

The charge of atheism against Hobbes was at least as dangerous as that of treason. And it was equally groundless and partisan. As Hobbes said in his own defense, "Do not many other men, as well as you, read my *Leviathan*, and my other books? And yet they all find not such enmity in them against religion. Take heed of calling them all atheists that have read and approved my *Leviathan*. Do you think I can be an atheist and not know it? Or knowing it, durst have offered my atheism to the press?"[32] Given that the charge was groundless, why was it made? It baffled Hobbes and he ruminated about Wallis's deep psychology. He speculated that Wallis was projecting his own doubts about the existence of God. Hobbes reasoned by analogy: Women of "poor and evil education" tend to call the people they dislike 'whores' rather than 'thieves' or 'murderers' because they attribute to other people what is true about themselves. For the same reason, Wallis calls Hobbes an atheist.[33]

Hobbes had earlier made these same points in *Six Lessons . . . to the Professors of the Mathematics* (1656). In *Considerations,* he gave a more reasoned defense: Every Christian believes that God is incomprehensible; Tertullian himself thought that God was corporeal; the term 'incorporeal' does not occur in the Bible, and Hobbes's own life testifies to his Christian faith. In general, his religious beliefs are unexceptionable because, as he wrote in *Leviathan*, he submits himself "both in this and all other questions whereof the determination depends on the Scriptures to the interpretation of the Bible authorized by the commonwealth whose subject I am." And he glosses it by saying, "What is there in these words but modesty and obedience?"[34] He travels the humble high road in contrast with Wallis's arrogant low one: "Is not Mr. Hobbes his way of attributing to God that only which the Scriptures attribute to him or what is never anywhere taken but for honor much better than this bold undertaking of yours [Wallis], to consider and decipher God's *nature* to us?"[35]

Hobbes's rage against Wallis mounts until at the end of *Considerations*, he can no longer maintain his civility: "In sum, it is all error and railing, that is, stinking wind; such as a jade lets fly when he is too hard girt upon a full belly. I have done. I have considered you now, but will not again, whatsoever preferment any of your friends shall procure you."[36]

The Cambridge Platonists

The Cambridge Platonists have enjoyed a certain respectability in the history of philosophy. They were not so respectable, however, in the late seventeenth century. Heresy was the chief charge against Ralph Cudworth, the greatest of them, and the Latitude Men more broadly. Henry More described some of the rhetoric against them: "some in their pulpits call them sons of Belial, others make the Devil a latitudinarian, which things are as pleasing to me as the raillery of a jack-pudding at one end of a dancing rope."[37] Although Cudworth's defense of free will was attractive to the Restoration Church of England, that doctrine was papist and out of temper with the Calvinism of the reformed Church of England.

The Cambridge Platonists were at least as rationalistic about religion as Thomas White, and rationalism is often a threat to revealed religion. Their assertion that the immortality of the soul could be proved by reason was a two-edged sword: It was reassuring to confirm a doctrine that most Christians took to be part of orthodoxy; but if it was a matter of reason, revelation was made superfluous, except for the stupid. So revealed religion was religion for the intellectually challenged.

Even worse was Henry More's doctrine that at death the human soul did not separate from matter but took up a new relationship to it. More claimed that there were three such relationships: the terrestrial, the aerial, and the celestial, each spiritually higher than the preceding one. This doctrine was taken by their enemies as a Platonized Roman Catholic purgatory, one of the hottest issues for Protestants. As late as 1678, Cudworth, who referred to White and Hobbes as "our Leucippus and Democritus,"[38] maintained that it was irrational to think that human souls could be "in an unnatural or preternatural separation from all body."

The idea that ordinary human beings, destined for heaven, cannot get there after death without some kind of purgation seems to be a powerful one. Even Richard Baxter, as reformed a Protestant as there was, felt he had to come up with some purgation in order to make people suitable for heaven. Joseph Glanvill, at once skeptic and Platonist, also defended the position that the human soul cannot become completely detached from matter at death by quoting numerous pagan philosophers. What does that have to do with Christianity? As Hobbes had written in 1662:

What kind of attribute, I pray you, is immaterial or incorporeal substance? Where do you find it in Scripture? Whence came it hither but from Plato and Aristotle, heathens, who mistook those thin inhabitants of the brain they see in sleep for so many incorporeal men, and yet allowed them motion, which is proper only to things corporeal? Do you think it an honor to God to be one of these? And you learn Christianity from Plato and Aristotle?[39]

A Reconciliation with White and Digby

The 1660s were not simply a daisy chain of debates and cavils for Hobbes.[40] He reconciled with Digby and White, kept up a correspondence with Continental friends, continued to publish, smoked for relaxation, and sang for health.

In the preceding chapter, we saw that Hobbes had had a falling out with Thomas White. White may have had a lingering irritation over Hobbes's rough handling of *De Mundo,* and his desire to get his faction of Roman Catholics accepted by the Commonwealth government aligned him with Wallis, against Hobbes. The opposite and more than equal reaction of Hobbes was not to associate with White. Like Descartes, White was a competitor whose views were too close to Hobbes's own for Hobbes's liking. White, like Hobbes, was trying to give a thoroughly materialistic account of the physical world, although he kept the soul in the wings. Both thought for some time that they had succeeded in squaring the circle. White, like Hobbes, opposed the Catholic doctrines of purgatory and papal infallibility. White was as odious to establishment Catholicism as Hobbes was to establishment Anglicanism. Hobbes even could have taken some pleasure in having made the Index of Prohibited Books before his Roman Catholic friend. White's Hobbesian defense of the legitimacy of the Commonwealth in *The Grounds of Obedience and Government* cost him dearly. Despite the best efforts of Digby, who had regained his post as chancellor of Henrietta Maria's court in 1660, Charles II was unwilling to forgive White: "No more of that," the king told Digby. "I know what man he is." For his efforts Digby was excluded from the court for a while.[41]

Digby was more successful in reconciling Hobbes to White. He had a kind of salon in his residence in Covent Garden. White, who lived close by in Drury Lane, would often attend as Hobbes would. To say that they were reconciled is not to imply that they agreed about everything. Anthony Wood reported:

Hobbes of Malmesbury had a great respect for him [White], and when he [Hobbes] lived in Westminster, he would often visit him, and he but seldom parted in cold blood; for they would wrangle, squabble and scold about philosophical matters like young sophisters, though either of them was eighty years of age, yet Hobbes being obstinate, and not able to endure contradiction (tho well he might, seeing White was his senior) yet those scholars, who were sometimes present at their wrangling disputes, held that the laurel was carried away by White.[42]

(There is at least some inaccuracy in this passage. Hobbes was in fact older than White. If the two men were about eighty, then Wood should be talking about meetings that occurred about 1668, three years after Digby died.) The reconciliation between White and Hobbes was probably aided by the fact that they were under attack from some of the very same people and for the same reasons. For example, Roger Coke, a relative of Edward Coke, attacked them in his book, *Justice Vindicated From the False Focus Put Upon it, by Thomas White Gent. Mr Thomas Hobbs, and Hugo Grotius* (1660). In another book, the anonymous *Evangelium Armatum. A Specimen or Short Collection of Several Doctrines and Positions Destructive to our Government both Civil and Ecclesiastical. Preached and Vented by the Known*

Leaders and Abetters of the Pretended Reformation (1663), Coke argued that
Hobbes was part of the papist conspiracy to overthrow Charles II, and
worse. In order to show that White and Hobbes approved of rebellion
against the king, Coke juxtaposed passages from works by White and
Hobbes with passages from presbyterians to show that they were all of the
same ilk. For Hobbes this would have been the unkindest cut of all.

Some critics did not need to associate Hobbes or White with presbyterianism to attack them. It was enough to show how Hobbes's theory was a
variation on the Roman Catholic threat. One Counter-Reformation argument for Roman Catholicism rested on a skeptical premise. There is no
way to know what the Bible means or what God wants without some
authority. There is no authority in the whole history of Christianity
except the Roman Catholic hierarchy. Knowledge requires certainty, and
the only ground of certainty for Christians is the infallibility claimed by
the Roman Catholic Church. White accepted a version of this argument.
Hobbes accepted the spirit but not the letter of it. Religion required
authority all right, but that authority was supplied by the sovereign, not
the Roman Catholic Church (except in Rome). Gilbert Burnet, bishop of
Salisbury, made this connection fairly explicit in his great history of the
Restoration:

And now that the main principles of religion were struck at by Hobbes and his
followers, the papists acted upon this a very strange part. They went so far even
into the argument for atheism, as that there was no certain proof of the Christian
religion, unless we took it from the authority of the church as infallible. . . . [The
Catholics] chose to make men who would not turn papists become atheists rather
than believe Christianity upon other ground than infallibility.[43]

Another way to attack Hobbes via Catholicism came from Archbishop
Talbot, who said that the "depraved doctrine" ("pravum dogma") of
White's protégé, John Sergeant, was basically the same as that of Hobbes.
Glanvill also associated White's Blackloism with Hobbism. Glanvill's first
of several attacks on White had appeared in the second edition of *The
Vanity of Dogmatizing* in 1661. Then, in response to White's defense of
himself, Glanvill wrote that White's philosophy was "irreligious" and had
"shaken hands with the *Leviathan*." Glanvill said that White was "in the
very road of the Hobbian hypothesis."[44] It would have been hard for
Hobbes not to like a person so in touch with his own philosophy.

Throughout the sixteenth and seventeenth centuries, skepticism was variously interpreted as an atheistic strategy against religion and as a religious strategy against atheism. Glanvill's own views are interesting insofar as they are an example of skepticism in the service of religion. Whether such skepticism was perceived as well intentioned or not depended to some extent on extraneous religious, social, and political factors. Glanvill's skepticism was religious because he was otherwise reputable, and so Hobbes's and White's dogmatism was irreligious because they were disreputable. But this formula does not always hold, as we shall see in the next section.

François du Verdus, 1663–66

Hobbes probably met François du Verdus (1621–75) in Paris in 1651. Du Verdus was described as Gilles Personne Roberval's best student in geometry, and he prepared the notes that Roberval, who held a chair of mathematics at College Royal, later used as the basis for his own lectures. Educated by the Jesuits, du Verdus traveled to Italy in the 1640s and met Torricelli and Digby, among others. He came to know Hobbes through their mutual association with Mersenne's circle and soon became intellectually and emotionally attached to the distinguished older man. After Hobbes returned to England, du Verdus began an ardent and faithful correspondence and translated Hobbes's trilogy, *Elementa Philosophiae,* into French. Only part of his translation of *De Cive* was ever published.

There are many surviving letters from du Verdus to Hobbes from 1663 to 1666. In them we get an embarrassing glimpse into his tortured soul. After years of anguish caused by long legal battles over the disposition of the estate he inherited, he became emotionally unstable. He believed that his guardian, his relatives, the Jesuits, and the archbishop of Bordeaux were using supernatural means to cheat him out of his inheritance. He said that Hobbes had talked about those very people in "Of the Kingdom of Darkness" in *Leviathan,* but even that description of them was "nothing compared with the reality."

Even if his beliefs about a conspiracy were true, he was also paranoid. Du Verdus thought that he had discovered the secrets of their diabolical machinations, and then that they found him out:

So, seeing that I was in possession of their secret, but knowing too that they knew that I knew it, I realized immediately that one of three things would have to happen. Either I would use that knowledge to destroy them; or they would destroy me; or we would make peace with each other. Destroying them seemed a great and fine thing, and perhaps not impossible: if I had one faithful ally I would have thought I could have achieved it, and turned the kings against them. But where could I find the faithful ally? That option therefore was difficult. Then again, should I agree with my destruction? One never agrees to that. So I sought out those gentlemen again. And since they went so far as to send me threats that they would have me seized, taken to Rome, and burnt alive . . .

And on and on.

Shortly later du Verdus entrusted Hobbes with a statement that was to be used if he met an untimely death. Part of it reads:

Slandered here by false rumors . . . about a secular nun, . . . suffering denials of justice, legal quibbles and breaches of trust; going for five years with only one suit of clothes, and living for three years on bread and water; poisoned twice; spending eleven months with my joints seized up throughout my body, alone and helpless all that time, and yet keeping up my spirits and not losing heart . . .[45]

And on and on.

What kept du Verdus going was his deranged religious faith. After reciting his litany of persecutions, ending with "I could also give a full account of their personal hatred for me," he abruptly says, "but one must be Christian and confide one's feeling to God." He also described for Hobbes "a tabernacle which I saw in a dream."[46] Mercifully, Hobbes did not point out to his friend that the correct rendering is: "you dreamed that you saw a tabernacle."

Since none of Hobbes's letters to du Verdus survive, we cannot be sure of how he responded. Du Verdus sometimes complains that he has not received any letters from Hobbes for a long time, but there is evidence that Hobbes was an indulgent and sympathetic friend. He dedicated *Examinatio et Emendatio Mathematicae Hodiernae* (1660) to him and acknowledged him ("honest friend") in his verse autobiography of 1672. Also, he graciously asked to see the entirety of a poem that du Verdus had written about a lesbian love affair between "Iris" and "Phoenix." The main action is Iris's dream of making love with Phoenix: "what pleasure, what delight there was / in the sucking of the lips / of their two mouths joined together – both kissing and kissed! – in the striving of each tongue to out charm the other." Inflamed by her nocturnal affair, Iris confesses her love to Phoenix, who thereupon reciprocates. After making love, they solemnize their love in "mutual, irrevocable pact / under the hands of a priest." The poem ends with the narrator wishing the lovers well as they "experience in reality / those pure delights, / those joys so pleasant and innocent" that they had dreamed of.[47]

As tiresome as du Verdus may seem to us, Hobbes remained faithful to him to the end.

Margaret Cavendish, Marchioness of Newcastle

One of Hobbes's admirers and one of the great characters of Stuart England was Margaret Cavendish (1623–73), Newcastle's second wife, thirty years younger than he. She wore outlandish costumes and expressed outlandish opinions that made her variously admired and disdained. She wrote an important, but uncritical, biography of her husband. Her nickname was "Mad Madge." According to one apocryphal tale, her train was so long that much of it was still in the anteroom when she was curtsying to the king. What was true was that "her carriage and her footmen were decked out in black and white velvet and trimmed with silver to match her clothes."[48] John Evelyn had a good opinion of her. He was "much pleased with the extraordinary fanciful habit and garb and discourse of the Duchess." Samuel Pepys disapproved of her but could not keep his lecherous eyes from exploring her exposed bosom. He called her a "mad, conceited, ridiculous woman, and he [Newcastle] an ass to suffer her to write what she writes to him and of him."

Among her many self-professed talents was literature of various sorts. In honor of the publication of her book, *Playes Written by the Thrice Noble, Illustrious and Excellent Princess, the Lady Marchioness of Newcastle* (1662), a book of letters and poems in her honor was assembled. Hobbes wrote a perfunctory piece for it, *Letters and Poems in Honour of Margaret, Dutchess of Newcastle:*

[Your book] is filled throughout with more and truer ideas of virtue and honor than any book of morality I have read. And if some comic writer by conversation with ill people has been able to present vices upon the stage more ridiculously & immodestly, by which they take their rabble, I reckon that amongst your praises. For that which most pleases lewd spectators is nothing but subtle cheating or filch, which a high and noble mind endued with virtue from its infancy can never come to the knowledge of.[49]

There is more here about the vulgar than about Margaret's work. Since, as we saw earlier, Hobbes thought that people should not make fun of others because comparisons imply that the ludicrous property is shared by oneself as much as the butt of the joke, it is possible that on this occasion he was subtly placing Margaret's work with the vulgar.

Margaret was also a philosopher, although not a very good one. Many of the themes in her philosophical work derived from things she heard being discussed by Descartes and Hobbes. She may have overheard the original debate between Hobbes and Bramhall on free will since she was with Newcastle in exile. She adopted Hobbes's reservations about the value of experiments: "our age being more for deluding experiments than rational arguments, which some call 'a tedious babble', does prefer sense before reason, and trust more to the deceiving sight of their eyes and deluding glasses, than to the perception of clear and regular reason."[50]

Margaret used to eavesdrop on conversations and recorded two involving Hobbes and her husband during the 1640s. One concerned whether humans could fly with artificial wings. Some of those present thought that they could. But Newcastle thought not, because human arms attach to their trunk opposite to the way that bird wings attach to theirs. Hobbes liked this observation so much that he used it in *Leviathan*, or so she thought. In fact, it does not occur in any of Hobbes's work. It is plausible that Hobbes announced his intention to include it in *Leviathan* and then never did. The other conversation involved witches. Newcastle, like Hobbes, did not believe that they existed in the normal sense of people actually getting supernatural powers through a contract with the devil. Newcastle thought that witches mistake their dreams for reality. Hobbes probably agreed since he explained in *Leviathan* that many people mistakenly think that they receive a revelation from God in the very same way. As was mentioned in Chapter 8, Hobbes, like John Selden, thought that self-styled witches ought to be executed, not because they are witches of course, but because they would injure people if they could. Unfortunately, the duchess claims that she never spoke more than twenty words to Hobbes. Such was the status of women, even when well placed. (Her claim may be hyperbolic because there is a story in which she invited Hobbes to dinner, after an evening of entertainment. More than twenty words must have been spoken on that occasion.)[51]

She wrote and worked for women's liberation, often arguing that women were equal to males by nature and only inferior as the result of cultural circumstances. She was at least as interested in natural science as her husband and wanted to visit the Royal Society. Pepys, like many others, opposed it; they were afraid that her mere visit to a session of the Royal Society would discredit the institution. Some of the ridicule that had been directed toward her might be deflected onto them. Eventually permission was granted due to the efforts of her friend Walter Charlton. In honor of her visit, Boyle operated his air pump, turned wine green by adding a certain chemical, and dissolved a piece of lamb in sulfuric acid. She viewed a telescope and watched a magnet disrupt a compass needle. Her earlier Hobbian skepticism about the value of experiments and the genuineness of the images from a telescope melted away.

Enough of these pleasantries. It is time to return to Hobbes's troubles.

The Plague of 1665 and the Fire of 1666

Epidemics were a regular occurrence in Stuart England, as they had been for centuries. Hygiene was bad. Knowledge of the causes was worse. Most people attributed them to God, the devil, or both. The etiology was sin. So the cure was to beg God for forgiveness and to reform one's life. In fact, bubonic plague was transferred from infected rats to fleas to human beings. The plague caused lymph nodes to swell. The victim suffered from high fever, chills, and delirium. Death usually occurred within ten days. Although Hobbes did not have detailed knowledge, his views about the plague were sophisticated for the time. He thought that it was spread by flies:

For first we know that the air is never universally infected over a whole country, but only in or near some populous town. And therefore the cause must also be partly ascribed to the multitude thronged together and constrained to carry their excrements into the fields round about and near to their habitation, which in time fermenting breed worms, which commonly in a month or little more, naturally become flies; and though engendered at one town, may fly to another. Secondly, in the beginning of a plague, those that dwell in the suburbs, that is to say, nearest to this corruption, are the poorest of the people, that are nourished for the most part with the roots and herbs which grow in that corrupted dirt; so that the same filth makes both the blood of poor people and the substance of the fly. . . . Thirdly, when a town is infected, the gentlemen and those that live on wholesome food, scarce one of five hundred die of the plague. . . . Fourthly, a man may carry the infection with him a great way into the country in his clothes and infect a village. Shall another man there draw the infection from the clothes only by his breath? Or from the hangings of a chamber wherein a man has died? It is impossible. Therefore, whatsoever killing thing is in the clothes or hangings, it must rise and go into his mouth or nostrils before it can do him hurt. It must therefore be a fly whereof great numbers get into the blood and there feeding and breeding worms, obstruct the circulation of blood and kill the man.[52]

In one of the worst and hence most famous of these plagues, the first few cases appeared in late 1664 in the parish of St. Giles. The problem grew early the next year, but it was still relatively restricted. In the spring of 1665, the cases became more widespread. Charles II's court left London in June for Oxford, not far behind many of the wealthy people who had already filled the roads going out of London. Neighboring villages required refugees of the plague to have a certificate of health issued by the mayor of London. He was only too willing to oblige. Hobbes probably left in late spring, as his correspondents surmise. One of the very few benefits of the plague was that the Inns of Court closed, no legal work got done, and the lawyers left the city. Arguably, it would have been better if the lawyers had stayed.

The plague was subsiding by September. A year later London was struck by an even worse disaster, the Great Fire of 1666. For most people, the two events were closely connected. The same mysterious offense against God was the cause of each, not to mention the war with the Dutch (1665–67). The fact that the fire broke out at a bakery in Pudding Lane was merely an instrumental cause. The destruction of four-fifths of the city, including St. Paul's Cathedral, the Royal Exchange, and other official buildings, was a sign of God's anger. Charles II and his brother, the duke of York, scored points with their subjects by staying in London and working hard to fight the fire. There is no record of Hobbes's whereabouts or behavior during the fire. It is unlikely that he was either wielding a fire ax or working in a bucket brigade. But the plague and fire would affect his life for the next several years.

Bishops and Heresy

For every event there is an explanation. Disasters are events. Sad to say, the explanations themselves are often disasters. The war, fire, and pestilence made Englishmen frantic for an explanation. A common explanation, as I have said, was that their own sinfulness was the cause. A more comforting explanation was that someone else's sinfulness was the cause.

Sometimes Roman Catholics and sometimes atheists were blamed. In October 1666, a bill was introduced into Parliament against "Atheism and Profanity." Hobbes and the Catholic priest Thomas White were to be investigated for "atheism, blasphemy, or profaneness." The investigation was to focus on "the book published in the name of one White, and the book of Mr. Hobbs, called *The Leviathan*."[53] A committee was supposed to report its opinions to Commons. The proceedings dragged on until 1668, but the investigation came to naught.

Still, Hobbes was rightly concerned about them. He was being investigated by fanatics and partisans. Innocent people need a defense as much as guilty ones. So Hobbes, lawyerlike, wrote several works that discussed the nature of heresy and explained why no one in the 1660s could be tried for heresy, why his views were not heretical, and why the views attributed to him were not his own. While he may have begun writing about the heresy laws as early as 1664, his major writings on the topic were the appendix to the Latin version of *Leviathan* (1668) and *An Historical Narration concerning Heresy and the Punishment Thereof* written at about the same time. There are also discussions of heresy in *Behemoth* and *A Dialogue of the Common Laws,* again dating from about the same time. The appendix to the Latin *Leviathan* has the most elaborately structured defense. It consists of three chapters in dialogue form between the one-dimensional characters A and B, titled 'On the Nicene Creed', 'On Heresy', and 'Objections to *Leviathan*'. Wallis once described these characters as 'Thomas' and 'Hobbes': "When Hobbes has occasion to assume what he cannot prove, Thomas, by a Manifestum est ["It is obvious"] saves him the troubles of attempting a demonstration."[54] The appendix as a whole, and not just the second chapter of it, constitutes his defense. If his explanation of the Nicene Creed is correct, then his views are orthodox. If his theory and history of heresy are correct, then he cannot be prosecuted for heresy. And, if his replies to the objections to *Leviathan* are cogent, then the attributed heretical views are not his. In effect addressing himself, Hobbes wrote, "So far you have explained the doctrine of the Nicene Creed in such a way that it does not seem to me that you have shaken the Christian faith at all; instead you have strengthened it, though in your own way."[55]

Hobbes's account of heresy is basically the same in all of his works. A heresy, he maintains, leaning on etymology, is any doctrine. So Plato and Aristotle were among the first heretics. In time, the term 'heresy' became restricted to religious doctrines. For the sake of civil order, some doctrines were made law, which thereby made others heresies. So it was important for people to know what those teachings were. Hobbes argues on the basis of the case of Eusebius and other bishops after the Council of Nicea that it is obvious that heresy was imputed only to a person that "in plain and direct words contradicted that form by the church prescribed, and that no man could be made *an heretic by consequence*."[56] In the Latin *Leviathan*, Hobbes explained: "For it is very difficult to judge the consequences of words. Therefore, if an accused person has said something against the letter of the law, because he did not know how to reason well, and has not harmed anyone, his ignorance will excuse him."[57]

Hobbes's historical conclusion is certainly meant also as a forensic one. The best case to be made against him was never more than indirect. He never contradicted prescribed doctrine. It was particularly absurd to charge the author of *Leviathan* with heresy for two reasons. First, it was written after the abolition of the court that had authority to judge the matter (the Court of High Commission), and there were no "human laws left in force to restrain any man from preaching or writing any doctrine concerning religion that he pleased." Second, it was written "in this heat of the war, [when] it was impossible to disturb the peace of the state, which then was none."[58] In other words, *Leviathan* is a product of the state of nature. If bishops and presbyterians do not like its doctrines, they should not undermine the authority that could prevent its publication, as they had in the 1640s. In making this point, Hobbes was as happy to be giving the presbyterians and the opponents of the king their comeuppance as he was to be defending himself.

Even if *Leviathan* were heretical, what should be the most severe punishment meted out? Originally, the penalty for heresy was relatively mild, deprivation of ministry for clerics, and exile for the most dangerous heretics. Excommunication was also a standard punishment. Eventually, some people were executed. The burning of heretics seems to have begun under Pope Alexander III in the twelfth century. In England, the Roman Catholic queen known as "Bloody Mary" executed Protestants as heretics, until succeeded by her Protestant sister, Elizabeth, who repealed Mary's heresy laws, declared that only doctrines considered to be heresies by the first four ecumenical councils would count as such, and ended burning as a punishment. In general, the Church of England under Elizabeth, James, and Charles was at least as good as the halcyon days of

Constantine, who ruled both the church and the Roman Empire. The reign of Constantine was glorified by John Foxe in *The Book of Martyrs*, for Protestants a book second in importance only to the Bible.

The clear implication of Hobbes's history is that heresy hunting and severe punishment are more characteristic of Roman Catholics than Protestants. The principal reason for punishing heretics is to prevent Christians from breaking up into "factions." Peace, not truth, is the purpose for imposing uniformity of doctrine on people.[59] Toleration of deviant religious beliefs was no part of Hobbes's brief. Since "disorders and civil wars" often result from "differences of doctrine and intellectual wrangling, there must be some restraint, in the form of punishment, on those who teach in books or sermons things whose teaching the laws of the prince or republic prohibit."[60]

Given that none of Hobbes's works on heresy were published until after the danger to him had passed, they could not have been the thing that kept him from being convicted. His innocence, in my opinion, was the evidence that weighed most strongly in his favor. He may also have received the help of Henry Bennet, who was Charles II's secretary of state for many years.[61] Bennet, as Lord Arlington, was one of the 'a's in the so-called Cabal that was believed to make policy in England after the fall of Clarendon in 1667. Arlington was a political enemy of Clarendon, a fact that would have helped to bond Arlington to Hobbes. Arlington, like several other converts to Roman Catholicism, had something of a reputation as an atheist. The evidence of Arlington's help is thin and ambiguous. In a letter of June 1667, Hobbes thanks Arlington (along with two of his aides) for his help, unspecified. In dedicating his *De Principiis et Ratiocinatione* (1666) to Arlington, Hobbes had acknowledged owing his "greatest comfort to my old age to your influence."[62] This could mean that Arlington helped get the investigation of Hobbes dropped. But since money is also a great comfort, Hobbes's gratitude may stem from Arlington's assistance in getting the royal pension paid to Hobbes. The next year Hobbes tried unsuccessfully to get Arlington's help in approving *An Historical Narration concerning Heresy* for publication.

Behemoth

As further evidence of his gratitude, Hobbes dedicated a finely written manuscript copy of *Behemoth* (located at St. John's College, Oxford) to Arlington. *Behemoth* is Hobbes's history of the English Civil War, written probably between 1666 and 1668. Its title is enigmatic. In a polemical passage, he suggested *Behemoth against Leviathan* as the title of a book to be written by his opponents against him. He himself usually referred to the book as *Dialogue of the Civil Wars of England*. Some of the earliest editions of the book, which were published without Hobbes's permission during his last year of life, had the title *The History of the Civil Wars of England* and others *Behemoth* plus some subtitle referring to the Civil War. The ominous title *Behemoth* stuck. It was one that Hobbes at least sometimes used himself, because it is on the copy of the manuscript that he dedicated to Arlington. Hobbes wrote, "Your Lordship may do with it what you please. I petition not to have it published." My guess is that Hobbes wrote this sometime after he had shown the work to Charles II, that is, about 1668. The king denied Hobbes's request to have it published. "Flatly refused," Hobbes wrote. Charles agreed with what Hobbes had written but knew that it would cause an unhelpful stir if it went into print.

Behemoth is in effect a case study of what Hobbes in *Leviathan* had claimed would go wrong with a government if his political principles were not followed. In short, a monarch must be an absolute sovereign, must function like one, must educate his subjects about their duties to the sovereign, and quash any opposition before it has any chance to do harm; otherwise, the government will disintegrate. To his sorrow and to the sorrow of the nation, Charles I was too accommodating to Parliament, allowed the universities to teach doctrines that subverted his authority, and acted too moderately when factions challenged first his policies and later his very legitimacy.

Hobbes does not always get his facts straight, but that hardly diminishes the interest of *Behemoth*. In philosophy it is often important not to confuse the issue with the facts. What concerned Hobbes was not so much the events of the Civil War as their causes, and he would not have altered his account of the causes even if the events had been somewhat different. His account varies depending on his mood and perspective. If the actions and personalities of the perpetrators are at issue, then the causes were "injustice, impudence, . . . hypocrisy, . . . knavery, and folly."[63] But he also had more historically specific accounts. One was that the king lacked the power needed to do his job. This lack of power consisted of inadequate money to run the government and incomplete control over the military. Another cause was the corruption of the people. Hobbes listed six main causes for this: Presbyterians; Roman Catholics;

Independents, Anabaptists, Fifth-Monarchy men, Quakers, and Ada-
mites; educated people corrupted by reading ancient Greek and Roman
political theory; London's imitation of the behavior of cities in the
Netherlands; and widespread ignorance about what a subject's duties are.
It is beyond the scope of this book to explain or evaluate these alleged
causes. What is significant about them is their complexity. He did not
oversimplify the number of things that contributed to the calamity. Some
of the causes are religious; some are political, and some are sociological.
Most of them were long-standing conditions that became part of the
complete cause of the Civil War when certain triggering events occurred.

Although most of the argument of *Behemoth* is consistent with his
theoretical principles, Hobbes made some concessions to the circumstances of the Restoration. His remark that Charles retained the right of
governing in 1646 although "the exercise [of it] was yet in nobody" is
inconsistent with his view that sovereignty requires having sufficient
power to protect one's subjects. His claim that nobody had "the right to
govern" in 1653 even though Cromwell had "the supreme strength"
could only have been defended with casuistic reasoning.[64] Yet Hobbes did
not exploit the execution of the king. His account is quite subdued in light
of the magnitude of the crime:

[The king was] executed at the gate of his own palace of Whitehall. He that can
delight in reading how villainously he was used by the soldiers between the
sentence and execution, may go to the chronicle itself; in which he shall see what
courage, patience, wisdom, and goodness was in this prince, whom in their charge
the members of that wicked Parliament styled tyrant, traitor, and murderer.[65]

When *Behemoth* was first published, Hobbes complained to Aubrey: "I
have been told that my book of the Civil War is come abroad, and am sorry
for it, especially because I could not get his majesty to license it."[66] An
authorized edition of *Behemoth* was published by Hobbes's official publisher, William Crooke, in 1682. After its initial success, the book was
relatively unread and unstudied until there was a resurgence of interest in
it in the last quarter of the twentieth century.

The Catching of Leviathan; or, The One That Got Away

We have already seen that 1668 was an important literary year for Hobbes.
A collection of his Latin works was published that included the Latin
version of *Leviathan.* The collection was put out by the Dutch publisher

Blaeu partially because in England there was a de facto ban on publishing Hobbes's works other than those on mathematics and science. Also, his Continental reputation was greater than his English one. His French promoter, Samuel Sorbière, was managing the project. He had arranged the publication of the second edition of *De Cive* and had translated that work into French. During his visit to England in 1663, Sorbière met with Hobbes and made plans to publish the Latin works. He wanted Hobbes to have a portrait made by the well-known artist William Faithorne to put at the front of a quarto edition. It was he that suggested that Hobbes think about translating *Leviathan* into Latin.

It has been suggested that at least part of the Latin version preceded the English one. This may be implied in Hobbes's verse autobiography when he says that he started *Leviathan* shortly around the time that he tutored the Prince of Wales and finished it in English. The phrase "finished in my native tongue" ("perfeci librum patrio sermone") suggests that it was started in some other language, presumably Latin. If this is correct, then the Latin version of *Leviathan* both antedates and postdates the English one. It makes sense that in the middle 1660s, Hobbes would have been more likely to produce a Latin version of *Leviathan*, the fourth version of his political theory, from a Latin manuscript that was already far along rather than starting the project from scratch. Nonetheless, the weight of scholarly opinion favors the view that Hobbes translated *Leviathan* from English into Latin for the Dutch edition of his Latin works and did it himself because he was not willing to entrust the job to anyone else.[67] Whatever the genesis of it is, the Latin *Leviathan* remains a translation of most of *Leviathan*.

The defense of his religious views that he wrote in 1668 but published posthumously was *An Answer to a Book Published by Dr. Bramhall . . . called the Catching of the Leviathan. Together with an Historical Narration Concerning Heresy, and the Punishment Thereof.* As the title indicates, it was two short works joined together. We have already discussed the *Historical Narration Concerning Heresy* (along with the appendix to the Latin *Leviathan*). His *Answer to . . . Dr. Bramhall* merits special attention.

The pretensions of the title of Bramhall's book, *The Catching of the Leviathan*, may remind us of Herman Melville's piscatorial tale, with Bramhall playing Captain Ahab to Hobbes's Moby-Dick. My sympathies are with the big fish. Bramhall's book, which had appeared a decade earlier, had one part devoted to Hobbes's political theory and one to his religious views. Only the latter concerned Hobbes in 1668. He said that he wrote his reply in order "to wipe off that unjust slander [of atheism]":[68]

Though I believe in the omnipotence of God, and that he can do what he will, yet I dare not say how everything is done, because I cannot conceive nor comprehend either the Divine substance or the way of its operation. And I think it impiety to speak concerning God any thing of my own head or upon the authority of philosophers or schoolmen, which I understand not, without warrant in the Scripture. . . . If I could find it there, I could believe it; and if I could find it in the public doctrine of the Church, I could easily abstain from contradicting it.[69]

In his preface "To the Reader," Hobbes legitimately complains that in large part Bramhall quoted *Leviathan* out of context and without the proofs that supported his conclusions. There is nothing ironic in his urging his readers to see "whether they be well proved and how to be understood."[70] If Hobbes actually wanted the reader to understand *Leviathan* as an antireligious text, then it would have been pointless for him to send readers back to his book. He should have been satisfied with Bramhall's digest of allegedly irreligious statements; they would be more than enough to convey that atheism, if it existed. It makes more sense to see Hobbes's request as being what he says it is: an attempt to correct the injustice of the accusation that his views amount to "atheism, blasphemy, impiety and subversion of religion."[71]

A regular refrain of Hobbes's defense of himself is that Bramhall misreads, misreasons, and misleads his readers: "this bishop . . . had but a weak attention in reading and little skill in examining the force of an argument."[72] To the extent that Bramhall's work is persuasive, it relies on rhetorical tricks, like putting "T. H. no friend of religion" in the margin even though that proposition is never proved in the text. Hobbes's gloss: "This behavior becomes neither a bishop, nor a Christian, nor any man that pretends to good education."[73] Bramhall's best strategy for proving Hobbes to be an atheist is to show that his principles lead to atheism. But even if Bramhall were to succeed in this, Hobbes points out, it would only show that Hobbes is "an atheist by consequence," not a witting or professing atheist. And this is a dangerous game for Bramhall to play. Hobbes says, "this atheism by consequence is a very easy thing to be fallen into, even by the most godly men in the Church."[74] Bramhall himself is an atheist by consequence, according to Hobbes. When Bramhall says that God is "wholly here and wholly there, and wholly everywhere," he is logically committing himself to the proposition that the whole world is in God and God in the world. This is pantheism, and pantheism is tantamount to atheism.[75] Much better, Hobbes maintains, to hold God to be "a most pure, simple, invisible, spirit corporeal."[76]

Like many of Hobbes's readers, Bramhall accused him of espousing inconsistent principles. Hobbes could not recognize that his principles were inconsistent, especially when Bramhall was making the accusation. Hobbes says, "[Bramhall thinks that] I am . . . a forgetful blockhead. I cannot help that: but my forgetfulness appears not here."[77] Bramhall was right in his belief that Hobbes's principles were inconsistent but not skilled enough to prove it.

The fundamental difference between Bramhall and Hobbes is not religious belief but philosophical theory. Bramhall was as much committed to obscurantist scholasticism as Hobbes was committed to the Bible and modern science. Hobbes rejects Bramhall's intellectually decadent vocabulary and dogmatism: God is *actus simplissimus;* God is indivisible; eternity is the divine substance, and eternity is a *nunc stans.*[78] It is all stuff and nonsense, according to Hobbes; it is Roman Catholic and not biblical. He is not the least bit moved by Bramhall's asseveration that God must be an "immaterial substance." The phrase is incomprehensible. The bishop has nothing more to support his views than "School-divinity," certainly not the Bible. Hobbes stands by the Bible and the Book of Common Prayer: "When the nature of the thing is incomprehensible, I can acquiesce in the Scripture; but when the signification of words is incomprehensible, I cannot acquiesce in the authority of a Schoolman."[79]

The Trinity

One of the few aspects of his philosophy that Hobbes could see was hopeless was his treatment of the Trinity. According to it, God is three persons because he was represented by three entities: Moses (God the Father), Jesus (God the Son), and the Apostles (God the Holy Spirit). As Bramhall pointed out, this view has the consequence that the Trinity is not eternal.[80] Also, since a divine person is created with each representation of him, God has "as many persons as there have been sovereign princes in the world."[81] Hobbes admits to a fault in his reasoning but "no impiety." He credits John Cosin, then bishop of Durham, with pointing out the problem with his interpretation of the Trinity. He modified the

Latin version to avoid the problem. One of the two interlocutors of the third chapter of the appendix, namely, B, says that Hobbes "wanted to explain the doctrine of the Trinity. . . . It is a pious wish, but the explanation is in error." B explains the error as a bit of carelessness that is easily corrected. Hobbes should have said, "God, in his own person, created the world, . . . [and], in the person of his Son, redeemed the human race, and . . . in the person of the Holy Spirit he sanctified the church."[82] In his *Answer*, Hobbes explains the source of his mistake as the result of his mistakenly using the phrase "in the person of Moses," when he should have used the phrase "by the ministry of Moses." The change strikes me as inconsequential, and I doubt that anyone other than Hobbes was or is satisfied with it.

Hobbes's treatment of the Trinity is unsatisfactory. But who has a completely satisfactory one? The distinguished Catholic theologian Bernard Lonergan said that the doctrine of the Trinity has four relations, three persons, two generations, one God, and no explanation.

Prophets

Bramhall doubts that Hobbes honestly believes that there have ever been prophets. He argues that according to Hobbes's view, "he that teaches transubstantiation in France is a true prophet; he that teaches it in England a false prophet; he that blasphemes Christ in Constantinople a true prophet; he that doth the same in Italy a false prophet."[83] Hobbes begins his reply by affirming belief in "true prophets in the Church of God from Abraham down to our Savior, the greatest prophet of all" and in "true prophets in the church of Christ" from Jesus until the "death of St. John the Evangelist."[84] After showing that Bramhall in fact holds some views that are the same as his own, Hobbes comes to answer the central objection. He denies that true prophets can teach contradictory doctrines. The reason is that a true prophet is one whose ministry is confirmed by miracles. So only one of two prophets teaching contradictory doctrines will have his ministry accompanied by miracles.[85] Finally, Jesus was a true prophet in virtue of having "the approbation of God, who was king of the Jews": "What other princes thought of his prophecies is nothing to the purpose."[86]

Hobbes does not deny that the legality of preaching a doctrine depends on the decision of the sovereign, but legality is not the same as truth: "I never said that princes can make doctrines or prophecies true or false; but I say every sovereign prince has a right to prohibit public teaching of them, whether true or false."[87] It should be obvious in light of the disaster of the English Civil War, instigated to some degree by fanatics representing themselves as prophets, and in light of the "controversy between Gomar and Arminius" in the Netherlands, that there has to be "a judge of doctrines." Who is it going to be? Hobbes wants it to be the king of England, who according to the Act of Supremacy is the head of the church.[88] But Bramhall wants it to be the bishops. What a self-serving position, Hobbes implies. Bramhall is trying to snatch the authority for himself. Not all of it, of course. He, "being too modest to undertake the whole power," is content to share it with the twenty-five other bishops of England.[89] Hobbes's charge that Bramhall's argument is nothing "but a heaving at the King's supremacy" is justified and politically astute.[90] In Restoration England, to defend the authority of the king was to stand behind a strong bulwark, and Hobbes had a right to be there.

Daniel Scargill

On March 12, 1669, Cambridge University punished one of its students:

> Whereas Daniel Scargill, late Bachelor of Arts of this university, & of Corpus Christi College, . . . [has been] legally convicted in the consistory before the vice chancellor and the major part of the Heads, to have asserted several impious and atheistical tenets, to the great dishonour of God, scandal of Christian Religion, and of the university: It is unanimously assented unto by the vice chancellor, and major part of the Heads, that he be forthwith expelled from this university.[91]

Scargill had entered Corpus Christi College on January 25, 1662, as sizar (a student receiving a stipend from the college). After his first tutor died, Thomas Tenison took on that role. Scargill's career through 1667 was quite successful. However, he took the heterodox side in public disputations on such issues as whether the origin of the world could be explained mechanistically, whether the moral law is founded on positive civil law, and whether God's law is founded in power. Worse, he also enjoyed drinking and carousing with men and women of the town who were his social inferiors: "His usual custom in the College was to begin the day with a pint of Sack or some other strong liquor, often to drink to distemper, and then used to shew himself openly to the just scandal of the Society." Several reprimands from the college court barely got his attention until December 7, 1668, when it suspended him until the next June. Scargill's response was to go out drinking with some friends. The next Lent, he was "several times disordered with wine and strong waters" and hung out with people of "inferior quality and young women." On March 12, 1669, the university expelled him. One of those signing the order was Ralph Cudworth.

It might seem that this dissolute youth would have had no recourse, but that would be wrong. He received the support of Charles II, Bishop Gilbert Sheldon, the chancellor of the university, and the earl of Manchester. Sheldon wrote to John Spenser, who was Scargill's superior, on June 28 and told him that Scargill had the support of the king. He then added: "My advice therefore to you is that you consider well whether it be not fit for you to readmit him [Scargill] without putting the King to the trouble of another letter, which (if you stand off) will certainly be sent to you." The university authorities were willing to be reasonable and ordered Scargill to prepare a recantation on July 7. He did not. Then he was ordered to prepare one for July 9. This he did:

Whereas I, Daniel Scargill, . . . being through the instigation of the Devil possessed with a foolish proud conceit of my own wit, and not having the fear of God before my eyes; Have lately vented and publicly asserted in the said University, diverse wicked, blasphemous, and atheistical positions, . . . professing that I gloried to be a Hobbist and an atheist; and vaunting, that Hobbes should be maintained by Daniel, that is by me. Agreeably unto which principles and positions, I have lived in great licentiousness, swearing rashly, drinking intemperately, boasting my self insolently, corrupting others by my pernicious principles and example to the high dishonor of God, the reproach of the university, the scandal of Christianity, and the just offense of mankind. . . . And I do profess . . . that the openly professed atheism of some and the secret atheism of others is the accursed root of all that abounding wickedness, perjury, sacrilege, debauchery, and uncleanness in this present age.

What this recantation makes clear is that Scargill was being punished primarily for his disruptive behavior. This was sufficient for censure. The supposition that Hobbism was the cause of his dissolute life simply made it worse. The moral consequences of Hobbism had always been perceived as its principal danger. As Bishop Laney would put it later, "when . . . he [Hobbes] labors to introduce a necessity into all men's actions . . . he takes away the nature of virtues and vices."[92]

Scargill may not even have had firsthand acquaintance with Hobbes's philosophy. Copies were expensive and in short supply in the late 1660s.

One of Scargill's interrogators, Dr. John Gunning, told Scargill that Hobbes did not hold some of the opinions that Scargill attributed to him. (It is possible that Hobbes attended Gunning's well-known worship services at Exeter House during the 1650s; this would explain Gunning's position with regard to Scargill.) When Gunning pressed Scargill to show him where Hobbes made certain alleged claims, Scargill replied that if Hobbes seemed to hold a different view, he "canted." Presumably, Scargill meant that Hobbes was prevaricating. But how could Scargill have known this? One of Scargill's sources for Hobbes's views may have been his tutor Thomas Tenison, who published *The Creed of Mr. Hobbes Examined* the very next year and dedicated it somewhat surprisingly to one of Scargill's champions, the earl of Manchester.

In early July, Scargill lost the support of Sheldon, who wrote to Spenser: "I am fully satisfied in the account you give me of Scargill. And I am of opinion with you, that it is better one foolish fellow be undone, than that he should be brought in again amongst you, to corrupt, or endanger (at least a whole society). I have so informed the secretary from whom the King's letters came in his behalf, that I think now you need not fear to be further pressed from thence." (I am amused that Sheldon's language ["it is better one foolish fellow"] wittingly or unwittingly echoes the language of the high priest who endorsed the execution of Jesus.) Given the Scargill case, it seems to me that Sheldon could have made a case against Hobbes himself if it was actually Scargill's doctrine and not his scandalous behavior that was the chief problem. Scargill was ordained two years later and spent a long, if undistinguished, life in the service of the church.

Hobbes has only a small part to play in the Scargill affair. After he learned of Scargill's expulsion, he wrote a letter that he wanted to get licensed to publish. The licenser, Sir John Birkenhead, refused, and the letter has disappeared from history. We have absolutely no knowledge of the content of that letter although it is plausible that Hobbes was critical of the university authorities.

Thomas Tenison

Scargill's tutor Tenison felt some anger about the affair and may have felt some guilt. In *The Creed of Mr. Hobbes Examined,* he alludes to the "error and recantation of an unhappy young man, committed sometime to my care" and is disconcerted that some people have been spreading it about that he (Tenison) was a Hobbist.[93] It was important to him to disavow that career-threatening rumor. His treatment of Hobbes is often irrelevantly abusive but does have the merit of just as often setting down Hobbes's opinions correctly because he quotes or paraphrases freely. But his treatment is also logically weak, often begging the question or relying upon non sequitur as if it were a rule of inference. Here, for example, is his refutation of Hobbes's claim that the Bible does not say that God is immaterial: "Concerning the Holy Scripture, it says that God created all things and fills all things, and therefore it teaches that He is immaterial."[94]

He is also impressed by some of Nostradamus's prophecies, one of which strikes him as having been fulfilled by the Great Fire of London. Further, he thinks that Hobbes's view that hell will be on earth cannot be right because it is plausible that as many as a billion people will be going to hell, and there is not enough room on earth for all of them. And heaven will not be on earth, because the talk of the New Jerusalem is not literally true. In contrast, Hobbes maintained the literal truth of as much of the Bible as he thought possible, given the results of modern science.

11

The Final Years, 1670–1679

My life has been consonant with my writings: I have taught and cultivated justice. Only greedy men are wicked, and no one greedy can produce excellent work. I have completed eighty four years: The long story of my life is almost over. ("Vita Carmina Expressa")

Hobbes wrote these words in 1672. His worst enemies (Boyle and Wallis) would outlive him, and his best friends would precede him in death. Most of his friends died in the 1650s and 1660s. A few lingered in the next decade. Newcastle died in 1676, but had much earlier become disillusioned with Restoration politics and had retired to his estates in the late 1660s. Several years earlier he had been too sick to accompany his wife's corpse to London for burial. Devonshire would outlive Hobbes, but he seems to have been demoralized by his treatment by Charles II at the Restoration and stayed away from court.

François du Verdus

One of Hobbes's oldest and last living friends was the unhappy du Verdus. His mind had broken under the strain of the legal wrangling that had gone on for more than a decade. He was being persecuted by his father's enemies, people who had "seized the divine throne, and had taken hereditary possession of the sanctuary of the true God." The title of his lawsuit, according to him, is "For the Oppressed Pupil of the Eighty-first Psalm, against the Council of Ten of Bordeaux, the Judges of That Psalm and the Governors of Lemuel." Du Verdus is referring to what is the Eighty-second Psalm in the King James Version, which says in part: "God standeth in the Congregation of the mighty; He judgeth among the gods. / How long will ye judge unjustly and accept the persons of the wicked?"

Much of what he reports seems to be a description of specters of his own mind. The named suit was supposedly filed "before the sovereign throne of the true God's mercy."[1] The articles of the suit included annulling the actions that had been taken against him by his enemies, entering the decree of annulment into the "hidden divine register which is kept in perpetuity for the great glory of God," and having "God's judges [investigate] . . . these malpractices." His suit should have been a complete success because God was his cocounsel. This much strikes me as fanciful. The part of his story that is not is that he filed suit in August 1672 and that he wrote compulsively about his troubles: a folio volume containing the history of his father's proscription and death, two quarto volumes describing further facts, two more quarto volumes, one containing 120 pages, the other at least 80, to mention just some of them. And he had plans for more.[2]

One dubious good result of the lawsuits was that du Verdus had figured out the meaning of his life, not by himself mind you, but through a revelation from God. In 1674, he wrote:

After all the great and special revelations which it has pleased God to vouchsafe me, I am confident that since he has always supported me with such strength, since he has performed so many miracles – true miracles, divine miracles – and since he has enabled me to expose these judges for their malpractices, I am confident, I say, that the true God will provide for the future. . . . Who would have thought it, Sir: that the true God should have chosen me – me, seemingly a poor witless fellow; me, whom those wicked judges had made to seem so witless; me, whom their unceasing succession of spells and curses had necessarily made to seem like a madman.[3]

I do not know who would have thought it, but it certainly would not have been Hobbes. Unfortunately again, we do not know how Hobbes reacted to the rantings of his old friend. But he obviously remained faithful to him. He had offered to dedicate *Rosetum Geometricum* to him, but du Verdus modestly refused the honor. The only mercy in these last struggles of du Verdus is that he died the next year.

Hobbes himself was not in good health during the 1670s. His shaking had gotten worse, and it was a struggle for him even to make his signature legible. He also had a bout of paralysis in 1671.

Gottfried Wilhelm Leibniz

Some people as they get older want to simplify their lives; they get rid of things that they have accumulated and avoid getting new things. It somewhat relieves the sadness of leaving behind what they love. They especially do not want to acquire new, young friends. In 1670, a young and unknown Leibniz wrote two unsolicited, solicitous letters to the superannuated Hobbes. He declared his admiration for Hobbes and his commitment to Hobbes's philosophy, rightly understood. He wrote that Hobbes's writings were unsurpassed even by "Descartes with his superhuman intellect." In the first of the two letters, the praise was prologue. Leibniz announced his own project of summing up the *Digest of Roman Law* in a few principles. Also, he had some questions about natural philosophy. Agreeing with the principle of inertia, the requirement that all motion is transmitted by contact, and the importance of understanding conatus (endeavor) as the beginning of motion, Leibniz wanted to know why the parts of an object stay together rather than flying apart when struck. Additionally, he wished that Hobbes had said more about the philosophy of mind. Leibniz, unlike Hobbes, did not think that sensation conceived of as permanent reaction can be explained unless some immaterial being is involved. Since brute animals do not have souls, Leibniz thought that they do not have sensations. Given these remarks, Hobbes probably would not have been impressed by the author of this letter. But he would have been discombobulated by Leibniz's desire that Hobbes would provide good reason for "our hopes of immortality."[4] The author sounded impertinent or stupid.

At the beginning of the letter, Leibniz had written, "If this letter from me is untimely, you may punish me by not replying." It is possible that the letter was never sent.[5] In any case, Hobbes did not reply. Leibniz drafted and may have sent one other letter to Hobbes three or four years later. Its subject was a problem in Hobbes's political philosophy. Leibniz noticed correctly that, on the one hand, Hobbes maintained that subjects transferred all of their rights to the sovereign and, on the other, that they retained their right to self-preservation. Hobbes cannot have it both ways. Also, since each person has the right to judge when his life is threatened and what he needs to do to preserve it, each person retains the right to make alliances to resist a tyrant. Leibniz naively thought that Hobbes would agree with the point.[6] Again, there is no evidence that Hobbes responded.

Oldenburg, Hooke, and Mathematics, 1672–73

His aches and pains notwithstanding, Hobbes was not going to "go gentle into that good night." He published three large-scale geometric works in the last decade of his life: *Rosetum Geometricum, Sive Propositiones Aliquot Frustra antehac Tentatae. Cum Censura brevi Doctrinae Wallisianae de Motu* (1671), *Lux Mathematica, Excussa Collisionibus Johannis Wallisii Theol. Doctoris, Geometriae in Celeberrima Academia Oxoniensi . . .* (1672), and *Principia et Problemata Aliquot Geometrica Ante Desperata, Nunc breviter Explicata & Demonstrata* (1674), not to mention his work of physics, *Decameron Physiologicum; or, Ten Dialogues of Natural Philosophy* (1678).

Wallis's review of *Lux Mathematica* published in the *Transactions of the Royal Society* angered Hobbes, who wrote to Henry Oldenberg, the secretary of the society. Hobbes requested that the society publish anything that he submitted on mathematics or philosophy because it had done the same for Wallis and, he adds as a final insult, because "it will save me some charges."[7] As an octogenarian living far from London, Hobbes had much less influence than he had had a decade earlier. Rather than writing on a clean sheet of paper, Oldenburg replied on the back of the letter that Wallis had sent to him about Hobbes. In that letter, Wallis said he had no interest in replying to Hobbes, and Oldenburg in his contribution wrote that the society was not going to arbitrate the dispute both because Hobbes was old and because he suspected that Wallis was in the right. Nonetheless, Oldenburg was willing to publish Hobbes's contributions on physics and mathematics as long as they were "not too long nor interwoven with personal reflections," the word 'reflections' being a replacement for the word 'criminations'. Oldenburg must have known that his offhand treatment of Hobbes's request would offend the old man. In fact, Oldenburg did not care for Hobbes. Sir John Hoskyns, who was a member of the society and who liked Hobbes, complained that Oldenburg "with some regret, grumbles out an account or notice rather of your Countryman Thomas Hobbes his last book."[8]

In early 1675, Aubrey informed Hobbes that Robert Hooke, curator of experiments at the Royal Society, would be happy to arrange to have anything that Hobbes wrote on mathematics published under the auspices of the society. Instead of being gracious, Hobbes used the occasion to vent his spleen against the snubs he had received from the society for more than a decade. He would not publish his mathematical or philosophical works with the society even if he had any – which he did not. How could Hooke expect him to submit anything to the society when it might have to pass by Wallis, who was like Cerberus at the mouth of Hades? Although Hobbes implies that his bile is not directed at Hooke, there is such a flood of it in the letter that Hooke is awash in it, too.[9] However, Hooke did not take offense, if Aubrey is to be believed. Described as "melancholy, mistrustful, and jealous" because of some bad experiences early in his professional life, Hooke had had his own troubles with Wallis and so was happy to hear him knocked. As far as Hobbes was concerned, Wallis was neither a philosopher nor a geometrician. For the wrongs it had inflicted on him, Hobbes wanted "reparation" from the society in the form of a public declaration attesting to his accomplishments. Varying the biblical complaint that a prophet is not without honor except in his own country, he says that his reputation among the learned in Europe is greater than the society can suppress.

Historia et Antiquitates Universitatis Oxoniensis, 1674

Hobbes's accomplishments were to be recorded in Anthony Wood's great history of the University of Oxford, though not without a fight. The antiquarian Wood had started his grand project in 1660. In 1669, John Fell, dean of Christ Church and former vice-chancellor of the university, was one of the most powerful people at Oxford. Dedicated to the good of the university, he offered to pay for the publication of Wood's book and suggested that it include biographies of Oxford's famous alumni. Since Hobbes undoubtedly qualified, Wood had Aubrey write up an entry for him. Fell hated Hobbes and was not pleased to be subsidizing a celebratory biography of him, so he altered Aubrey's work at various places. Where it had been written that Hobbes had a sober mind, Fell changed it to 'bitter'. Where it had been written that Hobbes was the author of *De Cive*, Fell glossed it as a book "destined to cause great confusion"; and he glossed *Leviathan* as "most monstrous" and famous "for the public harm it has caused." Fell also deleted information about Hobbes's international reputation and his friendship with the king.

Hobbes was not about to allow the insult to go unanswered. He had his publisher, William Crooke, print up a broadside detailing the changes that Fell had made. It took the form of a letter to Wood with the instruction that it be inserted between pages 444 and 445 in volume 2. Boastful yet accurate, Hobbes says that Fell's actions have not harmed him since his reputation "took wing a long time ago and has soared so far that it cannot be called back." Then, still boastful and prophetic, he says that even if his name is removed from *The Antiquities of Oxford*, his name will "still be praised by most of the scholars of the present time, and by even more (I believe) of those of the future."[10] In any case, Hobbes would not be injured by the slander because Fell's "moral vileness" would become known.[11] Unfortunately, the booksellers would not agree to the inclusion. Instead, Fell, getting wind of Hobbes's reply, prepared his own abusive reply to Hobbes and had it inserted at the beginning of the second volume. Fell, we might conclude, is the title character of the ditty:

> I do not love thee Dr. Fell.
> Why that is I cannot tell.
> But this I know and know full well.
> I do not love thee Dr. Fell.

Hobbes's relations with Oxford were not completely negative. In addition to the support he had from Aubrey and Wood, his alma mater asked him to send a copy of his *Opera Philosophica* to Josiah Pullen, the vice-principal of Magdalen Hall. Pullen's acknowledgment of the gift is gracious. (The copy is now in the library of Hertford College, Oxford.) He calls the books "condemned more frequently than understood."[12] Indeed.

Translations of the *Odyssey* and *Iliad*

Hobbes may have been obsessed with his disputes with Boyle, Wallis, and Fell, but he was not totally consumed by them.[13] He found time in the midst of these battles to return to one of the earliest loves of his life, translation. He anticipated his audience's wonderment about why he took on such a daunting task. His explanation was characteristically cheeky: "Why then did I write it? Because I had nothing else to do. Why publish it? Because I thought it might take off my adversaries from showing their folly upon my more serious writings and set them upon my verses to show their wisdom."[14]

His translations were much more highly regarded in the seventeenth and eighteenth centuries than they are now. When they are discussed at all, it is usually to denigrate them. Without denying their inadequacies, I think that they have not been given their due over at least the past century. Consequently, I will discuss them at much greater length than I otherwise would.

He published *The Travels of Ulysses*, a translation of Books 9 through 12 of the *Odyssey*, in 1673. A success, it was reprinted the next year. Perhaps this excerpt was a way of testing the waters. In 1675, he published a translation of the entire book. His translation of Homer's *Iliad* first appeared in 1676 and was similarly successful. Several editions of both works were put out during the seventeenth century. Both translations have been criticized for inaccuracies, omissions, and embellishments. Alexander Pope wrote that Hobbes's translation was "too mean for criticism." Pope's criticism is too harsh. I'll let Hobbes's translation speak for itself. Here are the first dozen or so lines from the *Iliad* and *Odyssey*, respectively.

> O Goddess sing what woe the discontent
> Of Thetis' son brought to the Greeks; what souls
> Of heroes down to Erebus it sent,
> Leaving their bodies unto dogs and fowls;
> Whilst the two princes of the army strove,
> King Agamemnon and Achilles stout.
> That so it should be was the will of Jove,
> But who was he that made them first fall out?
> Apollo; who incensed by the wrong
> To his priest Chryses by Atrides done,
> Sent a great pestilence to the Greeks among;
> Apace they died, and remedy was none.

> Tell me, O Muse, th'adventures of the man
> That having sack'd the sacred town of Troy,
> Wander'd so long at sea; what course he ran
> By winds and tempests driven from his way:
> That saw the cities, and the fashions knew
> Of many men, but suffer'd grievous pain
> To save his own life, and bring home his crew;
> Though for his crew, all he could do was vain,
> They lost themselves by their own insolence,
> Feeding, like fools, on the Sun's sacred kine;

Which did the splendid deity incense
To their dire fate. Begin, O Muse, divine.

Pope's poor opinion of Hobbes's translation did not keep him from echoing many of Hobbes's phrases and constructions. For example, one of Pope's most famous renderings derives from Hobbes:[15]

Hobbes: In hospitality this rule is true:
      Love him that stays, help forth the going guest.
Pope: True friendship's laws are by this rule exprest,
      Welcome the coming, speed the parting guest.

Another fair measure of Hobbes's aesthetic success is to compare it with what other translators of his time could do with the same material. I think that Hobbes's poetry is superior to that of the popular translation by John Ogilby, who rendered the opening lines of the *Odyssey* like this:

That prudent Heroes wandring, Muse rehearse,
Who (Troy being sack'd) coasting the Universe,
Saw many Cities, and their various Modes;
Much suffering, tost by Storms on Raging Floods,
His Friends conducting to their native coast;
But all in vain, for he his Navy lost,
And they their lives prophanely feasting on
Heards [*sic*] consecrated to the glorious Sun;

The abstractness of "universe" and "navy" are symptoms of the inferiority of Ogibly's verse. Hobbes's concreteness and Homeric realism is even better illustrated with a line like "And often on my breast you puked your wine,"[16] in contrast, say, with W. H. D. Rouse's overly delicate, "How often you have wetted my tunic, spluttering out drops of wine like a naughty child."[17] Pope omits the line completely.

To say that Hobbes's translation is better than Ogilby's is not a trivial claim. Pope, who denigrated Ogilby's translation, nonetheless often stayed close to it. As one critic commented, Pope "treads in the steps of Ogilby; below criticism, perhaps, but not imitation."[18] Ogilby's edition had other merits, too. It contained extensive, helpful notes to both poems and elegant illustrations. Hobbes himself was impressed by the scholarship, and, contrary to his usual practice, mentions Ogilby twice by name. He explains that his own translation contains no annotations, "Because I had no hope to do it better than it is already done by Mr. Ogilby."[19] And he meant it. Ogilby, who was well connected with Charles's court, may have been an acquaintance, but there is no hard evidence of that.

The aesthetic success (or failure) of Hobbes's translation might also be measured against Hobbes's own theory of epic poetry. The first edition of Hobbes's complete translation of the *Odyssey* (1675) had a preface, "Concerning the Virtues of an Heroique Poem," in which Hobbes stated seven characteristics of a good epic. First, the words used should be familiar ones. Second, the syntax should be simple and straightforward. These points are well illustrated by these economical lines from the beginning of Book 2 of the *Odyssey:*

> Soon as the rosy morning did appear,
> Telemachus himself array'd and shod,
> Puts on his sword, and takes in hand his spear
> And out he went appearing like a God.
> And straight unto the criers gave command,
> To call the people to the public place.

When critics object that Hobbes often omits stock epithets, they should at least mention that his practice fits his theory, and independently of that theory, many readers are irritated by Homer's seemingless pointless repetitions. Some contemporary translators vary the translations in order to ameliorate the stultifying effect.

In comparing Hobbes's translations with various others, I have been struck by how well many of his lines stand up even today. For example, compare these prose translations by Rouse with Hobbes's poetry:

Rouse: Alexandros replied: "That is true enough. Hector, that is true enough. Your heart is always hard as steel. Like a shipwright's axe when he slices off a spar from a tree with all the strength of a man! A hard heart indeed."

Hobbes: This answer then to Hector, Paris made.
Hector, since your reproof is just, said he,
And your hard language (as when help'd by art
A shipwright's axe strikes deep into a tree)
Like rigid steel has cut me to the heart.[20]

Rouse: All heard this in silence; then Menalaos cried out: "Hear me also! This touches me most nearly, but my mind is that Achaians and Trojans should now be reconciled."

Hobbes: When this was said, then Menelaus, spake,

> And both the armies with great silence sate,
> Hear me too then, said Menelaus, who
> By Alexander have been most offended.
> If you'll do that which I advise you to,
> The quarrel he began will soon be ended.[21]

The third characteristic of a good epic, according to Hobbes, is that the plot of a good poem should be advanced by the characters and not just the narrator. This needs no comment. Fourth, the poem should exercise our imagination ("fancy"). The fact that Hobbes says that this feature is usually considered the most important suggests that he thinks it is not. He also puts stringent conditions on the use of metaphors, which at their best are "not unpleasant." His general aversion to metaphor explains many of the omissions in his translations and led Pope to complain that Hobbes "omits whole similes." He also simplifies or omits Homer's stock epithets, as mentioned earlier. Homer's "early-rising rosy fingers of dawn" is simply "Aurora" to Hobbes. This explains both the nature of Hobbes's translation and Pope's low opinion of it. For Pope, imagination ("invention") is the most important quality of a poet, and he says that Homer is "universally allowed to have had the greatest invention of any writer."[22] So he thought that Hobbes had betrayed Homer.

The fifth characteristic is that the poet should be just and impartial in his opinions: "it is a very great fault in a poet to speak evil of any man in their writings historical."[23] Hobbes thinks that Homer is preeminently judicious.[24] Sixth, the descriptions of people and events should be sharp and precise, as I think they are in these lines from the beginning of Book 3:

> Up from the sea the sun leapt to the sky,
> To hold the light up before Gods and me;
> Telemachus, with all his company,
> Unto the town of Pyle arrived then.

Seventh, a good epic contains great variety.

Hobbes's adoption of these characteristics as virtues, and especially his description of them, makes him sound like a philistine. His theory was the (proto)Augustan equivalent of socialist realism: "bourgeois realism." John Dryden, the greatest of the Augustans, was not impressed with Hobbes's aesthetics. He expresses no admiration for him in his works of criticism, even though Aubrey said that Dryden was "his [Hobbes's] great admirer."

In his preface to *Fables* (1700), Dryden said that Hobbes began studying poetry, just as he had mathematics, "when it was too late." In particular, he objected to Hobbes's emphasis on "the choice of words and harmony of numbers." They are mere decorations. The essential ingredient of a poem is its structure, and immediately subserving structure is the way it gets conveyed and the thoughts expressed in the poem, conceived of as "the imitation of life." Although I concede that Dryden was the better critic, poet, and translator, it is arguable that "the choice of words and harmony of numbers" is more important to a poem than its structure.

Hobbesianism in the Theater and Other Arts

A different facet of Hobbes's relation to the arts was the creation of a Hobbism, causally, but not accurately, related to Hobbes's own doctrines. His philosophy, like Socrates', when mutilated in the right sort of way, made good material for theater, both drama and comedy, partially, I think, because the personalities of Hobbes and Socrates add spice to the raw doctrine. Aubrey said that Dryden "oftentimes makes use of his [Hobbes's] doctrine in his plays." The influence is greatly overstated; Dryden mentions Hobbes by name only three times in his published works. The following lines from Dryden's *The Conquest of Granada* (1672) are often identified as Hobbesian:

> No man has more contempt than I, of breath;
> But whence hast thou the right to give me death?
> Obey'd as Sovereign by thy Subjects be,
> But know, that I alone am King of me.
> I am as free as Nature first made men
> 'Ere the base Laws of Servitude began
> When wild in woods the noble Savage ran.[25]

Here are only a few of the genuinely Hobbesian doctrines that are misrepresented in these seven lines: All people fear death; each person has the right to kill every other person in the state of nature; no human being is a king in the state of nature; civil laws are not base; people in the state of nature are not noble savages. But *The Conquest of Granada* was good theater.

Dryden in fact knew Hobbes better than the preceding quotation indicates. Not only did he read *Leviathan*, but he was a client of and sometime collaborator with Newcastle, who could have set Dryden

straight if he really had such erroneous views about Hobbes. Genuine
Hobbesian views are expressed and endorsed in *Tyrannic Love* (1670) and
even more so in *Absalom and Achitophel* (1681). In the following lines from
the latter work, Dryden uses Hobbesian language and themes to criticize
rebellion:

> What standard is there in a fickle rout
> Which, flowing to the mark, runs faster out?
> Nor only crowds but Sanhedins may be
> Infected with this public lunacy;
> And share the madness of rebellious times
> To murder monarchs for imagined crimes.
> If they may give and take whene'er they please
> Not kings alone (the Godhead's images)
> But government itself at length must fall
> To nature's state, where all have right to all.
> Yet grant our lords the people kings can make,
> What prudent men a settled throne would shake?
> For whatso'er their sufferings were before,
> That change they covet makes them suffer more.

So far, the examples provided of Hobbes's influence on the theater
have concerned his political theory. His egoist psychology was taken over
even more, sometimes in dramas but especially in comedies by such well-
known playwrights as William Wycherley (*The Country Wife*, 1675),
George Etherege (*The Man of Mode*, 1676), and William Congreve (*The
Way of the World*, 1700). The characters are often lascivious (in order to
titillate the audience) but eventually frustrated (in order to keep on the
right side of the censors), just like network television shows.

One of the most notorious poets of the seventeenth-century was John
Wilmot, the earl of Rochester. He was an occasional patron of Dryden and
in poetry sometimes considered second only to Dryden. He traveled with
Devonshire's son, the future fourth earl and first duke of Devonshire, and
fought on his side against some French soldiers in a brawl that broke out
in a theater. He wrote vigorous and often bawdy poetry about some of the
most important people in the king's court. He was in and out of favor with
Charles because of his shenanigans. On one occasion, he meant to hand
Charles a satire about a courtier but mistakenly handed him the notorious
satire on Charles himself that begins,

> In the Isle of Britain long since famous grown
> For breeding the best cunts in all Christendom,
> There now does live – ah, let him long survive –
> The easiest king and the best bred man alive.

Thereafter it becomes more lewd. Rochester lived a dissolute life and died young, though not, supposedly, before getting religion.

Rochester was a cynic, possibly a misanthrope, and was influenced by Hobbes's philosophy, although the exact character of that influence is disputed. His most Hobbesian poem is "A Satire against Mankind" (1674). It begins on a skeptical note. Hobbes had called Aristotelian philosophy an ignis fatuus ("a false fire") in *Leviathan,* and Rochester seems to generalize the point to all reasoning, when he declares reason to be "an *ignis fatuus*" of the mind. All philosophy is vain, he appears to declare:

> Stumbling from thought to thought, [a philosopher] falls headlong down,
> Into Doubt's boundless sea where, like to drown,
> Books bear him up awhile, and make him try
> To swim with bladders of Philosophy.

In fact, philosophy is a big rock. In the end, according to Rochester, a philosopher comes to realize, "After a search so painful and so long, / That all his life he has been in the wrong."[26] His wisdom or the search for it has cost the philosopher his happiness. But this apparently blanket condemnation of philosophy is misleading. Rochester is condemning only Aristotelian and scholastic philosophy. He in fact endorses Hobbes's own view of reason. Reason must be restricted to the empirical world ("And he that thinks beyond thinks like an ass") and can instruct people on the way to become happy. He then explicates Hobbes's view further but in a rhetorically ambiguous way that is characteristic of Rochester's poetry. As we saw in Chapter 4, Hobbes thought that people who appeal to right reason are typically those who dogmatically try to impose their own beliefs on others: "And when men that think themselves wiser than all others, clamor and demand right reason for judge; yet seek no more, but that things should be determined by no other men's reasons but their own."[27] But Rochester's own voice seems to imitate exactly that kind of person, even though he is espousing the content of Hobbes's doctrine:

> Your reason hinders, mine helps to enjoy,
> Renewing appetites yours would enjoy,

My reason in my friend, yours is a cheat,
Hunger calls out, my reason bids me eat.
. . . .
This plain distinction, sir, your doubt secures,
'Tis not true reason I despise but yours.
Thus I think reason righted, but for man,
I'll ne'er recant, defend him if you can.[28]

In other words, the poet here adopts the voice of the dogmatist even as he scorns him. This is Rochesterian irony. Rochester's poem takes an un-Hobbesian turn in the end. It declares that hypocrisy means that "honesty is against all common sense." But Hobbes wants to make honesty profitable by having a strong system of laws and punishments. So, if Rochester was trying to give an accurate rendering of Hobbes's thought, then he got some of it right and some of it wrong, as did many of the people whom we have discussed. This is not surprising. The thoughts of great thinkers are almost always distorted or misunderstood by their contemporaries. The explanation is almost axiomatic. In large part their greatness is a combination of novelty and depth, and most ordinary people, even intelligent, ordinary people, find it very difficult to assimilate new thoughts and especially those that are profound.

Final Thoughts about Politics

Political intrigue was rampant in England during the 1670s. Charles II had made secret agreements with the Dutch and the French; an alliance would be made with one in order to make one with the other, which would call for breaking the first in exchange for a large sum of money. In the long run, Charles's sovereignty was compromised by having his foreign and domestic policy influenced by foreign money. In 1672, he issued a Declaration of Indulgence that allowed dissenting Protestants and Roman Catholics to worship, not simply because he had a soft spot in his heart for the Catholics, but because France insisted on it. This led England into the third war with the Dutch in twenty years. Hobbes does not comment on any of this, and, if he lived his theory, he thought it was none of his business. But Parliament did consider it its business and retaliated by passing a Test Act that required all government officials to be members of the Church of England. So the tension between the king and Parliament was increasing, just as it had in the early 1640s. The animosity was exacerbated by the fact that the king's brother and heir apparent to the throne, James, duke of York, declared his conversion to Catholicism, resigned his position as lord high admiral, and married a Roman Catholic princess. Most members of Parliament did not want a Roman Catholic monarch.

The political crisis erupted in 1678 into a nameable event, the Popish Plot, when Titus Oates, a religion-hopping liar and opportunist, claimed that he had evidence of a conspiracy engineered by the pope, the Jesuits, and the king of France to assassinate Charles, put James on the throne, and force England to convert. The charges were nonsense but credible to anyone who wanted to believe them. The earl of Shaftesbury did not believe them but nonetheless exploited the hysteria surrounding the event and pushed for excluding James from the hereditary succession as part of the Exclusion Crisis. This raised the general issue of sovereignty from another angle.

There is an undated manuscript in the Devonshire Collection of Hobbes's papers at Chatsworth with the title "Questions Relative to the Hereditary Right, Mr. Hobbes."[29] Some scholars think that it was written as a commentary on the Exclusion Crisis, and it may have been. Among Hobbes's papers is a copy of the Exclusion Act and a copy of a speech by Shaftesbury "against popery." Some have suggested that Hobbes's manuscript favors exclusion; I disagree. The question put to Hobbes is, "If a Successor to a Crown be for some reason or other which is notorious, incapable to protect the people, if the Government should devolve upon him, is not the Prince in possession obliged to put him by, upon the request of his subjects?" The question probably came from Devonshire's son, the first duke of Devonshire, who would receive that title as a reward for his support for William of Orange during the Glorious Revolution. The duke thought that his father had been badly treated by Charles II; he was strongly anti-Catholic, and he had a large number of duels to his discredit. I suspect that Hobbes did not like him. Hobbes begins his answer to the question peevishly: "Here again you mistake me." He affirms his belief that a king holds his title "by divine right" and then continues to charge his questioner with misunderstanding: "Nor did I mention the word 'Institution'; nor do I know what you mean."

The complaint against James's possible kingship was his Roman Catholic religion. But Hobbes's reply says nothing about that. Instead, he says that "the people ought to obey the King. For it is impossible for the best King in the world to protect his people, except his subjects furnish him with so much money as he shall judge sufficient to do it." Repeating himself somewhat, he says that if the "notorious incapacity" is the result of not having enough money, then the king should not disinherit him. Even if the incapacity is the result of stupidity ("want of natural reason"), the king need not disinherit, although he may. In any case, Hobbes refuses to say anything more about the topic "until we have such a weak king." None of this is strictly relevant to the Exclusion Crisis. But to the extent that it is, Hobbes supported the conservative cause against exclusion: "Who shall force him [the king]; for I suppose the sound King living cannot be lawfully deposed by any person or persons that are his subjects; because the king dying is ipso facto dissolved, and then the people is a multitude of lawless men relapsed into a condition of war of every man against man. Which by making a king they intended to avoid."[30]

Decameron Physiologicum, 1678

Hobbes had as much right to be proud of *Decameron Physiologicum*, published at the age of ninety, the year before he died, as anything that he had written in the previous decade. It is a spirited defense of almost all of the physical theory that he had been advancing for three decades or more. In ten dialogues between his beloved characters, A and B, he defends philosophy against philosophers many of whom are "foolish and ridiculous."[31] He lays out in a clear and summary fashion his axioms of physics: (1) No two bodies can occupy the same place at the same time; (2) nothing moves itself; (3) all motion occurs by contact; that is, there is no action at a distance; and (4) nothing is absolutely at rest.[32] Later he asserts the conservation of all matter, but not as an axiom.[33]

He asserts that God is "the most real substance that is; who, being infinite, there can be no place empty where He is, nor full where He is not."[34] So it is implausible that a vacuum exists. He also has various scientific arguments against the existence of a vacuum. Refining an argument he had used in *Dialogus Physicus*, Hobbes contends that if the vacuumists were right in holding that sucking makes a vacuum, then nursing mothers would collapse into themselves. Hobbes's own view is that air from the infant passes through the mother's milk to fill the space left by the milk being ingested.[35] Many of his other arguments are repeated from earlier works. And of course the views of John Wallis are criticized.

Abuse and Misinterpretation of *Leviathan*, 1670–79

Misinterpretation of Hobbes's *Leviathan* had begun not long after it had been published. In *The Unreasonableness of Atheism Made Manifest* (1666), Charles Wolseley maintained that Hobbes grounds all religion in human authority, when in fact Hobbes holds only that human authority makes a specific religion law, not that it makes anything to be a religion, much less a true one. A worse distortion of Hobbes's views occurs in "The Atheists' Catechism," which Wolseley appended to his book:

Q. Do you believe there is a God?
A. No: I believe there is none.
Q. What is the true ground of your belief?
A. Because I have no mind there should be one.
Q. What other reason do you give for it?
A. Because I never saw him.
. . .
Q. What is it that men call Religion?
A. A politick cheat put upon the world.
Q. Who were the first contrivers of this cheat?
A. Some cunning men that designed to keep the world in subjection and awe.

Hobbes would never maintain, pace Wolseley, that God did not exist simply because he never saw him. He believed in the existence of bodies even though he thought that they are never actually seen. Rather, bodies act on sense organs and thereby cause motions that are phantasms. Belief in bodies is justified by the fact that the only sensible way to explain phantasms is to infer that bodies exist and act in the way described. Even if we posit a sense in which people perceive bodies, Hobbes believed that the basic particles of matter are much too small to be perceived by humans. But he knew that they exist because any body can be divided infinitely, and at some point such division would yield a body imperceptibly small. It is most likely that Hobbes, like virtually everyone else before the mid-eighteenth century, could not conceive of the world existing without some cause or explanation. Hobbes also did not believe that "the first contrivers" of religion were "cunning men that designed to keep the world in subjection and awe." Even on the atheistic interpretation of

Hobbes, he maintained that the source of religion is curiosity and a mistaken understanding of causality.

At least in the 1650s and 1660s, Hobbes still had the vigor and sometimes the interest to defend his religious doctrines. But for the most part, he ignored his critics. In the preface to *An Answer to . . . "Catching of the Leviathan,"* Hobbes wrote that he had not known for ten years that Bramhall had written his book because "so little talk there was of his Lordship's writings." My guess is that in addition to insulting Bramhall, Hobbes is indicating how indifferent he usually is to criticism. More than once he had said that he did not dispute but taught. It was worth his while in the mid-1660s to defend his religious and, to a lesser extent, his political views, because of the practical threat to his safety. He wrote no defense of *Leviathan* after 1668 because he felt no need to. He had had his say.

His critics during the 1670s, virtually all of them superficial and bigoted, had a field day. He was blamed for the libertinism of the age, partially because he was a safer target than Charles II, "the Merry Monarch." Wolseley in *The Reasonableness of Scripture-Belief* (1672), wrote, "'Tis but of late that men come to defend ill living and secure themselves against their own guilt by an open defiance to all the great maxims of piety and virtue; . . . and most of the bad principles of this age are of no earlier a date than one very ill book, are indeed but the spawn of the *Leviathan*." Robert Sharrock outdid Wolseley in misinterpretation the next year. He stupidly attributes the following injunctions to Hobbes: "Fill yourselves with costly wine and ointments and let none of you go without some part of his [Hobbes's] voluptuousness, . . . oppress the poor righteous man, spare not the widow and (which is perfect Hobbism) let your strength be the law of justice and what is feeble count it little worth. Lay wait for the righteous man."[36] This characterization of Hobbesianism is absurd. Hobbes was well known for his charity; he thought that letting each person's strength be the law of justice was the formula for solitude, poverty, and wretchedness, and he thought that lying in wait for the "righteous" would probably result in one's own demise in the not too distant future. Hobbes was unalterably opposed in theory and practice to licentious living. Licentiousness, that is, living in complete liberty, was living in the wretched state of nature, and the critics who knew him personally, such as Bramhall and Clarendon, testified to Hobbes's personal sobriety and integrity.

Sharrock was in effect making Hobbes out to be Friedrich Nietzsche, and two philosophers are hardly farther apart. Nietzsche praises what is natural and condemns what is artificial, celebrates the exercise of power for its own sake, and disdains conventional morality; Hobbes praises what is artificial and is wary of what is natural; the exercise of unrestrained power inevitably ends in premature death, and conventional morality is an essential part of self-preservation. Nietzsche is the philosopher of the strong; Hobbes is the philosopher of the weak.

Samuel Parker, who was sometimes accused of being a Hobbesian in spite of himself, thought that Hobbes maintained that "Power is right, and justifies all actions whatsoever, whether good or bad." He was woefully confused. Hobbes thought that the only power that justifies everything is the irresistible power of God; such power, by definition, cannot justify anything bad. What God wills is good.

What the words of Hobbes's critics set the criterion for is rhetoric. Their abuse is often better than Ronald Reagan's attacks on the country formerly known as the Soviet Union and Saddam Hussein's on the United States. Here's a sample from Charles Robotham's *Idea Theologiae Leviathanis* (1673):

Malmesburian hydra, the enormous Leviathan, the gigantic dragon, the hideous monstrosity and British beast, the Propagator of execrable doctrines, the Promulgator of mad wisdom, the herald and pugilist of impious death, the insipid venerator of a material God, the renowned fabricator of a monocondyte symbol, the depraved renewer of old heresies to the faith, the nonsensical roguish vendor of falsifications, a strenuous hoer of weeds and producer of deceits.[37]

Hobbes's Alleged Atheism

The misinterpretations of Hobbes's philosophy contributed to his reputation as an atheist. And it is not surprising that it was misinterpreted. People find it difficult to assimilate conceptually new information for the simple reason that it has no preexisting place in their scheme of beliefs. Rather than understand the material to be genuinely new, they tend to relegate it to a familiar, if inappropriate, category. Since Hobbes's treatment of Christianity was obviously not a familiar one, many people thought of it as atheistic. Even the early Christians were thought of as atheistic because they denied the existence of the Roman gods.

Related to the tendency to conflate conceptually new material with preexisting concepts is the phenomenon of slippery thinking, for example, the belief that heterodoxy (or deism) inevitably leads to anticlericalism (or irreligion) and then to atheism. It is not so. Anyway, at least a prima facie case for taking Hobbes to be deistic and anticlerical was made within a few months after his death by people sympathetic to his thought. Two broadsheets were published containing select excerpts from his writings along with some comments ascribed to him that cannot be found in his surviving works. Taken out of context and gathered together as they are, they do convey deistic anticlericalism. Both broadsheets run toward deism. "Memorable Sayings of Thomas Hobbes" begins with Hobbes's proof for the existence of God. One of the more offensive sounding propositions in the other broadsheet, "The Last Sayings or Dying Legacy of Mr. Thomas Hobbs of Malmesbury," is that God is "Almighty Matter." This sentence, which is not in any known work by Hobbes, would accurately express his view, if it meant that God is material and is almighty. However, the proposition is more likely to be taken to mean that God is all matter and all matter is what is almighty. And Hobbes never asserted that.

"The Last Sayings" purports to have been "Printed for the Author's Executors." Hobbes's executor was his longtime secretary and companion, James Wheldon, who wrote an account of Hobbes's last days. There is no evidence that Wheldon had anything to do with the publication of either broadsheet. Rather, the first and possibly the second seem to be the work of Charles Blount (1654–93). Blount is an odd character. He was the author of a variety of works about politics and religion, supported the exclusion of James II, and was a member of the Green Ribbon Club, made up of Whigs. His bête noire was the immortality of the soul, about which he wrote several works. Part of his affection for Hobbes was the latter's antipathy for the concept of an immortal soul. In 1678, Blount sent a copy of his book *Anima Mundi* to Hobbes along with a letter that praised his views about heresy. There is no evidence that Hobbes ever met or corresponded with Blount. Most of all, Blount was a deist and wrote a defense of John Dryden's *Religio Laici* that made Dryden out to be one. Dryden's biographer cannot determine whether Blount's misrepresentation was due to "stupidity or malice."[38] It may have been largely enthusiasm.

One characteristic of Blount's literary style was plagiarism. A large part of his *Religio Laici* was taken from Lord Herbert of Cherbury. A large part of his letter to Hobbes uses passages from Henry Stubbe's *An Account of Mohametanism* without attribution. And his *Miracles, No Violations of the Laws of Nature* uses material verbatim from Hobbes and Spinoza, again without attribution. Deist or not, Blount took priests too seriously. Having been refused ecclesiatical permission to marry his dead wife's sister, he committed suicide.

Aubrey indicated that Blount was responsible only for "The Last Sayings." It is possible, however, that Blount at least had a hand in both, since one of his notebooks contains quotations that correspond closely to both broadsheets. Given that some of these quotations are longer than the ones in the broadsheets and also that some get divided between the two, he may have used the notebook version as something like a master from which the two broadsheets were edited.[39] According to Aubrey, "Memorable Sayings" was the project of Francis and Charles Bernard, who were surgeons, royalists, and High Churchmen. It is slightly less anticlerical than "Last Sayings." It also bears some marks of having been produced by acquaintances of Hobbes. For example, one remark is prefaced with the words "Drinking a glass of wine, he said," and the next with, "And after another glass, speaking of government." Some of the remarks may be apocryphal. The last one reads, "When he was dying, he called for his chair (in which he died) saying, *Oportet philosophum sedentem mori* ('A philosopher should die sitting up')." It is a nice sentiment, but, as we shall see, it does not fit the firsthand account we have of his last days. It is possible that "Memorable Sayings" was the work of a larger group since, when Aubrey attributes it to the brothers Bernard, he alludes to "a club."

Hobbes was only one of many distinguished thinkers to be accused of atheism in the sixteenth and seventeenth centuries. A partial list includes Luther, Calvin, Sir Walter Raleigh, and Thomas Browne. The case of Browne is especially interesting because what the redoubtable Samuel Johnson says about Browne applies equally to Hobbes:

There remains yet an objection against the writing of Browne, more formidable than the animadversions of criticism. There are passages, from which some have taken occasion to rank him among Deists, and others among Atheists. It would be difficult to guess how any such conclusion should be formed had not experience shewn that there are two sorts of men willing to enlarge the catalogue of infidels. . . . [One group are atheists and infidels.] In proportion as they doubt the truth of their own doctrines, they . . . eagerly catch at the slightest pretense to dignify their sect with a celebrated name.

The others . . . [are] men so watchful to censure, that they have seldom much care to look for favorable interpretations of ambiguities, . . . or to know how soon any slip of inadvertency has been expiated by sorrow and retraction; but let fly their fulminations without mercy or prudence against slight offenses or casual temerities, against crimes never committed or immediately repented. . . .

Men may differ from each other in many religious opinions, and yet all may retain the essentials of Christianity. . . . Whether Browne has been numbered among the contemners of religion by the fury of its friends or the artifice of its enemies, it is no difficult task to place him among the most zealous Professors of Christianity. He may perhaps in the ardor of his imagination have hazarded an expression which a mind intent upon faults may interpret into heresy, if considered apart from the rest of his discourse; but a phrase is not to be opposed to volumes: there is scarcely a writer to be found whose profession was not divinity that has so frequently testified his belief of the Sacred Writings, has appealed to them with such unlimited submission, or mentioned them with such unvaried reverence.

It is indeed somewhat wonderful that he should be placed without the pale of Christianity who declares [here I replace quotations from Browne with some by Hobbes]: "This I know; God cannot sin, because his doing a thing makes it just, and consequently no sin; as also because whatsoever can sin is subject to another's law, which God is not. . . . yet I know this, that in the court of heaven there is no such difference between saying, signing, and sealing, as his Lordship seems here to pretend. I am baptized for a commemoration that I have enrolled myself. I take the sacrament of the Lord's supper to commemorate that Christ's body was broken and his blood shed for my redemption."[40]

The Old Philosopher in the Country

One of the few glimpses of the bucolic life that Hobbes lived in Derbyshire over the last decade of his life comes from a man who detested him. In his *Memoirs of the Cavendish Family*, White Kennet wrote:

His method of life was said to be very singular. His professed principle was to dedicate the morning to his health, and the afternoon to his studies; and therefore at his first rising he walked out, if the weather was dry, or else within doors, so fatigued himself as to be in a sweat, recommending that practice upon the opinion that an old man had more moisture than heat, and therefore by such exercise heat was to be acquired and moisture expelled. After his walk or other motions, he took a comfortable breakfast, and then went round the lodgings to wait upon the earl and the countess and all the children, paying some short addresses to them. He kept these rounds till about 12 a clock, when he had a little dinner provided for him, which he always ate by himself. Soon after dinner, he had his candle and 12 pipes of tobacco laying by it, then shutting his door, and darkening some part of his windows, he fell to smoking and thinking and writing for several hours. He had very few books, and those he read very little, thinking he was now only to digest what he had formerly fed upon.

He used to be thinking of his epitaph while he was living and would suffer some friends to dictate inscriptions for him, among which he was best pleased with this humor for a gravestone: This is the true Philosopher's Stone.[41]

Death Be Not Proud

About mid-October 1679, it became extremely painful for Hobbes to urinate.[42] The diagnosis was strangury or an ulcerated bladder. A physician gave Hobbes medicines to take, but to no avail. When Hobbes asked whether his condition could be cured, the physician said "No." The most that the doctor could do would be to reduce the pain a bit. Echoing his autobiography, in which he called himself a "little worm," Hobbes said that he would "be glad to find a hole to creep out of the world at." He was more afraid of the pain than of his impending death. Near the end of November, the Cavendish family was preparing to move from Chatsworth to the more moderate climate of Hardwick for the holidays. They wanted to leave Hobbes at Chatsworth because of his dire condition, but he refused and insisted on coming with them. He had overcome poverty and nastiness; his life certainly had not been short. His life had never been solitary except when he sought it, so why in these last days should he return to the state of nature and die in solitude? He wanted the artificial consolation of his adopted family.

He was wrapped in a feather comforter and placed in a coach for the ten-mile ride to Hardwick. Some days later, he suffered a stroke that paralyzed his right side and struck him speechless. His eyes wandered around the room but he seemed to have lost his senses and ability to recognize anyone. He was unable to "take the sacrament," although he had received it several times shortly before his last illness. On those occasions he had taken it "with seeming devotion, and in humble and revered posture," according to Devonshire's chaplain. He was unable to eat and died, in the judgment of his executor, James Wheldon, "rather for want of fuel (which was spent in him) and mere weakness and decay than by the power of his disease, which was thought to be only an effect of his age and weakness."

He had first taught that death was the greatest evil that could befall a human being. Later, he said that it was a painful death that was the greatest evil. Finally, in a variant ending to his verse autobiography, he wrote, "Et prope stans dictat Mors mihi, 'Ne metue'." ("And Death, standing close to me, says, 'Do not be afraid'.") He knew that death was not the greatest evil for everyone all the time.

He died on Thursday, December 4, 1679.

His body was wrapped in a woolen shroud and placed in a casket that was covered first with a white sheet and then on top of that a black hearse cloth. The casket was carried on the shoulders of some men to St. John the Baptist Church, the parish church of Ault (Hault) Hucknall, about a mile from Hardwick. The minister of the parish conducted the burial service, which was attended by the Cavendish family and their neighbors. Hobbes had outlived all of his friends. Afterwards the mourners were given "wine, burned and raw, cake, bisquit, etc."

On his tombstone is an inscription in Latin that means:

Here are buried the bones of Thomas Hobbes of Malmesbury, who for many years served two earls of Devonshire, father and son. He was a virtuous man and his reputation for erudition both at home and abroad is well known.

The secretary to the earl of Devonshire wrote a brief account of Hobbes's last days: "Mr. Hobbs calmly departed this life after he had lain speechless and with one side of the palsy a full week and some hours. . . . there passed nothing remarkable or extraordinary either in his sickness or at his death." Those who hated him were dissatisfied that he had died peacefully; it was hard enough for them to explain how God could have kept the wretch alive for more than ninety years. Consequently, they littered London with the lie that he had refused communion on his deathbed.

Hobbes left a substantial estate, calculated by Aubrey to be worth about £1,000, equivalent to wages for ten to twelve years. In his will, made up on September 25, 1677, he made provisions to leave his brother Edmund's two daughters £40 each. He left £200 to Elizabeth Alaby, the orphaned daughter of Thomas Alaby. He must have been her guardian because he committed her to the care of his executor, Wheldon, until she reached the age of sixteen. At that time, she was to receive £200, either as a dowry or "to dispose of as she please." Since he had already given a plot of land to his brother's grandchild Thomas, no further provision was made for him. But £100 was to be split evenly between four other grand-children. The remainder of his estate, including whatever the king might be willing to pay from the arrears of Hobbes's pension, was to go to his loyal aide, Wheldon, except for £10. In a codicil, that money was stipulated for an otherwise unidentified Mary Dell. In a poem written late in his life, Hobbes confessed his love for a young woman:

> Tho' I am now past ninety, and too old
> T' expect preferment in the course of Cupid,
> And many winters have me ev'n so cold
> I am become almost all over stupid,
> Yet I can love and have a mistresse too,
> As fair as can be and as wise as fair;
> And yet not proud, nor anything will doe
> to make me of her favor to despair.
> To tell you who she is were very bold;
> But if I' th' character your selfe you find
> Think not the man a fool tho he be old
> Who loves in body fair a fairer mind.

Could it have been Ms. Dell? We shall never know. What we do know is that overall his life was neither solitary, poor, brutish, or short.

Still, it had more than its share of nastiness. Much of Hobbes's life had been a struggle for survival. His family was lower middle class; his father abandoned the family when Hobbes was an adolescent. Much of what he did was motivated by fear. He lived in exile for a decade because he was afraid of being killed in the English Civil War. He returned to England because he feared the French and some exiled English clergy and the possibility of assassination by resentful royalists. There he feared prosecution for atheism, both during the Commonwealth and the Restoration. He also came to fear the loss of his mathematical reputation and battled furiously, if not wisely, some of the most powerful members of the Royal Society. In short, much of his life was spent in fear of war. All other time was peace.

A Bibliographical Essay

For Hobbes's life, the best place to begin is with Aubrey's *Brief Lives* (various editions), both because it is the most engaging account ever written and because one can then read around in the book to find out more about Hobbes's friends and enemies. The modern equivalent of Aubrey is the two volumes of *The Correspondence of Thomas Hobbes,* edited by Noel Malcolm (Oxford: Clarendon Press, 1994). It is as scholarly as Aubrey's book is charming and has rightly been called "stupendous." Good general biographies of Hobbes have been written by Miriam Reik, *The Golden Lands of Thomas Hobbes* (Detroit: Wayne State University Press, 1977); Johann Sommerville, *Thomas Hobbes: Political Ideas in Historical Context* (New York: St. Martin's Press, 1992); and Richard Tuck, *Hobbes* (New York: Oxford University Press, 1989). Anything written by the prolific Tuck is valuable. For example, he emphasizes Hobbes's changed attitude toward the competence of clerics in religious matters from *De Cive* to *Leviathan.* I especially recommend his *Philosophy and Government, 1572–1651* (Cambridge: Cambridge University Press, 1993) and "Hobbes and Descartes," in *Perspectives on Thomas Hobbes,* ed. G. A. J. Rogers and Alan Ryan (Oxford: Clarendon Press, 1988). All the essays in this latter collection are valuable. A biography that is both very good and very bad is Arnold Rogow, *Thomas Hobbes: Radical in the Service of Reaction* (New York: Norton, 1986). It contains information not found in any other published source. Unfortunately, it is sometimes inaccurate and often presents implausible speculations about Hobbes's psychological life.

The master of historically informed, philosophically sensitive treatments of Hobbes's philosophy is Quentin Skinner. His latest book on Hobbes is the magisterial *Reason and Rhetoric in the Philosophy of Hobbes* (Cambridge: Cambridge University Press, 1996). His articles, listed in the bibliography of that book, are extraordinarily valuable.

359

There are many fine editions of Hobbes's *Leviathan*, each with its own merits. Overall the best in my opinion is the one by Edwin Curley, published by Hackett. I have used his translation of parts of the Latin *Leviathan*.

Good, straightforward accounts of Hobbes's philosophy are given in my own *Thomas Hobbes* (New York: St. Martin's Press, 1997), Richard Peters's *Hobbes* (Harmondsworth: Penguin, 1956), Tom Sorell's *Hobbes* (London: Routledge & Kegan Paul, 1986), *The Cambridge Companion to Thomas Hobbes*, ed. Tom Sorell (Cambridge: Cambridge University Press, 1996), and J. W. N. Watkins's *Hobbes's System of Ideas*, 2d edition (London: Hutchinson University Library, 1973). Hobbes's philosophy is also presented in easily digestible bites in my *A Hobbes Dictionary* (Oxford: Blackwell, 1995).

A good selection of some of Hobbes's best and earliest critics is in *Leviathan: Contemporary Responses to the Political Theory of Thomas Hobbes*, ed. G. A. J. Rogers (Bristol: Thoemmes Press, 1995).

The relationship between William and Fulgentio Micanzio and its relevance to Hobbes is discussed in Noel Malcolm's *De Dominis (1560–1624): Venetian, Anglican, Ecumenist and Relapsed Heretic* (London: n.p., 1984). Hobbes's activities as a member of the Virginia Company are discussed in Noel Malcolm's "Hobbes, Sandys, and the Virginia Company," *Historical Journal* 24 (1981), 297–321.

Hobbes's use of rhetoric is masterfully treated by David Johnston in *The Rhetoric of Leviathan* (Princeton: Princeton University Press, 1986) and by Quentin Skinner in the book mentioned earlier. The place of Hobbes's rhetoric within rhetorical studies of the period is examined by Walter J. Ong, "Hobbes and Talon's Ramist Rhetoric in English," *Transactions of the Cambridge Bibliographic Society* (1951), 260–69.

On the Newcastle circle and Walter Warner in particular, an excellent book is Jan Prins's *Walter Warner (ca. 1557–1643) and His Notes on Animal Organisms* (Utrecht: n.p., 1992). Unfortunately, in the United States, it is available to my knowledge only in the Widener Library of Harvard University. On Robert Payne, see Mordechai Feingold's "A Friend of Hobbes and an Early Translator of Galileo: Robert Payne of Oxford," in *The Light of Nature: Essays in the History and Philosophy of Science Presented to A. C. Crombie*, ed. J. D. North and J. J. Roche (Dordrecht: Martinus Nijhoff, 1985), pp. 265–80.

The single best work on Hobbes's philosophy of science and debate with Robert Boyle is Steven Shapin and Simon Schaffer, *Leviathan and the Air-Pump* (Princeton: Princeton University Press, 1985). For the background to Hobbes's complaints about the universities, see Alan Debus, *Science and Education in the Seventeenth Century: The Webster-Ward Debate* (New York: American Elsevier, 1970).

Two works that deal in a more general way with the people and ideas of Stuart England as they relate to Hobbes are Hugh Trevor-Roper, "The Great Tew Circle," in *Catholics, Anglicans, and Puritans* (London: Fontana, 1989), and Francis Bickley, *The Cavendish Family* (London: Constable, 1911).

Abbreviations

AW = *Anti-White* (aka *Hobbes's Critique of Thomas White's De Mundo*, trans. Harold Whitmore Jones [London: Bradford University Press, 1976])

B = *Behemoth*, ed. Ferdinand Tonnies (London: Simpkin, 1889)

Correspondence = *The Correspondence of Thomas Hobbes*, ed. Noel Malcolm (Clarendon Press, 1994)

DC = *De Cive*

DCo = *De Corpore*

DP = *Dialogus Physicus*, in Steven Shapin and Simon Schaffer, *Leviathan and the Air-Pump* (Princeton: Princeton University Press, 1985)

EL = *The Elements of Law, Natural and Politic*

EW = *English Works*, ed. William Molesworth

HS = *Horae Subsecivae: Observations and Discourses*

L = *Leviathan*

LN = *Of Liberty and Necessity*

OL = *Opera Latina*, ed. William Molesworth

PW = *The Peloponnesian War: The Complete Hobbes Translation*, ed. David Grene (Chicago: University of Chicago Press, 1989)

SL = *Six Lessons to the Savilian Professors of Mathematics*

ST = *A Short Tract on First Principles*, ed. Tonnies

TO = *Tractatus Opticus* in OL, vol. 5

Notes

In general, I provide references to quotations from Hobbes and to those secondary works to which I owe a special debt. Seventeenth-century letters are typically referred to simply in the text by sender and addressee. I have not given references to Hobbes's autobiographies, except to credit a translator, or to John Aubrey's biography of Hobbes, or to unpublished material in archives.

I occasionally give my own translations for and alter the punctuation of quotations when I refer to a standard edition.

1. Malmesbury and Magdalen Hall, 1588–1608

1. On Hobbes's early life, I found helpful Arnold Rogow, *Thomas Hobbes: Radical in the Service of Reaction* (New York: Norton, 1986).
2. Quoted from Rogow, p. 27.
3. Quoted from Rogow, p. 29.
4. Quoted from G. R. Elton, *The Tudor Constitution*, 2d ed. (Cambridge: Cambridge University Press, 1982), p. 338.
5. Rogow (p. 35) denies that Hobbes had a position in Charlton.
6. According to Joseph Foster, *Alumni Oxonienses* (London, 1887–88), 3:884b, and Andrew Clark, *Register of the University of Oxford*, vol. 2, part 3, p. 168.
7. L 30.7.
8. *Register of the University of Oxford*, vol. 2, part 1, pp. v–xi.
9. Quentin Skinner, *Reason and Rhetoric in the Philosophy of Hobbes* (Cambridge: Cambridge University Press, 1996).
10. *Register of the University of Oxford*, vol. 2, part 1, p. 176.
11. C. E. Mallett, *A History of the University of Oxford*, vol. 2 (New York: Longmans, Green, 1924), p. 132.
12. L 4:12.
13. B, p. 147.
14. John Nichols, *The Progresses, Processions, and Magnificent Activities of King James the First, etc.* (London, 1745–1826), 1:530ff.

15. Some sources say 1607, but they probably are not taking into account the fact that the English began the New Year on March 25.

2. Tutor and Companion, 1608–1620

1. On Elizabeth of Hardwick and the Cavendish family, I benefited from A. S. Turberville's *A History of Welbeck Abbey and its Owners*, vol. 1 (London: Faber and Faber, 1938), and Francis Bickley's *The Cavendish Family* (London: Constable, 1911).
2. Quoted from Bickley, *The Cavendish Family*, p. 22.
3. Page references to *Horae Subsecivae* are to the original edition; these page numbers are inserted into a modern edition, *Three Discourses*, ed. Noel Reynolds and Arlene Saxonhouse (Chicago: University of Chicago Press, 1995). HS, p. 382.
4. HS, p. 384.
5. John Venn and J. A. Venn, *Alumni Cantabrigienses* (Cambridge: Cambridge University Press, 1922), 1:311.
6. Correspondence, p. 856 n. 5.
7. HS, p. 149.
8. HS, pp. 163, 168.
9. Quoted from Roger Lockyer, *The Early Stuarts: A Political History of England, 1603–1642* (London: Longman, 1989), p. 186.
10. Linda Levy Peck, "Hobbes on the Grand Tour: Paris, Venice, or London?" *Journal of the History of Ideas* 57 (1996), 177–82.
11. HS, pp. 340–42.
12. HS, pp. 365, 366.
13. HS, pp. 367, 368, 371, 372.
14. HS, pp. 374, 375.
15. HS, pp. 390–91, 392.
16. HS pp. 331–33, 337.
17. Niccolò Machiavelli, *Discourses*, trans. Leslie J. Walker (London: Penguin Books, 1970), pp. 102–3.
18. HS, pp. 340, 343, 345; L 45.33.
19. L 6.36.
20. HS, p. 397.
21. HS, pp. 399, 403.
22. HS, p. 400.
23. HS, p. 402.
24. HS, pp. 402–3.
25. HS, p. 406; L 38.25.
26. HS, p. 417.
27. William Bouwsma, *Venice and the Defense of Republican Liberty* (Berkeley: University of California Press, 1968), p. 526.
28. The original translation of the letters from Micanzio to Cavendish is at Chatsworth and a copy is in the British Library.

29. Lawrence Stone, *The Crisis of the Aristocracy, 1558–1641*, abr. ed. (London: Oxford University Press, 1967), pp. 50–51.

30. AW, p. 87.

3. Secretary and Humanist, 1621–1629

1. On the influence of Tacitus in Tudor England, I have been guided by Ronald Mellor, *Tacitus* (New York: Routledge, 1993), pp. 148–52.

2. HS, pp. 295, 261, 271, 291.

3. L 11.7; HS, pp. 279–80.

4. L 11.8; HS, p. 281.

5. HS, p. 224.

6. HS, p. 238; L 21.8.

7. HS, pp. 269, 272–73.

8. HS, p. 267.

9. HS, pp. 306–7.

10. HS, pp. 323–24.

11. HS, pp. 505, 542.

12. HS, pp. 507–8.

13. HS, pp. 512, 512–13.

14. HS, pp. 506–7.

15. HS, pp. 528, 529.

16. Correspondence, p. 3.

17. See Glenn Burgess, *The Politics of the Ancient Constitution* (University Park: Pennsylvania State University Press, 1992), p. 176.

18. I have relied on Noel Malcolm, "Hobbes, Sandys, and the Virginia Company," *Historical Journal* 24 (1981), 297–321; and Frank Craven, *The Dissolution of the Virginia Company* (New York: Oxford University Press, 1932). Quotations from this section can be found in these works unless otherwise noted.

19. Quoted from Craven, *The Dissolution of the Virginia Company*, p. 238.

20. Quoted from Craven, *The Dissolution of the Virginia Company*, p. 309.

21. L 10.49, 27.35.

22. B, p. 126.

23. L 22.16.

24. Correspondence, p. 32.

25. L 24.14.

26. EW 7:112.

27. DCo 1.6.

28. *The Advancement of Learning and New Atlantis*, ed. Arthur Johnston (Oxford: Clarendon Press, 1974), p. 128.

29. L 4.13.

30. Francis Bacon, *The Essays* (London: Penguin, 1985), p. 126.

31. B, p. 38.

32. *The Essays*, pp. 270–71.

33. DC, "Preface," 2.

34. Correspondence, p. 7.
35. PW, pp. 204–5.
36. PW, p. xxi.
37. PW, p. 577.
38. PW, p. xxii.
39. HS, pp. 194–95.
40. PW, p. 579.
41. PW, p. 581.
42. PW, p. 582.
43. PW, pp. 570–71.
44. EW 6:97.

4. Early Scientific Studies and Religious Views, 1629–1640

1. Quoted from "The Life of Thomas Hobbes of Malmesbury," trans. J. E. Parsons Jr. and Whitney Blair, *Interpretation* 10 (1981), 2.
2. Correspondence, p. 12 n. 1.
3. Correspondence, p. 12 n. 1.
4. Quoted from Francis Bickley, *The Cavendish Family* (London: Constable, 1911), p. 44.
5. On the issue in this and the following two paragraphs, see Arnold Rogow, *Thomas Hobbes* (New York: Norton, 1986), pp. 112–17.
6. Rogow, *Thomas Hobbes*, pp. 115–16.
7. Joseph Quincy Adams, ed., *The Dramatic Records of Sir Henry Herbert* (New Haven: Yale University Press, 1917), p. 55.
8. Translated by Noel Malcolm in Correspondence, p. 151.
9. Correspondence, p. 29.
10. DCo 20.1.
11. "The Life of Thomas Hobbes of Malmesbury," p. 3.
12. DCo 25.2.
13. Correspondence, p. 23.
14. Correspondence, p. 37.
15. Correspondence, p. 41.
16. Correspondence, p. 46.
17. Correspondence, p. 50.
18. Correspondence, p. 52.
19. Correspondence, p. 53.
20. EL 9.13.
21. Correspondence, pp. 52–53.
22. DC 1.2.
23. Quentin Skinner, *Reason and Rhetoric in the Philosophy of Hobbes* (Cambridge: Cambridge University Press, 1996), pp. 198–211.
24. Correspondence, p. 53.
25. Quoted from *The Cavendish Family*, p. 52.

26. Leo Strauss, *The Political Philosophy of Hobbes* (Chicago: University of Chicago Press, 1952), pp. 35–43.

27. EW 6:464.

28. EL 9.12.

29. EW 6:433.

30. DH 11.14.

31. Correspondence, p. 38.

32. Edward Hyde, *The Life of Edward, Earl of Clarendon* (Oxford: Oxford University Press, 1761), part 6, p. 249.

33. See Jean Jacquot, "Sir Charles Cavendish and His Learned Friends," *Annals of Science* 3 (1952), 13–27.

34. Correspondence, p. 29.

35. J. O. Halliwell, ed., *A Collection of Letters Illustrative of the Progress of Science in England, Etc.* (London, 1841), p. 68.

36. Correspondence, p. 41.

37. EW 7:342.

38. Halliwell, *A Collection of Letters*, p. 65.

39. Correspondence, p. 28.

40. ST 3.2.

41. Jan Prins's *Walter Warner (ca. 1557–1643) and His Notes on Animal Organisms* (Utrecht: n.p., 1992), p. 270.

42. Unless otherwise noted, quotations from this section can be found in Hugh Trevor-Roper, "The Great Tew Circle," in *Catholics, Anglicans, and Puritans* (London: Fontana, 1989), pp. 166–230.

43. Quoted from Robert Orr, *Reason and Authority* (Oxford: Clarendon Press, 1967), p. 36.

44. EW 5:2.

45. Anthony Wood, *Athenae Oxonienses*, 3d ed., ed. Philip Bliss (London: Rivington, 1817), 3:90.

46. Quoted from Orr, *Reason and Authority*, p. 198.

47. Quoted from J. P. Kenyon, *The Stuart Constitution*, 2d ed. (Cambridge: Cambridge University Press, 1986), pp. 18–19.

48. L 32.2.

49. William Chillingworth, *The Religion of Protestants* (London, 1638), p. 284.

50. L 32.4.

51. Quoted from C. Hill, *The English Bible and the Seventeenth-Century Revolution* (London: Penguin, 1994), p. 417.

52. On Socinianism and the Great Tew circle, see Trevor-Roper, p. 189.

53. Richard Tuck, *Philosophy and Government, 1572–1651* (Cambridge: Cambridge University Press, 1993), pp. 272–78.

54. Chillingworth, *The Religion of Protestants*, p. 461.

55. Quoted from Orr, *Reason and Authority*, p. 71.

56. EL 25.13.

57. EL 25.5.

58. EL 25.6.

59. EL 25.10.
60. EL 25.12; see also L 29.7.
61. EL 6.8.
62. EL 25.13.
63. EL 25.3.
64. EL 28.8.
65. EL 25.5.
66. EL 26.1.
67. EL 26.7.
68. EL 26.7.
69. EL 26.8.
70. EL 26.9.
71. EL 26.10.
72. EL 26.10.
73. EL 26.11.
74. B. H. G. Wormald, *Clarendon* (Cambridge: Cambridge University Press, 1989), p. 256.
75. Richard Tuck, "Hobbes and Descartes," in *Perspectives on Thomas Hobbes*, ed. G. A. J. Rogers and Alan Ryan (Oxford: Clarendon Press, 1988), pp. 11–41.

5. The Elements of Law, Natural and Politic, 1640

1. See *Ceremonies of Charles I*, ed. Albert Loomie (New York: Fordham University Press, 1987), pp. 270–71.
2. Quoted from Correspondence, p. 171 n. 2.
3. EL 19.7; cf. 19.10.
4. EL 28.7.
5. Samuel Gardiner, *History of England from the Accession of James I to the Outbreak of the Civil War, 1603–1642* (London, 1884), 9:130.
6. EL 12.2.
7. EL 5.11.
8. EL "Dedicatory Letter."
9. EL "Dedicatory Letter."
10. L "Review and Conclusion," 4.
11. L "Review and Conclusion," 4.
12. L 15.12.
13. L "Review and Conclusion," 4.
14. EL 23.1.
15. EL 2.10.
16. EL 3.1.
17. L "Introduction," 1.
18. EL 5.6.
19. EL 6.1.
20. EL 6.1.
21. EL 7.1.

22. EL 9.7.
23. DCo 15.2.
24. EL 7.2.
25. EL 7.2.
26. EL 9.5; see also L. 6.18.
27. EL 7.3.
28. EL 7.7.
29. L 11.1.
30. L 6.7.
31. EL 9.12.
32. EL 9.16, 9.17.
33. EL 9.19, 9.21.
34. EL 11.2.
35. John Calvin, *Commentary on Ezechiel 9:3–4;* quoted from Edward Dowey, *The Knowledge of God in Calvin's Theology* (Grand Rapids, Mich.: Eerdmans,1994), p. 4 nn. 1 and 2.
36. See A. P. Martinich, *The Two Gods of Leviathan* (Cambridge: Cambridge University Press, 1992), pp. 190–97.
37. Quoted from Dowey, *The Knowledge of God in Calvin's Theology,* p. 4 n. 2.
38. EL 11.2.
39. Quoted from Dowey, *The Knowledge of God in Calvin's Theology,* p. 6.
40. *The Philosophical Writings of Descartes,* vol. 2, trans. John Cottingham (Cambridge: Cambridge University Press, 1984), pp. 126–27.
41. EL 11.2; L 11.25.
42. EL 11.2.
43. EL 11.3.
44. See Ian Ramsey, *Religious Language: An Empirical Placing of Theological Phrases* (New York: Macmillan, 1957).
45. L 31.28.
46. AW, p. 417.
47. EL 11.4.
48. L 34.2.
49. EW 4:305.
50. EW 4:305.
51. EL 11.5.
52. EL 11.5, 11.6.
53. L 34.24.
54. DC, "Author's Preface to the Reader," 3.
55. EL 14.2.
56. EL 17.1.
57. EL 14.2.
58. EL 14.3–6.
59. EL 14.4.
60. EL 14.10, 14.7.
61. EL 15.1.

62. EL 15.1.
63. L 14.5.
64. EL 16.9.
65. EL 17.1.
66. L 15.41.
67. EL 17.12, 18.1; DC 2.1.
68. L 14.31.
69. EL 15.3.
70. EL 15.3.
71. EL 19.7; also 20.8; cf. 19.10.
72. EL 15.11.
73. L 18.3.
74. L 13.13.
75. EL 15.13.
76. DC 6.13.
77. EL 20.7, 20.9.
78. EL 20.9.
79. EL 20.19.
80. EL 20.19.
81. EL 20.13.
82. EL 24.2.
83. EL 22.4, 22.5, 24.2.
84. EL 27.4.
85. EL 20.13.
86. EL 21.1.
87. DC 7.5.
88. EL 21.1.
89. EL 22.1.
90. EL 23.1.
91. EL 23.3.
92. EL 23.8.
93. DC "Author's Preface," 3.
94. EL 23.4.
95. EL 24.3, 24.4, 24.3.
96. EL 24.4, 24.8.
97. EL 24.4, 24.8.
98. EL 27.1.
99. EL 27.2–3, 27.13, 27.15.
100. EL 27.4; also 27.10.

6. A Decade of Exile, 1641–1651 (I)

1. Correspondence, pp. 115–16.
2. Samuel Gardiner, *History of England from the Accession of James I to the Outbreak of the Civil War, 1603–1642* (London, 1884), 9:240.

3. Correspondence, p. 115.

4. Richard Tuck, "Hobbes and Descartes," in *Perspectives on Thomas Hobbes*, ed. G. A. J. Rogers and Alan Ryan (Oxford: Clarendon Press, 1988), pp. 11–41.

5. Correspondence, p. 57.

6. *The Philosophical Writings of Descartes*, trans. John Cottingham et al. (Cambridge: Cambridge University Press, 1991), 3:170.

7. Correspondence, p. 71.

8. Correspondence, p. 85.

9. *The Philosophical Writings of Descartes*, 2:126.

10. *The Philosophical Writings of Descartes*, 2:133.

11. Correspondence, p. 83.

12. *The Philosophical Writings of Descartes*, 2:122–33.

13. Correspondence, p. 118.

14. EW 7:340–41.

15. Correspondence, p. 119.

16. Correspondence, p. 100.

17. Quoted from *The Protectorate of Oliver Cromwell and the State of Europe, etc.*, ed. Robert Vaughan (London, 1838), 2:363–64.

18. DP, p. 359.

19. EW 7:136.

20. Quoted from Anthony Fletcher, *The Outbreak of the English Civil War* (London: Edward Arnold, 1981), p. 100.

21. Correspondence, p. 120.

22. Quoted from Fletcher, *The Outbreak of the English Civil War*, p. 286.

23. Correspondence, p. 120.

24. EW 4:364.

25. Correspondence, pp. 120–21.

26. Quoted from B. H. G. Wormald, *Clarendon* (Cambridge: Cambridge University Press, 1989), p. 282.

27. L 47.20.

28. Tuck, "Hobbes and Descartes," p. 16.

29. TO 5:217.

30. OL 5:309.

31. OL 5:217.

32. *The Protectorate of Oliver Cromwell and the State of Europe, etc.*, pp. 363–65.

33. Correspondence, p. 129; Tuck, "Hobbes and Descartes," p. 21.

34. Tuck, "Hobbes and Descartes," pp. 20–22.

35. Correspondence, pp. 133, 177.

36. Tuck, "Hobbes and Descartes," p. 19.

37. DC, "Author's Preface to the Reader," 7.

38. DC, "Author's Preface," 7.

39. DC, "Author's Preface," 2.

40. DC, "Author's Preface," 2.

41. DC, "Author's Preface," 8.

42. AW, p. 474. I have modified the translation of Harold Whitmore Jones.

43. AW, p. 477.
44. Quoted from and translated by James Miller Lewis, "Hobbes and the Blackloists" (Ph.D. diss., Harvard University, 1976), p. 79.
45. "Hobbes and the Blackloists," p. 27.
46. Thomas Browne, *Religio Medici* 1.17; L 32.9; L "Introduction," 1; *Religio Medici* 1.27.
47. AW, pp. 23, 24, 256.
48. AW, pp. 310, 25.
49. AW, p. 30.
50. AW, p. 32; see also pp. 306 and 357.
51. AW, p. 38; see also p. 311.
52. AW, p. 54; see also pp. 306–7.
53. AW, p. 162.
54. AW, pp. 326, 341; see also p. 391.
55. AW, p. 162.
56. AW, p. 305.
57. AW, p. 305.
58. AW, pp. 305, 306.
59. AW, pp. 40–41; DCo 7.2.
60. Correspondence, p. 382.
61. AW, pp. 148–49.
62. AW, pp. 311, 320, 339.
63. AW, p. 313.
64. AW, pp. 315, 358, 401.
65. AW, p. 317.
66. AW, pp. 453–54.
67. AW, pp. 321, 318.
68. AW, pp. 323, 321.
69. AW, p. 324.

7. A Decade of Exile, 1641–1651 (II)

1. Quoted from *The Protectorate of Oliver Cromwell and the State of Europe, etc.*, ed. Robert Vaughan (London, 1838), 2:367–68.
2. EW 5:2.
3. EW 4:256–57.
4. EW 4:236; an allusion to Romans 9:20.
5. EL 25.9.
6. EW 5:3.
7. EW 5:3.
8. John Calvin, *Institutes of the Christian Religion*, 2.4.1; see also 2.3.5.
9. EW 4:239–40.
10. AW, p. 424.
11. EW 4:241.
12. AW, pp. 428–29.

13. AW, p. 460.
14. EW 4:256.
15. EW 5:110–11.
16. EW 4:253, 259–60.
17. EW 4:250.
18. EW 4:250.
19. John Bramhall, *Works* (Oxford, 1842), 4:581.
20. Calvin, *Institutes of the Christian Religion*, 2.4.2.
21. Quoted from Peter White, *Predestination, Policy and Polemic* (Cambridge: Cambridge University Press, 1992), p. 19.
22. EW 4:250–51.
23. EW 4:258.
24. AW, pp. 460–61.
25. EW 4: 249–50.
26. Samuel Gardiner, *History of the Commonwealth and Protectorate* (London: Longmans, Green, 1903), 1:133.
27. Correspondence, pp. 128–29.
28. Correspondence, p. 151.
29. See Douglas Jesseph, "Hobbes on the Methods of Modern Mathematics," *Revue d'Histoire des Sciences* 46 (1993), 157 n. 6.
30. DC "Preface to the Reader," 3.
31. DC 5.2.
32. L 13.10.
33. Correspondence, p. 133.
34. Correspondence, p. 167.
35. Correspondence, pp. 168, 173.
36. L 3.3.
37. Correspondence, pp. 157, 158.
38. Correspondence, p. 170.
39. EW 4:444.
40. EW 4:447.
41. EW 4:449; see also L 8.3.
42. EL 10.4.
43. L 8.3.
44. L "Review and Conclusion," 3.
45. L "Review and Conclusion," 4.
46. Edward Hyde, *A Brief View and Survey of the Dangerous and Pernicious Errors to Church and State etc.* (Oxford, 1676), pp. 8–9.

8. *Leviathan* and the Engagement Controversy, 1651–1653

1. *Table Talk*, 2d ed. (London, 1696), p. 186.
2. L 2.8.
3. EW 1:viii–ix.
4. EW 7:337.

5. DP, p. 350.

6. EW 7:120.

7. Quoted from Geoffrey Keynes, *The Life of William Harvey* (Oxford: Clarendon Press, 1978), p. 462.

8. Walter Pope, *The Life of the Right Reverent Father in God Seth Ward etc.* (London, 1697), pp. 117–18.

9. *Nicholas Papers,* ed. Sir George F. Warner (n.p.: Camden Society, 1886), 1:284–86.

10. L "Review and Conclusion," 5.

11. EW 7:335.

12. EW 4:420, 423, 423–24.

13. Quoted from John Wallace, *Destiny His Choice* (Cambridge: Cambridge University Press), p. 50.

14. *The Case of the Commonwealth of England, Stated,* ed. Philip Knackel (Charlottesville: University Press of Virginia, 1969), p. 129.

15. Quoted from Wallace, *Destiny His Choice,* p. 32.

16. Robert Filmer, *Patriarcha and Other Writings,* ed. Johann Sommerville (Cambridge: Cambridge University Press, 1991), p. 285.

17. Filmer, *Patriarcha and Other Writings,* p. 285.

18. Quoted from James Miller Lewis, "Hobbes and the Blackloists" (Ph.D. diss., Harvard University, 1976), p. 129.

19. L 46.18.

20. L "Review and Conclusion," 6.

21. DC 8.2–3.

22. L "Introduction," 1.

23. Correspondence, p. 124.

24. "A Speech to the Lords and Commons of the Parliament at White Hall" (1610).

25. L 17.13.

26. Filmer, *Patriarcha and Other Writings,* p. 184.

27. L 13.5.

28. DC "Author's Preface to the Reader," 3.

29. L 13.13.

30. L 14.8.

31. EL 24.4.

32. L "Dedication."

33. EL 24.1.

34. EL 24.5.

35. EL 24.2.

36. L 6.36.

37. DC 16.1.

38. L 12.6.

39. Quoted from A. P. Martinich, *The Two Gods of Leviathan* (Cambridge: Cambridge University Press, 1992), p. 63.

40. L 32.1.

41. L 7.7.

42. L 32.5.
43. L 36.11, 36.13, 36.13.
44. L 36.9.
45. L 36.7.
46. L 36.19.
47. DC 16.12.
48. L 36.20.
49. L 36.20.
50. Correspondence, p. 702.
51. L 37.7, 37.1.
52. L 37.6.
53. L 37.4.
54. L 37.5.
55. L 38.25.
56. L 41.5.
57. EL 11.8.
58. L 33.21.
59. EL 11.9, 11.10.
60. EL 11.9.
61. DC 17.28.
62. L 33.21.
63. L 33.20.
64. Charles Wolseley, *The Reasonableness of Scripture Belief* (London, 1672), pp. 218–20.
65. L 38.4.
66. L 38.5.
67. L 35.1–3.
68. L 35.3.
69. L 35.4; also DC 16.4.
70. L 35.11.
71. L 38.14.
72. *Leviathan,* ed. Edwin Curley (Indianapolis: Hackett, 1994), pp. 624–25; see also p. 507.
73. L 44.26.
74. Quoted from EW 4:359.
75. L 44.1.
76. L 47.30.

9. Demonstrations and Disputations, 1652–1659

1. Correspondence, p. 787.
2. Correspondence, pp. 420, 421.
3. Clarendon, *A Survey of Mr Hobbes His Leviathan,* in *Leviathan: Contemporary Responses to the Political Theory of Thomas Hobbes,* ed. G. A. J. Rogers (Bristol: Thoemmes Press, 1995), pp. 181, 182.

4. Seth Ward, *A Philosophicall Essay* (Oxford, 1652), "To the Reader."
5. Alexander Ross, *Leviathan Drawn Out with a Hook* (London, 1653), "To the Reader."
6. James Harrington, *The Prerogative of Popular Government* (London, 1658), p. 36.
7. Marchamont Nedham, *Case of the Commonwealth of England, Stated* (London, 1650), p. 139.
8. Ross, *Leviathan Drawn Out with a Hook*, "To the Reader."
9. Walter Pope, *Life of the Right Reverend Father in God Seth Ward etc.* (London, 1697), p. 118.
10. *Theoremata Theologica* (London, 1654), p. 230.
11. Robert Filmer, *Patriarcha and Other Writings*, ed. Johann Sommerville (Cambridge: Cambridge University Press, 1991), pp. 184–85.
12. John Tulloch, *Rational Theology and Christian Philosophy in England in the Seventeenth Century* (Edinburgh: William Blackwood and Sons, 1874), 2:26.
13. Filmer, *Patriarcha and Other Writings*, pp. 187, 188.
14. Correspondence, pp. 331–32.
15. L 17.13.
16. Barbara Shapiro, *John Wilkins, 1614–1672* (Berkeley: University of California Press, 1969), p. 97.
17. *Academiarum Examen* (London, 1654), p. 88.
18. Shapiro, *John Wilkins*, p. 101.
19. Shapiro, *John Wilkins*, p. 107.
20. L Conclusion, 16; EW 7:335.
21. L 4.16; EW 7:335; also 7:343–44.
22. John Bramhall, *Works* (Oxford, 1844), 4:580.
23. EW 7:340.
24. Quoted from Shapiro, *John Wilkins*, p. 110.
25. EW 5:25–26.
26. EW 5:1.
27. See Samuel Mintz, *The Hunting of Leviathan* (Cambridge: Cambridge University Press, 1962), p. 127.
28. Correspondence, p. 277.
29. EW 5:454.
30. Ross, *Leviathan Drawn Out with a Hook*, pp. 89–90.
31. EW 5:112.
32. EW 5: 111.
33. Quoted from Peter White, *Predestination, Policy, and Polemic* (Cambridge: Cambridge University Press, 1992), p. 7.
34. EW 5:55.
35. Quoted from Mintz, *The Hunting of Leviathan*, p. 131.
36. DCo 1.2–3.
37. DCo 1.3.
38. DCo 25.1.
39. DCo 25.2.
40. DCo 1.6.

41. DCo 1.7.
42. DCo 1.9.
43. L 9.4.
44. Concerning Hobbes's mathematical views, I have found the following works helpful: Hardy Grant, "Hobbes and Mathematics," in *The Cambridge Companion to Hobbes*, ed. Tom Sorell (Cambridge: Cambridge University Press, 1996), pp. 108–28; and three works by Douglas Jesseph: "Hobbes and Mathematical Method," *Perspectives on Science* 1 (1993), 306–41; "Hobbes on the Methods of Modern Mathematics," *Revue d'Histoire des Sciences* 46 (1993), 153–94; and "Hobbes and the Method of Natural Science," in *Cambridge Companion to Hobbes*, pp. 86–107.
45. Jesseph, "Hobbes on the Methods of Modern Mathematics," p. 173.
46. EW 7:343.
47. Quoted from Miriam Reik, *The Golden Lands of Thomas Hobbes* (Detroit: Wayne State University Press, 1977), pp. 178–79.
48. John Wallis, *Hobbius Heauton-timorumenos* (Oxford, 1662), pp. 8, 6.
49. Tenison, *The Creed of Mr. Hobbes Examined* (London, 1670), "Epistle Dedicatory."
50. EW 7:352–56.
51. EW 7:205.
52. EW 7:200–1.
53. DCo 6.6, 15.1; EW 7:219.
54. Quoted from Jesseph, "Hobbes and Mathematical Method," p. 323 n. 20.
55. EW 7:59.
56. Quoted from Jesseph, "Hobbes and Mathematical Method," p. 323 n. 21.
57. EW 7:67.
58. EW 7:68.
59. EW 7:59–60.
60. OL 5:96–97.
61. OL 4:441.
62. EW 7:194.
63. EW 7:187–88.
64. EW 7:316.
65. EW 7: 329
66. OL 4:97.
67. L 11.21.
68. EW 7:248.
69. EW 1:141; DCo 12.5.
70. EW 1:141.
71. EW 1:18.
72. EW 7:184.
73. OL 4: 421.
74. EW 7:201.
75. Euclid, *Elements*, I, def. 2.
76. EW 7:202.

77. OL 4:393; DCo 12.4.
78. OL 5:96.
79. EW 7:324.
80. Thomas White, *Chrysaspis to Querula* (London, 1660), C2v–C3.
81. Quoted from James Miller Lewis, "Hobbes and the Blackloists" (Ph.D. diss., Harvard University, 1976), p. 227.
82. "A Letter from a Gentleman to his Friend in London," quoted from "Hobbes and the Blackloists," p. 228.
83. EW 7:392–94.
84. EW 7:392.
85. Wood, *Athenae Oxoniensis,* ed. Philip Bliss, 3d ed. (London: Rivington, 1813–1820), 3:1072.
86. See EW 7:415ff.
87. DCo "Epistle Dedicatory."
88. Correspondence, p. 456.
89. EW 7:340.
90. EW 4: 439.
91. EW 7:331, 332, 341.
92. EW 7:356, 427.
93. EW 7:387.

10. Baiting the Bear, 1660–1669

1. Correspondence, pp. 513–14.
2. "Declaration of Breda," in Samuel Gardiner, *The Constitutional Documents of the Puritan Revolution,* 3d ed. (Oxford: Clarendon Press, 1906), pp. 465–66.
3. John Wallis, *Hobbius Heauton-timorumenos* (Oxford, 1662), p. 154.
4. DP, p. 379.
5. EW 4:437.
6. Quoted from Noel Malcolm, "Hobbes and the Royal Society," in *Perspectives on Thomas Hobbes,* ed. G. A. J. Rogers and Alan Ryan (Oxford: Clarendon Press, 1988), pp. 57–58. I have relied heavily on Malcolm's treatment of Hobbes's relationship to the Royal Society.
7. Malcolm, "Hobbes and the Royal Society," pp. 62–64.
8. L 31.33.
9. L 47:21.
10. Quoted from Malcolm, "Hobbes and the Royal Society," p. 57.
11. Quoted from Malcolm, "Hobbes and the Royal Society," p. 65.
12. Quoted from H. G. Lyons, *The Royal Society* (Cambridge: Cambridge University Press, 1944), pp. 54, 55.
13. Malcolm, "Hobbes and the Royal Society," pp. 57–58.
14. Lyons, *The Royal Society,* p. 58.
15. The phrase comes from Michael Hunter, *Science and Society* (Cambridge: Cambridge University Press, 1981), p. 178.
16. A letter from Hooke to Robert Boyle in the British Library.

17. EW 7:463–64.
18. My discussion in this and the next section is greatly indebted to Steven Shapin and Simon Schaffer's *Leviathan and the Air-Pump* (Princeton: Princeton University Press, 1985). References to quotations in this section can be found in Shapin and Schaffer's book unless otherwise noted.
19. Shapin and Schaffer, *Leviathan and the Air-Pump*, p. 78.
20. Hunter, *Science and Society*, p. 57.
21. L 46.15.
22. Correspondence, pp. 530ff.
23. Correspondence, p. 577.
24. Correspondence, p. 725.
25. Correspondence, p. 583.
26. Correspondence, p. 584.
27. Correspondence, p. 603.
28. EW 4:416, 418.
29. EW 4:419.
30. EW 4:414.
31. EW 4:420; cf. 415.
32. EW 7:350.
33. EW 7:353.
34. EW 4:420, 425.
35. EW 4:426.
36. EW 4:440.
37. Quoted from M. Nicolson, "Christ's College and the Latititude-Men," *Modern Philology* 27 (1929–30), 51.
38. Quoted from James Miller Lewis, "Hobbes and the Blackloists" (Ph.D. diss., Harvard University, 1976), p. 261.
39. EW 4:427.
40. My discussion in this section is indebted to Lewis, "Hobbes and the Blackloists."
41. See letter from Digby to Wallis (and Brouncker) in J. Wallis, *Commercium Epistolicum de Quaestionibus quibusquam Mathematicis* (Oxford, 1658).
42. Wood, *Athenae Oxoniensis*, ed. Philip Bliss (London: Rivington, 1817), 3:1247–48.
43. Quoted from Lewis, "Hobbes and the Blackloists," p. 258.
44. Quoted from Lewis, "Hobbes and the Blackloists," p. 260.
45. Correspondence, p. 653.
46. Correspondence, p. 653; see also p. 691.
47. Correspondence, p. 661.
48. Kathleen Jones, *A Glorious Fame* (London: Bloomsbury, 1988), pp. 160–61. My discussion of Margaret Cavendish is indebted to this book. Quotations about Margaret come from this book, unless otherwise noted.
49. Correspondence, p. 524.
50. Quoted from Shapin and Schaffer, *Leviathan and the Air-Pump*, p. 31 n. 14.
51. Geoffrey Trease, *Portrait of a Cavalier* (New York: Taplinger, 1979), p. 170.
52. EW 7:136–37.

53. Historical Manuscripts Commission, 8th report (1881), p. 111a; see also p. 112a.
54. *Hobbius Heauton-timorumenos* (Oxford, 1662), pp. 15, 103.
55. *Leviathan,* edited and translated by Edwin Curley (Indianapolis: Hackett, 1994), p. 512.
56. EW 4:397.
57. *Leviathan,* ed. Curley, p. 529.
58. EW 4:407, 406.
59. *Leviathan,* ed. Curley, p. 531; EW 4:393.
60. *Leviathan,* ed. Curley, p. 526.
61. My discussion of Bennet is influenced by Peter Milton, "Hobbes, Heresy and Lord Arlington," *History of Political Thought* 14 (1993), 501–46.
62. OL 4:387.
63. B, pp. 119–20.
64. B, p. 180.
65. B, p. 154.
66. Correspondence, p. 772.
67. EW 4:317. See Cornelis Schoneveld, *Intertraffic of the Mind* (Leiden: Brill, 1983), pp. 45, 150 n. 64.
68. EW 4:384.
69. EW 4:296.
70. See also EW 4:334.
71. EW 4:281.
72. EW 4:291, 338, 363.
73. EW 4:284, 286.
74. EW 4:384.
75. EW 4:296.
76. EW 4:313.
77. EW 4:286.
78. EW 4:301, 303, 304, 301.
79. EW 4:305, 300, 314.
80. EW 4:315.
81. EW 4:315.
82. *Leviathan,* ed. Curley, p. 543.
83. EW4:325.
84. EW 4:326–27.
85. EW 4:328, 330.
86. EW 4:329.
87. EW 4:329.
88. See also EW 4:338, 340.
89. EW 4:330; see also 4:363.
90. EW 4:340.
91. Cambridge University Library, MS. Mm 1. 38, p. 143.
92. Benjamin Laney, *Observations appended to Thomas Hobbes, A Letter About Liberty and Necessity* (London, 1677), pp. 102–4.
93. Tenison, *Creed of Mr. Hobbes Examined* (London, 1670), "Epistle Dedicatory."

94. Tenison, *Creed of Mr. Hobbes Examined,* p. 17.

11. The Final Years, 1670–1679

1. Correspondence, p. 741.
2. Correspondence, pp. 740, 739ff.
3. Correspondence, p. 742.
4. Correspondence, p. 720.
5. Correspondence, p. 721.
6. Correspondence, p. 735.
7. Correspondence, p. 726.
8. Quoted from Michael Hunter, *Science and Society in Restoration England* (Cambridge: Cambridge University Press, 1981), p. 178.
9. Correspondence, p. 751.
10. Correspondence, pp. 746, 747.
11. Correspondence, p. 747.
12. Correspondence, p. 730.
13. On the relations between the translations of Hobbes, Pope, and Ogilby, I am indebted to Maynard Mack's edition of Pope's translation. See note 15.
14. EW 10:x.
15. There is a partial list of parallels between Pope and Hobbes in *The Odyssey of Homer, Books XIII–XXIV,* ed. Maynard Mack (New Haven: Yale University Press, 1967), pp. 492–512.
16. EW 10:105.
17. *Homer: The Iliad,* trans. W. H. D. Rouse (New York: New American Library, 1950), p. 111; *The Iliad of Homer, Books I–IX,* ed. Maynard Mack (New Haven: Yale University Press, 1967), p. cxxii.
18. *The Iliad of Homer, Books I–IX,* ed. Mack, p. lxxii.
19. EW 10:x; see also p. viii.
20. *Homer: The Iliad,* p. 40; EW 10:30–31.
21. *Homer: The Iliad,* p. 41; EW 10:31.
22. See "Introduction" to *The Iliad,* ed. Mack, pp. xlvii, 3.
23. EW 10:vi.
24. EW 10:viii.
25. *The Conquest of Granada,* part 1; 1, ll. 203–9.
26. "A Satire against Mankind," ll. 18–21, 27–8.
27. L 5.3.
28. "A Satire against Mankind," ll. 104–13.
29. The text is printed in Quentin Skinner, "Hobbes on Sovereignty: An Unknown Discussion," *Political Studies* 13 (1965), 213–18.
30. Skinner, "Hobbes on Sovereignty," p. 218.
31. EW 7:71.
32. EW 7:85–87.
33. EW 7:133.
34. EW 7:89.

35. EW 7:90; DP, p. 367.
36. *De Finibus Virtutis Christianae* (Oxford, 1673), quoted from *The Hunting of Leviathan,,* pp. 135–36.
37. Quoted from *The Hunting of Leviathan,,* p. 56.
38. John Anderson Winn, *John Dryden and His World* (New Haven: Yale University Press, 1987), p. 380.
39. Cf. Correspondence, pp. 793–94.
40. EW 4:250–51, 4:342.
41. In Anthony Wood *Athenae Oxonienses,* 3d ed., ed. Philip Bliss (London: Rivington, 1817), 3:1218.
42. This section is indebted to Allan Pritchard, "The Last Days of Hobbes," *Bodleian Library Record* 10 (1980), 178–87.

Index